SPECIAL FORCES

NOVELS BY TOM CLANCY

The Hunt for Red October
Red Storm Rising
Patriot Games
The Cardinal of the Kremlin
Clear and Present Danger
The Sum of All Fears
Without Remorse
Debt of Honor
Executive Orders
Rainbow Six
The Bear and the Dragon
Red Rabbit
The Teeth of the Tiger

SSN: Strategies of Submarine Warfare

NONFICTION

Submarine: A Guided Tour Inside a Nuclear Warship
Armored Cav: A Guided Tour of an Armored Cavalry Regiment
Fighter Wing: A Guided Tour of an Air Force Combat Wing
Marine: A Guided Tour of a Marine Expeditionary Unit
Airborne: A Guided Tour of an Airborne Task Force
Carrier: A Guided Tour of an Aircraft Carrier
Special Forces: A Guided Tour of U.S. Army Special Forces

Into the Storm: A Study in Command (written with General Fred Franks, Jr., Ret., and Tony Koltz)
Every Man a Tiger (written with General Charles Horner, Ret., and Tony Koltz)
Shadow Warriors: Inside the Special Forces (written with General Carl Stiner, Ret., and Tony Koltz)
Battle Ready (written with General Tony Zinni, Ret., and Tony Koltz)

TOM CLANCY

SPECIAL FORCES

A Guided Tour of U.S. Army Special Forces

WRITTEN WITH

John Gresham

BERKLEY BOOKS, NEW YORK

THE BERKLEY PUBLISHING GROUP
Published by the Penguin Group
Penguin Group (USA) Inc.
375 Hudson Street, New York, New York 10014, USA
Penguin Group (Canada), 10 Alcorn Avenue, Toronto, Ontario M4V 3B2, Canada
(a division of Pearson Penguin Canada Inc.)
Penguin Books Ltd., 80 Strand, London WC2R 0RL, England
Penguin Group Ireland, 25 St. Stephen's Green, Dublin 2, Ireland (a division of Penguin Books Ltd.)
Penguin Group (Australia), 250 Camberwell Road, Camberwell, Victoria 3124, Australia
(a division of Pearson Australia Group Pty. Ltd.)
Penguin Books India Pvt. Ltd., 11 Community Centre, Panchsheel Park, New Delhi—110 017, India
Penguin Group (NZ), Cnr. Airborne and Rosedale Roads, Albany, Auckland 1310, New Zealand
(a division of Pearson New Zealand Ltd.)
Penguin Books (South Africa) (Pty.) Ltd., 24 Sturdee Avenue, Rosebank, Johannesburg 2196,
South Africa

Penguin Books Ltd., Registered Offices: 80 Strand, London WC2R 0RL, England

This book is an original publication of The Berkley Publishing Group.

Copyright © 2001 by Rubicon, Inc.
Author photograph by John Earle.

PRINTING HISTORY
Berkley trade paperback edition / February 2001

Library of Congress Cataloging-in-Publication Data

Clancy, Tom, 1947–
    Special forces : a guided tour of U.S. Army Special Forces / Tom Clancy,
    written with John Gresham.
        p. cm.
    Includes bibliographical references.
    ISBN 978-0-425-17268-1
    1. Special forces (Military science)—United States—History.   2. United States.
    Army—Commando troops.   3. U.S. Special Operations Command—History.
    I. Gresham, John. II. Title.
        UA34.S64 C58   2001
    356'.1673'0973—dc21

                                                        00-065121

PRINTED IN THE UNITED STATES OF AMERICA

15   14   13   12   11

DISCLAIMER: The views and opinions expressed in this book are entirely those of the author, and do
not necessarily correspond with those of any corporation, military service, or government organization
of any country.

Some projects run longer than others. Some years are tougher than others. In the almost two years that went into this book, we have come to know many fine people within the Special Forces community, some have become close friends. Sadly, with all the happy times have also come darker moments. It goes without saying that what Special Forces professionals do is dangerous. The years 1998 and 1999 were no exception. Casualties were suffered. The United States lost Special Forces soldiers. We wish to remember them here:

Sergeant Ronald K. Fairchild	September 3, 1998
Specialist Henry W. Lane	October 20, 1998
Specialist Evitt D. Thirrel	December 30, 1998
Chief Warrant Officer Thomas Brooks	January 9, 1999
Master Sergeant Carl P. Dalton	January 17, 1999
Specialist Roy B. Rogers	March 6, 1999
Specialist Ralph K. Ingram	March 8, 1999
Chief Warrant Officer Rohn E. Jolly	April 6, 1999
Lieutenant Colonel Timothy A. Boyles	September 9, 1999
Sergeant Eric T. Ellingson	September 9, 1999
Command Sergeant Major Peter G. Bell	October 30, 1999
Master Sergeant Tony J. Sangueza	November 19, 1999

Specialist Terry L. Pope   November 20, 1999

Staff Sergeant Joseph E. Suponcic   December 15, 1999

None of these losses made the national news. Like the community they served and the company they kept, these men died quietly keeping the faith in their "special" profession. They asked for nothing more than the chance and a place to serve. It is to these special men that that this book is dedicated. Fighting men, of the Green Beret.

Contents

Acknowledgments

This book—like all the others in this series—has been a team effort; no one person can take total credit for it . . . or total blame.

None of the team deserves more credit than my longtime partner and researcher, John D. Gresham. As always, John traveled the world, met the people, took the pictures, ate MREs, spent cold, sleepless nights in the field, and did all the things that make readers feel they are there for all the action. Next, I have to praise the literary skills of Tony Koltz. Without his constant, passionate prodding and brilliant way with words, this book would never have seen the light of day. We have also again benefited from the wisdom, vision, experience, and efforts of series editor Professor Martin H. Greenberg, as well as Larry Segriff and all the staff at Tekno Books. Laura DeNinno is again to be saluted for her wonderful drawings, which have added so much. This team has brought these books to you, and I hope we all get together again. It was great, guys!

Any book like this would be impossible to produce without the support of senior service personnel, both retired and in top positions. In this regard, we have again been blessed with all the support that we could have needed or wanted. Great thanks for two retired senior Army officers: General Carl Stiner and Lieutenant General Bill Yarborough. Both gave us their valuable time and support, and we can never repay their trust and friendship. In the office of the Chairman of the Joint Chiefs of Staff, we had the best: General Henry Shelton, Colonel (and Dr.) David Petreaus, Captain Steve Petropelli, and Carolyn Piper made our much delayed interview finally happen. Over in Army Public Affairs, we had the pleasure of doing another book with Colonel John Smith. We also had Lieutenant Colonel Ray Whitehead at *Soldiers* magazine. Down at U.S. Special Operations Command in Florida, General Peter Schoomaker and his staff were generous with their support as well. It's nice to have friends.

At Fort Bragg, the home of Army Special Forces, Lieutenant General William P. Tangney, Major General William G. Boykin, and Major Generals Kenneth R. Bowra and John Scales were kind enough to open up the community for our research. Over at the JFK Special Warfare Center, Colonel Remo Butler gave us time and access to his command, which produces Special Forces soldiers. We also need to thank the media relations team at U.S. Army Special Operations Command, who held our hands throughout the project. Major Tom McCollum was there at every turn, was with us on every trip and visit, and did a job no paycheck could ever compensate for. Backing him up was Lieutenant Colonel Tom Rhinelander and Carol Jones, who made sure we walked the line and stayed safe.

Out in the field, there was the wonderful staff at Fort Polk, who took care of us on our JRTC visits. Major Tom Costello and the incomparable Paula Schlag run a media relations shop that has no equal anywhere in the military today. They put the public face on the world's finest training center, whose commanding officers, Brigadier Generals Sam Thompson and Charles Swannack, Jr., made us welcome again and again. Down at the SOT-D shop, Colonel Mike Rozsypal, Lieutenant Colonel John Smith, and Major Tim Fitzgerald took good care of us from Yuma to Mississippi. Finally, special thanks to Major Bill Shaw and his lovely wife, Mary Kay, who took us in, fed us, and made us welcome in their home. As friends and professionals, we thank them for their efforts.

The real story of this book took place out in the Special Forces Groups (SFGs) and Teams, and we never lacked for material. Normally, we would have a long list of the young men and women who helped us, but such a roster is not possible because of the continuing nature of downrange Special Forces operations. As you read this, almost everyone we might talk about is probably on a foreign mission or getting ready for one. Thus, for reasons of personal respect, safety, and security, we have avoided providing names (except where they are already known), and our pictures have been shot to protect identities. We do want to make special thanks to Colonels Ed Phillips and James "Roy" Dunn, along with Lieutenant Colonel Joe Smith, who tolerated our continued presence and questions. And our finest wishes must also go to the teams who let us into their deployments, missions, and lives. In the 1st, 3rd, 5th, 7th, 10th, 19th, and 20th SFGs, there are a lot of Special Forces soldiers who took us with them in the field and downrange. To those men, I hope we got your stories right, because you sure told them well. You know who you are. Thanks, too, to the fine folks from the 160th Special Operations Aviation Regiment (the Nightstalkers), who took us on several exciting rides. We need to thank Colonel Marcos Rojas of the Guardia Nacional's GAC FAC and Colonel Jose Grant of the 107th SF Battalion in Venezuela. In a bad part of the world, these two fine officers are part of the long-range solution and they are our friends. And for all the folks who took us for rides, jumps, shoots, and exercises, thanks for teaching the ignorant how things really work.

We must again extend thanks for all of our help in New York, especially to Robert Gottlieb and Matt Bialer at the William Morris agency, and Robert Youdelman and Tom Mallon, who took care of the legal details. Over at Berkley Books, our regards to our series editor, Tom Colgan, as well as to David Shanks.

And of course, for our friends, families, and loved ones—we thank you once more. We're finally coming home.

Foreword

President John F. Kennedy was a voracious reader. Early in his presidency, at the urging of Roger Hilsman (who was then Director of the State Department's Bureau of Intelligence and Research and a World War II OSS veteran with guerrilla warfare experience), the president made himself familiar with the revolutionary writings of Che Guevara and Communist China's Mao Tse-tung, as well as the military philosophy of the Vietnamese General Vo Nguyen Giap, whose book *People's War, People's Army* offered JFK a revealing taste of the future. As he reflected on these and other sources, our dynamic young president came to feel that the threat to the security of the United States posed by irregular, clandestine, and covert politico-military aggression was grave enough to demand special attention. And he concluded that in the turbulent world of the 1960s, the forces of instability and conflict were largely not vulnerable to attack by conventional military weapons and tactics. As a student of international affairs, President Kennedy was convinced that:

> *" ... [A] whole new kind of strategy, a wholly different kind of force, and therefore a wholly different kind of military training ... was called for."*

Few of the president's peers would pursue his studies of unconventional warfare, or reach the conclusions he reached. This failure would later haunt the United States.

In the early 1960s it was generally accepted in America's high military command and staff circles (including the Joint Chiefs of Staff) that there was nothing unique about Ho Chi Minh's war then smoldering in Southeast Asia. Public statements by very high-ranking Army officers made light of the idea that guerrilla warfare was important or posed any serious problems, and rejected any inference that an intense political struggle was woven through the fabric of Communist military action in Southeast Asia.

As far as the majority of senior leaders were concerned, the basic training, leadership, motivation, organizational principles, tactics, and strategy that had won America's wars in the past could handle any conflict situation, and would be more than adequate for Indo-China—or any other land infected with guerrilla warfare.

It was the president himself, and not his military advisors, who first perceived that the front line of defense against paramilitary aggression had to be in the hearts and minds of the threatened population. Though the Joint Chiefs of Staff and other high level military leaders did not share his enthusiasm for the development of an unconventional military capability, there was within the ranks of the U.S. Army a small element whose genes had been inherited from the behind-the-lines OSS warriors of World War II. These unconventional soldiers had been given the label of *Special Forces.*

It was President Kennedy's desire that Special Forces become an elite corps of experts both in guerrilla warfare and in counterguerrilla operations, and he made his wishes known to the Joint Chiefs of Staff in very firm terms. Even so, several aspects of the Special Forces Prototype, which was being crafted in response to the desires of the Commander in Chief, were in for heavy going. The reasons were traditional. Unlike the armies of other great powers past and present, the United States Army has always looked with disfavor upon the concept of elite military organizations. Both *special warfare* and *special forces* were terms that raised hackles among conventional regulars.

Which meant there was, for example, minimal official Army support for the philosophy of the great Sun Tzu, which held that special men and units could be found and formed: "When all troops are encamped together, the general selects from every camp its high-spirited and valiant officers who are distinguished by agility and strength and whose martial accomplishments are above the ordinary. These are grouped to form a Special Corps. Of ten men, but one is selected; of ten thousand, one thousand."

By way of contrast, the U.S. Army's vast personnel system was designed to handle the manpower requirements that our nation of over two hundred million souls would generate in time of war. This system focused with reluctance and some hostility on the Special Forces microcosm from which only minuscule conventional fighting power was expected to emerge. For example, the smallest unit of Special Forces, the "A" Detachment, had only two officers, with ten enlisted men (each a noncommissioned officer or rated specialist) under their command. These men were *not* expected by Special Forces leaders to directly face a heavy, mechanized division. They had other, far more valuable uses. The point was that no unit of similar size had anything like their many capabilities and skills.

Sergeant Barry Sadler's famous "Ballad of the Green Beret" made this point well. To a number of members of the U.S. Army's General Staff, Sergeant Sadler had put to music the chief reasons why they supported an expansion of Special Forces reluctantly or not at all:

> *"Silver wings upon their chest, These are men, America's best.*
> *One hundred men we'll test today. But only three win the Green Beret."*

The first chapter of Robin Moore's 1965 best seller, *The Green Berets,* outlined just how tough it was to become a fully qualified Special Forces soldier. As Moore pointed out, most demanding of all were the unbending requirements that the products of this unprecedented training exhibit character, moral courage, dedication, honesty, and true patriotism, in addition to the technical military skills and physical standards that set them apart from "general purpose" troops. They were anything but run-of-the-mill. They were "special" in every sense. And it was precisely this category that placed Green Berets in frequent jeopardy of being at war with the rest of the Army.

The Vietnam chapter of American military history reflects little in the way of strategic, tactical, or political credit upon our beloved United States. On battlefields that rarely resembled those Americans had seen—or expected—the massive battering ram of American firepower proved no answer to a will-o'-the-wisp adversary who was more vulnerable to the weapons of political and psychological warfare than to bullets and bayonets. The United States Army's Special Forces were perhaps the only element of U.S. military power in Vietnam that practiced the art of persuasion as a major weapons system. Their influence resulted in psychological denial to the VC and the NVA of human and geographic areas that would otherwise have fallen under their control.

In time, media emphasis on the educational and humanitarian side of the tough, all-purpose Special Forces soldiers led to invitations from other countries . . . countries that would previously have rejected out of hand the presence of Green Beret soldiers whose only skills appeared to lie in the murky area of guerrilla warfare. Serving in hundreds of localities around the world and in some of the most complex politico-military environments imaginable, they have provided a type of support for America's strategic aims possible to no other forces within the U.S. inventory.

President Kennedy's name will be linked forever with the history and ideals of the United States Army's Special Forces—and with their proud symbol, the Green Beret. On the 12th of October 2001, forty years will have passed since a group of regular Army soldiers appeared before their Commander in Chief wearing a distinctive type of headgear never before authorized by the U.S. Army, but now approved by the president himself. The Green Beret had emerged from the unauthorized—even prohibited—category to become the distinctive badge of the most carefully selected and highly trained body of American soldiers that had ever been part of any fighting force.

Among those present was Francis Ruddy, a soldier whose outstanding leadership qualities had resulted in his promotion to the position of Command Sergeant Major of the Special Warfare Center. Ruddy had set standards of conduct and performance that would be associated with his name wherever Special Forces were in action.

Following the president's assassination, it was Special Forces Command Sergeant Major Francis Ruddy who proposed that the Special Warfare Center be called the John F. Kennedy Special Warfare Center. And it was Command Sergeant Major Ruddy who, in Arlington National Cemetery, emotionally and reverently removed his precious Green Beret and placed it gently upon the fresh grave of his slain president.

Since those long-ago events, the Special Forces of the United States Army have in every way lived up to President Kennedy's hopes and expectations.

During the years that I spent personally engaged with the alchemy and philosophy that led to today's Special Operations Forces, one of my major challenges was to explain Special Forces to our own military brothers in arms. Though this new phenomenon had grown from old roots that were deeply imbedded in America's history, it was always difficult to explain the phenomenon's esoteric nature.

One vehicle I quickly discovered for communicating some of this to my military colleagues and the thousands of other visitors and trainees hosted by the Special Warfare Center during my 1961 to 1964 tenure was what we called the "Gabriel Demonstration" (named for a Special Forces hero of the Vietnam conflict).

At a "Gabriel," Special Forces soldiers in a field setting and surrounded by the tools of their trade explained to their audiences the nature of their training and how they related to the then little known "A," "B," and "C" Detachments.

And yet, as effective as this visual and hands-on educational effort proved to be, it only partially explained the nuances of a mechanism and philosophy aimed at focusing paramilitary power upon targets that were not always vulnerable to the fire and movement of conventional military force.

Now, finally, I have a book to give to people who want to understand our community. Tom Clancy's guided tour of our beloved Special Forces demonstrates a truly remarkable grasp of the intangibles and intricacies that characterize the unconventional element of our national defense system. I hope that you enjoy it as much as I have, and take away some of the lessons that I have spent a lifetime trying to get across to people in all walks of life, from presidents to housewives.

—Lieutenant General William P. Yarborough,
USA (Retired)
Southern Pines, North Carolina

Introduction

I like to think of myself as a fairly well-informed individual on military matters, having spent half my life either writing about or studying the armed forces of the world. It was therefore with some level of surprise that I found myself constantly being corrected, astonished, and educated as I moved through the world of the U.S. Army Special Forces (SF). Perhaps my biggest surprise was just how little I truly knew about this fascinating community and the people in it. My first error came with the original name for this book. I had planned to call it *Snakeater*, an old Vietnam-era slang term used to describe special operations personnel and their skills in the field. *Big* mistake on my part! The first of many as it turned out. Despite a heritage going back almost five decades, SF soldiers have worked hard to throw off their Vietnam reputation for reckless behavior, made popular by actors and movies portraying their exploits. By far the best movie ever made about the Special Forces, John Wayne's *The Green Berets*, is little more than a World War II–era propaganda film wrapped in a Vietnam suit of clothes.[1] Notwithstanding my personal love of Duke Wayne, the overall media presentation of the Army Special Forces has generally been one of contrived crap. This was perhaps the most compelling reason for writing this book.

Far from their "kick ass, take no prisoners" public personas, today's SF soldiers are perhaps America's most professional and capable warriors. Despite being publicly called *Green Berets*, they prefer the simple title of *Special Forces Soldiers*. Most members of the SF brotherhood (still men only as of the year 2000), while proud of their famous headgear, cringe at being called by that name. Inside their own ranks, they call themselves the "quiet professionals," a name that reflects the very private and discretionary nature of their trade. Given a choice, SF soldiers would prefer that nobody take notice of their work, and just ignore their presence within the military in general. Much of this comes from the poor way in which they have been portrayed to the world. As I learned the first time that this project was turned back in my face (and there were several!), the men of the Special Forces are very picky about what

---

1 Despite the unrealistic portrayal of Vietnam, it is something of a SF tradition that any Special Forces unit on a mission or training exercise has a copy of this movie in their traveling video library. SF soldiers respect the image of the Duke, and often show the movie to their foreign hosts.

journalists and other media personnel say and write about them. Too often, they have been accused of crimes and misconduct they had nothing to do with, or policies they had no input in formulating.

Perhaps the most egregious of these media assaults came from CNN and *Time* magazine several years ago. In what came to be known as the Operation Tailwind Scandal, *Time* and CNN accused SF personnel of using chemical weapons on defecting American personnel in Cambodia in the early 1970s.[2] While a subsequent Department of Defense investigation showed the story to be a fabrication, the fact that such a tale ever saw the light of day is a sign of the total public and media ignorance of the SF community. Anyone who takes the time to look at their community motto, *De Oppresso Libre* (To Free the Oppressed) automatically knows that such a crime is outside the values and standards of *every* SF soldier. If anything, the Special Forces have a well-earned reputation for rescuing people, preserving human life and rights, and generally supporting freedom wherever their boots hit ground. For some SF soldiers, like the legendary Colonel Arthur "Bull" Simons and Major Dick Meadows, this "code" became a personal obsession that drove them until their dying days. These men are perhaps two of the most highly regarded humans America has ever produced—respected for their personal morality and honor as much as their physical and mental capabilities. If you have not yet guessed, I like these guys a lot. The reasons, though, have to do with more than just their membership in an elite military force.

One of the first things I came to respect about the Special Forces was their sense of history and heritage. Though officially created in 1952, their roots date back almost a decade prior to that, as members of the Office of Strategic Services (the OSS: America's first real intelligence agency) and the joint American/Canadian 1st Special Service Force (the famous Devil's Brigade). Strangely, this makes them direct contemporaries of the Army's airborne troopers and the Marine Corps heritage of amphibious operations in World War II.[3] Starting with a small cadre of mostly Eastern European immigrant soldiers, the Special Forces formed a regimental-sized unit in 1952 devoted to behind-the-line guerrilla warfare. Known as the 10th Special Forces Group (SFG), they were led by Colonel Aaron Bank, a veteran of service in the OSS during the Second World War. Since that time, the Special Forces have been America's forward-deployed eyes and ears, seemingly always the first U.S. troops on the scene in a crisis zone.

Another thing I like about Special Forces personnel is that they are not the sort of folks who like to show off. Anything but, in fact. The first time you meet a SF soldier you may not even know it. Unlike the famous Navy SEALs (Sea-Air-Land special operations personnel) or Army Rangers, they are not necessarily physically

---

2 It appears that several overzealous reporters and producers from *Time* and CNN attempted to take the story of Operation Tailwind and fabricate a story that would gain them publicity and disgrace the Special Forces. When the truth came out and the story backfired, all concerned suffered appropriate professional punishment and disgrace, including firing for those most involved.

3 Though the Marine Corps was formed in 1775, their acknowledged mission of amphibious assaults from the sea only dates from 1942. Though they have a history of raids and operations from the sea that dates back 225 years, their formal mission of amphibious warfare was only conceived in the 1920s and implemented during World War II.

imposing or overtly dangerous-looking. SF soldiers also lack some of the more destructive or confrontational qualities of some other American Special Operations Forces (SOF) personnel. If you're looking for a Sylvester Stallone or Arnold Schwarzenegger, don't expect to find them in today's Army Special Forces. On the contrary, SF soldiers like to blend in, quietly taking in their surroundings and trying to learn something of the people and situations they have come into contact with. To do this, they use well-honed language skills and regional cultural training, so that they can act like something other than a normal heavy-handed American. They also have a well-developed sense of proportionality, knowing just how much force or energy to apply to a given situation, and exactly when to do so. A trip into a Persian Gulf shopping bazaar is living proof of their skills in these areas.

Perhaps their most attractive quality, and certainly the one that makes them so valuable to leaders throughout the government, is their adaptability across the full spectrum of warfare. In previous volumes of this series, readers have been shown some of the most versatile and important of military units. America and its allies can be rightly proud of the array of talent and capabilities these units provide. Nevertheless, not one of the more conventional units shown in previous books of this series is as capable and versatile as a Special Forces A-Team. While that may seem a bit of a stretch given the fine things I've said in previous books, trust me when I say that the SF soldiers I know are as a group America's finest warriors. A single twelve-man A-Team might one day be conducting medical and civil engineering training for a foreign government, and the next helping conduct the evacuation of an American embassy. If you think this sounds unlikely, talk to the kids from the 3rd SFG who helped evacuate Sierra Leone a few years back. In a given year, a team might have a peacekeeping mission in Bosnia for a few months, then help train officers in the countries of the former Warsaw Pact for a few more months. On top of this, each SFG has a dedicated wartime mission, supporting the interests and tasks of regional commanders around the globe. Clearly, these are the folks you want on the ground first when trouble breaks out somewhere, which is exactly how they are being used today. That's a lot of value for a surprisingly small investment in personnel, real estate, and equipment. All this out of a community of around 10,000 men—less than you would find in a single Army light infantry division or Marine brigade. Personally, I feel like I'm getting my money's worth.

I'd like to say that I knew all these things when I started this book. I didn't though. The two years that were spent researching and writing this book were a long and hard trek around the world and into unknown venues. Frankly, it was not always comfortable or even pleasant. I had to forget much of what I already believed I knew, and learn new truths that sometimes were hard to accept, even though these sometimes occurred in front of my own eyes. Nevertheless, I now look back with pride on what went into this volume, and how it has worked out. As this seventh book closes out my guided tour series, I hope that you will find it the best of the bunch. A lot of fine people have put their hearts and souls into helping me get things right, and I hope that you see their hand in what is presented in the pages that follow. And as you read, remember that unlike some of the other books of this series, which have focused on technology and the instruments of warfare, this book is all about people. People who are, in my personal opinion, some of the finest Americans to have ever worn a uniform. The men of the Green Beret.

—Tom Clancy
Peregrine Cliff, Maryland
June 2000

Special Forces 101

Fighting soldiers from the sky, Fearless men who jump and die,
Men who mean just what they say, The brave men of the Green
Beret.
Silver wings upon their chests, These are men, America's best,
One hundred men we'll test today. But only three win the Green
Beret.
Trained to live off nature's land, Trained in combat, hand to hand,
Men who fight by night and day, Courage taken from the Green
Beret.
Silver wings upon their chests, These are men, America's best,
Men who mean just what they say, The brave men of the Green
Beret.
Back at home a young wife waits, Her Green Beret has met his fate,
He has died for those oppressed, Leaving her this last request:
Put silver wings on my son's chest, Make him one of America's best,
He'll be a man they'll test one day, Have him win the Green Beret.

Staff Sergeant Barry Sadler, "Ballad of the Green Beret"

Most of us probably think of them as Green Berets—just like the song says. But some—usually their detractors—call them *Snakeaters*, after the fearsome reputation they gained during the Vietnam War. In their own minds, however, they are *Special Forces*—or officially, the U.S. Army Special Forces. The green beret they consider just a nice piece of headgear.

The past of the Special Forces is wild and colorful, and the nicknames reflect it; but in fact, the preferred name more accurately speaks to their more sophisticated and professional present.

Organizationally, the Special Forces is part of a relatively new community within the American military known as Special Operations Forces—SOFs. Created as a result of the Nunn-Cohen Amendment to the 1986 Goldwater-Nichols Defense Reform Act, they operate under the U.S. Special Operations Command—SOCOM—which is based

The Special Forces soldier memorial at Fort Bragg, outlined against the North Carolina sky. Located next to the headquarters of the U.S. Army Special Operations Command, it symbolizes the dedication of all Special Forces professionals past, present, and future.

JOHN D. GRESHAM

at MacDill Air Force Base near Tampa, Florida. SOCOM is the newest of the eight "unified" commands that make up today's U.S. military.

Practically speaking, there are significant differences between SOCOM and the other seven unified commands. These differences will gradually become clear. Meanwhile, let's take a look at what Special Forces do.

Or, to put this another way, why Special Forces?

Warfare wears many faces. There is, for example, the official face, with large standing armies, rigid discipline, formal uniforms, and formalized battles (though these are always characterized by rampant chaos). The form and the discipline seem to be the best defense against the inevitable chaos.

War also wears a less formal face. Call it shadow war, clandestine war, or sometimes guerrilla war. Throughout history, small bands of warriors have used unusual and unconventional weapons, tactics, and organizations to fight and often defeat larger and more powerful conventional forces. Such bands were a very potent weapon during our own American Revolution. And in the Vietnam War, shadow warriors proved to be an equally potent weapon against the large and inflexible American Army.

One obvious drawback to the "normal" practice of shadow warfare is its potential for lawlessness. That is to say, shadow warriors rarely obey international laws and rules of warfare. To shadow warriors, for example, the distinction between combatants and noncombatants is usually meaningless. They rarely hesitate to attack civilian personnel and targets, and often use civilians as human shields. Shadow warfare tends to be nasty, savage, and frustrating. . . . Who are the bad guys?

Warfare is hardly an inherently moral act; yet America's SOF warriors have set as their aim to come as close to the moral high ground as possible. Their goal, in other words, is not only to become the most useful, resourceful, and dangerous group on the planet, but to bring some semblance of morality and civility into the least moral and civil form of warfare . . . and to teach these attitudes to those who need it most. By using their superior training and knowledge of small unit warfare, as well as by providing guidance and leadership, their hope is to instill in emerging nations that are under attack (or under threat of attack) the kinds of values and ideals civil society requires.

This is not an easy sell. It is hard to imagine Che Guevara, Slobodan Milosevic, or the Taliban giving lessons in ethics to their irregular troops.

Such missions—it should be added—are far from the only jobs given to the Special Forces. Because they can operate in a relatively clandestine or "discretionary" fashion, with a small on-the-ground "footprint," American SOF units are proving to be useful in a number of other areas. SOFs are *precision* weapons, with great sensitivity to political control, regional cultures, rules of engagement, and many other factors that frequently make them superior to conventional forces in many types of missions.

By comparison, the commitment of a conventional military unit like an aircraft carrier battle group or an airborne brigade is a major political—and news—event.

Unlike conventional forces, which have utility only when an international crisis is already brewing, SOF units have value across the full spectrum of conflict—from anticipation (by providing defense training and assistance) to cleanup (by helping enforce peace in a postwar situation). SOFs, in short, have value in almost any kind of situation, including open combat, where they provide the American military with deep reconnaissance and ground strike forces.

First use of SOF units in a crisis gives politicians a chance to achieve their goals quietly, with risk to only a handful of personnel and resources. Later, if a larger and more conventional response is needed, then that option is still available. For heads of state, such options and capabilities are more precious than gold.

With all of this in mind, it is easy to understand why SOCOM has seen its budget and responsibilities grow—even as almost every other American military community has been slashed to the bone. It also explains why units like the Special Forces have the heaviest operations tempo (OpTempo) in the U.S. military community. The Army Special Forces, for example, frequently spend more than six months out of every twelve on deployment—or "downrange," as they call it.

Special Operations Forces: What Are They?

Just what are "Special Operations Forces" and what do they do?

The short answer is this: They are specially selected, specially trained, specially equipped, and given special missions and support.

SOF units are a natural development of modern military doctrine, which tends to create purpose-designed forces for a wider variety of specific roles and missions. By creating superbly trained specialized units for specialized tasks, roles, and missions, particular problems that prove beyond the capabilities of general-purpose forces can be handled by smaller, more focused units.

There is a downside, however. Elite units come with a high price tag, not only

Special Forces soldiers hang from a 160th Special Operations Aviation Regiment MH-60 Blackhawk. Special Forces are part of a large joint-service special operations community, capable of deploying anywhere in the world.

MAJOR MARK

in terms of what they cost to build and maintain, but also in the effect they have on the structure and attitudes of other units. As always, those who dare to rise above the crowd and distinguish themselves will spark envy and resentment. In the highly competitive world of the military, this tendency is even more pronounced. This partly explains why SOFs are often disliked by their more conventional brothers in arms. SOF units and their men are frequently seen as "sponges," sucking up prized personnel and funds at the expense of "regular" units. There is also a very thin line between the necessary freedom to act according to the demands of the situation (that higher command may have no idea of) and the long demonstrated tendency of SF personnel to do what they please. How current SF commanders have managed to keep the independence, creativity, and resourcefulness that SOFs must have, while maintaining proper command authority, will become clearer in a later chapter.

It is not surprising that something resembling open warfare has from time to time broken out between the SF leadership and the generals at the top of what they call "Mother Army." Even a decade after the legislation that set the SOFs free of their parent services, animosity remains. Both sides have nevertheless lowered the volume of their rhetoric, and are working hard to develop ways to merge their capabilities for their own and their country's good.

What, then, is the makeup of an SOF unit? First of all, those on the "muscle" end of things will all be men. While this restriction is in principle based upon U.S. Code Title 10[4] limits upon the units women can be assigned to, the truth is that very

---

4 Title 10 of the U.S. Code lays out the requirements for personnel serving in various kinds of units. As of 1999, Title 10 restricts women from serving in frontline combat infantry units—the core of SOF forces today.

few women will be able to stand up under the physical strains and exertions special operations require of personnel. This is not male chauvinism so much as a statement of fact. SOF combat personnel must be able to carry—on foot—heavy loads over long distances, and do it quickly.

After the basic physical prerequisites have been satisfied, there are other, less obvious requirements:

Specialized missions (paradoxically) require a broad range of general capabilities and skills. So, for example, the Army's Special Forces soldiers, while physically fit, tend to be more balanced (like triathletes) than specialized (like marathoners or weight lifters). Don't expect to find Rambos in the Special Forces.

Most are senior enlisted personnel in their thirties, with at least ten years of military service. They possess above-average intelligence, have attended numerous service schools, and are voracious readers and "news junkies" (who keep one ear tuned to a radio or CNN). They tend to be mature "self-starters," with excellent problem-solving abilities and better than average people skills; all speak a minimum of one language in addition to English (many speak several); and they are optimists, who see opportunity when others are ready to quit and go home.

Despite their inherent intelligence, few come to Special Forces with college degrees (but those without degrees usually pick them up).

Most have been divorced (sometimes more than once). Youthful marriages don't stand up well under the strain of time spent deployed away from home (added to the normal personal problems of the young). Despite the strains, SF personnel tend to be married. In the marriages that last, you're likely to find in the mate the same qualities of independence, intelligence, and caring that you'll find in the SF guy.

Finally, most are solitary and shy, yet most associate comfortably with each other (the traditional rewards and badges of rank and accomplishment count for very little among SFs). Unlike the rest of the (more traditional) Army, where officers and enlisted personnel are rarely seen together away from their units, SF soldiers of all ranks enjoy socializing with their own kind. In fact, they prefer it. Getting asked into this family is not easy, but once you're in you're *in*.

Once men have been chosen for Special Forces, they are formed into tightly bonded teams, usually composed of a dozen or so specialists who train together intensively and for a very long time. Each team member is skilled in a variety of tasks.

SF units are not new. Throughout history we find stories of men of extraordinary training and dedication conducting tremendously difficult feats of military arms. One only need look at the Spartans at Thermopylae, King Henry's archers at Agincourt, or Stonewall Jackson's "foot cavalry" in the Shenandoah Valley to understand what well-led elite forces can do.

The first application of modern Special Forces principles occurred during World War I, when the German Army trained special infiltration units prior to their western offensive in the spring of 1918. After four years of stalemated trench warfare, the Kaiser's generals were seeking a way to break through the Allied lines into the clear countryside of Flanders. To accomplish this, they created specially trained *Stosstruppen* (shock troop) squads, designed to infiltrate the Allied trenches and open breaches for followup infantry units. The strategy worked, creating havoc in the Allied armies before the German tide was stemmed.

Specially selected and trained units were used even more widely in the Second World War.

The Germans under Adolf Hitler (who loved elite forces more than he loved women) created a variety of SOF units in the Wehrmacht and SS, in the Luftwaffe, and in the Kreigsmarine, and some of these proved very successful. The Koch Assault Detachment, for example, stormed the Belgium fortress of Eben-Emael in the war's early days; and Hitler's greatest commando, Otto Skorzeny, led elements of General Kurt Student's 7th Parachute Division to rescue Benito Mussolini (after his first fall from power) from captivity in a mountain fortress. By the end of the war, however, the Axis forces were so overendowed with SOF units, that they were falling over each other, fighting for resources, men, and missions.

The Allies used SOF units in a much more balanced way, and British and American SOF units made major contributions to the eventual victory—from British commandos conducting raids along the Atlantic coastline, to American agents of the Office of Strategic Services (OSS) supporting native guerrilla fighters against the Japanese in Burma.[5]

The OSS, led by the legendary "Wild Bill" Donovan, was a centralized agency, with not only intelligence collection and analysis bureaus, but the ability to conduct clandestine paramilitary and other special operations behind enemy lines. For these missions, Donovan recruited America's best and brightest—physically, mentally, and even spiritually—to become his foot soldiers. The best source for the best and brightest, in his view, was Ivy League colleges, and that's where he obtained them. Though he was arguably mistaken in this judgment, these recruits became not only the backbone of the OSS, but the core of the postwar intelligence community leadership.

By contrast with the German proliferation of SOF units, Allied SOF units were generally kept small and few, thus allowing them to retain the core characteristic that made them "special" in the first place: special people. In any pool of military recruits, only a select group of personnel can thrive under the rigors and requirements needed by SOF units. These are just a tiny percentage of the total, maybe as small as one or two percent. Any attempt to force into SOF units personnel who are not endowed with the necessary requirements is a futile exercise.

In short, "It's the people, dummy!"

What can you do with such units? The principal SOF missions can be broken down as follows:

- **Counterproliferation (CP)**—It's hard to turn on the news or read a newspaper without hearing about the dangers of the uncontrolled spread of weapons of mass destruction (WMDs—nuclear, chemical, and biological weapons). SOF forces have taken an active role in limiting the acquisition of WMDs by rogue nations. Their

---

5 I should note that Douglas MacArthur hated unconventional units, including the American OSS and the British SOE, SAS, and SBS, and did all he could to keep them out of his territory.

U.S. Special Forces soldiers supervise men of the Venezuelan Guardia Nacional in antiterrorist training. Such training is a significant part of current-day American foreign policy.

CP missions include intelligence gathering and analysis, site surveys, and even force protection of "special" personnel (such as diplomats, scientists, etc.), diplomatic support, arms control, and enforcing import/export controls, sometimes in concert with other government and Allied agencies. They also might be tasked with going in and taking out a site where WMDs are being developed or produced.

- **Combating Terrorism (CBT)**—CBT continues to be a critical SOF mission, especially as the terrorist threat evolves from hijackings and hostage taking to use of truck bombs and WMDs to send political messages. The range of CBT tasks encompasses not only antiterrorism and counterterrorism missions, but also actual prosecution and resolution of terrorist situations.

- **Foreign Internal Defense (FID)**—In these missions, SOF forces organize, train, advise, and assist military, paramilitary, and national police forces of foreign host nations. These forces can then be used either to protect their societies or free them from subversion, lawlessness, insurgency, and terrorism.

- **Special Reconnaissance (SR)**—One of the traditional SOF missions—usually covert. SR teams conduct reconnaissance and surveillance activities in support of national, military, and other governmental agencies. These clandestine missions are a key SOF contribution to the national defense.

- **Direct Action (DA)**—Another long-time SOF mission, DA is a fancy term for a raid. Designed to be conducted as a short-duration operation, a DA mission can be tailored to seize, capture, recover, or destroy designated personnel, equipment, or facilities in a particular area.

A soldier of the 7th Special Forces Group instructs Venezuelan Guardia Nacional soldiers in ground tactics and movement. By providing such training, the quality of allied armed forces is enhanced, as is U.S. influence in the region.

JOHN D. GRESHAM

- **Psychological Operations (PSYOP)**—One of the most subtle and effective of SOF missions, PSYOPs are designed to positively reinforce and tailor the attitudes of enemy combatants, noncombatants, and other individuals toward friendly forces and operations. PSYOPs are made of various mixes of news, entertainment, information, and coercion. Properly planned and executed, PSYOPs have toppled governments and won wars without a shot being fired in anger.

- **Civil Affairs (CA)**—CA missions are aimed at the civil population of an area where friendly military forces are going to operate. The idea is to keep the indigenous population's attitude toward our forces as positive as possible. Thus their mission is part intelligence, a bit of civil engineering, lots of public relations, and a dash of theater. CA units tend to be made up of Reservists and National Guard troops, whose skills are based upon what they do in everyday life—that is, public relations and advertising professionals, as well as civil servants and media personnel. Properly executed, CA missions act as "grease" for military units who might normally be disruptive to the civilian population in the area of operations (AOR).

- **Unconventional Warfare (UW)**—UW is a long-duration version of the FID mission, where SOF teams actually form part of the fighting forces engaged. A more common term for UW is *guerrilla warfare*.

- **Information Operations (IO)**—A relatively new type of SOF mission, IO missions are designed to adversely affect enemy information and information systems (computers, phones, networks, etc.). The idea is to disrupt these systems (to limit the enemy's information and his command and control) as well as to confuse, decoy, or even deceive him about our intentions or actions.

In addition to their primary missions, U.S. SOF units also conduct a number of collateral missions, which include the following:

- **Coalition Support (CS)**—This is a kind of military diplomacy. CS missions are designed to help integrate the units of various partner nations into a single cohesive fighting force.

- **Combat Search and Rescue (CSAR)**—CSAR is a morale-critical mission designed to retrieve military personnel or downed aircrews from behind enemy lines before they can be captured by hostile forces.

- **Counterdrug (CD) Operations**—SOF CD missions are designed to train host nation military forces and law enforcement personnel in critical skills required to interdict drugs at the source. The skills taught include detection and monitoring, as well as interdiction of cultivation, processing, and transportation of illegal narcotics.

- **Humanitarian Demining (HD) Operations**—SOF teams train foreign personnel to survey, identify, neutralize, and remove mines and other unexploded ordnance so that hazards to civilians are removed and useful land is reclaimed.

- **Humanitarian Assistance (HA)**—SOF personnel support relief operations during natural disasters, refugee crises, or other events that disrupt mass populations. The services delivered by SOF units can range from on-site observation and assessment of the scope of the crisis, to actually directing relief efforts from military, governmental, and nongovernmental agencies.

- **Peace Operations**—SOF units are frequently called upon to support so-called "peace" operations. These can include monitoring of peacekeeping operations, enforcement of terms among warring factions, and other missions promoting peaceful relations in troubled regions of the world.

- **Security Assistance (SA)**—SA operations are congressionally mandated programs to provide training and assistance to nations obtaining and assimilating U.S. equipment, in support of U.S. national policy.

- **Special Activities**—The *really* "sticky" SOF missions—the ones you hardly ever hear about. These operations are in direct support of national policy; they are designed with "credible deniability" as a goal; and if successful, they are *never* exposed or acknowledged. They are usually covert and clandestine, and are sometimes just barely legal (under the U.S. Code). That means they normally require a presidential authorization (called a *finding*), as well as mandated congressional oversight. Examples might include clandestine reconnaissance inside a foreign country prior to an air strike, as apparently occurred in Khartoum, Sudan, prior to the August 1998 cruise missile strike. Another might be to kidnap or eliminate a key personnel target, such as a war criminal or despot leader. Such "snatches" have occurred several times in Bosnia over the last few years, though exactly which units were involved and their tasking remain highly classified.

All of these missions add up to the day-to-day workload of America's SOF warriors around the world . . . hardly the standard military missions. SOF missions are "on-the-margins"—and thus difficult and potentially controversial.

Because SOF operations tend to be on-the-margins, there have been occasions when units have performed not only with a degree of operational freedom greater than was in the best interests of the U.S. and our allies, but even outside the international laws of warfare. With some justice, the press, politicians, and non-SOF military leaders have labeled these units "rogue"—with the added implication that the epithet applies to SOFs in general.

The fact is that virtually every military operation has a rogue potential (all military units operate near the edge of morality, and, to repeat, warfare is itself not inherently moral). Mistakes will be made. There will be moral lapses. Some of these are tragic, obscene, and hideous. And, of course, the mistakes have to be corrected once they occur; and where appropriate, the rogues themselves have to be punished. But to blame all special forces for the mistakes of a few, much less to question the validity of the special forces mission—on that account—is simply absurd.

SOF units are worth the price that sometimes needs to be paid.

Trail of Tears: The Road to SOCOM

No branch of the American military has had a more tortured or prolonged birth than U.S. Special Operations Command. The story of that birth is important, because it shows not only the process that made Special Forces a virtual fifth American service (after the Army, Navy, Air Force, and Marines), but also the dangers of "inside-the-box" military thinking. That is, thinking that is conventional, predictable, unoriginal, and boring. In the world of the "quick and the dead," the dangers of inside-the-box thinking are obvious.

Without the birth of SOCOM in the late 1980s, the options of American leaders would be terribly limited in the post–Cold War world.

The story begins in 1947, when President Truman signed the National Security Act, which created the Department of Defense, as well as the Departments of the Army, Navy, and Air Force. Quietly tucked into the fine print of that document was the enabling legislation for America's first full-time intelligence department, the Central Intelligence Agency (many of whose personnel had previous service with Donovan in the OSS, and were looking to start where they had left off at the end of World War II; they formed the core of the new agency). At the time, the CIA's charter was to collect and analyze foreign-related intelligence, and then distribute it to various government leaders and organizations, but there was also a snippet of text mandating "other related duties as required," which left the door open for the former OSS veterans to enter the world of covert, clandestine, and unattributed operations (what they technically called "denied" operations).

After some early successes (such as influencing elections in Italy, Greece, and France), the CIA was given much of the responsibility for conducting special military operations in the Korean War (which broke out in 1950). And there they ran into problems. Virtually every CIA behind-the-lines operation in Korea failed. The reasons for failure were many, but the key was the CIA's lack of focus on regional and cultural issues in East Asia. (They hadn't done their homework.) And these failures led to the ending of CIA involvement in special military operations.

For the military forces that had depended upon the CIA, there was more than just disappointment. There was out-and-out resentment against what they saw as the OSS old boys' club.

Out of that experience came early attempts to build SOFs that would be attached to the various military services, and beholden to those forces alone. The first of these was the Army's 10th Special Forces Group, which was created in 1952. The 10th SFG was to provide a "stay behind" SOF capability against the perceived threat of a European invasion by the Soviet Union and their Warsaw Pact allies. Other SOF units created during this period included the Navy's Sea-Air-Land (SEAL) teams and the Air Forces "Air Commando" units. At first, these were just small units with minuscule budgets, and did little to attract the notice (or envy) of the leadership of their parent services.

President John F. Kennedy and Vietnam changed all that.

In the late 1950s and 1960s, as the old colonial empires of Europe were crumbling, "wars of liberation" seemed to erupt throughout the Third World. In Cuba, Vietnam, the Belgian Congo, and in a bewildering assortment of little-known and once sleepy places in Latin America, Africa, and East Asia, guerrilla forces—usually backed by communist patrons like China and the Soviet Union—were rolling back a century of colonial stability . . . and colonial profits. Kennedy perceived a worldwide threat from these wars, and sought ways to fight the growing insurgent tide. Unfortunately, he was prone to taking shortcuts. He wanted to win . . . but he wanted to win easy. Early in his presidency, he tried to use the CIA to stop Fidel Castro's Cuban revolution. The result was disastrous—the Bay of Pigs fiasco and Operation Mongoose (an attempt to assassinate Castro that was run by the CIA out of Miami and supervised personally by Robert Kennedy).

Stung by these failures, Kennedy turned away from the intelligence community as a counterinsurgency force. Now it was the small military SOF community that caught the dramatic and excitable young president's eye. Taking a special shine to the men of the Army Special Forces, whose distinctive green berets he admired, he ordered a vast expansion of SOF units in all services. And when he began to take seriously the communist threat in Southeast Asia, he began to deploy his new favorites to fight the North Vietnamese forces of Ho Chi Minh and the Vietcong rebels.

The tale of America's 1960s and 1970s nightmare in Southeast Asia needs no retelling. But a few points should be made.

What few realize is that our war in Vietnam was actually a series of parallel campaigns, including the "big" ground war in the south, air campaigns all over Southeast Asia, and a number of covert actions. In the process, the pool of SOF units was vastly expanded . . . so much so that they began to lose much of what was "special" about them in the first place. Men became Green Berets or SEALs who never should have been Green Berets or SEALs (much to the contempt of professional warriors). Even today, senior military leaders remember with loathing snake- and lightbulb-eating Special Forces hooligans making a mockery of discipline and order. (Based on his own bad experiences with SFs in Vietnam, H. Norman Schwarzkopf did everything in his considerable power to keep SOFs out of Desert Shield and Desert Storm.)

After the war, and especially during the Carter presidency, SOF-related funds were scarce (as was funding for the rest of the military). With all the services scraping for dollars to upgrade equipment, hold onto personnel, and keep units intact and in operation, SOF units were hard-pressed to keep any sort of capability alive. And like the rest of the U.S. military, SOF units sank into a dark morass, with little trust or support from the country or its leadership.

The one bright spot during the 1970s came when a few Army officers realized that the U.S. would have to deal with the growing threat of international terrorism.

As a small start, an antiterrorist unit was created in Europe—code-named Blue Light. Blue Light was a small company-sized force modeled on existing antiterrorist units in Europe and the Middle East, but since the Blue Light force was equipped and trained for only a few possible contingencies, its usefulness was limited.

A more permanent solution came with the development of Detachment Delta, better known today as the Delta Force, which was based upon the organization, training, and tactics of the British Special Air Service.[6]

Unfortunately for Delta, their first major mission (which was also America's first major attempt to use SOF units in the post-Vietnam era) developed into a chaotic debacle. In 1980, Delta, along with Blue Light, was assigned the job of rescuing American hostages in Iran. During the operation, the helicopters that were to transport the rescue teams into Tehran broke down and the entire Joint Task Force had to be withdrawn. Failure turned into a flaming fiasco when several aircraft collided on the ground in Iran while refueling.

The immediate cause of this disaster was lack of foresight and planning by the U.S. civilian leadership.[7] But deeper down, America's SOF units had much more systemic problems. Like the rest of the U.S. military of that time, SOF units of each service were focused only upon the roles and missions of their parent force . . . meaning that they lacked the ability either to operate together or to integrate units from nonSOF forces (such as transport helicopters and aircraft) into their own task forces. These skills—the core of "joint" (interservice and/or multinational) military operations—had not been practiced since the end of World War II. These limitations left the U.S. entering the 1980s ill-equipped for the terrorist and insurgency battles they would have to fight in the years ahead.

One might have imagined that the arrival of the Reagan presidency in 1981 would have provided SOF forces with the financial and other benefits soon enjoyed by the rest of the American military. However, since most senior leaders during the Reagan era were the same people who had most hated SOF units during their days as junior

---

6 The British SAS dates from the Second World War, when it served in North Africa against the units of Erwin Rommel's Afrika Korps. Originally designed as a long-range reconnaissance and raiding force by its founder, Major David Sterling, it has evolved today into perhaps the world's finest such unit. Man-for-man, it continues to be among the busiest and best-trained SOF forces, with capabilities in counterterrorism, reconnaissance, raiding, and other aspects of unconventional warfare.

7 One of the primary shortcomings of Operation Eagle Claw, as it was called, was that all the services had to operate jointly to covertly transport the strike force to its target in Iran. The lack of long-range helicopters with in-flight refueling capabilities proved to be the most obvious of many weak links in the capabilities of America's SOF community.

officers in Vietnam, that was anything but the case. Thus, for example, the Air Force leadership refused to buy new aircraft and helicopters for their own SOF units, even when directly mandated by congressional legislation. The Army and Navy were likewise doing all they could to starve their own SOF units (over the objections of Congress and the few visionary civilian leaders within the Department of Defense).[8]

Another problem during the Reagan Administration was its love affair with clandestine and covert action (even as it allowed the deterioration of those special forces units already in place). Thus a number of so-called "black" SOF units were created.[9] These included Sea Spray (a clandestine helicopter unit) and Yellow Fruit (a behind-the-lines reconnaissance unit). Though some of these units (Yellow Fruit, for example) transitioned to join the larger SOF community, where they serve today, others went "rogue" (always a temptation among black units), and their commanders had to be indicted and tried for misappropriation of funds and other charges. In consequence, several of the Reagan-created black units were dissolved . . . and conveniently forgotten by those who had created them.

Congress would not forget.

During the early 1980s a series of terrorist incidents against American citizens and property overseas caught the attention of Congress, and special operations became a congressional passion. What particularly bothered Congress was the impotence of U.S. SOF units. In those days, *joint* (i.e., multiservice) was an oxymoron. The community had no centralized leadership, and thus no one had any idea of the extent of our SF capabilities. What clearly was needed was a joint command and operations structure for the entire U.S. SOF community. Yet this was exactly what the various service chiefs wanted to avoid.

Though the buildup and renewal of the military during the early Reagan years was on the whole a good thing, it came with a downside: an increase in interservice rivalries and squabbles. All the services did their best to upstage the others in operations and funding. Clearly, the various services were not going to become "joint" on their own.

Meanwhile, the inability of U.S. forces to conduct joint operations had become intolerable to Congress. The worst offense against "jointness" remained the failed Iran hostage rescue mission in 1980, but the 1983 invasion of Grenada (Operation Urgent Fury) also pointed up serious weaknesses. The actual structure of the U.S. military had not been changed since the 1947 National Security Act, almost four decades earlier. By the mid-1980s, it was clear to almost everyone in the Congress that reform was needed.

We needed a "joint" military.

But what *is* "jointness"?

---

8 One of the few SOF supporters was an Undersecretary of Defense, Noel Koch, who single-handedly kept elements of the community alive during the early years of the Reagan administration. Today, Koch is celebrated as one of the founding fathers of USSOCOM.

9 "Black" units and programs are so secret that they are denied publicly, and do not appear in the funding documents submitted annually to Congress. Examples of such programs include the development of the U-2 and SR-71 spy planes, the F-117 Nighthawk stealth fighter, and the founding of the Delta Force.

Military operations conducted jointly yield three major benefits: economy, efficiency, and effectiveness.

Economy: A military force must operate under tight budget restrictions. If military services were to fight together under joint leadership, unnecessary duplications of capabilities could be ended. Thus, for example, in the mid-1990s two separate fleets of U.S. tactical jamming aircraft were eliminated (the Air Force's EF-111A Raven and the Navy/Marine EA-6B Prowler). Now the U.S. air services jointly operate a single force composed only of EA-6Bs.

Efficiency is a direct result of the elimination of redundant units and organizations within the services. Years ago, each service developed its own weapons, munitions, and systems, and there was little crossover of ideas or designs. Today, very few procurement programs can even get started unless they benefit at least two of the services. The new series of satellite-guided (using the NAVISTAR GPS system) air-to-ground weapons used during Desert Fox and Allied Force provide an excellent example of these improved efficiencies.

Effectiveness builds on the benefits made possible by forcing the services to work together. Service personnel spend most of their time with members of their own branch. Yet when these soldiers, sailors, airmen, and Marines train and fight together, the result is a better and more powerful (person-for-person) military force.

The new reform legislation establishing a joint military, the Goldwater-Nichols Act (after the two legislators who introduced the bill), was passed in 1986. It led to a true revolution in military affairs for the American armed forces, and provides the basic structure under which they fight and train today. Along with a restructuring of various commands and their relationships, Goldwater-Nichols removed functional control of operational forces from the service chiefs and gave it to a group of "unified" commanders in chiefs (CINCs). Each CINC and his staff were charged with responsibility over particular regions or missions.

There was, however, a notable early "hole" in Goldwater-Nichols, for the act only "suggested" that the Department of Defense create a unified command for SOF units. Since it was only a suggestion, it was almost immediately ignored by the various services, who wanted nothing of the kind.

It is hardly surprising that ignoring an act of Congress is a good way to encourage more powerful and direct legislation. And this is exactly what happened in 1987, when an amendment to Goldwater-Nichols was passed. Introduced by two of the Senate's most respected legislators, Sam Nunn and William Cohen,[10] the Nunn-Cohen amendment directed in exact terms the creation of USSOCOM. From now on, SOCOM would control all the SOF units of the three parent services.[11] Nunn-Cohen also created a new funding source (as part of Title 10 of the U.S. Code) for SOF training,

---

10 Senator Sam Nunn (D-Georgia) was chairman of the Senate Armed Services committee prior to his retirement, and Senator William Cohen (R-Maine) would become the Secretary of Defense in 1997.

11 Because the USMC had encouraged special operations development, and had invested heavily in their own SOF capabilities, it was excepted from the Nunn-Cohen legislation and retained control of its Force Reconnaissance teams, as well as various SWAT teams and other units. Today, these are located within the seven Marine Expeditionary Unit, Special Operations Capable—MEU (SOC)—forces deployed worldwide. For more information on MEU (SOC)s and Marine Corps doctrine, see: *Marine: A Guided Tour of a Marine Expeditionary Unit* (Berkley Books, 1996).

procurement, and operations, and effectively ended the ability of the service chiefs and DoD (Department of Defense) bureaucrats to starve SOF units. In the process it created a *de facto* fifth military service.

With their leadership and funding protected, USSOCOM was ready to head into the brave new world offered by the collapse of the Soviet Empire and the end of the Cold War. They did not have to wait long to prove their worth.

In 1989, a decade of bad relations with the government of Panama came to a head with the indictment on drug-trafficking charges of General Manuel Noriega (the commander of the Panamanian Defense Force and Maximum Leader of Panama). When a PDF-sponsored coup failed to oust him as Maximum Leader, the administration of President George Bush began to lay out plans to remove him with military force. The U.S. force charged with maintaining U.S. interests in the region was called SOUTHCOM (Southern Command, which included all of Central and South America), whose new commander, General Maxwell Thurman, knew *exactly* how he wanted to take down Noriega and the PDF. His plan, which became known as Operation Just Cause, would be an SOF tour de force. Elements of almost every Special Operations unit in the U.S. military (SEALs, Rangers, etc.) were packaged by SOCOM to be launched as soon as the "go" order came from the White House. All they needed was a provocation. This Noriega provided in midDecember, 1989.

In two separate incidents, PDF troops assaulted American service personnel (and in one case also a dependent wife). After one of the servicemen died, Operation Just Cause was unleashed. Panama was not, obviously, a serious obstacle to American forces, and the operation was effectively over in a matter of hours—with surprisingly light casualties. The SOF forces SOCOM had packaged for the Panamanian operation had fought in the first true joint combat operation of the Goldwater-Nichols era. Their next test would come in the form of an enemy who would prove to be far tougher than Manuel Noriega: General H. Norman Schwarzkopf.

Nobody has ever accused General Schwarzkopf of keeping his opinions to himself. Or of having a small ego. He is especially famous for verbally eviscerating those in his staff who displeased him. While Schwarzkopf commanded the U.S. Central Command (CENTCOM), the phrase *CINC Abuse* was coined to describe his tirades during meetings and planning conferences.

Schwarzkopf had equally strong—not to say violent—opinions about SOF units and their personnel. The bad feeling started in Vietnam, and later, in 1983, he was present during the Grenada Invasion, where he witnessed a poor performance by Army Rangers, Navy SEALs, and other SOF units.

Based on these experiences (and because he was a supporter of strong conventional force units), Schwarzkopf excluded SOFs from his plans when he became CINC of CENTCOM. Thus, from the very beginning of Desert Shield in August 1990, Schwarzkopf made it clear that he wanted no SOF units in the Persian Gulf.

Meanwhile, Schwarzkopf's MacDill AFB neighbor, General Carl Stiner (then the SOCOM commander), had extensive plans for SOF operations in the Persian Gulf. These ranged from support of a behind-the-lines Kuwait resistance movement to attacks on Iraqi infrastructure targets deep in enemy territory. Initially, Schwarzkopf would have none of it.

The official emblem of the U.S. Special Operations Command
OFFICIAL DEPARTMENT OF DEFENSE GRAPHIC

In time, however, the CENTCOM commander began to allow SOF units into the region, but under highly restrictive rules and oversight that none of the other component forces (air, naval, ground) had to endure. And yet, in the event, it turned out that even the strong-willed Norman Schwarzkopf couldn't fight his war without them. By the time Desert Storm broke out in January 1991, SOF units had thoroughly imbedded themselves into the CENTCOM war plan.

They took part, in fact, in the mission that fired the first shots of the war.

On the war's first night, Air Force MH-53J Pave Low Special Operations helicopters led the way for two teams of Army AH-64 Apache attack helicopters to destroy a pair of important radar installations. Later, Green Berets from the 3rd and 5th SFGs conducted deep-reconnaissance missions in Iraq; SEALs helped divert Iraqi attention toward the sea; and other SOFs, along with their British counterparts from the Special Air Service, helped hunt down the Iraqi SCUD missile force. By the time the war was over, Schwarzkopf had no choice but to give credit to the various SOF units, although it probably pained him to do so.

With two successful armed conflicts behind them, the personnel at USSOCOM could finally look forward to a real future. Their four decades of uncertain existence were over. It was a rough pregnancy and a messy birth, but SOF warriors are now equipped and positioned to give service to the nation and the world at the very moment when they seem to be most needed.

American Special Operations Forces: A Roadmap

We'll shift our focus now from history to organization—and we'll look specifically at the units that make up the command.

Warning: What follows will necessarily include an array of acronyms and overlapping responsibilities and capabilities. This partly results from the nature of the business, which is often clandestine and therefore outside the control and view of mainstream military authority. But it is also a consequence of interface lines in what the military calls areas of responsibility (AORs). Thus the SEALs focus on maritime and littoral operations. The Delta Force focuses on land operations, and so on.

U.S. Special Operations Command: CINCSOC

At the top of the SOF food chain is the U.S. Special Operations Command, which is based at MacDill AFB near Tampa, Florida, and is commanded by a four-star flag officer (normally a full U.S. Army general).

Because SOCOM is now one of the eight "unified" commands that make up the actual fighting muscle of today's U.S. military, and stands equal with the other seven unified commands, Special Forces now no longer live at the bottom of the financial priority lists of their parent services. SOCOM has its own funding sources in the annual Department of Defense budget and (under Title 10 of the U.S. Code) does not need to go to the service secretaries or joint chiefs for money to buy new gear or pay for training, operations, maintenance, and other vital functions. In other words, in the high-pressure world of the U.S. defense budget, this means relative freedom from interservice politics and squabbling.

SOCOM is unusual in other ways as well.

First, most other unified commands either "own" (that is, train and equip) or "fight" units, but not both. When a unified command is about to "fight," the units it needs are "chopped" to it from the commands that "own" them. Though the original "owners" will still be expected to provide supplies, maintenance, and replacements of personnel and equipment, the units are now "owned" by the command that is "fighting" them. This works out much more smoothly in practice than it reads on paper (Desert Shield/Storm provide a good example).

SOCOM, however, doesn't work that way. It is the only unified command that can both commit units in combat and train and package SOF components for other CINCs.

Second, USSOCOM does not have a particular service or regional affiliation. The other unified CINCs have a territorial responsibility. U.S. Central Command (CENTCOM) protects U.S. interests in the Middle East, South Asia, and northeast Africa (i.e., the Muslim world). EUCOM's primary interest is in Europe; PACOM's is in areas that ring the Pacific.

SOCOM, however, has responsibilities across the entire world, and these responsibilities include the full spectrum of missions, from counterterrorism to all-out war.

Third, SOCOM is the smallest of unified commands . . . and by a wide margin. When CENTCOM went to war during Operation Desert Storm in 1991, it fought with almost 500,000 personnel under its control. In the spring of 1999, SOCOM had something less than 30,000 people in its various components. All of SOCOM, in other words, is smaller than a normally staffed and equipped Army or Marine division.

Such a diverse command requires a leader who can bridge the multitude of service, cultural, financial, and material challenges that SOCOM presents.

SOCOM has recently been blessed with exceptional leadership in the top position (CINCSOC).

In 1996 and 1997, the CINCSOC was General Henry Hugh Shelton, USA. During his tenure, Shelton did much to "sell" the command's units and capabilities to its "customers" around the world (that is, to bridge the problems and differences between

General Peter Schoomaker, the commander of
the U.S. Special Operations Command based at
MacDill AFB in Florida.

John D. Gresham

SOCOM and the other seven unified commanders and our allies). So impressive were his achievements in this and previous assignments that he was appointed Chairman of the Joint Chiefs, the first time a Special Operations professional has held the position.

When Shelton left SOCOM, in September of 1997, he was replaced by General Peter J. Schoomaker, USA. Though Schoomaker is another SOF professional (he had previously commanded the Joint Special Operations Command that handles antiterrorism), he began as an armor officer, and his career has been a mix of assignments to both armor and SOF units, as well as a host of important "joint" assignments. In the process, he attended almost every important school and qualification course the Army has to offer (as well as the Marine Corps Amphibious Warfare School). All of this experience has provided him with a vast reservoir of knowledge about the many communities his command has to work with and serve, and has greatly enhanced his ability to continue General Shelton's efforts to "sell" special forces.

Though SOCOM is now built on a solid organizational foundation, General Schoomaker and his staff have more than their share of problems.

On the low end of the spectrum: They have to share MacDill AFB with the commander and staff of CENTCOM, probably the busiest of the unified commands over the past decade. Base traffic jams and seating problems at official functions aside, there is a serious struggle going on at MacDill . . . and it's not about whose name is mentioned first on the base phone roster. Though only a few short blocks separate the two headquarters buildings, the gap between the two is considerable. CENTCOM represents the "big" U.S. military (it has successfully fought America's largest military action since World War II), while SOCOM represents a "new" kind of warfare, one that frequently threatens the very unified commands it is mandated to support.

The component commands of SOCOM. From left to right, USASOC, NACSPEC-WARCOM, AFSOC, and JSOC

OFFICIAL DEPARTMENT OF DEFENSE, U.S. ARMY, U.S. NAVY, AND U.S. AIR FORCE GRAPHICS

Unconventional warfare is the antithesis of the large unit operations that most of the Army is trained to perform. That such small forces *might* do the same job, and *perhaps* do it better, is *very* threatening to "Mother Army."

This means that General Schoomaker, his staff, and the 30,000 or so personnel under them have to face a great deal of friction. It is far from easy to operate and maintain what is for all practical purposes a fifth military service . . . all of whose pieces must be supplied by three different branches of the military, none of which ever wanted SOCOM to see the light of day. In other words, CINCSOC is now in charge of the most hated (or at least feared and misunderstood) command in the U.S. military, yet he must also act as the chief salesman for that command and its services to customers who often include the very people who are doing the hating.

It is a tough job. Thankfully, the top leadership at SOCOM has come a long way from the cavalier attitudes of some of the command's early leaders. General "Hugh" Shelton's ascendancy from CINCSOC to Chairman of the Joint Chiefs says much about how far the command has come.

SOCOM Components: SEALs, Air Commandos, and Army

Within SOCOM, General Schoomaker commands a collection of SOF units from the Army, Air Force, and Navy.

As previously mentioned, SOCOM has no U.S. Marine Corps units. The Marines have always integrated their SOF units (Force Reconnaissance, Raiders, etc.) into the

The official emblem of NAVSPECWARCOM

operation doctrine and structure of the USMC. In recent years, they have concentrated their Special Operations capabilities into the specialized afloat units, creating the Marine Expeditionary Unit, Special Operations Capable—MEU (SOC). Thus, the Marines were excluded from the Nunn-Cohen Amendment. The rest of the services, however, had no choice about the future of their SOF units.

Each service's SOF units were grouped into a separate "component" command within SOCOM. These break down as follows:

- **Naval Special Warfare Command (NAVSPECWARCOM)**—NAVSPECWAR-COM controls the famous Sea-Air-Land (SEAL) teams and their supporting special boat squadrons, submarines, and delivery vehicles. These units handle Special Operations missions in the littoral zones of the oceans and coasts. NAVSPECWAR-COM is based at Coronado, California, near San Diego, and has units stationed around the world.

- **Air Force Special Operations Command (AFSOC)**—Based at Eglin AFB, Florida, AFSOC is composed of specialized helicopter and transport aircraft units that formerly made up the old Air Commando squadrons. Though primarily focused on transporting units from other commands to their destinations, and then supporting them, AFSOC not only delivers a considerable combat punch on its own, but also supports the preparation of landing zones and airfields for followup units.

- **Joint Special Operations Command**—JSOC is a multiservice/interdepartmental command, with antiterrorism as its primary job. It is based at Fort Bragg, North Carolina, and includes a command staff that oversees training and operations of the Army's Delta Force, the Navy's SEAL Team Six, and reportedly elements of the FBI's Hostage Rescue Team (in time of national emergency or insurrection).

- **U.S. Army Special Operations Command (USASOC)**—Something like 25,000 SOCOM personnel are contained in this single component command, which includes the U.S. Army Special Forces Command (Airborne), the 75th Ranger Regiment, the 160th Special Operations Aviation Regiment (SOAR), the JFK Special Warfare Center and School, the U.S. Army Civil Affairs and Psychological Operations Command, the U.S. Army Special Operations Support Command, and assorted chemical reconnaissance units. Headquarters is located at Fort Bragg.

All of these components make up one of the busiest and most powerful commands of its size in the world, and man for man, they can probably stand up to any other unit in the world.

The official emblem of AFSOC

In addition to the basic SOCOM command structure, there are Special Operations component commanders within each of the other warfighting CINC staffs around the world. For example, just a few blocks from SOCOM headquarters at MacDill AFB, Special Operations Command, Central (SOCCENT), has an office at the CENTCOM building. This is the CENTCOM element that would utilize any special operations forces that SOCOM might be ordered to package and send to them.

The following table shows the various CINC component command elements and shows how major special operations forces are laid out within the command structure set forth in Goldwater-Nichols and Nunn-Cohen:

Unified Military Commands and Special Operations Assignments

Command Component	Designation	Assigned Unified Command	Area of Responsibility
Special Operations Command, South	SOCSOUTH	U.S. Southern Command (SOUTHCOM)	Latin America/Caribbean Basin
Special Operations Command, Atlantic	SOCACOM	U.S. Atlantic Command (USACOM)	Continental United States/ North Atlantic Basin
Special Operations Command, Europe	SOCEUR	U.S. European Command (EUCOM)	Europe/West and Southern Africa
Special Operations Command, Central	SOCCENT	U.S. Central Command (CENTCOM)	Central and Southwest Asia/ Middle East/Eastern Africa
Special Operations Command, Pacific	SOCPAC	U.S. Pacific Command (PACOM)	Pacific Basin/Eastern and Southern Asia

Let's now look more closely at the Special Forces located within USASOC.

U.S. Army Special Operations Command (USASOC): Rangers, Nightstalkers, and Special Forces

The largest of SOCOM's component commands, USASOC is housed in a massive new headquarters building on the southeastern side of the Fort Bragg reservation in North Carolina. Well separated from the other Army units based on the post (the XVIII Airborne Corps and 82nd Airborne Division are located there as well), they live in some of the newest and most secure quarters you are likely to see.

Commanding the roughly 25,000 personnel of USASOC is Army Lieutenant

The official emblem of JSOC

OFFICIAL DEPARTMENT OF DEFENSE GRAPHIC

General William P. Tangney. Originally an artillery officer, he became a Special Forces soldier in 1969, and has remained in the special operations community ever since. Along the way, he has acquired an awesome resume of assignments and schools, including a course at the Naval War College at Newport, Rhode Island. His mission is to make USASOC the command of choice for special operations missions around the world. He certainly has the tools to make that a reality.

USASOC is composed of six basic parts (or communities), each of which is important to its roles and missions. To understand them better, let's look at USASOC's component units, and some of their capabilities:

- **75th Ranger Regiment**[12]—The 75th, which is based at Fort Benning, Georgia, is the descendant of the famous Ranger battalions that "led the way" during many of the famous assaults of the Second World War. Composed of three highly trained and jump-qualified Ranger battalions, the 75th is equipped to occupy or destroy large targets such as airfields and ports . . . or even small countries. They did this twice in the 1980s when they jumped as the lead elements of Operations Urgent Fury (Grenada, 1983) and Just Cause (Panama, 1989).

- **160th Special Operations Aviation Regiment (SOAR—the "Nightstalkers")**— The most secret and technologically advanced unit in USASOC, the Nightstalkers provide the rest of the command with the aviation support that was lacking during the Iranian hostage rescue in 1980. Headquartered at Fort Campbell, Kentucky (also the home of the 101st Airborne Division, Air Assault), the 160th flies a mix of helicopters, which are all heavily modified and specialized. These include:

  —**MH-47D/E Chinook**—The long-range, heavy-lift component of the 160th, the MH-47 is a heavily modified variant of the Army's famous twin-engine/rotor Boeing Chinook helicopter. Equipped with a specially engineered mission equipment package (terrain following radar—TFR; forward-looking infrared scanner— FLIR; radar, electronics countermeasures—ECM; an in-flight refueling probe,

---

12 The term "ranger" has a dual meaning in the U.S. Army. For most Army personnel, Ranger training is an advanced course, which can be taken by virtually anyone in any branch of the service. The Ranger course is a physically and mentally arduous school, which is designed to toughen a soldier, and give him advanced training in combat skills, field craft, and small unit leadership. It is a tough course, with an extremely high dropout rate. Most of the men I know who wear the Ranger tab on their uniforms will tell you it was the roughest training they ever survived! The 75th Ranger Regiment is a formation composed exclusively of jump-qualified personnel who have also completed the Ranger training course. As such, they are an elite light regiment of shock troops, with few equals in the world.

The official emblem of USASOC

etc.) and computer system, the MH-47 is able to do the kinds of nonstop missions that were impossible in Iran back in 1980. A single MH-47 can carry up to twenty fully equipped Special Operations personnel or a rubber boat with a dozen men.

—**MH-60K/L Pave Hawk**—Based upon the popular UH-60 Blackhawk, the MH-60 is the little brother to the MH-47 Chinook. Equipped with a similar mission equipment package, the Pave Hawk is designed to conduct similar missions of shorter duration and with smaller payloads. However, the MH-60K model is equipped with an in-flight refueling probe so that longer missions can be flown, as well as air-to-ground rockets and machine guns. There are also unconfirmed reports of an attack version of the MH-60K, known as the AH-60. It reportedly has a laser designator in addition to the normal mission equipment package, as well as a pair of 30mm chain guns. This gives it firepower similar to that of the AH-64 Apache attack helicopter, which includes both Hellfire and Stinger missiles for attacking ground and air targets respectively.

—**A/M/TH-6 "Little Bird"**—The most secret of the 160th's aircraft, the Little Bird is actually a family of light attack, assault, and surveillance helicopters that are based upon the H-6/MD-500 series helicopter built by Boeing (formerly McDonnell Douglas and Hughes). Though the details surrounding these birds are highly classified, we know that most are equipped with a lightweight FLIR system, and can be armed with 7.62mm six-barreled miniguns and air-to-ground rockets. The Little Bird can also be used as an urban assault transport helicopter, equipped to "fast rope" up to six special operations personnel into built-up environments like cities and industrial zones.

The Nightstalkers specialize in night operations, where their advantages in sensors, navigational equipment, weapons, and crew skills can translate into a potent edge in combat; and they have seen their share of action since they were formed in the early 1980s. From the invasion of Grenada to operations in Bosnia today, the 160th owns the night, and stays busy!

• **Civil Affairs/Psychological Operations Command**—As mentioned earlier, one of the most effective ways to get your way is to "persuade" the other guy to give up . . . or else to decide that you are right. "Persuasion" (PR, advertising, rhetoric, call it what you like) applies as much in warfare as it does in a schoolyard or politics. It therefore makes sense that the Army's repository of expertise in these

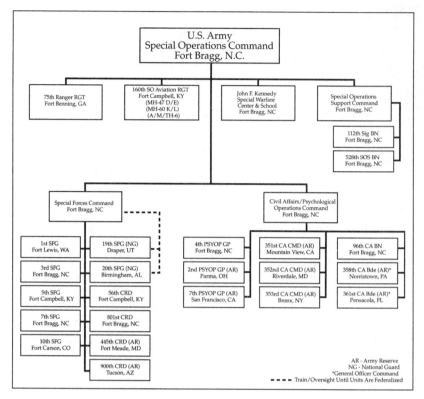

US. Army
Special Operations Command
Fort Bragg, N.C.

| 75th Ranger RGT
Fort Benning, GA | 160th SO Aviation RGT
Fort Campbell, KY
(MH-47 D/E)
(MH-60 K/L)
(A/M/TH-6) | John F. Kennedy
Special Warfare
Center & School
Fort Bragg, NC | Special Operations
Support Command
Fort Bragg, NC |

112th Sig BN
Fort Bragg, NC

528th SOS BN
Fort Bragg, NC

Special Forces Command
Fort Bragg, NC

Civil Affairs/Psychological
Operations Command
Fort Bragg, NC

1st SFG Fort Lewis, WA	19th SFG (NG) Draper, UT	4th PSYOP GP Fort Bragg, NC	351st CA CMD (AR) Mountain View, CA	96th CA BN Fort Bragg, NC
3rd SFG Fort Bragg, NC	20th SFG (NG) Birmingham, AL	2nd PSYOP GP (AR) Parma, OH	352nd CA CMD (AR) Riverdale, MD	358th CA Bde (AR)* Norristown, PA
5th SFG Fort Campbell, KY	56th CRD Fort Campbell, KY	7th PSYOP GP (AR) San Francisco, CA	353rd CA CMD (AR) Bronx, NY	361st CA Bde (AR)* Pensacola, FL
7th SFG Fort Bragg, NC	801st CRD Fort Bragg, NC			
10th SFG Fort Carson, CO	445th CRD (AR) Fort Meade, MD			
	900th CRD (AR) Tucson, AZ			

AR - Army Reserve
NG - National Guard
*General Officer Command
■ ■ ■ Train/Oversight Until Units Are Federalized

USASOC Organization Chart

RUBICON, INC., BY LAURA DeNINNO

areas resides in one of the "smartest" commands in the Army. Headquartered at Fort Bragg, the CA/PSYOPS Command is composed of nine component units. These include:

—**2nd, 4th, and 7th PSYOP Groups**—These three groups are the core of the Army's PSYOPs capability. The 4th PSYOP Group is based at Fort Bragg, while the 2nd and 7th Groups are members of the reserve, and are based at Parma, Ohio, and San Francisco, California, respectively.

—**96th CA Battalion**—The 96th is based at Fort Bragg, and is the only active-duty CA unit in the Army.

—**358th and 361st CA Brigades**—These are two large CA brigades assigned to the reserves. They are based at Norristown, Pennsylvania, and Pensacola, Florida, respectively.

—**351st, 352nd, and 353rd CA Commands**—These three reserve units are smaller than their brigade counterparts, and are based at Mountain View, California; Riverdale, Maryland; and the Bronx, New York, respectively.

- **Special Operations Support Command (SOSCOM)**—Logistics and communications are never "sexy." But without them, no military operation will go well or far. The Army's SOS Command provides spare parts, supplies, and a huge variety of services for USASOC. The two major component units are:

  —**528th SO Support Battalion**—Based at Fort Bragg, this unit provides the basic supply and service function for the rest of USASOC.

  —**112th Signal Battalion**—Also based at Fort Bragg, the 112th services the wide range of communications, data processing, and networking requirements for USASOC.

- **U.S. Army John F. Kennedy (JFK) Special Warfare Center (SWC) and School**—This is the USASOC schoolhouse. Originally formed to support the training and selection of new Special Forces soldiers, it has grown into a center of learning for the entire USASOC special operations community. In 1999, it taught everything from trauma medical techniques to satellite communications. Along the way, it is the repository for everything the Army has ever learned about special operations, unconventional warfare, and all the other tricks of this deadly and valuable trade. A number of subsidiary schools around the country teach specialties like SCUBA diving and free-fall parachute jumping and there are several field schools, as well.

- **Special Forces Command (SFC)**—This is the home of the Green Berets, and is composed of approximately 10,000 personnel. It is thus the largest single component within both SOCOM and USASOC. SFC is made up of active-duty and National Guard Special Forces Groups (SFGs), as well as active and reserve Chemical Reconnaissance Detachments (CRDs), and is the "brains" portion of USASOC (as opposed to the 75th Ranger Regiment's "muscle"). The command, based at Fort Bragg, breaks down as follows:

  —**1st SFG**—Based at Fort Lewis, Washington (with one of its battalions forward-deployed to Okinawa), the 1st SFG provides services to PACOM/SOCPAC.

  —**3rd SFG**—Assigned to support EUCOM/SOCEUR operations in western and southern Africa, the 3rd SFG is based at Fort Bragg. They also support CENTCOM/SOCCENT operations as needed.

  —**5th SFG**—Perhaps the best known and most decorated of the groups (as a result of its service in Vietnam), the 5th SFG is assigned to support CENTCOM/SOCCENT in eastern Africa, the Middle East, and southwest/central Asia. The 5th Group calls Fort Campbell, Kentucky, home.

  —**7th SFG**—Also based at Fort Bragg (with a company forward-based in Puerto Rico), the 7th SFG handles operations for SOUTHCOM/SOCSOUTH in Latin America and the Caribbean Basin.

  —**10th SFG**—Just moved into their new quarters at Fort Carson, Colorado (with a forward-based battalion in Germany); the 10th SFG was the first such unit formed (back in 1952), and covers Europe for EUCOM/SOCEUR.

—**19th SFG**—The 19th is one of two National Guard SFGs, which help "backfill" various missions for the active-duty groups. Based at Draper, Utah, the 19th is composed of units from all of the western United States, and tends to focus on missions for PACOM/SOCPAC and CENTCOM/SOCCENT.

—**20th SFG**—The other National Guard group is the 20th SFG, which is based in Birmingham, Alabama. The 20th provides missions for SOUTHCOM/SOC-SOUTH, with a concentration on the Caribbean Basin.

—**56th and 801st CRDs**—Based at Fort Campbell and Fort Bragg respectively, these are the only active-duty units of their kind in the Army.

—**445th CRD**—This reserve unit is based at Fort Meade, Maryland, where it provides CRD support for the eastern U.S.

—**900th CRD**—The other reserve CRD, the 900th is based at Fort Carson, Colorado.

SFC has the highest operations tempo (OpTempo) within SOCOM, with the average SF soldiers spending more than six months per year in the field. By comparison, a Navy carrier battle group or MEU(SOC) only spends six months out of every eighteen on cruise. To better understand why, let's look a bit closer at SFC.

Special Forces Command: The Green Berets

Just what are Special Forces, and what do they do? What value do they give the nation? And what roles and missions do they fulfill?

For starters, though they are indeed fearsome warriors, their *primary* focus is not necessarily on combat. While they have conducted significant combat missions since the end of the Cold War, and they will continue to operate in a combat role, this is just a tiny fraction of the overseas work that they have done (and will do). In short, this highly flexible combat force has vast utility in peacetime.

Let us not forget the core truth of the special forces profession: They are special people, given special training, and provided with unique opportunities for service to the Army and the country. SF soldiers are recruited from around the Army to undergo what is perhaps the longest and most rigorous qualification and training program anywhere in the U.S. military. Once these men finish this initial curriculum (called the "Q" Course—for Qualification), they are assigned to the various SFGs around the country. They then undertake further training in the languages and culture of the regions covered by their assigned group. Once they have become proficient in these, they are assigned to a fourteen-man team, the basic building block of the Special Forces, known as an "Operational Detachment Alpha," or ODA (also known as "A-Teams," though that term has fallen into disfavor since the airing of the television show of that name).

It is in peacetime operations, however, that the Special Forces normally earn their pay, and to understand them we need to return back to that basic building block, the ODA.

Each ODA is a carefully balanced team, which can split into two evenly matched units with duplicate capabilities. These capabilities include civil engineering, medical skills, communications, and various kinds of military training. Additionally, SF soldiers are trained specialists, with a high level of technical, cultural, and combat skills; they are chosen for their ability to work together and solve problems; and they are each natural leaders, with what can only be described as an entrepreneurial spirit.

So just what good do they do for America?

SF soldiers like to refer to themselves as "the quiet professionals." Though they sometimes take their taciturnity just a bit too far (they don't have to be *that* reticent about what they do), their quiet discretion nevertheless makes the ODA the unit of choice for a variety of difficult and sensitive jobs.

For this reason, organizations like the Departments of Defense and State trust sending a single ODA led by an Army captain to another country to run an entire mission: perhaps an FID course of instruction to a national police force or military unit. Another ODA might support the training of personnel involved in the removal and deactivation of mines and other unexploded ordnance. Still another team might help a rebel force develop an insurgency against a government opposed by the U.S. and its allies.

Though all of these missions have "high adventure" written all over them, they all also require a delicate touch. For this reason, some people have wryly begun to call the Special Forces, "the Peace Corps with guns," or "the armed branch of the State Department."

Looking at this another way: Not only has Special Forces Command cast off its "Snakeater" image, it is hard to find more professional or more flexible warriors in the U.S. military.

The Road to the Top:
An Interview with
General Henry H. Shelton

The Chairman of the Joint Chiefs of Staff commands no units of his own and has no authority to issue orders to troops in the field. He normally serves two two-year terms, but can serve up to six years at the discretion of the President of the United States, and requires the approval of the Senate to even walk into his office on the Pentagon's E-Ring. To accept the job means an end to personal privacy and endless scrutiny from an inquisitive press and members of Congress. Yet the Chairman of the Joint Chiefs of Staff is the highest-ranking military officer in the United States and has no military equal anywhere in the world.

The list of men who have served as "Chairman" (as the job is called by Washington and military insiders) is a "who's who" of recent American military leadership. The first was General of the Army Omar Bradley, the "Soldier's General," who led Army units from North Africa to the German heartland during World War II. Others included legendary warriors like General Maxwell Taylor, Admiral Thomas Moorer, and General David Jones.

These were all great men, but it is the four most recent chairmen who have defined the job as we know it today.

Following the passage of the Goldwater-Nichols defense reform act (officially known as the Department of Defense Reorganization Act of 1986) in the 1980s, Admiral William Crowe successfully transformed the position into the powerful advisory post it would become in the post–Cold War world, while his successor, General Colin Powell (the youngest man to hold the chairmanship, as well as the first African-American and ROTC officer), set the standard for the revised position, helping lead America to victories in Panama and the Persian Gulf, and in the endgame of the Cold War. Powell's replacement, General John Shalikashvili, (the first foreign born chairman), brought his own unique perspective to the chairmanship. Gentle and soft-spoken, General "Shali," as he was affectionately known, led the U.S. military through a critical period of downsizing and consolidation, while at the same time watching over America's myriad interests around the globe. When the time for his retirement came in 1997, it was clear that whoever would replace him would have huge responsibilities to shoulder and a vast job to do.

The man who would take over that job had made his first notable appearance on the public scene in 1994 as the Joint Task Force commander for Operation Uphold

General Henry H. "Hugh" Shelton, USA. General Shelton is the Chairman of the Joint Chiefs of Staff, the first special operations professional to achieve the position.

Official Department of Defense Photo

Democracy in Haiti, when (with TV cameras rolling) Lieutenant General Henry Shelton emerged from a helicopter having flown in from three miles off the Haitian coast abroad the U.S.S. *Mount Whitney* (LCC-20), his command ship for the operation. Shelton's quiet, professional handling of the Haitian operation quickly demonstrated to the world at large why he had been a rising star in the Army.

In the next three years, Hugh Shelton was promoted to general (four stars), given command of the U.S. Special Operations Command at MacDill AFB, and in 1997 was nominated to replace "General Shali" as chairman. In 1999, at the completion of his first two-year term, he was renominated for a second, which runs through October 2001.

To meet General Shelton is to be impressed—and not just for his distinguished Army career. While many people who encounter him focus on his physical presence (he's six feet, five inches tall and built like John Wayne) and quiet authority, a small and elite community takes a special pride in his present position and achievement: special operations professionals. General Shelton is the first member of the Special Operations Forces to be appointed to the chairmanship.

Hugh Shelton started his career as a Special Forces soldier during Vietnam. And his subsequent story is in many ways the story of the SOF community. It was with an eye to learning this story that I went to the Pentagon to meet with this man over lunch in late 1999. It proved to be an enlightening and powerful experience.

General Henry H. Shelton (USA), came into the world in January 1942, in a North Carolina coast farming family. As you listen to his sometimes thick Carolina drawl

The author and General Henry Shelton shake hands during their interview. A tall man, General Shelton combines an impressive physical presence with quiet Southern charm as his leadership style.

JOHN D. GRESHAM

and soft-spoken words, you can't help but wonder how his Carolina background formed his personality:

Tom Clancy: Can you tell us a little about your early years in North Carolina? What was your hometown like back then?

General Shelton: I was born in Tarboro, which is a small town, though the little town I was actually raised in is called Speed. Back when I was growing up, Tarboro had about 5,000 people, while Speed had around 250. My girlfriend, who would one day become my wife, lived in Speed with her parents; her sister still lives in their family home, while my family lived several miles out in the country.

Both communities experienced terrible flooding during Hurricane Floyd [in October 1999]. You may have seen pictures of it on TV. The church in which I was raised was badly flooded, and my brother told me that our eighty-two-year-old mother was down on her hands and knees helping to clean it up. She's been the organist there for sixty years.

Tom Clancy: What memories of growing up in that community in the 1950s shaped your desire to join the military?

General Shelton: Now that I can look back and think, it was a tremendous place to be raised in. The folks there were good, basic, hard-working, God-fearing people. The churches and schools were the centerpieces of their lives, and you had a lot of veterans in the community. These were folks who had taken four years out of their lives to go off and fight World War II. The emphasis was on hard work, honesty, integrity, and your word was your bond. There was a great emphasis on these and all the other attributes that we try to perpetuate in today's military.

Tom Clancy: Did your family have a tradition of military service prior to your going in?

General Shelton: I did not come from a military family, though I had three uncles that served during the Second World War.[13] I remember listening to their stories and was very impressed. There were a lot of other people in our community who had also served, so you picked up other stories, too . . . though not everyone who went to war talked about it.

As I think about it [General Shelton added thoughtfully], I've never really talked to my own sons about my experiences in Vietnam, and the more I think about it, the more I think that I probably should, so they will have a feeling and better understand what that was like.

After a childhood on his family's farm, Hugh Shelton began to think about a career that would both challenge him personally and allow him to exercise the values that had been instilled in him. This led him to seek his college education at North Carolina State University in Raleigh, North Carolina, just as America was entering the 1960s. His observations of those days are a flashback to the days before Vietnam, assassinations, and the bad race relations that defined that revolutionary decade.

Tom Clancy: You went to North Carolina State [in Raleigh, North Carolina] back in the early 1960s. What was the campus like then, and what led you to your own ROTC experience there?

General Shelton: Well, first of all, I was raised in a family that included a *lot* of NC State graduates. As you know, there is a tremendous rivalry in North Carolina between universities. I'd grown up as a Wolfpack fan, and had since early childhood desired to attend NC State in Raleigh. I'd never even thought of the military as a career, or as something I would want to do or be interested in. But as it happened, NC State was a land grant college and ROTC training was mandatory for the first two years at these institutions. That went away around 1966 or 1967, but was mandatory for men of my generation. That got me involved in ROTC for the first two years, and I really liked it—the people that were in it, the organization, and everything about it.

In those days after the first two years in ROTC, they would pay you about $27.50 a month to stay. Not much by today's standards, but real money back then! Some people may have called that "beer money," but to me it was "survival" money. At any rate, that got me interested in staying on, and I did. At that time, signing up meant a two-year obligation on active duty following graduation, and I said, "Fine." I figured I could serve in the Army for two years and stuck with it.

---

13 General Shelton's father was given a 4-F (medically unsuitable) status during the Second World War; but his brothers were all able to serve with honor during the conflict.

Tom Clancy: Give us a little "snapshot" of American life at that time if you will. What was NC State like in the early 1960s?

General Shelton: It was a conservative era for NC State. We really had not gotten into Vietnam yet, and student activism was not a "big" thing. Of course Communism could get you into some heated discussions, and you had a few students who would say that there was nothing wrong with it, and you would get a heated debate going. It's what we got for letting Yankees into the school!

Seriously though, in those days most of our basketball team came from New York or Indiana, and they were quite good! The big thing on campus was to go down and have a big pep rally around the Capitol, and show everybody that we could pull against UNC [University of North Carolina, in nearby Chapel Hill].

The bottom line was that NC State worked us hard, with a lot of academic discipline required. It was a technical school, with basically an engineering and agricultural curriculum. There was very little of what we now call "liberal arts," though that has subsequently been added as well.

Tom Clancy: What did you study while you were there?

General Shelton: I started out in aeronautical engineering and I ended up in textiles. The academic discipline required taught me a lot and it expanded my horizons.

Hard as it may be to believe, today's Chairman of the Joint Chiefs at one time thought his vocation would be to manage one of Carolina's many cloth mills. Let's let him tell the story:

Tom Clancy: You graduated in 1963, and then received your reserve commission in the Army. Can you trace for us the early years of your career?

General Shelton: When I graduated from NC State, I was high enough in my ROTC class that I could have accepted a commission into the regular Army. However, I saw my future in the field I had studied in school: textiles. I had signed a contract with a company called Riegel Textile Corporation. After graduation, my plan was that when my two year Army commitment was up, I would come back [to Greenville, South Carolina] and go to work as a management trainee in one of their mills.

So I went off to the Army with a reserve commission to serve my commitment, fully intending to return in two years to work in the textile business. I was on orders for Fort Benning, Georgia, to the 2nd Infantry Division, which became the basis for the experimental 11th Air Assault Division. This eventually became the 1st Air Cavalry Division, which deployed to Vietnam in 1965. Along the way I went to the Jump and Ranger schools, and I really liked that a lot. Coming off a farm where I had worked as a youth, I did not find either of those terribly challenging from a physical point of view. I did enjoy the time with the air assault division a lot, and my commanders were pitching hard for me to stay in. But my word is my bond: I had made a commitment to Riegel and my wife and I headed off to civilian life.

When I got there, though, I found that the challenges of the textile industry did not match those I had encountered in the Army. Furthermore, I discovered that what the military had taught me had made me really effective in private industry. But then after about a month, I started missing the daily challenges of the Army, and I talked it over with my wife, Carolyn. We decided that I should reapply to the Army for a regular commission, which took about a year to obtain. When the telegram arrived from the Army, the Riegel management tried hard to keep me, even offering to double my salary. Eventually, the company president and I had a talk, and after he tried one last time to convince me to stay, he shook my hand and said, "God bless you and the best of luck!" The rest, as they say, is history.

Having cut his ties to the civilian world, then-1st Lieutenant Shelton embarked upon a truly challenging enterprise: Special Forces and the U.S. Army JFK Special Warfare School at Fort Bragg, North Carolina.

Tom Clancy: What was it like in those days to go through the Q Course [Special Forces Qualification Course]?

General Shelton: It was tough training. In fact, I think Barry Sadler's song summed it up best. You know, "One hundred men will test today, but only three will win the Green Beret." While I don't think the statistics were quite that bad, it was very rigorous physically and mentally. It was twelve weeks long, with a lot of emphasis on getting ready to go into Vietnam in the Unconventional Warfare (UW) role. I count it as some of the very best training I've ever received.

Tom Clancy: What was the actual focus of SF training in those days? Was it strictly UW, or were you doing the kinds of training that we would recognize today in realistic field exercises like Robin Sage?

General Shelton: Robin Sage was called "Cherokee Trail" then, but it did the very same kinds of things. That part of the course has been very consistent. I think that today's course is a little bit tougher than it was when I went through, to tell you the truth. Certainly the great work that we do on the front end throughout SOF now, in the assessment and selection process, is primarily responsible for the tremendous force that you have in the community today. I mean you start off with great people, physically and mentally up to the challenge, and then build on that.

Tom Clancy: Did the local North Carolina residents help out as they do today, formed into the "Pineland Auxiliary" [locals who play roles in the excercises]?

General Shelton: I've never forgotten it, without a doubt! I mean the compartmentation among the locals in terms of knowing whose side everyone is on is incredible. It's become a multigenerational family affair, and they're always trying to "break" the other side in terms of the various "cells." For example, is the guy who runs the (dry) cleaners working for "Pineland" [the bad guys] or the local insurgent militia [the good guys—our allies]?

The reason I mention the guy who was the dry cleaner was that when I took the course, he had a step van. Of course, he was the guy who came by and rendezvoused with us out on the road at a predetermined point and transported our demolition team through two checkpoints that were out looking for us. He delivered us to the bridge that we were going to blow up, where we all jumped out almost on the fly. We made our way down the bank, rigged the bridge for destruction, got back up and rendezvoused, and he got us back through the checkpoints. He just looked at them and said, "Hey, Joe, I'm just delivering my dry cleanin'!" It was the damnedest thing I'd ever seen! I'll bet he's still down there with the same van today.

Once he'd earned his Green Beret, Captain Shelton left his wife and young son behind, and headed to Vietnam for the first of two combat tours in Southeast Asia.

Tom Clancy: Would you please tell us a little about your first tour in Vietnam with the 5th Special Forces Group?

General Shelton: I actually went into Fort Bragg in about August of 1966, working at the JFK Special Warfare Center. I then went through the "Q" Course, with my first son being born on the same day that Cherokee Trail started. I graduated about two weeks later, took some leave, and then departed for Vietnam in December of 1966.

Tom Clancy: Where were you initially assigned in 5th SFG?

General Shelton: I went into, as everyone else did at the time, the 5th Group headquarters at Nha Traug, and they asked me what I desired to do. You know, typical administrative kind of thing, what kind of assignment was I looking for?

My thought process was that I was a good swimmer. There's a lot of water down in IV Corps. I like the water. Why not go to IV Corps? So I told them I wanted to go to IV Corps down in the Mekong Delta. The officer noted that on the form, and after a little discussion, he departed.

There were about eight or nine of us who arrived that day, all lieutenants. We reported back around four or four-thirty that afternoon, and he handed me my paper and said that I was going to Detachment B-52, 5th SFG. When I asked what Detachment B-52 was, he told me that it was Project Delta, and that it was right down the street.[14]

Back at (Fort) Bragg, Project Delta had a reputation as one of those super-secret organizations that does a lot of "behind the lines" operations, has a high mortality rate, etc. When I pointed out that I had requested duty down in IV Corps, he told me that they needed eight more captains over at Project Delta right now, and that I was one of them. I said, "Okay, I've got it." So I went down, and I'll never forget it.

The XO [Executive Officer] of Project Delta, a major (who shall remain nameless), got three of us that reported in first and said, "I'll brief you on what this is all about."

We went into this supersecret conference room, which had all kinds of video equipment and was pretty "high speed" for those days. The place even had sliding doors that were electronically controlled. Once inside, he gave us the command briefing. He then told us, "Now you three guys need to understand one thing. Statistically, two out of three of you are going to die, so make sure you've got your affairs in order."

How's that for a welcome? I might add that this was just after Charlie Beckwith had left, having taken a .50-caliber round in the gut. That really set the stage for us. I mean, here's the commander of the outfit getting whacked!

From there on, we went out and tried to make the best of it, and we went to see what kind of training we were going to get.

Then I met the group of the NCOs that were there, many of whom had been there for quite some time, over a year, and I saw in them a great group of professionals and felt pretty good about being there.

The next day the commander (a lieutenant colonel) called me back in and said, "Listen, I've decided I'm gonna send you back." He told me I was too tall! This was because they worked with South Vietnamese and former North Vietnamese and he felt I would stand out like a sore thumb. He said that if I was out with a recon team, I would be the target of choice, because the enemy would know I was an American. So all of a sudden I found myself begging him not to send me back. I liked this outfit, this was what I wanted to do. He finally acquiesced, and said, "Okay," and a few other "choice" things that I won't repeat here, and told me, "You're staying!"

I said, "Thank you!" and departed. It turned out to be a great assignment.

Tom Clancy: General, if you were losing two out of three of your lieutenants, how was it for the NCOs?

---

14 Project Delta was a unique SF reconnaissance unit formed and initially headed by Major Charles "Chargin' Charlie" Beckwith, and based upon his own experiences during a tour with the British Special Air Service. Though wounded while extracting several SF soldiers from behind enemy lines, Beckwith survived and used his Project Delta to design and stand up the Army's antiterrorist (Detachment Delta or Delta Force) in the late 1970s. Project Delta teams, along with other special SF units, provided much of the muscle to the clandestine Military Assistance Command—Studies and Operations Group (MACV-SOG) in the 1960s, as America's commitment to South Vietnam grew.

General Shelton: Well, we took casualties, though I'm not sure of the exact statistics. There were a lot more NCOs in the unit than there were officers. We ended up with eight officers, and we had a total of thirty-two two-man teams we could put together. Each was composed of two NCOs, or an NCO and an officer. So the NCOs casualty rate was not as high as the officers, but we still lost a lot of good people in the process.

The most important thing, though, was that it was a really good organization! We had our own helicopters, for example, eight [UH-1 "Huey"] "slicks" [transports] and four [UH-1] gunships that stayed with us; we trained together as teams. When you were "put in" [inserted] with your team, the same pilot that put you in was going to come back and get you. And if he went down in flames, the guy who was his alternate was going to come in and get you. So, it really tightened things up, in terms of everyone understanding what the other one was doing, and having a good, tight team.

Despite his positive first-tour experience, Hugh Shelton did not come away unscathed. Like other veterans of the Vietnam conflict, he saw his share of bad policy decisions.

Tom Clancy: What are a couple of your most important memories and lessons that you brought back from that first tour in Vietnam?

General Shelton: By the time I came back around December of 1967, there was starting to be a lot of debate about Vietnam, and whether we should be there or not, etc.

But it was a debate I had a hard time with. The Montagnards, who I had served with in my area, were basically good, hard-working people who were really oppressed and taxed heavily by the Viet Cong and NVA [North Vietnamese Army]. Therefore, my initial impression was that we were right, that we were going to make a difference if we stayed with it and helped keep these people from having to live under that regime.

In other words, I believed that what we were doing at the time was right, but I really did not fully understand the great debate that was going on. Certainly, as a young captain, I accepted the orders to go and do my duty; and I went over trying to do the very best that I could, given what I had been trained to do.

Tom Clancy: Like many senior officers of your generation, you have the experiences of Vietnam and the post-war 1970s as part of your personal memories. Can you share with us some of the personal lessons and promises that you made to yourself in these tough times?

General Shelton: Vietnam was a watershed event for all Americans, not just for those of us who served in uniform. There are four distinct lessons that I took away from Vietnam.

The first was that Vietnam underscored the importance of recognizing that every war has its own military, cultural, geographic, political, and economical context. What works in one conflict will not necessarily work in another.

Second, Vietnam showed the need to carefully consider the costs, and to fully and publicly debate them before embarking on a major foreign policy commitment. The political objectives may or may not turn out to be obtainable through the use of military forces. It also showed us that we need to consider the end state that we're looking at before making a commitment to use our military forces.

Third, Vietnam taught us that while military force is a powerful and effective tool, it is only one of the foreign policy tools that is available to the president. As someone once said, "The military is a great hammer, but not every challenge that we face is a nail!"

Lastly, if we commit our military, we need to do it in an overwhelming manner, using every element of our military power available to win decisively and expediently. And we must not allow the enemy to have sanctuaries or to have any aspects of his resources or his power base that is placed off-limits to the military forces.

I hope these lessons are really never forgotten, because if we send America's sons and daughters to fight and die on foreign soil, we as a nation must be prepared up front to support them.

Tom Clancy: You were obviously in Vietnam during the heyday of Special Forces operations there. Do you have any memories of any particularly colorful or interesting SF?

General Shelton: My experience in Special Forces at that time caused me to come away with two different views. First and foremost, what a tremendous asset Special Forces provides to our nation in terms of augmenting our conventional forces, in terms of being a multiplier to what the conventional guys bring. Consider the counterinsurgency scenario we were in then. With every twelve-man "A-Team" [Operational Detachment Alpha, the basic building block of Special Forces units], I was able to support five South Vietnamese/Montagnard companies. We then were able to go out and expand the influence the United States had. It was a great multiplier.

Second was in the area of people. The Special Forces selection process in those days was not anywhere near what it is today, in terms of the selection and assessment up front. You didn't weed out the way we can today some of those who should not have been there. What I found was one of the most professional Non-Commissioned Officer corps I've ever known. I've always had very fond memories of our NCOs.

That was not true, though, on the officer side. When I looked at the senior officer leadership, and General Lindsay [the first CINCSOC] and I shared this one day talking about our own Special Forces experience in Vietnam, we didn't see senior officers that we wanted to be like or emulate, per se. There was not a lot of coaching, teaching, or mentoring, and you did not see very many you aspired to say, "I want to be like that someday."

What has changed so drastically since then is that today, especially since the Army has made Special Forces its own branch, we have grown those kinds of individuals.

But to go back to the original question about special or unique individuals.

One I remember particularly was Doug Coulter, a Harvard graduate who came to Vietnam when that was not a very popular war and said, "I'm going to do my duty. My number came up and I'm going." He did and was a very professional guy, one of the best officers I saw during my two years over there. Today he teaches Harvard business case studies in China. Before that, he also taught in Russia. He's as professional as they come, and went out on some missions and did some things that would make the hair on the back of your neck stand up. All out of range of U.S. forces and artillery (though we did have air support we could call in). He was truly good. Then there was a guy named "Doc" Simpson, an 18D medical technician, and an NCO in Delta. Doc never smiled, and I always worried about him, because we could not make him laugh. Yet anybody going out on patrol would want Doc as a partner, because this guy knew the [Special Forces] business backwards and forwards. I mean he knew the business cold! He was the most experienced guy we had, and Doc was on his second or third year in Delta when I got there, and he'd been doing this for a living.

Most people after about six months of that would just as soon go do something else for a living. And until about the time I got there, for every three missions you went on, MACV-SOG [the parent organization of Project Delta] used to give you a week's rest and recuperation back in your choice of locale— Hong Kong, Bangkok, Hawaii, etc. But Doc Simpson didn't bother to do that very often. He'd rather go out and do another mission. I don't know exactly what happened to him. I lost track of Doc later. Hopefully, he's still alive and prospering.

Then finally, back at the "C" Team in Da Nang [Operation Detachment "Charlie," the battalion headquarters], there were a couple of NCOs, sergeant majors by the name of Hodge and Thomas. Hodge's nickname was Preacher, while Thomas was part American Indian. These two guys were the living embodiment of your Special Forces sergeants. I mean, if you wanted to cast a guy [in a movie about Special Forces], it would not be John Wayne. It would be Hodge or Thomas. Very competent, very professional men, and you looked at them and could say, "There lies the real strength of the Special Forces, in its NCOs."

Tom Clancy: By the way, were you wounded in Vietnam during any of your tours?

General Shelton: I was. We were on a patrol one night, looking for a Chinese hospital. Supposedly the Chinese were advising the [North] Vietnamese, but we never did find the hospital.

But right at nightfall, our point man was shot and killed, and we came under tremendous fire from the top of a hill. We knew we were close and it [the hospital] had to be in the immediate area. So from there we fanned out the Montagnard company that was with us (myself and an NCO). We pressed them up and started running up the hill to try and get them [the Montagnards] to move in. The enemy were fairly good woodsmen and had good fieldcraft. They had in fact put out early warning devices [noisemakers on tripwires] and Pungi Sticks.[15] All of a sudden, I felt a sharp, searing pain and got jerked to a stop. I reached down and felt the tip of the stick that had come out of my calf and gone in the front. I was able to get out my trusty K-Bar [Marine] knife, and with great pain was able to slice the ends of the Pungi Stick off, then went up the hill.

Later on that night, we took the rest of the stick out. The NCO I was with was a medic also, and he was saying that we need to call a medevac [Medical Evacuation helicopter—Dustoff]. I was saying, "No, we've got to finish the job we were sent in for." So the next day they flew me out to have it [the wound] treated and sewn up. To this day, I know to be careful when you run in the dark! Ironically, we had the boots with the steel sole inserts, but the stick actually went above that into my calf. It was coming up out of the ground at an angle, and it turns out there were quite a few of them [Pungi Sticks] around there. I was able to see that the next morning when we walked back down into the area where I had been wounded.

One would think that with such a powerful first-tour experience behind him, Hugh Shelton would want to make Special Forces a career. Unfortunately, there was a problem—one of the many that would haunt Army SOF professionals for the next two decades: The Army did not then recognize SF as a career specialty. Special Forces were then part of the Infantry community, which meant that if an officer wanted to pursue promotion possibilities, he would be forced to leave SF for a more "balanced" Army career. That meant that he had to leave the SOF world for what turned out to be a two-decade hiatus. Nonetheless, the lessons he had learned at the JFK School and with the 5th SFG would stay with him.

What followed were tours with some of the top infantry units in the Army, including the 173rd Airborne Infantry (with which he served his second Vietnam tour) and in the 1980s command in the 82nd Airborne Division.

Tom Clancy: Moving forward a bit, after you finished your first tour in Vietnam, it seems that your career took a move back toward the conventional forces. Can you tell us a bit about that?

General Shelton: I've been really fortunate in that way. When I came back from Vietnam after the Special Forces tour, I wanted to go to Fort Bragg and the 82nd

---

15 A Viet Cong invention, Pungi Sticks—sharpened sticks about the diameter of a finger—were designed to maim enemy soldiers walking through heavy ground cover or rice paddies. The sticks were grouped into fields or belts around terrain that was to be denied to an enemy, or emplaced in hidden holes that a soldier could stumble into. Both sides used Pungi Sticks as a defensive or ambush measure.

Airborne. I sent my "dream sheet" [career preference statement] in, and I got orders to go to Fort Jackson, South Carolina. For the first and only time [in my career], I called up the personnel guys and said, "Why are you doing this to me?"

They said, "You deserve a company, but there's a lot of competition for a company right now; and Fort Jackson is the best place where you can get one." So there I was, and I screamed and shouted at them, but they said, "You're going."

As it turned out, it was an absolutely great assignment. I ended up with the 3rd AIT [Advanced Infantry Training] Brigade training guys, every one of whom graduated and was sent to Vietnam. I was able to capitalize on my experience and taught them how to deal with the whole "Vietnam Experience"—from booby traps to the rest.

I mentioned role models a while ago. The other important thing at that point was that my love was first and foremost with the special operations/light side of the force. The Special Forces, however, were not then a formal branch within the Army. So like [Army] Aviation at the time, you had to walk a fine line. If you served in one of the nonbranch communities, you had better not do it for too long, or the Army would "grind you off." I mean, your career could come to a screeching halt, and you would not go any further; you'd be one of those "guys over there" or "Snakeaters," as they used to refer to us.

So building an Army career required you to come back into the "conventional" side of the force. Then, once you had done that, it was tough to get back to an SOF assignment. So literally, after I came back from that experience at Fort Jackson, I was selected early for major, and that almost terminated my ability to jump back and forth. This was because I went off from there to do my troop duty as a major—four years in the 25th Division. Then I came back to work on a staff in the personnel business, and was selected for battalion command, again on the conventional side. So once my career started moving, it was almost like there was not much influence I could have. They select you for command and assign you to a specific unit, so you don't have a "say-so" in the process. So I was just very fortunate that I ended up in the great units that I did.

Later on, when I was a Brigadier [General], and they asked me which division I wanted to go to, my top two choices [divisions] were both in Europe, both heavy [armored and mechanized]. Where did they send me? Back out to the 101st Airborne (Air Assault) at Fort Campbell, Kentucky [a "light" division, which usually got to where it was going in helicopters].

The good news is that being on the "light" side, I've been with the forces that have been in the "action." Desert Storm being the one exception that gave the "heavy" forces a good shot at combat. But all the rest of the operations, from Panama to Somalia to whatever, focused predominately on the "light" side.

Tom Clancy: During the command phase of your career you seem to have spent much of your time in units of the XVIII Airborne Corps. Units like the 10th

Mountain, 82nd Airborne, 101st Airborne (Air Assault), etc. Was this by design or just the luck of the draw?

General Shelton: From the time that I entered the military service and attended the Airborne and Ranger schools, I was always drawn toward units that could move rapidly, fight decisively, and had a lot of esprit and charisma. I guess I've liked units that basically could come at the enemy from where he might least suspect it. I believe it was Benjamin Franklin who said, "Where is the country that can protect itself against 10,000 men descending from the skies?" So I had a natural propensity to seek out and desire to serve in Airborne, Ranger, and Special Forces types of units.

At the same time I recognized the need to be well rounded, to have a good, solid infantry background, which included not only light units and Airborne and Special Forces, but also time with mechanized forces. So if you ask any officer in the Army what would be their ideal assignment, it would probably be to one of these elite units. However, that doesn't mean you don't need experiences in other types as well.

As luck would have it, by virtue of my experience and my previous assignments, I tended after my early days to be steered in that direction by the Army's institutional assignment processes. But I do think that the missions, the experiences, and the association in these units really allowed me to be with some of the very finest soldiers to ever wear an Army uniform, and of course those are wonderful memories that I will have forever.

Like every other U.S. Army officer in the 1970s, Hugh Shelton endured the lean years following Vietnam. These were hard times for the Army. It had to endure not only a drying up of money and the transition to an all-volunteer force, but severe cultural, social, and morale challenges. No group within the Army suffered more than the young officers who were rising to command their first battalions and brigades, and trying to hold their units together in the face of all that.

Tom Clancy: You were part of that generation of senior officers who had to deal with the trauma of the post-Vietnam era in the Army. What are your memories of what the Army was like in the late 1970s?

General Shelton: It was an abysmal experience, to be frank. It came partly from the impact of the post-Vietnam attitude toward the military, and the fact that a lot of good people got disgusted and decided to hang it up and leave the service. Combined with that was the now acknowledged mistake in recruiting personnel who were not physically and mentally qualified. It was bad! A lot of the people who were brought in during those days were given a "choice" of going to jail for criminal convictions or going into the armed forces. I had a lot of those [individuals] as a battalion commander.

At the same time all that was going on, [unit] strengths were declining rapidly into what was called the "Hollow Army." I know what the Hollow Army was all about. As a battalion commander, I actually briefed a Major General division commander about going to just one platoon per [infantry] company, which normally has three or four per.

In particular, we had a problem with our NCOs. A lot of our NCOs in those days had been left over from Vietnam. During that time, we had promoted them very rapidly, and they were at grades that were much higher that they should have been, without the real underpinnings of [professional] education and an understanding of what their [job] responsibilities entailed. It was so bad that as a battalion commander in the 1979 to 1981 timeframe, I seriously considered leaving the service.

That's where we were. The drug problem was tremendous, even in line outfits, though to a lesser degree than support units. They kept us busier and in the field, which held that back a little bit.

Tom Clancy: When did you begin to see things get better?

General Shelton: I came back from my battalion command tour, and became the G-3 [Operations Officer] of the 9th Light Infantry division. I then went to the War College, got selected for colonel and programmed to go to the 82nd Airborne Division for [brigade] command. In those years after 1982, when I left the West Coast and moved to Fort Bragg, you literally could see the Army turning around. So by the 1983–1984 timeframe, there was a noticeable improvement starting to take place. By the time I left Fort Bragg [in 1985] and went up to Fort Drum as the 10th Mountain Division Chief of Staff, you could really see the Army turning around. Of course, the new Non-Commissioned Officer education system had kicked in at the same time, and you were starting to see really top-notch, fine young men who are continuing to serve us today. You were seeing a real difference!

The end of the 1980s and the Cold War saw General Shelton rising to the top levels of leadership in the U.S. Army. By 1990, he was a Brigadier General and Assistant Division Commander of the famed 101st Airborne Division (Air Assault) at Fort Campbell, Kentucky. When Iraq invaded Kuwait in August of that year, his division commander was away on leave, and it fell on Hugh Shelton to get the Screaming Eagles ready to move to the Saudi desert and eventual combat in Operation Desert Storm.

Tom Clancy: You were assistant division commander of the 101st Airborne Division (Air Assault) during Desert Storm and Desert Shield. Can you tell us about your experiences there and your impression of the division's actions during the war?

General Shelton: I was the assistant to Major General Bennie Peay, the division commander. I was his Assistant Division Commander for operations, but also had the (101st) Aviation Brigade under my supervision, which was a nine battalion aviation brigade, with about 350 to 400 helicopters.

What jumps out at me in that period of time was that we trained hard back at Fort Campbell, and we had our "eyes on the ball" in terms of our deployed goals. So when I went to the 101st, we had a lot of emphasis on deployment training, and "how to get out of Dodge" in a hurry.

All that came in handy when General Peay, for the first time in about a year, had gone on leave. General Ed Burba [the commander of FORSCOM— U.S. Forces Command at Fort McPherson, Georgia] called me on August 3rd, 1990, while General Peay was gone, and said, "Are you ready to go?" And I said, "We're ready to go!" He came back and said, "Well, I sure hope so, because it looks like you're going!" When I asked if he meant the whole outfit [the entire division], he said to me, "The whole outfit!" General Burba then asked, "Is there anything you need?" And I told him that CH-47 pilots were still in short supply, and we had put that in our readiness reports at the time. He said he would fix that, and I told him then that we would start moving.[16]

We started moving in a hurry, and I went on the first plane, a C-5 Galaxy, with the six Apache helicopters. I still remember that when we got to Dhahran and got off the plane and walked away, I thought I was still in the jetwash of the engines. It was about five P.M. in the afternoon when I got there, and the heat was up to about 137° to 140°F there on the tarmac. It was unbelievable!

I immediately began coordinating with XVIII Airborne Corps to find out where we would go, so I could start making arrangements for the division to receive the flow [of units and equipment] that was supposed to come in right behind us. I soon came to find out that they were going to put us at King Fahd Airbase. So I ran out the next day to look at what was available there.

Meanwhile, the SOF [units] had been flown out of Riyadh the day before by General Schwarzkopf. He had told Colonel Jesse Johnson [his SOF component commander] that the Saudis were concerned about the American presence, with so many [personnel] in Riyadh, and had asked him to move out. So the SOF guys had leapfrogged out to this airfield, and now I've got to go in and coordinate it. My real concern was that there was no place to put anybody [from the 101st], except in the middle of the desert. I knew the troops would die coming into that. So I immediately set out to try to get tents put up so that at least they could get out of the sun. That turned out to be a real challenge, and wrung me out, no question about it! I'm telling you that the August/September timeframe [in the Persian Gulf] is absolutely incredible weatherwise!

Tom Clancy: You said that you had around 400 helicopters to move over to Saudi Arabia. How did you eventually get them there?

General Shelton: We had to break them down, load them onto ships, then unload them on the other end and put them back together. It would have been nice if

---

16 General Edward Burba was one of a handful of senior officers, like Don Starry and Fred Franks, who helped hold the Army together in the 1970s and rebuild it in the 1980s. Such officers helped get the Army ready to fight the battles that would come with the end of the Cold War. For more on this, see my book with General Fred Franks, *Into the Storm* (Putnam, 1998).

the Navy could have loaned us an aircraft carrier to do the job, but "jointness" was not quite as developed then as it was a few years later in Haiti.

We did get them to do it later during Uphold Democracy [in Haiti, 1994], but that wasn't easy either. Those Rangers embarked on the *America* [CV-66] just about put the ship out of business with all the chow they were consuming! We figured that they ate about three times the rate that the sailors were eating. They were spending all day down on the lower decks doing PT trying to stay in shape.

Tom Clancy: When the war [Desert Storm] actually started in 1991, did things go about the way you expected?

General Shelton: I was initially the senior guy for the 101st Airborne Division up front inside of Saudi Arabia, near the Iraqi border with the assault command post. Of course we were ready to prevent Saddam from being able to roll south out of Kuwait and down into Saudi Arabia and catch the units there off guard.

The 101st was a really great outfit! After we had gotten everyone in and settled down, I took the forward command post of the 101st up north about a hundred miles along the Tapline Road [which roughly paralleled the Kuwait/Iraq/ Saudi border]. We had one brigade that stayed forward. I kept AH-64 Apaches and other aviation assets up there, so that if the Iraqis had decided to come south, we would be the covering force. The 101st would take them on initially and hold them where they were until the rest of the force [JTF] could start deploying or get ready to reinforce. I stayed up there for almost six months until we kicked off the ground campaign.

The good news was that we trained hard, and Brigadier General Keith Huber [later the SOUTHCOM J-3] was my major in charge of the command post. He and I put together a training program, and we exercised it. We would launch at night, and assume that the Iraqis were attacking, and see how fast we could get our command post back to where it would be more survivable, set up again, and got a real battle or team drill down. We had made the team so sharp that when the war kicked off, I told General Peay that the forward CP should be the one to move forward. We would control the 101st's one hundred–mile leap into Iraq [as part of XVIII Airborne Corps' rush on the western flanks of VII Corps' armored attack into the Republican Guards], and then bring the "big" [division-level] CP forward at some future time.

As it worked out, the forward CP functioned so well that he decided that we should continue to fight the war with it.

Even before the ground war started, our AH-64 Apache helicopters had captured a couple of [Iraqi] infantry battalions. Our biggest concern was how do you accept the surrender if you're up in an aircraft? We had to fly some people out there just to do that job.

Then the first day, we ran into another battalion right on the planned perimeter of our Forward Operating Base [FOB Cobra].[17-18] So immediately we came under fire, and the Apaches returned fire. We had sent recon teams up there the night before to look over the area so we would not hit a real "hot" spot, but they had not detected this one. We started getting another battalion ready to go against one of the flanks, but it turned out to be unnecessary because the Iraqis surrendered.

One of my most memorable experiences occurred with the 101st on the third day after the war began. I was flying over to a site that was going to be one of our advanced command posts, and it required me to basically do a flight in a lateral manner across the front lines, east toward Basra. In doing that I flew over and followed the armored forces [VII Corps] that were moving north. There were about two hundred rooster tails of sand and dust coming up from the desert. As far as you could see there were rooster tails. This was the sand that the armored vehicles kick up as they move forward.

Coming behind them was a big five- or ten-ton supply truck, and it had the biggest flag—I believe it was a garrison flag—but the biggest flag I think I've ever seen that was stuck up on a long, tall pole on the truck. Of course, as he was driving forward at thirty or forty miles an hour trying to keep up with the tanks, this flag was sticking straight out to the rear. I'll never forget looking at that. I thought to myself, "Saddam, I hope you know what you've asked for, because here comes the United States Army at its best!"

Of course a day later the decision was made to stop. I felt then as I feel now that it was the right decision—even though Saddam has continued in power and has continued to cause a headache for America and the rest of the world. By that time it was no longer a real fight. Iraqi soldiers were dying needlessly. The leadership had been pulled out of the units, and for the most part, Saddam had decided that he would allow the battalions to surrender. This was because the privates out front would either be killed or surrender anyway. So he had pulled the majority of his leadership back to Baghdad obviously to try to save them or to preserve them for another day. To continue the killing was not something we felt good about, and I thought we made the right decision on day four to stop.

Tom Clancy: Thanks to its early emphasis on air mobile operations the 101st had a hand in a number of special operations missions such as Task Force Normandy.[19] Tell us, if you can, about your work on these operations and how your own Special Forces experience helped you in understanding and supporting their execution.

17-18 FOB Cobra was a huge logistics and operations base that was established over a hundred miles into Iraq at the start of the ground war in February 1990. Completed in a matter of hours, the move to FOB Cobra remains the largest and most difficult airmobile operation of all time.

19 Task Force Normandy was assigned to take out a pair of Iraqi radar sites (Objectives Oklahoma and Nebraska) that might have detected Allied strike aircraft headed into Baghdad and western Iraq. For more on the mission and on AH-64 Apaches, see *Armored Cav* (Berkley Books, 1994).

General Shelton: As I indicated earlier, we had spent a lot of time at Fort Campbell training in air assault techniques, developing tactical techniques and procedures to survive in combat as an air mobile or air assault outfit. And so the missions that we were asked to do then tied right in with what we had trained to do. In essence, we carried them out as we had trained for them back at Fort Campbell.

Of course, Task Force Normandy was a special request from the Air Force to take out the forward-looking [low frequency] radars [in southern Iraq]. This would provide the Air Force with even greater capabilities to get into Iraq before hitting the surface-to-air missile engagement zone near Baghdad. As is pretty much public knowledge by now, that was a highly successful operation, and it really showed the value of those Apaches. [Air Force] SOF helicopters [MH-53 Pave Lows], because of their great navigational capabilities actually led the Apaches in. This was because they had GPS, whereas we were still using Doppler [AHARS] systems on the Apaches.

The MH-53s flew to a designated point. When they crossed over the border, they threw out a bunch of chemlites to mark the checkpoint, and that was the signal to punch right in onto the targets. The ability of our Apaches to go deep and to carry out the air attacks as part of Operation Normandy was something we felt very comfortable with and were well-prepared to do.

We [the 101st] also put in our own recon teams, along with those from the 3rd and 5th SF Groups. The thing that jumped out most of all, though, was that we trained hard to do this. We made a concerted effort back at Fort Campbell to really make our long-range reconnaissance assets work, and to do it the same way that I had learned to do it in Project Delta back in Vietnam. The way we had put them in and taken them out back then had been very successful. Without a doubt, my prior SOF experience made me a better recon planner in conventional operations. The good news was that by using those techniques, we put our five teams in, and none of them were detected (though we wound up having to take out some teams). Still, all in all, it worked well.

After the 101st returned from the Persian Gulf, Hugh Shelton was promoted to major general and given command of a division.

Tom Clancy: After you left the 101st, you got to command the 82nd Airborne Division. What kind of a thrill is it to command that unit?

General Shelton: Well, once you have served there one time, and you see the great quality of the people, particularly the NCOs, you realize that they are tremendous Americans. Everyone—the sergeant majors, junior NCOs, etc.—are as good as anywhere in the Army, maybe even as good as the ones in the SOF community. To go back and command is the dream of a lifetime for anybody who's familiar with the 82nd.

To give you a quick story, General Peay, who I worked for in the desert, found out that General Vuono [the Army Chief of Staff] was coming over to Saudi to visit. The way you get to command a division depends a lot upon who

General Hugh Shelton and other dignitaries at a ceremony to dedicate the Arthur "Bull" Simons memorial at Fort Bragg. Though he heads the Joint Chiefs of Staff, he often can be found supporting Special Operations events like this.

JOHN D. GRESHAM

recommends you among the senior officers. Well, General Peay said he'd really like to see me replace him as commander of the 101st. I was by then [already] on the promotion list to major general, and he tells me, "When the chief comes tomorrow, I can either try to get you the 82nd [Airborne Division] or the 101st to be my replacement. Which one would you rather command?"

Of course, here I am in the middle of the desert with the great Screaming Eagles, and nobody can complain about that. I looked back at him and said, "That's like asking me to tell you which son I love the best. They're both great! But I would never forgive myself if I did not choose the 82nd. I like to jump out of airplanes! I like the exercises they go on. I like the level of readiness they have. And, of course, they're from North Carolina, my home state. I even went to ROTC summer camp with the 82nd, which sponsored the camp. I had admired the 82nd since my days in ROTC."

After two years commanding the 82nd Airborne Division, Shelton, now a lieutenant general, moved down the road at Fort Bragg to command the XVIII Airborne Corps. There Hugh Shelton inherited problems that would define much of his career in the next few years. First was to deal with the simmering political problems in Haiti. Second was to make XVIII Airborne Corps ready for the challenges of the post–Cold War world.

Tom Clancy: You have a reputation—not unlike that of the Special Forces—of being a quiet man. What do you think of that assessment?

General Shelton: That ties into the SOF community—"quiet professionals." They are nice people, very competent, and [also] professional. I think it serves them well to be "quiet professionals," because they just add to the great capabilities that are resident in their parent services. The various services now are beginning to love the capabilities that they provide. Along with that, they don't come around looking for glory or fame. They just say, "What do you want done?" and "Here's what we can do . . ."

One of my favorite SOF/"joint" operations stories involves Admiral Jay Johnson, who commanded the naval task force for me down in Haiti in 1994. One of the things that really impressed Jay was when the Army SOF aviators [from the 160th Special Operations Aviation Regiment—the Nightstalkers] came to pick him up to take him over to a JSOC [Joint Special Operations Command] change of command ceremony over aboard the USS *America* [CV-66].[20] General Brown was coming out of command, and he sent a 160th chopper over to pick us up, as I was the JTF [Joint Task Force] commander. It landed on the *Mount Whitney* [LCC-20—the Haiti JTF flagship], and as they landed, the crew chief jumped out to come get us, and the guy was dressed in solid black. He had kneepads on, elbow pads, a black helmet and flight suit, and a smoked face shield. As he walked over, he motioned for us to follow, and then turned around. As he did that, we saw in big words on his back, "NO FEAR!" I remember Jay looking over at me, and it clearly made a big impression!

Tom Clancy: You took over XVIII Airborne Corps in 1993, and you had to deal with the crisis in Haiti for much of your tenure there. Can you please give us some general impressions of Operation Uphold Democracy, and what you had originally planned if General Cedras (the Haitian dictator) had not resigned and gone into exile?

General Shelton: When I took over XVIII Airborne Corps, I remembered that as a brigade commander for the 82nd Airborne during the 1983–1985 timeframe, I had been told that some day we might have to do a parachute operation with a brigade-sized element into Haiti. We would have jumped into Port-au-Prince Airfield to either rescue the Americans that were there or to help stabilize the situation until other forces could arrive. So in '93 when we were asked by ACOM [Atlantic Command—now Joint Forces Command] to take a look at our plans for Haiti, I was quite surprised to see that it was the same contingency plan I had been asked to do some eight years earlier. I looked at it and I said, "There has got to be a better way to do this."

So we put together what eventually became the Uphold Democracy plan. It involved an amphibious landing by the Marines, a large parachute operation by the 82nd Airborne Division, and a reserve consisting of the Joint Special Oper-

---

20 To support the planned invasion of Haiti, the Navy removed their aircraft from a pair of Atlantic Fleet carriers and loaded aboard helicopters from the 160th Special Operations Aviation Regiment and the aviation brigade of the 10th Mountain Division. Though controversial at the time, the operation was highly successful, and remains an option today.

ations Command. We knew we were up against about 7,000 members of the Haitian Defense Forces, which included not only military but also the police. Our goal was to hit them in the middle of the night, take over every one of their police stations and all of their key military installations, so that by the time daylight came we basically would be in charge. If they wanted to fight, they would have to do that in a very disorganized manner.

To execute Uphold Democracy, we had the capabilities resident within XVIII Airborne Corps, with some augmentation with the Marines. We had trained hard with the 2nd Marine Division and II MEF down at Camp LeJeune, along with the 2nd Fleet in Norfolk, and felt very comfortable that in a joint environment this would be a relatively easy operation.

Tom Clancy: As the Uphold Democracy Joint Task Force Commander you had control of a wide variety of units, including a large Special Operations Forces component. Would you please describe those units and how you eventually wound up using them?

General Shelton: As a result of my prior training and of knowing a lot of the individuals in Special Operations (Fort Bragg[21] is a *very* tight community), I was well aware of what they did, who they were, and how they did their jobs. Therefore, when we put the plan together, one of the first units I got involved in it was the Joint Special Operations Command at Fort Bragg. At the same time, Special Forces teams were designed to be spread throughout the country in about twenty key towns and villages, and to show that we had a presence all over the island, not just in Port-au-Prince. They had tremendous capabilities, and we had planned to use all of these, including the hostage rescue element, as a part of our backup plans in case things did not go as planned.

Tom Clancy: Haiti eventually evolved into a long-term peacekeeping and nation-building effort. How did the particular capabilities and skills of Army Special Operations units make this easier for the U.S., and what special contributions did you see them make?

General Shelton: Special Forces have contributed immensely from day one in the operation, right up through and including the recent days there. For a long time, a lot of our humanitarian efforts (such as the building of schools and medical treatment facilities) were directed at Port-au-Prince. These were done for the most part by conventional units, but our Special Forces soldiers for a long time continued to operate out in the hither and yon. They were out in some of the more desolate places in Haiti, and the U.S. presence they showed added to peace and stability within the region.

---

21 Fort Bragg is home of the XVIII Airborne Corps and the 82nd Airborne Division, and SOF is headquartered there.

Among the seldom mentioned groups that played a major role from day one were the civil affairs and psychological operations (CA and PSYOPs) troops that came in. The CA did everything from helping open schools to the PSYOPs that helped tell the Haitian people why we were there and what we wanted them to do in support of Operation Uphold Democracy. Those efforts continued for a long time.

Almost across the entire spectrum of operational capabilities, the Special Operations community has been a key part not only in Haiti but in many other areas throughout the world.

General Shelton's command tour of XVIII Airborne Corps provided him with a high level of visibility. He was seen as having handled the difficult and potentially embarrassing Haiti problem successfully, and thus worthy of greater rank and responsibility. Thus, when it came time to pick a new head for the U.S. Special Operations Command in 1996, he was given the nod.

Tom Clancy: In early 1996 you were promoted to general and given the job as Commander in Chief of Special Operations Command. At the time some observers considered this an unusual move, given the credentials of your predecessors, General Carl Stiner and General Wayne Downing. Both had been longtime SOF professionals, while your career had followed a more conventional track. What do you feel made you the logical candidate for this position, and what were your early goals once you took command of SOCOM?

General Shelton: First, I would say that I considered my nomination and eventual selection to be CINCSOC as one of the greatest honors that has ever been bestowed upon me. This is a community of great Americans, who bring to this nation a great deal of capabilities. They are great force multipliers for our conventional forces. As we have already seen, I had been involved in Special Forces early on as a young officer and gone through qualification, spent a year in combat with the 5th SFG, and then worked as a joint forces commander having SOF units under my command.

My predecessors, Wayne Downing, Carl Stiner, and before him Jim Lindsay, all had served in Special Operations, but to some degree had had very similar types of experiences to mine. Jim Lindsay and Carl Stiner, for example, had both joined Special Forces early on, yet their careers had also followed a more conventional pattern until they were selected from XVIII Airborne Corps to command SOCOM. Wayne Downing had not been in Special Operations until he joined the Rangers. Of course after that he commanded the 75th Ranger Regiment and then went into JSOC and ultimately into the U.S. Army Special Operations Command. So his experience was on the "Black Hat"—or the Ranger side of Army SOF—and not so much on the Green Beret side.

I felt fortunate in my case to have been both in the Rangers as well as the Green Berets, so I understood the abilities that the Special Forces troops brought, along with the capabilities of the Rangers, and therefore felt very well-prepared to take Wayne Downing's place at SOCOM.

To be very frank, my goal when I went into SOCOM was to try to extend the role of Special Operations Command. I needed to tell my fellow CINCs about the great capabilities that Special Operations Command provided so Special Forces units would be properly integrated into future contingency operations. This was so that the tremendous talent that SOF units could bring to bear could be applied in a correct manner by our conventional force commanders. That meant that I had to be a "quiet professional" who educated the conventional side of U.S. forces into all the capabilities of the unconventional side of the military, so to speak.

At the same time I felt it was incumbent on me to look ahead, to see where we needed to head as a command and as a community in the future. That led me to publish *Joint Vision 2020 for Special Operations Command*, which would leverage off of the conventional version of *Joint Vision 2010*. Our goal was to look much further into the future for Special Operations Command, so we could make sure that we always were on the leading edge, both in terms of technology and preparation, to make a difference in today's environment or in a future conflict.

Those were the two goals that I set out. The first one being the enhanced integration of SOF into conventional operations; and second, preparing for the future of Special Operations Command.

Tom Clancy: How did you go about educating your fellow CINCs in the capabilities of the units in SOCOM?

General Shelton: As I indicated previously, this was one of my key goals as CINC-SOC, because I felt that this was where our greatest effort was needed. Frankly, my efforts were supported by my credentials on the conventional side of the military profession. Having established my credentials as a Joint Task Force Commander, XVIII Airborne Corps Commander, 82nd Airborne Division commander, and also having a Special Operations (Green Beret) background, allowed me to bridge the gap. Approaching the conventional side of the armed forces in that manner showed that we had great capabilities and were there to support *them*. It was not a matter of choosing between Special Ops or conventional forces, but a matter of integrating them to achieve the complementary capabilities for the joint warfighters.

Tom Clancy: You took over SOCOM during a time when the early gains made by the community under the 1980 Goldwater-Nichols and Nunn-Cohen legislations were being consolidated, and procurement efforts began to result in deliveries of aircraft and other hardware. Can you talk to us about how these events and new systems affected your ability to conduct operations as well as your ability to support your fellow CINCs?

General Shelton: I don't think there's any question that the arrival of new platforms and new technology into the community began to show the conventional side of

General Shelton makes points during his interview
with the author.

the armed forces just how effective the SOF elements could be and what they could provide for them. Capabilities ranging from the AC-130U Uniform gunship with its tremendous capabilities and all-weather look-down/shoot-down capabilities, to the infiltration aircraft used by the 160th Special Operations Aviation Regiment, to the low observable technology that was available in several forms within the SOF community. Everywhere you turned there was leading-edge technology being applied.

But also, and perhaps more important, as a result of the personnel assessment and selection process, we had seen the transition of the individuals within SOF into a first-class—a world-class—force. From the officers to the noncommissioned officers, they were quality troops. Everyone began to appreciate that, particularly as they had a chance to work with them and see them and integrate them into their operations and see what they could do for them. Suddenly it was that technology in our platforms and the quality of our people that really began to sell Special Operations. That continues today.

Tom Clancy: You had less than two years in command of SOCOM . . . not a very long time. This said, what are the achievements that you are most proud of when you look back on that time?

General Shelton: That's a great question; and it really strikes a nerve, since it was the best job a four-star could possibly have in the armed forces—a chance to be associated with such a great group of top-notch professionals. Also a chance to jump out of airplanes with them, to participate in operations, and to see them at work was always a reward in itself. I would also say that to be Commander in

General Shelton makes points during his interview with the author.

JOHN D. GRESHAM

Chief of SOCOM was a pinnacle of achievement for me, and a tremendous assignment.

To put what I've already said another way, when I took over SOCOM, what I really set out to do was to sell Special Operations Forces to the rest of the CINCs and the services. I wanted them to know what superb people and capabilities the Special Forces would bring to the joint fight. Warfighting in the future has got to be done by the total force. That was my goal, and I think we were successful.

At the same time, when I took over, we were then entering into the 1996 Quadrennial Defense Review, and the second goal I had was to make sure that I protected SOF. We wanted to do this by making sure that everyone understood what this very small investment of personnel did for the nation. We made sure in the war games conducted as part of QDR to determine future force structures that the capabilities SOCOM units provided would be incorporated into the final report.

Also, because of my SOCOM funding authority, we were like a separate service. And I insisted that SOCOM sit at the table when funding and programming decisions were being discussed and that we were fully integrated into the Quadrennial Defense Review. I basically committed the Deputy CINCSOC, at that time Admiral Ray Smith, to go to Washington with a first-class team. We did this during QDR to make sure that we were present at all the key decision points and showed what SOF could contribute to each of the war games that they ran.

The final thing I remember being proud of was *Joint Vision 2020*, making sure that we had a vision for the future that would help lead to a pursuit of technology, and the types of individuals that we would need to fight in future environments. This way, SOCOM units would continue to be key players in joint warfighting into the future.

The official seal of the Joint Chiefs of Staff.
General Henry Shelton heads the Joint Chiefs,
and is the first special operations professional
to hold the post.

In 1997, General Shelton was nominated to take over the post of Chairman of the Joint Chiefs of Staff. Like his two predecessors, Generals Powell and Shalikashvili, he brought his own unique experiences and perspectives to the post that he has occupied since that time. And like both of them, he had been commissioned from the ranks of ROTC officers. He was also the first Special Operations professional to ever serve on the Joint Chiefs. This background has provided him with an unprecedented view, both for the worth of SOF units and their place in America's military and the world.

Tom Clancy: In 1997, the president nominated you to become Chairman of the Joint Chiefs of Staff. What are your memories of receiving the nomination, and what were your personal feelings about rising to this position within the American military?

General Shelton: Any time a president appoints you to a position it's an enormous privilege and it's hard to say no. I was humbled and honored by the trust and confidence that President Clinton had placed in me. I thought of all those many people—family, friends, soldiers, and bosses—who had helped mold me into the person that was ready to take on this job as America's top soldier. I certainly understood the responsibility that comes with the job and I accepted it willingly and without any reservation, knowing that it meant longer hours—there's never enough hours in the day—and a lot of travel miles. But, I also knew it would be rewarding and would give me the opportunity to serve with America's best for a few more years. I can tell you there is no greater job than to represent America's men and women in uniform and to champion their interests and concerns before the president, Congress, and the American public.

Tom Clancy: When you relieved General Shalikashvili, you became the first officer from the SOF community to rise to Chairman of the Joint Chiefs. What do you think that this meant to the SOF professionals back at SOCOM, and how does your own special operations experience affect your day-to-day approach to the job?

General Shelton: SOF professionals have a long and proud history of serving their country in war and peace. I don't want to speak for the community, but I think they were proud of my nomination. Their good wishes certainly indicated as much. There's not a day that goes by that I don't call on some experience along the way in my career, SOF or otherwise, to help me. There are many tough issues facing our nation that require that I make the right decisions, give the right advice—and I'm thankful that I had an opportunity to learn and to serve with the very best.

Tom Clancy: You are the fourth chairman of the Joint Chiefs of Staff to operate under the Goldwater-Nichols/Nunn-Cohen legislation passed in the 1980s. Will you please talk a bit about how you benefit from the actions of your three predecessors (Admiral Crowe along with Generals Powell and Shalikashvili), and what benefits that legislation has provided the four of you in the decade since its passage?

General Shelton: In 1999, we celebrated the 50th anniversary of the establishment of the position of Chairman of the Joint Chiefs of Staff. I'm only the fourteenth person in all those years to hold the position. Admiral Crowe was the chairman when the Goldwater-Nichols legislation was signed in 1986 and did a superb job in guiding the transition. By the way, I served on the Joint Staff in J-3 (Joint Operations) during his chairmanship. The legislation brought obvious changes that enhanced the influence of the chairman—making the chairman the principal military adviser, as opposed to being part of the corporate body that provided advice; giving the chairman a deputy; and assisting the secretary in providing for the strategic direction of the armed forces. But, if I had to single out one thing that my predecessors bequeathed to me it would be a premier Joint Staff—and that's with an emphasis on JOINT. They helped to create the fully qualified joint specialty officer, making it important for officers to have a joint assignment as well as a good service assignment. In doing that, they assured that the best and the brightest are assigned to the Joint Staff.

Another aspect would be the advice that is rendered to the president and the Secretary of Defense. Many will recall that one of the criticisms of the old system was that the advice to the president and the secretary was watered down because they had to reach a consensus. If there were any kinks in the rendering advice under Goldwater-Nichols, they were ironed out before I arrived in the job. I serve with a great vice chairman and a great group of chiefs—men who are at the top of their profession and services—and we have a good process of airing out issues. When all is said and done, I am responsible for the advice, but I can tell you all perspectives have been thoroughly examined.

Goldwater-Nichols was enacted some fourteen years ago and, as anyone will tell you, it's been an evolutionary process. We're looking now at follow-on to Goldwater-Nichols, so it's still developing. But, the bottom line is—we have a superb and effective joint military force. We saw that evidenced in the Persian Gulf, in Haiti, in Bosnia, and Kosovo. Our goal is to ensure that our Joint Force has the personnel and the resources to meet the challenges of the twenty-first century.

Tom Clancy: For the last few years, you've been teamed up with Secretary of Defense William Cohen as your civilian counterpart. How has the relationship between you two worked out and what kind of a man is he to work for?

General Shelton: It's worked extremely well. He's very good to work for. His time in Congress has given him a great understanding of the military and the issues. In Bill Cohen, our men and women in uniform have a true friend and he has been a champion for increased pay and retirement reform, improved medical care, and in general improving the quality of life for our service members. He has set a goal to ensure that the American people have a better understanding of its military—he calls it reconnecting with America—which will ensure that support, so absolutely essential for us who wear the uniform, is continued.

Tom Clancy: During your tenure as chairman, you've had the responsibility for running the American military in its busiest nonwar period in history. Would you please talk a little about how busy things have been for you these last few years, and how the operations tempo [OpTempo] has affected the forces.

General Shelton: First let me say, America's military strength is built on a foundation of quality people, trained and ready forces, and an effective modernization program. While each of these elements is essential, number one remains—people! Without trained, well-motivated, and committed people, we could not have the successes we have had. Our young men and women—and their families—are absolutely tremendous.

It is clear that the current tempo of operations [OpTempo] continues to have a significant impact on service members and their families, and therefore is a concern for the chiefs and me. It is no secret that frequent and persistent deployments have stressed the force and stretched assets that degraded readiness and increased the risk to our ability to execute the most demanding operations. Just as important, OpTempo impacts quality of life and we believe jeopardizes our ability to retain the high-quality people we need for tomorrow's force. We continue to assess how Operation Allied Force and the long-term deployments in both Bosnia and Kosovo have affected the force. However, long-term deployments will be with us for some time to come. We all know operational tempo can be and often is a function of unpredictable world events and global commitments—that is why the services, the Joint Staff, the CINCs, and I are all taking steps to reduce its impact. First, we have increased our global sourcing of units to fill deployment commitments, and more equitably distribute the workload across the force.

Second, we have expanded our Global Military Force Policy (GMFP) to improve worldwide management of Low Density/High Demand (LD/HD) assets. The Joint Staff, in conjunction with the services, is assessing each of our LD/HD capabilities to determine which force structure increases will best meet CINCs' requirements. For some of our most overworked assets, we have already acted to increase our numbers. We have reduced our Joint Exercise program by fifteen percent . . . and we are looking to make further reductions.

The chiefs and I know there is much work to be done and we will do all we can to balance the pace of operations against our ability to complete the missions given by the president.

While General Shelton serves as the top officer for all of America's soldiers, sailors, airmen, and Marines, he still traces his roots back to SOF. His views on the value of SOF units, and Army Special Forces in particular, are insightful.

Tom Clancy: You are surely the first Chairman of the Joint Chiefs of Staff to have a fully matured Special Operations community to work with. How well have they performed and are they properly sized, manned, and equipped to fulfill the jobs that you have in mind for them?

General Shelton: First, let me say without reservation, our SOF forces are the best in the world, and they provide our armed forces and our nation with unique, one-of-a-kind capabilities. We've been able to develop them because of the foresight of Congress in creating USSOCOM and by providing the tools they need to get the job done. Continued support and key investments in quality people, readiness, and modernization are essential if SOF is to continue to be ready and responsive. SOF is experiencing some of the same recruiting concerns we have heard and read about—after all, they take their people from the services. I've spoken about these recruiting concerns before. The manpower pool from which SOF must recruit is shrinking. So it is more important than ever that our efforts are redoubled to recruit the right young people and retain highly qualified and experienced soldiers, sailors, and airmen. We anticipate that the individual SOF operator of the twenty-first century, just as the worker of the twenty-first century, will most likely require greater math, computer, and language skills. That means we will need to determine what skills will be resident in our recruiting pool and what skills must be developed with SOF resources.

Tom Clancy: You've been using the Army Special Forces a lot over the last few years. Can you explain for our readers the value of JCS mandated and funded missions like those run under the Joint Combined Engagement Training (JCET) program?

General Shelton: Quite simply, the JCET program exists primarily to broaden and deepen the practical, cultural, and language skills of SOF personnel when deployed in foreign countries working closely with foreign militaries. I believe—and others will verify for you—the training is extremely valuable and producing big dividends. Just think what it has done—JCET has allowed our soldiers to refine area skills and, most important, has added a key ingredient to the success of our operations—because SOF will bring with them in times of crisis or conflict language skills, as well as firsthand knowledge of customs, terrain, environment, infrastructure and, in many cases, a network of personal relationships with key leaders of foreign militaries.

Tom Clancy: You've managed to have Special Forces teams forward-deployed on missions during a number of fast-breaking contingencies these last few years. Places like Sierra Leone, the embassy bombings in Kenya and Tanzania, and the World Trade Center bombing and firefight in Ceylon have all seen SF soldiers as some of the first responders to crisis and disaster. How valuable to you has it been having such "eyes and ears" on the ground, ready to respond and provide on-site intelligence and support?

General Shelton: Extremely valuable. All of our military leaders today know the value of SOF forces far better than their predecessors and what they bring to the joint warfighting effort. As we have seen our personnel numbers and resources decrease, our SOF forces will continue to grow in importance. But, without being too specific, let's look at why they are "global scouts" and what unique capabilities are offered as they deploy continually worldwide. We've talked about the JCET program and the benefits it provides. Just think about how that training can reduce tensions, build trust among nations, and oftentimes resolve situations before they get out of hand. SOF personnel are often the first Americans—military or otherwise—that foreign nationals come in contact with, and can set the stage for the employment of conventional forces, if that is deemed necessary. They are often the only force that is acceptable early on because they can operate with a small number, a "reduced footprint," if you will. The SOF deployments establish important contacts for all of our forces and establish the links that make coalitions effective, and that's because they know military leaders in most of the countries of the world where we are likely to deploy U.S. forces.

Tom Clancy: With the need for services from Special Operations units growing, has there been consideration to the idea of expanding the base of Reserve and National Guard SOF units that augment the active duty force?

General Shelton: The role of our Reserve Components has grown markedly as the active force has drawn down. In virtually every domestic and overseas mission—

from disaster relief in our own country to humanitarian assistance in Central America to ongoing operations in Iraq, Bosnia, and Kosovo—our Reservists and National Guardsmen, both SOF and regular units, have performed magnificently in some very important roles. Readiness issues have a high priority with me—they did when I was the CINC at Special Operations Command and now as Chairman. Effective integration and utilization of the men and women in our Reserve Component are key elements of Joint Personnel Readiness and absolutely critical to the success of the total force. Often the capabilities—such as civil affairs, psychological operations, and civil support—are found predominantly in the Reserve Components. We saw how important these were in Desert Shield and Storm, and again in Bosnia and Kosovo. Clearly, the wide range of contributions by the Reserve Components continues to be a bright spot as we strive to match available resources to a demanding mission load. Their service demonstrates the enduring value and relevance of the citizen soldier. We must continue to look for innovative ways to capitalize upon the strengths of our Reserve Components, our trump card for maintaining high readiness levels in these challenging times.

As the interview wound down, I wanted to know something of the *person* I was talking to. My final questions were directed toward General Shelton the man, and how he deals with the awesome stresses, strains, and challenges of the chairmanship.

Tom Clancy: General Colin Powell was known to relax by doing "shade tree" restorations of old Volvos. What hobbies or sports do you enjoy to unwind?

General Shelton: I have a number of hobbies. I enjoy playing the guitar and banjo. That's relaxing for me—I'd probably like to be better, but I do find it relaxing. I've always liked water sports. Carolyn and I enjoy boating, although we had more of an opportunity to do that in Tampa. Boating was a family activity and when my sons were younger it was fun for us to get away and spend time together.

Tom Clancy: You've had an extremely busy year, with Operations Desert Fox and Allied Force, the African embassy bombings and retaliations, Kosovo, and East Timor to deal with—there may be others. How do you deal with the stress and strain, and how tough has the job been personally?

General Shelton: It's been a challenging three years—no doubt about it. But, it's been a rewarding time for me both personally and professionally. In spite of the hard work and the challenging days, one of the things you have to do is maintain a sense of humor and a balance. Carolyn is a great help in keeping me centered and focused. I enjoy running, and try to do that most days, whether it's early in the morning before I come to work around 0500 or at midday on days when I can get away. I run about four or five miles, it clears the mind, and it's a good time for thinking. It works well for me.

Tom Clancy: You have a reputation for still wanting to maintain your roots back to the Airborne and Special Forces, and you still make the occasional parachute jump. We've heard that you recently did a jump with former President George W. Bush. Would you please tell us about that jump? And in fact, why do you still love to "jump out of perfectly good airplanes?"

General Shelton: President Bush sent a letter inviting me to jump with him in part to celebrate his seventy-fifth birthday. I was delighted to accept. It gave the military a chance to participate in the birthday celebration of a former president. I just recently went back to Fort Benning for the sixtieth anniversary of the Airborne. It was a great occasion, and being at Benning brought back great memories of my time at Jump School—at least they are great now. At the end of the second week of Jump School, I was getting a bit nervous about my first jump—so I asked the Black Hat if the 'chutes were safe. He barked back at me that if the parachute didn't work, I could bring it back and get another one. This improved my comfort level a bit, but I was still concerned and asked another question, "Just in case my main 'chute doesn't work, how long do I have to pull my reserve?" The Black Hat replied without hesitation, "Airborne, you have the rest of your life to pull the reserve." I once heard one of our great Airborne leaders comment, "I don't like jumping out of airplanes, but I sure like being around people who do!" For me, I like both—and have always liked jumping out of "perfectly good airplanes," as you say. I like the dedication . . . the courage . . . the esprit de corps—all wonderful characteristics of the Airborne soldier . . . that appealed to me as a young officer and still do today.

With this, the interview came to a close.

As I was leaving, General Shelton kindly offered me a hearty handshake and a coin with the JCS emblem. On the way out, I reflected upon this very quiet and private man, who has so much responsibility . . . and started to appreciate just how much America needs men like him. It is unfortunate that fewer and fewer Americans have served within the military, making the pool of leaders who can lead the world's most powerful fighting force ever smaller.

General Shelton is a man from another time, when honor and one's word were more important than personal gain and the fiscal bottom line. Had he taken another path, I have no doubt he would have become a wealthy and successful businessman in the textile industry. Luckily for America, he took the path of greatest resistance and challenge, and we are all the better and safer for his choice. I hope there are more like him out there. We need them now, more than ever.

Creating Special Forces Soldiers

Eagles don't flock. You have to find them one at a time!

H. Ross Perot

What kind of man undertakes a career where he can expect to spend up to six months a year away from home, where he is paid roughly half what his similarly qualified friends are making, where—if he is married—he is almost guaranteed a divorce, and where he has a pretty good chance of getting injured, wounded, or killed?

Sound like an attractive profession?

To a few . . . To a *precious* few.

The recruiters within Special Forces Command face the daunting challenge of identifying and training almost a thousand men every year who are not only unfazed by these challenges but are *surpassingly* capable in a breathtakingly large number of military and nonmilitary skills . . . the Renaissance Men of the military. The task is a big one; and it has recently grown even bigger, as the combination of an exceptionally healthy civilian economy and extreme operations tempos (OpTempos) makes the lure of civilian life ever more attractive.

It is not surprising that SFC has had a difficult time recruiting enough new SF soldiers to replace those who have retired or else have left the service for civilian jobs and more "normal" lives.[22]

This leaves SFC with a difficult challenge: either reduce the standards for new recruits and accept a potentially less capable SF soldier, or hold the current high standards and hope that better recruiting will eventually turn the tide of attrition. Right now, SFC has chosen to maintain the highest possible standards, even if that means they are able to take on fewer missions. It is a lousy choice.

So how would we describe their standards for selecting, recruiting, and training new SF soldiers? Well, it's a little hard to do that.

---

[22] The total Special Forces community numbers approximately 10,000. These days, about 1,000 leave that community every year, while something like five to six hundred replacements are now being trained every year. This deficit has been gradually slowed through better retention, but it still leaves ODAs as much as 25% to 33% under strength.

The official shoulder flash (emblem) of the John F. Kennedy (JFK) Special Warfare Center (SWC) and School

OFFICIAL U.S. ARMY GRAPHIC

For starters, it must be understood that the personnel assigned to U.S. Special Operations Forces are not simply highly trained soldiers, but *special* people given training that is not just specialized but *extreme*. It is this distinction that separates SOF personnel from conventional units assigned to unusual missions. A good example of the latter would include the B-25 bomber crews led by Jimmy Dolittle on the aerial raid on Japan in April 1942. These were selected from several line medium bomber units, given special training in Florida, then used on a one-time basis for the raid.

At the same time, it's clear from my conversations with folks in the organization that there is no such animal as an *ideal* Special Forces soldier . . . or, for that matter, an *ideal* Special Forces recruit. And *that* may be the point. In diversity there is strength and depth. And *that* is exactly what folks like Colonel Remo Butler are looking for.

Colonel Butler is commander of the 1st Special Forces Training Group—Airborne (1st SFTG [A]), a part of the much larger John F. Kennedy Special Warfare Center (JFK SWC). The colonel, a most impressive human being (something like a cross between a college professor and a world-class athlete—he coaches boxing in his spare time), is very particular about the men who are allowed into the SF training program, and even pickier about those who survive to graduate. Along with his boss, Major General Kenneth R. Bowra (the commander of the JFK SWC), Butler has been leading the fight to hold onto the qualities that have made the individual SF soldier legendary.

The organization where they work, the JFK SWC, is housed in two main buildings on the main post at Fort Bragg (Kennedy and Bryant Halls), as well as a host of subsidiary facilities across the country. It is the institutional keeper of all U.S. Army SOF knowledge, and it is responsible for a wide range of training, procurement, design, and development tasks for the entire Army SOF community (which, in addition to the Special Forces, includes the 75th Ranger Regiment, the 160th Special Operations Aviation Regiment (SOAR), the Delta Force, and the various other units

General Ken Bowra, USA, leads a party of dignitaries (including H. Ross Perot and Generals Shelton and Schoomaker) during a Fort Bragg dedication ceremony. General Bowra commands the John F. Kennedy Special Warfare Center at Fort Bragg, North Carolina.

of USASOC). General Bowra and his staff control everything from a museum and archives to jump and SCUBA schools. Truly, if you want to know about Army SOF, you start at the JFK SWC.

Perhaps the biggest misconception about SOF units is that they are all brawn and combat skills and short on brains and judgment. "A Detachments" are not "Dirty Dozens," as a visit to the JFK SWC will quickly demonstrate. Over the years I've visited scores of military schools in many countries, and none of them has the academic diversity and depth you find at the JFK SWC.

So, just what kind of warriors are the Special Forces looking for?

- **Gender**—Forget political correctness and the advancement of women. The existing Congressionally mandated Title 10 restrictions deny women the opportunity to serve in front-line infantry units, such as the Special Forces. Until that mandate is changed, the SF world will remain an all-male bastion.
- **Rank/Experience**—The top leadership of the Special Forces likes its personnel to be older and more mature than the American military average. Thus, entry into SF is restricted to officers who are captains (O-3) or 1st lieutenants (O-2) already selected for captain. Enlisted personnel must either have reached the rank of specialist (promotable) E-4 and sergeants (E-5), or Special Forces recruits will usually

be in their mid- to late twenties or early thirties—hopefully old enough to know what and when to do things, and perhaps more important, when *not* to.

- **Branch Experience**—Though SF candidates are recruited from every branch of the Army, the majority of Special Forces recruits have come from a traditional pool of personnel within the Army's infantry community—men who have risen from line infantry units to the 82nd Airborne Division, and then into a Ranger unit. However, since recent military drawdowns have been drying up this source, the SF leadership has had to cast a wider net, looking deeper into a greater variety of personnel skills and specialties. Today, an average Special Forces training class will include soldiers from the armor, signals, supply, and aviation branches, as well as the more traditional infantry career path. This trend has an upside: The personnel entering the teams have a broader than ever range of talents and skills, and these are proving valuable in the field on missions.

- **Physical Attributes**—No, SOF personnel do *not* look like Arnold Schwarzenegger, Sylvester Stallone, or Jesse Ventura (though you will run into Chuck Norrises). Raw strength is not usually seen as a plus. In fact, Special Forces physical requirements are weighted more toward endurance and mental toughness. Sure, SF soldiers tend to be well muscled, shaped, and toned, but they are not taut hardbodies. In other words, they're more like distance swimmers or triathletes than Nautilus nuts; and mental qualities are far more valuable than physical strength to future SF soldiers. More on this later.

- **Airborne Qualification**—As mentioned earlier, the names of Special Forces units always include an "Airborne" designation. This means that everyone who aspires to the SF trade will either have successfully attended the Army Airborne School at Fort Benning, Georgia, or be prepared to do so prior to Special Forces Training. This course is a major hurdle in itself, one of the toughest obstacles to getting selected into SF training.

- **Language Skills**—By the time a new SF soldier reaches his first team, he will have been assigned at least one foreign language to learn. Some of these are quite easy (like Spanish), while others might require more than a year of study (like Chinese or Arabic). On the other hand, candidates who are already proficient in one of the languages on the SF qualification list have an especially useful edge over other potential Special Forces candidates.

- **Racial/Ethnic Background**—Over the years, the SOF community has had difficulty recruiting minority candidates. There are several reasons for this. For starters, there are simply far too few qualified minority candidates, while at the same time, the rest of the Army—not to mention the other military services, governmental agencies, and private industry—has proved to be especially attractive to those who are qualified. All the same, minority recruitment has become an increasingly important priority for the SF leadership, especially in light of the growing overseas commitments where a Hispanic, Slavic, Arabic, or Asian member might open doors that would remain closed to Anglo personnel.

Since all of these items will be listed in any soldier's personnel file, the first step in finding the men who will eventually become new SF soldiers will be a close look at the paperwork.

But the clerical work is only a start. The *real* character traits that will qualify a recruit for Special Forces training are far deeper and harder to pin down than the qualities that find their way into personnel files. Let's call the *real* traits "survival skills," that is, those skills held by "survivor types." Survivor types are the ones still standing after insanely tough or deadly encounters. They are the ones who will seize the opportunities available, steer through chaos, and win.

How can you tell in advance who the survivor types are? You actually can't with accuracy, because there is always an element of luck, but you can select for traits that survivors usually possess—and then hope.

When I asked the trainers of the 1st SFTG to identify the chief of these traits, I kept hearing a single word—"agility."

Cats are agile, as are most animals in the wild. And most SF soldiers are agile in that sense. But they are also agile in senses that go far beyond mere animal grace and quickness. To better understand, let's contrast agility with another term often used in military circles—"flexibility." Flexibility is of course a good thing. It means you can adapt, change; it means you are not rigid or hidebound.

But for the Special Forces, this is not enough. To be flexible, in their view, is to be reactive. It's a way of responding to problems or situations rather than mastering them. On the other hand, agility, whether mental or physical, is a proactive quality. Those who have it have an edge in almost every kind of situation. In fact, to many SF personnel, their agility is their armor. With it they provide themselves with protection lacking in conventional Army units.

Agile men are hard to find anywhere, but they are especially hard to find in the U.S. military, where the usual policy is to drive qualities like agility out of young soldiers, sailors, Marines, or airmen. The agile ones are seen as rebels, mavericks, or misfits, usually to the detriment of a long-term military career. And yet, *such* men are *exactly* the types that the Special Forces need.

What are some of the other traits one can expect to find in a Special Forces soldier?

- **Military/Combat Experience**—Because SF recruits will normally be 03/E-4, they will arrive with the benefit of from five to ten years of invaluable Army experience . . . probably including deployed or combat duty (the Army has been *very* busy since the end of the Cold War). Anyone who has led troops will tell you that soldiers come in two flavors: those who have "seen the elephant" of combat and those who have not. Clearly, the combination of years of experience and a taste of combat is the best litmus for determining who will not freeze or hesitate in a critical situation.

- **Leadership**—Leadership is an indefinable quality. Nevertheless, a few years of Army service tend to point out those who possess it. And for both officers and NCOs there are particular times when leadership qualities like initiative and self-motivation skills are most likely to appear. For officers, this time comes during their tours as platoon leaders. For NCOs, it most often comes when they serve as fire team and squad leaders or platoon sergeants.

- **Education**—Special Forces leaders look for a solid knowledge base in each potential soldier, along with an indication that he wants to continue learning. Special Forces soldiers will not be academics, but they *are* intellectually curious: They are voracious readers; they soak up knowledge. Officers (who already possess a college degree when they enter the Army) will attend the staff and continuing education courses that are part of the normal Army career path, but they will also tend to find time for post-graduate programs. Enlisted personnel and warrant officers will work toward—and usually achieve—their own undergraduate or graduate degree. It's also common to take additional night or continuing education courses.

- **Interpersonal Skills**—Military officers and enlisted men are not famous for smooth, skilled interpersonal relations. And too often they are clumsy and abrupt enough to make civilians uncomfortable, threatened, or even hostile. Such an outcome is not an option to SF personnel if they are to successfully accomplish the range of overseas missions they'll be called upon to do. If they are not already comfortable dealing with other people, other communities, other cultures, or other races, Special Forces soldiers have to learn how to do that. Not everyone has the temperament for that kind of openness, and that quality is closely monitored during the selection process.

- **Entrepreneurial Spirit**—This is almost cognate with agility. The greatest entrepreneurs have vision. They're adaptable. They take risks, but the risks more often than not pan out. They are alchemists, who can create a successful enterprise from nothing but raw ideas. They have incredible drive and energy. And they can focus the drive, energy, and ideas of others toward a desired outcome. Given the nature of Special Forces missions and the variety of circumstances they encounter, there is a pressing need for an entrepreneurial spirit within each SF soldier. The leadership, understandably, selects for it.

Let me add a last, sobering observation to the above thoughts: During any given year, the number of candidates eligible for recruitment into the Special Forces is just a few thousand out of the more than one million soldiers (active, reserve, and National Guard) in the Army. Out of these few thousand, fewer than four hundred will successfully complete the journey to the awarding of the Green Beret.

Special Forces: The Mix

All military units require a balanced mix of personnel whose skills are matched to their potential missions. Nowhere is this truer than in those small combat units that the Special Forces have designated as Operational Detachment Alphas (ODAs or "A" Detachments). The ODAs are the basic building blocks of the Special Forces. We'll talk more about how these fit into the larger picture of SF organizations and missions later on, but right now I want to concentrate on how they are put together.

Officially, each ODA is composed of twelve Special Forces soldiers. It is commanded by a captain (O-3), who is assisted by an assistant detachment commander, normally a warrant officer. They lead ten SF soldiers, whose skills cover six specific specialties, or technically, five Military Occupational Specialty (MOS) codes.

Special Forces branch codes all begin with the number 18 (the number reserved for them in the Army system). These are broken down as follows:

- **18A (Officer/ODA Commander)**—The 18A branch code is reserved for Special Forces officers who will command ODAs on missions. 18As also provide the leadership for every other significant leadership position within the Special Forces community. Each ODA has one 18A assigned to it.

- **180A (Warrant Officer/Assistant Detachment Commander)**—To back up the 18A commanding the ODA, each A Team is assigned a 180A warrant officer to act as the assistant detachment commander.[23–24] When the team operates together, he backs up the 18A and is prepared to take command in the event that the captain is absent or incapacitated. Also, should conditions or the mission dictate it, the ODA can be split into two equal teams, with the 18A and 180A each commanding one part.

- **18B (Sergeant/Weapons)**—The ODA 18Bs are the weapons specialists, and they are capable of operating and maintaining a wide variety of U.S., Allied, and other foreign weaponry. This includes not only personal weapons like the M4 carbine, M249 light machine gun, and M203 40mm grenade launcher, but also larger and more powerful weapons like the M2 .50-caliber machine gun, Javelin antitank missile, and mortars. 18Bs who have attended one of the Army's two sniper courses can also act as snipers. Each ODA is normally assigned two 18Bs.

- **18C (Sergeant/Engineering)**—Since an ODA may be called upon to blow up a bridge one day, and then help rebuild it on another, each team is assigned two 18C engineering sergeants. 18Cs are specialists across a range of disciplines, from demolitions and construction of field fortifications, to topographic survey techniques. This means they are a significant force multiplier for planners in missions ranging from direct action strikes against enemy targets in wartime to humanitarian operations in time of crisis or natural disaster.

- **18D (Sergeant/Medical NCO)**—Since ODAs may have to operate behind the lines for months at a time, it is essential that each team have an organic medical capability. The two 18Ds who provide those services to each ODA are generally considered to be the finest first-response/trauma medical technicians in the world. Though primarily trained with an emphasis on trauma medicine, they also have a working knowledge of a range of skills such as dentistry, veterinary care, public sanitation, water quality, and optometry.

- **18E (Sergeant/Communications NCO)**—Another organic capability within each ODA is the ability to communicate back to base from virtually any point on Earth. A pair of 18Es provides these services. 18Es can operate every kind of commu-

---

23–24 Warrant officers' MOS codes always have an "0" added.

A Special Forces engineering sergeant (18C) places a cutting charge of C4 plastic explosive on a steel I-beam during training. Along with demolition duties, 18Cs can also construct bridges and other useful items while on missions.

JOHN D. GRESHAM

nications gear, from encrypted satellite communications systems to old-style high-frequency (HF) Morse key systems, but they also have serious computer/networking skills.

- **18F (Assistant Operations/Intelligence NCO)**—Since many ODA missions involve behind the lines activities in denied (i.e., hostile) territory, each ODA is assigned one 18F intelligence specialist. The 18F is fully qualified to collect and evaluate information for transmission back to higher headquarters, as well as to supply vital data on enemy units, targets, and capabilities. He will also provide the team with an interrogation capability should enemy prisoners be captured.

- **18Z (Sergeant/Operations NCO)**—Though shown on the organizational chart as an "operations planner," the 18Z is actually the senior enlisted man in the team. Usually flagged as the "team sergeant," the 18Z is responsible for making sure the entire team runs as a unit and is properly outfitted and supplied. While looking after the other sergeants on the team, he relieves the 18A and 180A of more mundane tasks, which allows them to concentrate on leading and planning missions for the ODA.

ODAs are probably the finest and most capable light infantry units in the world, and they can conduct a variety of missions across the full spectrum of warfare and conflict.

A Special Forces communications sergeant (18E) works on the networking gear for a large command post exercise, R-3. 18Es are among the most valued of military personnel for their extensive communications, encryption, and networking skills.

JOHN D. GRESHAM

There are, of course, downsides:

Downside One: There are only about 6,500 combat-ready SF soldiers to go around at any time: about the same number as half of a single light infantry division.

Downside Two: SF soldiers are expensive to train and support.

Downside Three: They are frequently the targets of recruitment by civilian businesses. Companies who are looking for exactly that mix of technical skills and mental agility so prized by the Special Forces covet men from every one of the various 18-series MOS codes.

Maintaining the organizational integrity of the Special Forces is a constant challenge.

Recruiting: The First Step

How do they build these unique warriors?

First, SF soldiers are not born. They have to be handcrafted one at a time by a time-tested process, which begins with the initial step of recruitment.

Second, finding "the best of the best" is extremely difficult . . . and not just because the sort of man with the necessary qualifications is a rare bird. All too often, the quiet professionalism of the Special Forces works against them. Because the Special Forces are not very good self-advertisers, potential recruits are often unaware what Special Forces can offer them . . . or what they themselves can bring to Special Forces.

The thin trickle of volunteers has left the staff of the 1st SFTG with a big job getting the word out about their community. Through a program of posters, newsletters, and command magazines, the various Army SOF units try to educate potential candidates on the possible career paths open to them. Since the military overall already has such a wide variety of jobs and careers open to its personnel, this is tougher than it sounds. It's not easy to persuade people to leave a branch or community after they have already invested as much as five or ten years in it.

To help make those sales, a number of Special Forces recruiting teams make the rounds of Army posts around the world.[25] These serve a dual mission: to inform soldiers that the Special Forces have openings and are recruiting, and to perform preliminary screening of possible SF candidates. Like any other recruiting detail, it is hard and terribly tedious work, and now that the total pool of Army personnel has been reduced by almost half from what it was a decade ago, while the number of SF soldiers needed to man the seven Special Forces Groups has not changed, it has become almost impossible.

Still, the SFC recruiting teams manage to deliver a quality man to the 1st SFTG; the raw material for the Special Forces soldiers factory is as good as it has *ever* been . . . and in some ways it may be even better. The move to recruit from branches other than the infantry has expanded the skill base of the entire SF community, and this has served them well in the post–Cold War world.

Once a soldier has determined that he wants to join up, he volunteers.[26] Assuming that he has met the necessary criteria and has completed his Jump School qualification, he can go into the queue for the next open spot in the Special Forces Assessment and Selection (SFAS) course.

Into the Fire: Special Forces Assessment and Selection

At a minimum, a successful training evolution for a single SF soldier takes a full year, and costs a minimum of $100,000. It makes sense, therefore, to arrange for attrition to take place within the pool of potential recruits early in the training process, so as to minimize costs. This attrition is accomplished by means of the Special Forces Assessment and Selection (SFAS) course.

Seven times a year, Company "G" of the 1st Battalion, 1st SFTG gathers SF candidates for SFAS at the Colonel Nick Rowe Special Forces Training Facility at Camp MacKall, North Carolina.[27] Located in the sand hills west of Fort Bragg, Camp

---

25 A number of foreign exchange military personnel are also recruited for Special Forces training. These soldiers (normally officers) are picked by their home governments, and training is provided by the U.S. government. They tend to be well-qualified for the SF trade, since a failure during training would reflect poorly upon their home country, military service, and government.

26 Along with women, the Army will not allow the recruitment into Special Forces of military doctors or aviators. Since an impressive investment has already been lavished upon them, they are far too valuable to risk in an SF environment.

27 Colonel Nick Rowe was a legendary Special Forces soldier. While serving in Vietnam, he was captured. After five years in captivity, he managed to escape and make his way back to friendly lines (a story eventually chronicled in the book *Five Years to Freedom*). A quarter century later, he was killed in the Philippines by a bomb set by insurgent forces.

MacKall is a satellite facility adjacent to a number of range facilities used to train personnel from every part of the Army SOF community. Here every SF soldier's career is born. At this humble location in the North Carolina pines, up to three hundred candidates (officers, warrant officers, and sergeants all together) are run through SFAS to determine their suitability to continue to the Special Forces Qualification Course (SFQC)—the "Q" Course.

SFAS is twenty-four days of hell on earth; and it is probably the single biggest hurdle between a soldier and the Green Beret he will be awarded if he makes it to the end of the "Q" Course. Survivors of the SFAS test get an invitation to the SFQC. The alternatives are to return to their original Army service branch, or to try the SFAS again. Return to the original branch is not exactly an attractive choice, since it frequently leads to an early exit from the Army.[28] But who in his right mind wants to go through the SFAS again?

SFAS is designed to provide a raw test of body, mind, and soul that will allow the 1st SWTG staff to confidently send candidates forward, sure that they will be worth the money and effort that will be expended upon them during the "Q" Course. During those miserable twenty-four days, the candidates will suffer sleep deprivation, limited rations, and physical exertions bordering on the inhuman. At the same time, they will be required to demonstrate fieldcraft skills, mental toughness, and most of all, the *refusal* to give up. SFAS is not at all a builder or measure of qualities like intelligence, resourcefulness, or agility. It's a straight-up, in-your-face test of an individual's basic suitability for the Special Forces.

Attrition is heavy. In one recent SFAS class, 7–99 (the final SFAS class of Fiscal Year 1999), 236 students started, and 78 successfully finished—an attrition rate of 67 percent. With dropout rates like this, it's easy to understand the line from "The Ballad of the Green Berets": "One hundred men will test today; but only three win the Green Beret!" By the time the entire recruitment, selection, and qualification process is done, three percent may actually be an overestimate.

SFAS begins with up to three hundred candidates reporting to Camp MacKall. If they have been clever, they will have taken the advice of their SF recruiter to get into a regular physical fitness regime before they come. For most, this involves lots of distance walking with heavy loads in a rucksack. But swimming skills are even more important, since the ability to stay afloat and move in water is a requirement for all SF personnel, and the swim test often ends prospective Special Forces careers. By the way, wood chopping is an excellent preparation for the swim test, an SFAS instructor explained to me, since it builds upper body muscles.

Another problem for SFAS candidates is that the course is never the same. In order to prevent potential SF soldiers from "figuring out" the course and outsmarting the instructors, events and goals are constantly changed from class to class. For example, though distance marches with loaded packs are a staple item in SFAS life, the

---

28 Because those in a soldier's parent branch (armor, infantry, aviation, etc.) tend to view a Special Forces candidate as a "traitor" or malcontent, a failure to qualify frequently results in his leaving the service entirely. This is another reason why the SF leadership tries to make sure that the bulk of the dropouts or failures occur early, while there is still a chance for candidates to regain their position back in their home branch.

Along with their other skills, all Special Forces soldiers are fully jump qualified prior to attending their qualification course. These soldiers are practicing parachute and water infiltration skills, which are organic to each Special Forces Group.

actual distances vary,[29] and many times the students are not told how far they will go on a particular march, only that they will carry a weighted rucksack (the weight varies, but usually is over 50 lb./22.67 kg.) until the instructors tell them to stop. These marches are run in all sorts of conditions, from the humid heat of summer to the ice storms of winter.

To make life even more interesting, the students gradually have their sleep patterns and sleep periods altered, so that they are rapidly sleep deprived.

Meanwhile, the SFAS staff packs a lot into the twenty-four days:

- **Obstacle Courses**—SFAS has a good one. It incorporates a variety of barriers from walls and jumps to climbing ropes and underground sewer pipes. This course not only provides the SFAS cadre with a means to evaluate the overall physical fitness of the candidates, it lets them note specific shortcomings, such as fear of heights, inability to climb, or claustrophobia. All of these are important to know early, as any one of them can make a soldier worthless to SFC teams in the field.

- **Runs**—While much of the military has taken the view that high-impact aerobic activities like running can be bad (with good reason—it's hell on joints), the Special Forces take the view that their entire profession is "high impact," and Special

---

29 The SFAS staff is *very* protective of their event parameters. When I asked for a general range of distances, they gave me a steely look and said, "Next question?" There were, I might add, no smiles.

Special Forces applicants endure the agonies of the ammo box carry during a Special Forces Assessment and Selection course. Survival of this endurance contest is needed to move on to the Special Forces Qualification Course.

JOHN D. GRESHAM

Forces soldiers simply have to deal with it. Since SFAS aims to shake and rattle an SF candidate within an inch of his life, medium distance runs are an excellent way to start the day.

- **Marches**—Dozens of marches with packs are conducted during the twenty-four days of the course. All are designed to wear down a candidate to the point of mental and physical exhaustion.

- **Land Navigation/Fieldcraft**—Along with physical and mental stamina, there is no other skill so vital to a Special Forces soldier as land navigation. While most Army units take it for granted that they will have a NAVSTAR Global Positioning System (GPS) receiver and satellite photo-based maps, SF units are expected to maneuver to pinpoint, time-on-target objectives with nothing more than a compass, protractor, and map. Just to make things interesting, they must also do it in the dark and bad weather. Remember that batteries run down and electronics break, yet the magnetic field of planet Earth has proven comfortingly reliable. Though SFAS candidates go through a whole series of exercises on the ranges around Camp MacKall, this fixation on navigational skills is continued during the "Q" Course.

- **"Situation and Reaction"**—These exercises take students who are already sleep deprived and on the edge of a physical collapse and test their problem-solving skills in a real-world situation. They are faced with a problem that is only a half a degree of separation from absurd. Then using simple materials supplied by the

Special Forces candidates carry a log in a "Situation and Reaction" exercise. Such exercises are used during Special Forces Assessment and Selection courses to help identify those with the aptitude and physical qualities necessary for life in the teams.

JOHN D. GRESHAM

staff or by nature, they must find a way to solve it. Over the years, the SFAS staff has devised dozens of these "Situation and Reaction" situations, so that particular events are rarely repeated in a given year.

For example, imagine a 5,000-lb./2,267-kg. M151 jeep with a wheel missing. Now consider how a group of ten SFAS candidates might use only poles and ropes to move the crippled vehicle, along with a load of water cans, a mile or two.

One of the more creative solutions involves removing a wheel, leaving only two on opposing corners, and then running poles across the hood and rear bed and tying them down with ropes. Next, the water cans and everybody's packs are loaded onto the jeep, along with a (preferably light) soldier to steer. Two other soldiers balance the vehicle with the poles, while the other seven push. This really works!

- **Team Events**—Though SFAS is a highly personal event for an individual soldier, a few team-oriented events allow the cadre to evaluate a candidate's ability to work with others. These are normally variations on "Situation and Reaction"-type events, and have similar goals.

  For example, consider a wooden box with rope handles, about 3-ft./1-m. long, weighing about 60 lb./27.2 kg. loaded, and containing 5.56mm rifle ammunition. Such boxes are generally considered miserable to move more than a few hundred yards/meters (after that, the rope handles start cutting into the carrier's hands).

Now, imagine a twelve-man squad of SFAS students toting their weighted field packs having to move four or five of these containers several miles.

To begin with, putting a pair of SFAS candidates on each will not do (because of the rope handles problem). And there is the further problem that the weight of the boxes is sufficient to require that now and again the carriers will have to be relieved. Clearly, the job will take a concerted team effort.

I saw a number of solutions: One was to build a rope and pole platform that could be rested on the packs of six marching candidates. They would then trade off every few hundred yards/meters. Another team had a volleyball-style rotation, with eight or ten candidates carrying, while the other two walked behind and "rested."

Since SFAS events are designed to eliminate SF candidates who do not have the "right stuff" to move on to the "Q" Course, the whole thing must be, in all honesty, brutal. This is by no means a judgment on anyone's personal or "human" qualities (Mother Teresas need not apply). You are evaluated purely on your performance.

For that reason, SFAS cadre personnel avoid sympathetic reactions or evaluations; and they do not get to know the students. The entire SFAS cadre is fully aware that in a year or two, one of these candidates could be in the field on a mission with them. Who do you want at your side when your life hangs in the balance? Much like the Navy's famous TOPGUN school for fighter pilots, "There are no points for second place."

The vast majority of SFAS attrition takes place during the second week, during which time the class will be trimmed to about half its starting size. Most will drop out on marches or during training events. A candidate will hit a "wall," much like marathon runners during the twenty-first mile of a race. Something breaks inside, and he will raise a hand to call a cadre member, who quickly takes him aside to minimize the shock and shame. Though this is hardly a shameful failure (anyone with courage enough even to try SFAS is a special kind of human being, and should be admired for it), the prospect of returning home is always a tough one.

Sometimes the SFAS cadre will see someone who is simply not physically or mentally up to the challenge. They will then either counsel the candidate to drop out, or else just fail him on their own. Other times an otherwise qualified candidate suffers an injury during the course, which presents the SFAS staff with a difficult problem.

There are several ways to deal with it. If the injury is minor (say a stress fracture or a pulled muscle or tendon), then the candidate will probably be given a chance to heal and try again in the following SFAS class. Should the problem be more serious, the staff may send the candidate back to his home base to heal and (if he's willing) get himself ready for another try the following year. If the injury is even more serious, he will have to be dropped, and advised not to return. Though these last losses are heartbreaking, the good news is that many of the injured candidates choose to try SFAS again. Such men are exactly the kind of people that the Special Forces want— men who would rather die trying than fail. These "retread" candidates have an extremely good completion rate.

By the end of the third week of SFAS, most failures and dropouts will have taken place, and the survivors are starting to think ahead to entering the "Q" Course.

A Special Forces Assessment and Selection candidate just after falling out of a march—deciding to drop out. While such moments are heartbreaking, they help ensure the extremely high quality of every Special Forces soldier.

However, nobody should assume he will finish SFAS without going through *every* wicket thrown up by the cadre. For example, the land navigation portion of the course frequently causes problems even for experienced infantrymen, and can cause a "drop" just as easily as an injury. Nothing at SFAS is easy, and none of the students knows until the last day if they have made it or not.

Finally, on day twenty-four, the tests come to an end, and the successful candidates will begin to look forward to what is to come. There are no fancy graduation ceremonies or presentations. SFAS is about survival, pure and simple. But there *is* a prize: an invitation to the Special Forces Qualification Course.

Unfortunately, the SF candidates don't just finish up SFAS and head into the "Q" Course. Usually, the candidates must wait for a while between the end of one and the start of the other (and the wait can be as long as a year). This is a good time to take some leave, or possibly a military school course, and, of course, they are expected to stay in top physical condition.

Longer waiting periods have to be dealt with back at the soldier's home base, which can be an uncomfortable time (not a few candidates will undergo some harassment from their conventional force brethren). While nobody in SFC or the rest of the Army cares to say it, the wait leaves candidates in a limbo, between their old and new lives.

The Special Forces Qualification Course

SFAS does not make a Special Forces soldier. Surviving SFAS merely shows an aptitude to *become* an SF soldier. Actuating that potential requires a lot more training and persistence. The "Q" Course takes a qualified and experienced soldier and turns him into a basically trained Special Forces soldier, ready to join a team in one of the SFGs and head "downrange" on missions.

The SFQC functions as a graduate-level training course, providing everyone who completes it with a common set of skills and experiences to take with them into their teams. At the same time it provides a final filtering element that allows the Special Forces community to confirm that a soldier is both ready and worthy for the responsibilities ahead.

Today's "Q" Course essentially follows the syllabus laid out a half-century ago by Colonel Bank and his original 10th Special Forces Group (SFG) cadre. Run in three parts (or phases), SFQC is designed to give each SF candidate not only the field and combat skills he will need, but also the technical and professional training to fulfill his particular MOS code. The three phases are broken down this way:

- **Phase I**—Centering on basic skills training, Phase I is thirty-nine days long and is designed to provide a common level of field skills for all participants, no matter which branch they may come from.

- **Phase II**—In Phase II the group is broken up according to the students' various MOS specialties, and it varies in length depending upon the technical skills code assigned to a particular soldier.

- **Phase III**—During Phase III, students are familiarized with their core mission: unconventional warfare . . . the "muscle" end of the Special Forces trade. Thirty-eight days long, Phase III culminates in a large-scale field exercise, known as Robin Sage.

Four courses are run each year. But because of the varying lengths for Phase II training, most students wind up finishing Phase III with a different group of students than they started with. Since many SF missions involve "pickup" teams thrown together at the last minute, this inconsistency is probably an aid to training and not a hindrance. Every part of SFQC is designed to mimic the real-world situations that SF troops will inevitably encounter in the field.

The "Q" Course: Phase I

The goals and objectives of Phase I of the SFQC are fairly simple: A soldier who successfully completes this part of the course will be ready to plan, conduct, and lead a squad-sized patrol, accurately navigating cross-country movements with a full combat load to a planned schedule in darkness and bad weather.

While these skills may seem basic, you'd be surprised how few soldiers around the world can actually run such an operation. To the leadership of most armies it is virtually inconceivable that *every* member of a squad or platoon (the equivalent of a Special Forces ODA) could bring it off. At SFQC such an accomplishment is only a "passing" grade.

For most students, the "Q" Course begins with a return to Camp MacKall and the Rowe Training Facility, where they endured the SFAS. However, whatever the

A member of the Special Forces Assessment and Selection cadre at Camp MacKall, North Carolina. Such Special Forces professionals are the keepers of their almost tribal knowledge, and ensure that every new soldier they mint is as good as those who have come before.

JOHN D. GRESHAM

memories they may have of the SFAS (usually unpleasant), there is a basic difference between the SFQC and SFAS. Though failures and dropouts will still happen, at the SFQC the cadre will do everything they can to help the SFQC students win their Green Berets at the end of Phase III.

The instructors are drawn from Company "F" of the 1st Battalion/1st SWTG, who also run Phase III and some elements of the Phase II training.

From the moment a student arrives, every hour of each day is carefully scheduled for maximum training value. The focus is on building a common set of field and combat skills, no matter what a soldier's background or previous service specialty may be. Phase I levels the playing field of skills, and prepares the students for what follows.

So for example, to folks from branches like armor or logistics, much of what they learn there is brand-new, while infantrymen who have gone through Ranger training probably have much of the Phase I curriculum down cold, and for them it is a refresher course. But—and this is a big but—they are expected to mentor those from other communities, and are judged on how well they do this.

The table below lays out the entire thirty-nine days of Phase I:

Timeframe	Activity
Day 1 to 10	Land Navigation
Day 11 to 14	Common Task Training/Fieldcraft Skills
Day 15 to 21	Patrolling Basics

Timeframe	Activity
Day 22 to 24	Leadership, Ambush, and Reconnaissance Training
Day 25 to 31	Squad-Level Patrolling Field Exercise (FTX)
Day 32 to 33	Platoon Operations Training
Day 34 to 38	Platoon-Level Patrolling Field Exercise (FTX)
Day 39	Outprocess to Phase II Training

Not surprisingly, Phase I begins with a heavy dose of land navigation—a continuation of the skills that they demonstrated during SFAS. The exercises are designed to make the students confident of their movement skills under any conditions imaginable; and they must do this without GPS receivers.

Obviously, every SF ODA deploys with GPS navigation gear, and they are trained to use it capably. However, batteries run down and satellites can be disabled by solar storms or enemy action. A compass and paper map always work. Therefore, the SFQC makes certain that these are a SF candidate's primary navigation tools.

Actually, proficiency at manual land navigation is not terribly difficult. It just takes preparation time and practice.

For starters, each student must discover exactly how long his stride is. This is done on a measured course, either fifty or a hundred meters long. (Because metric measurements are the standard in civilized countries, and maps everywhere are *always* drawn in metric measures, the U.S. military has gone metric. The old imperial measures used by the rest of Americans are now Neanderthal . . . though I have to confess that I still find comfort in them.)

Usually the students measure their stride (one step with each leg) over several kinds of terrain, so they can bias their measurements accordingly. Let's say a student measures sixty strides per hundred meters, and this is fairly constant over most kinds of terrain and tactical movement. He can then calculate distance traveled fairly easily. And to make this easier, he is encouraged to use "Ranger beads," a sort of field abacus that can be hung from his uniform blouse. (Ranger beads don't crash; they have no batteries to fail; and they work in the dark in any weather.)

Once a student can reliably measure distance, his next problem is to make sure he is going in the right direction. This is done by means of what is called "point to point" movement: The student figures a base course from the start point to the objective. But, if necessary, the journey can be broken into smaller legs to accommodate difficult terrain or covert movement. The student then calculates a bearing from "point to point," and proceeds on his way. The trick to staying on course is to take bearings on significant terrain features (trees, rocks, poles, etc.), and move between them. By regularly checking his bearings, tracking the distance with his beads, and looking for intermediate calibration points shown on the map (road junctions, buildings, etc.), the student should be able to move quite accurately.

Following land navigation training, the trainees move on to a four-day course in common soldier tasks (marksmanship, first aid, etc.), along with fieldcraft skills (which are not all that different from what you might encounter at a good Boy Scout summer camp).

This training is followed by a week of learning patrolling and other soldier skills.

Tactical movement and observation skills are emphasized, but there is also additional weapons training. By the end of the third week of Phase I, the students are ready to move into a series of more complex skills training and exercises.

Week four of Phase I begins with a three-day introduction to the art of ambushes and field reconnaissance. These bread-and-butter SF missions begin to give the trainees an idea of what they will be in for if and when they move on to an SF ODA.

This is followed by a week of field exercises, where the lessons of the previous twenty-four days are put to practical use. The students are broken into six-man squads, and sent out into the countryside around Camp MacKall to conduct simulated ambushes, reconnaissance missions, and other assorted tasks. During this period the instructors get their first real look at how individual students function in the field, and how they interact with team members. Those who clearly do not meet the required performance standards will be dropped (or sometimes counseled to recycle and try again later).

Just as at SFAS, injuries can cause unwanted problems, but the instructors try to nurse the injured along to the extent that is possible. If it is not, the injured candidate is evacuated to the medical facilities at Fort Bragg for treatment, and perhaps a chance to try again during another SFQC session. Generally, a student can take two tries at the "Q" Course.

Day thirty-two begins a two-day session on platoon operations, which is then followed by another five-day field exercise. This time, twelve-man platoons/ODAs are sent out into the forests and fields to run various kinds of missions. Once again, the Phase I cadre can judge whether or not candidates are ready to move on to Phase II training. This is a critical moment, because the really difficult and expensive part of a SF soldier's training begins in Phase II, and the cadre wants to make sure that only qualified students go further.

The students spend Day 39 doing paperwork and outprocessing, getting ready to head into Phase II.

The "Q" Course: Phase II

Once Phase I is completed, each Special Forces trainee will begin to train for his own unique MOS specialty code, often at facilities other than Fort Bragg or Camp MacKall. For example, the 18Es (communications sergeants) do much of their training at Camp Gruber, Oklahoma, while the 18Ds (medical sergeants) perform trauma room rotations in hospitals located in New York City and Tampa, Florida. In all, eight separate 18-series courses are run for Phase II training, varying in length from six to twelve months.

The courses break out this way:[30]

- **18A (Officer)**—Run by Company "A" of the 1st Batallion/1st SWTG (A), this course is six months long. The 18A course is designed to take officers from con-

---

30 The courses for 180A (warrant officers), 18F (intelligence), and 18Z (operations) are handled elsewhere by the JFK Center and School, as follow-on qualification classes.

Special Forces officer candidates attend an operations planning lecture during Phase II of their qualification course. The "Q" Course has a heavy academic component, which prepares young officers and noncommissioned officers for duty in the field.

JOHN D. GRESHAM

ventional line Army units and turn them into leaders capable of running an ODA in the field thousands of miles from home base. During the 18A course, the students get a heavy dose of unconventional warfare (UW) training, with a particular emphasis on mission planning and logistics. There is also a great deal of academic work, focused specifically on guerrilla warfare and insurgency operations.

- **18B (Weapons Sergeant)**—Company "B" of the 1st Batallion/1st SWTG (A) runs the course for weapons sergeants, which is designed to teach advanced weapons skills for a wide variety of ordnance. An 18B candidate is expected to learn how to operate and maintain every kind of weapon from pistols to rocket launchers. And not only U.S. and Allied weapons, but also firearms from around the world.

- **18C (Engineering Sergeant)**—Also run by Company "B" of the 1st Batallion/1st SWTG (A), the 18C Phase II training (at Camp MacKall) is simply a course in how to build things, and then blow them up. This seemingly odd combination of skills actually makes a lot of sense for those who may have to build a dam one day on a peacekeeping mission, and then blow up a bridge in combat on another.

- **18D (Medical Sergeant)**—The longest of the Phase II training courses (at twelve months), the medical sergeant's course is run by the Special Operations Medical Training Battalion at Fort Bragg (which also trains combat medics for the Rangers, Navy SEALs, and others), and it is quite simply the finest first-response medical training in the world. One reason for this is the emphasis on quick response to trauma, especially gunshot wounds. To give the student 18Ds the necessary experience, each candidate conducts rotations at innercity hospitals in the Bronx and Tampa.

- **18E (Communications Sergeant)**—SF operations make a lot of demands upon communications—the responsibility of the 18E. Trained by Company "E" of the 1st Batallion/1st SWTG (A) at Camp Gruber, Oklahoma (an Army National Guard post), the SF 18Es are among the most talented and skilled communications personnel in the world. Their six-month course covers everything from basic Morse code training to advanced computer networking and encryption techniques. These are "shade-tree" radio operators, who can design and string homemade wire antennas one day and install computer network routers the next.

This set of courses is the distinguishing element that sets the Special Forces apart from other SOF communities. Here SF candidates learn not only their particular MOS skills, but also the key principles of UW, such as combat tactics and warfare abilities, and also noncombat and political principles. Because they carry both an olive branch and a gun in their rucksack of skills, SF soldiers can cover a much broader spectrum of warfare than any other SOF community in the U.S. military. This is another component of their "agility."

One of the more interesting challenges in Phase II is to work the "conventional" Army mentality out of candidates. What do I mean by that? Though many of my friends in the Army will disagree with me, let's say that in its conventional manifestation it is big, slow, ponderous, resistant to change, resistant to innovation, dogmatic, bureaucratic, closeminded . . . "Mother." For many, leaping out of the lap of Mother Army is far from easy, so deeply imbedded are the Pavlovian responses learned during their years of service in "the big green machine."

One sharp-looking and obviously talented young captain from the armor community showed me how hard it can be. During a map exercise with other 18A candidates, he proceeded to break a simulated operational area into squares (which is the way the "regular" Army does things), with no consideration of the nature of the terrain or of the various groups that might have to operate on it. The Army likes lines and grids; UW is nonlinear. The young captain clearly had trouble with the nonlinear nature of unconventional warfare, and the Phase II cadre criticism hit him so hard that he visibly sagged.

But he learned. His second try was better: He broke the zones by roads, streams, and county boundaries. Later he learned to draw his demarcation lines along impassable or difficult terrain, since these are rarely in dispute between guerrilla bands and military units.

The 18-series Phase II training also includes a heavy dose of teaching skills, since so much of a SF soldier's time downrange will be spent on training foreign military personnel. There is also an additional dose of cross-cultural skills training, so the students will be ready for their next challenge: Phase III and the Robin Sage field exercise.

The "Q" Course: Phase III

The home stretch of the "Q" Course starts with the beginning of Phase III, which is the advanced training portion of the SFQC, and which concludes with a large-scale final examination known as Robin Sage. At only thirty-eight days long, Phase III is the most concentrated part of the course, and the final chance for the training cadre to evaluate a student prior to certification as a Special Forces soldier. The course schedule is broken out in the table below:

Timeframe	Activity
Day 1	Inprocessing/Equipment Issue
Day 2 to 3	Intelligence Preparation of the Battlefield (Officers)/Mission Planning (NCOs)
Day 4 to 6	Air Operations and Parachute Extractions
Day 7 to 10	Direct Action Practice Isolation
Day 11	Practice Airborne Operation
Day 12 to 14	Unconventional Warfare Classes
Day 15	Cross-Cultural Communications Training
16 to 20	Robin Sage Isolation/Planning Period
Day 21 to 22	Robin Sage Mission Rehearsals
Day 23 to 37	Robin Sage Field Exercise
Day 38	Outprocessing

Over half of Phase III is dedicated to the preparations for and the running of Robin Sage, which probably gives you some idea of how much weight the SFQC cadre places on it. Robin Sage ties everything together, and shows once and for all whether or not a student really has the "right stuff" for the Special Forces trade.

Phase III begins with a day of inprocessing and issuing equipment. At the same time, the students are grouped into student SF ODAs, where they will operate for the rest of Phase III (after days two and three).

On days two and three, officers are lectured on Intelligence Preparation of the Battlefield (IPB—a fancy military term for getting the lay of the land and sizing up possible opponents and targets), while the sergeants learn about mission and operations planning.

Then the students are given refresher training on air, helicopter, and parachute operations and procedures, in preparation for a series of field exercises.

Days seven to ten are used to indoctrinate the student ODAs into the SF practice of premission isolation for planning, training, and packing. Going into ISOFAC (short for Isolation Facility) is one of the cornerstones of SF combat operations, and is drilled hard into the minds of the new SF candidates. The idea is to isolate the SF ODA personnel, so that they can plan their missions with a minimum of outside influence and interference.

Their first chance to try out their new planning skills is on an airborne (parachute) field exercise, which is run on day eleven. This acts as a refresher jump for those who may be out of practice, and gets everyone ready for the Robin Sage insertion two weeks later.

The jump exercise is followed by the last four days of academic instruction, which covers UW and cross-cultural communications skills.

Day sixteen begins the run-up to Robin Sage. Each ODA is given a simulated set of tasks that must be accomplished during the exercise. The teams then go into ISOFAC, and begin to run their planning and preparations. This includes a series of rehearsals on days twenty-one and twenty-two, as well as evaluations of planning and proposed courses of action by the Phase III cadre.

Once all the preparations are completed, it is time for the "Q" Course's final examination: Robin Sage.

Final Exam: Robin Sage

In military circles the rule is that if you train for the most difficult and dangerous kind of combat operation, you can probably handle the operations that are easier than that. This is the working philosophy behind the final Phase III field exercise, which is designed to test everything the candidates have been taught in their Army careers. The exercise also has some history behind it: Robin Sage attempts to simulate the missions of the World War II Jedburgh teams that were dropped into Europe by the OSS prior to the D-Day invasion in 1944. On the ground, these teams linked up with local resistance bands and partisans, and helped them to fight the Axis forces. . . . *Extremely* difficult and dangerous missions.

Such missions still represent the most difficult tasks that SF ODAs might be assigned to accomplish, and they are a unique training challenge that is not practiced anywhere else in the U.S. military.

To the north and west of Fort Bragg and Camp MacKall lies the vast rural area of North Carolina's sand hills (which is mostly made up of farms and retirement/ vacation communities). The people here not only support their military neighbors, they actually love to take part in the exercises. So much so that many of them offer their time and land at no charge to help the Special Forces practice their trade. By enlisting hundreds of these patriotic Americans, the staff of the SFQC can vastly expand their normal training ranges during Robin Sage, and has free rein over the imaginary nation they call "Pineland"[31] (a number of counties in the Uwharrie Forrest, totaling several hundred square miles), where bands of resistance fighters are trying to overcome an oppressive government. As an added bonus, the local residents have formed a loose association known as the "Pineland Auxiliary," which supplies civilian roleplayers to augment military personnel who run the exercises.

Robin Sage is the largest and (despite the unpaid help of local residents) most expensive continuing exercise run by the Special Forces. (They have run this, or very similar, exercises for more than forty years.) Each of the four Robin Sage events run each year requires several hundred SF soldiers from the 1st SWTG (A) and active groups, and these will have to assemble and operate in the field for several weeks at a time. There are also enormous expenditures by Air Force and Army aviation units

---

[31] "Pineland," of course, refers to the marvelous pine forests of North Carolina. The SF staff uses the pine tree as a symbol for Robin Sage and other exercises.

in order to support simulated infiltration and resupply missions throughout the exercise.

The scenario of Robin Sage is actually quite simple. The Phase III staff prepares up to a dozen twelve-student ODA teams. Each is assigned an insurgent group within Pineland for link up and support. The student ODAs are then infiltrated into Pineland by land, air, or water, after which they march to safe meeting places with the guerrilla groups (called "G Bands"). The ODA's job is to integrate into the insurgent organizations, build a rapport with the guerrilla leadership, and attempt to organize them into more effective military units. It will also assist the insurgent bands in striking at enemy targets within Pineland, in anticipation of a future liberation by Allied forces.

Each Robin Sage simulates a seventy-five day campaign, but this is compressed into an exercise timeframe of fifteen days.

All of this action requires a great deal of supervision and observation, and the Phase III cadre stays busy making sure things run smoothly. Each student SF ODA has an observer/controller (O/C) assigned to monitor its actions, and provide advice and guidance when it is needed. Other O/Cs assess combat drills, the meetings with guerrilla bands, and almost everything else that a dozen men might do in two weeks of field activity.

Every Robin Sage begins with a forced entry into "Occupied Pineland," and it is run exactly as it would be in combat. Many teams will ride into the exercise area by air. Some may then parachute down from an Air Force C-130 or C-141 transport. Others may ride one of the Army's 160th SOAR MH-47 or MH-60 special operations helicopters. But to make things more interesting, the Phase III cadre will often switch delivery methods at the last minute in order to create what the Prussian military philosopher Clausewitz called friction—the inevitable messes, confusions, hang-ups, and breakdowns in real-world combat operations that cause plans to come unraveled and schedules to grind to a halt. A major objective of Robin Sage is to view how the students deal with "friction." How they manage it is a good test of agility. The ones who possess agility will find ways to overcome or bypass friction. They are worth their weight in gold. The ones who constantly get bogged down may not have the temperament for the Special Forces.

Robin Sage traditionally begins on a Saturday night, a few hours before midnight with between ten and twelve student ODAs fanning out across central North Carolina.

The night I watched a Phase III group head out, six teams were going to be dropped by parachute from two C-130s, and four more were to be delivered by 160th SOAR MH-47s and MH-60s. As they trundled toward their aircraft, every man was carrying a full combat load of weapons and ammunition, together with enough rations for five days without resupply. Average pack weight was between 100 and 125 lb./45 and 57 kg. Those carrying parachutes had another 50 lb./23 kg. and literally waddled out to the C-130s. At around 2100 hours, the aircraft and helicopters began to lift off, and over the next several hours, the skies over resorts like Pinehurst and manufacturing towns like Dunkirk droned with the sounds of turboprops and rotor blades.

Once student ODAs hit the ground, their first order of business is a tactical movement off of the landing zone and assembly at a rally point to count heads and get themselves aligned. This is another chance for the cadre to apply "friction," and occasionally a team is diverted away from their planned drop or landing zone. This requires a quick adjustment, since teams of Opposing Force (OpFor) troops are out there trying to capture or "kill" them.

Most of what's left of the first night will be spent marching to a link-up point, where the teams will meet representatives of the guerrilla band they are assigned to work with. Along the way, they will find a safe place to hide the bulk of their ammunition, food, and explosives, and bury it in what is called a cache.

I need to note here that the guerrillas they will meet are not "nice" or "well-behaved" people, and they are not necessarily eager to experience the benefits of democracy or the American way of life. In other words, they will have their own agenda—primarily to get rid of the bastards who run their country. There is no guarantee that they themselves will not also be bastards. The ODAs will not have an easy time of it.

The leader of the guerrilla band (called a "G" Chief) is an experienced SF officer, selected for his ability to role-play a local rural warlord. A mixed team of SF personnel and 82nd Airborne Division/XVIII backs up the "G" Chief and acts as guerrilla role-players in his band. Their job in general is to act as provocateurs. But specifically, it is to obtain supplies and weapons from the ODA with no strings attached. That is, without *any* commitment in return. The goal of the ODA captain is to negotiate with the "G" Chief and persuade him to allow the student team into the camp to train and professionalize his band.

The problems usually begin when the student ODA team arrives at the "G" camp, attempts to make contact, and finds that their training and instructions have not prepared them for what they encounter.

The student SF ODA captain will attempt to introduce himself and his team, but finds that the "G" Chief does not treat them like saviors. In fact, they are kept at arm's length. The next few hours are normally tense and unpleasant for the SF candidates. First the "G" Chief will make it *very* clear that he is the one in charge around here, they do not count for much in his scheme of things, and he has nothing but contempt for the U.S. military in general and for them in particular.

Since their mission specifically orders them to build rapport with the band, the student SF ODA members just have to take all this. Thus, the ODA captain must patiently listen and wait until (hopefully) an opening appears that will allow him to explain how they will give the guerrillas something far more valuable than weapons, and can make the guerrilla band stronger and more effective.

Even if that point does get made, the sparring between the "G" Chief and student ODA members will likely go on for days. Establishing credibility and trust takes time. And the rural freedom fighters are *far* from achieving sanctity. Sometimes they will try to steal ammunition, food, and weapons from the students (or cheat them out of them). Other times, an ODA gaff, misstep, or cultural insensitivity will sit very badly with the guerrillas, and chill the relationship, which will then have to be patiently

The "G" Chief of a simulated guerrilla band during Robin Sage. Such roles are played by experienced Special Forces soldiers, and provide a realistic final examination for the "Q" Course.

JOHN D. GRESHAM

renegotiated. In some cases things go badly enough that the team's attached O/C may coach the students to get them back on track.

At some point during the opening days of the exercise, the student ODA captain and team sergeant will be taken to a meeting with the guerrilla chief of the whole region, who is usually played by a member of the Pineland Auxiliary. There the ODA captain is expected to speak in general about U.S. policy toward Pineland, and specifically about how he plans to help the resistance forces. Predictably, these meetings do not turn out to be a piece of cake for the young captains. Tempers flare, tough, demanding words fly; it's all very confrontational . . . and there is always the possibility of further deterioration in ODA-guerrilla relations. Or worse.

The rapport-building phase of Robin Sage lasts until D+3, at which point the scenario jumps forward thirty days in simulated time. The table below shows how the next events break out:

Actual Timeframe	Simulated Timeframe	Activity
D-Day	D-Day	Nighttime Infiltration
D+1	Day 1	Phase I—Link-up with "G" Band
D+2	Day 2	Phase I—Rapport-Building
D+3	Day 3	Phase I—Meeting with Area Commander
D+4	Day 34	Phase II—Resupply
D+5	Day 35	Phase II—"G" Training
D+6	Day 36	Phase II—Strike on "Confidence" Target

Actual Timeframe	Simulated Timeframe	Activity
D+7	Day 37	Phase II—Student ODA Counseling
D+8	Day 68	Phase III—Landing Zone Operations
D+9	Day 69	Phase III—Meeting with Area Commander
D+10	Day 70	Phase III—Mission Planning
D+11	Day 71	Phase III—Final Target Strike
D+12	Day 72	Phase III—Link-up with Conventional Forces/ "G" Demobilization
D+13	Day 73	Phase III—Civil Affairs Program
D+14	Day 74	Counsel ODA Students/Equipment Turn-In
D+15	Day 75	Return to Forward Base, North Carolina

The second part of Robin Sage opens on D+4. The ODA members will now teach the guerrillas important military skills, like weapons and demolitions training and field medical procedures. But the training is not limited to strictly operational subjects. For example, the student SF soldiers will also teach the guerrillas the rudiments of the laws of war, and at some point they will try to sign them into the Free Pineland Army (which means, practically, that the guerrillas can be "paid," and will have "service records"). This last is no small matter. In many countries their service may well be rewarded with pensions and decorations (*if* the freedom fighters win).

Teaching the guerrillas the laws of war is also hugely practical, for they are not normally observed in the kinds of insurrections and unconventional wars fought by guerrillas. And this means that our young ODAs will have still more bad problems to handle. Acts in combat that would normally be considered "war crimes" or "atrocities" are just the ways things are done in the less-developed regions of the world. The student ODA will frequently be faced with a situation that may or may not be a war crime. They will have to evaluate the situation, try to decide if it *is* a crime, and then figure out some way to resolve the situation without wrecking the rapport they have built with the "G" Band. It can (and *should*) be a tough judgment call.

The second phase of Robin Sage ends on D-7 (day thirty-seven in simulated time), with a combined ODA/"G" Band raid or ambush on OpFor forces (drawn again from the 82nd Airborne Division or XVIII Airborne Corps). The student ODAs will guide their "G" Band through the planning and execution of the mission, doing their best to build up the skills and confidence of the guerrillas. During the actual event, the ODA members will then make sure the guerrillas are out front in the action. And after it is over, they will try to spread as much credit as possible out among the guerrillas for any successes they achieve. By means of this kind of intensive care, feeding, and attention to detail, you take ragtags like the Afghan mujahideen and turn them into the kinds of organized forces that can kick butt on a major army like the former USSR's.

D+8 (day sixty-eight in simulated time) begins the final phase of Robin Sage. There are a series of training operations of helicopter/airborne landing zone procedures to teach the guerrillas how to support conventional forces (a conventional invasion will come later). The student ODA and "G" Band also prepare and execute a simulated precision raid on an infrastructure target such as a bridge, a dam, or a power plant. On this operation the guerrillas will do much of the technical work, and (if all goes well) lead the mission on their own.

A number of significant events end the exercise.

D+12 (day seventy-two in simulated time) involves a simulated link-up with conventional forces (i.e., after the "conventional" invasion), after which comes the very difficult process of demobilizing the guerrilla forces and supervising the turn-in of their weapons (a very large real-world problem; insurgents aren't necessarily eager to give up their weapons or become peaceful citizens . . . see Northern Ireland). The guerrillas will then receive "medals" and "certificates of service" to liberated Pineland.[32]

When all this is done, the student ODA is extracted and returned to their forward operating base where they will turn in equipment, write reports, and wait for the final judgments of the Phase III cadre. The tough job of informing those who have failed or must try again is done on the afternoon the student ODAs return to Camp MacKall. And then they are moved out swiftly to their next assignment.

A happier fate awaits those who have made the grade. They are allowed a night of rest and time for clean up. Then the "Q" Course graduates are marched into the Camp MacKall mess hall for an awards ceremony and dinner. Here they are inducted into the 1st Special Forces Regiment, and are presented with their Green Berets and the badge for their newly assigned SFG (which goes on the front of the beret). It is a powerful moment, and there are often tears of pride.

Into the Teams

The "Q" Course graduates now have their Green Berets and group assignments. Even so there are still a number of challenges to overcome before they are assigned to their first ODAs. First on the list (preferably after some leave) is language school. With the exception of their combat skills, nothing is more useful to a SF soldier than the ability to speak the language of the people he will live and work with. The skill does not come easy or cheap. Consider the following list of operational theaters and their major languages:

EUCOM	PACOM	SOUTHCOM	CENTCOM
Russian	Chinese	Spanish	Arabic
German	Russian	Portuguese	Persian
Czech	Korean		Pushtu
Hungarian	Indonesian		Urdu
Portuguese	Thai		
French	Tagalog		

32 To show their appreciation for the civilian members of the Pineland Auxiliary, each ODA also does some work fixing fences and other chores around the private property used during Robin Sage. It is the Special Force's way of saying thank-you to the civilian role-players, and is an excellent example of real-world winning of "hearts and minds."

EUCOM	PACOM	SOUTHCOM	CENTCOM
Arabic			
Polish			

Every new SF soldier is expected to learn at least one foreign language, depending upon the theater his group is assigned to and the needs of the group. Some (like Romance languages: Spanish, French, etc.) are relatively simple to learn, and students can be conversational (what the Special Forces call Level I proficiency) in just a few months, while Level III proficiency (speaking the language like a native) might take only nine months for a well-motivated student. On the other end of the spectrum, Level I proficiency in complex languages like Chinese and Arabic can take over a year.[33] In any event new SF soldiers must learn their language prior to reporting to their SFG. At times, this training can actually take longer than the combined SF selection/qualification process (up to three years).

After language school, each SF soldier must attend the Survival, Evasion, Resistance, and Escape (SERE) school at Fort Bragg. The SERE course is run for at-risk personnel who may be captured and tortured, and it is quite difficult—and much dreaded (there is no training experience in the American military that is more hated).

Without going into the highly classified details of the SERE curriculum, let me say that the course shows soldiers how to avoid becoming a prisoner of war . . . or (if that proves impossible) how to survive captivity, and (if the opportunity arises) how to escape. It is now time for the new Special Forces soldiers to head to their first SFG assignment.

There they will be given very little time to get used to the new routine. The current operations tempo of the SF community means that they will probably spend at least ninety days out of their first year overseas, with the only break being an opportunity to attend either military free-fall parachute or combat diver training.

The advanced parachute training is conducted at the Military Free-Fall Course at Yuma, Arizona. This is a "joint" (multiservice) school, with instructors from all the military services. Free-fall jumping requires a *far* higher level of training and skill than conventional military parachute jumping (where the parachutes are deployed with static lines). It also is *far* more technical and dangerous.

Currently, the Special Forces qualify their personnel in two major forms of free-fall jumping. These are:

- **High Altitude-Low Opening (HALO)**—In HALO deliveries, personnel wearing special breathing (force-fed oxygen) apparatus jump from high altitudes. They then free-fall for up to two minutes at speeds greater than 125 mph/205 kph. At an altitude of only a few thousand feet, they pop their parachute canopy. The extremely small radar signature of an individual HALO means that a whole ODA can be delivered undetected deep into denied territory.

---

[33] Students tasked with learning these high-level languages are normally dispatched to the Defense Language School, which is located at the Naval Postgraduate School in Monterey, California.

Students at the joint Military Free-Fall School at the Army's Yuma Proving Ground in Arizona. These students are being taught high-altitude precision parachute insertion techniques.

JOHN D. GRESHAM

- **High Altitude-High Opening (HAHO)**—Not as well-known as the HALO technique, HAHO is actually the more tactically useful delivery method. While the equipment is generally similar, the opening altitude for the MC-4 steerable parachute is much higher. By opening the parachute just after exiting the aircraft, the jumper can glide for upwards of 25 miles/50 kilometers from the drop point. For example, a jumper equipped with a small GPS receiver can drop just outside an enemy's boarder, and then glide to a precision landing well inside denied territory. This is a really slick way to accomplish a tactical insertion, and like the HALO jump technique, cannot easily be picked up on radar or other sensors.

High-altitude jumping allows Special Forces soldiers to make discrete, covert insertions. A military transport aircraft flying at extremely high altitudes (over 30,000 feet/9,144 meters) can look like a commercial flight, and deliver a force of SF soldiers stealthily.

Tactical infiltration from underwater requires the use of Self-Contained Underwater Breathing Apparatus (SCUBA) gear. Though SOCOM also operates the Navy's SEAL teams, which have *serious* underwater capabilities, Special Forces also has its own underwater capability. To this aim it has established a Combat Diver certification program, which is located at a state-of-the-art facility in Key West, Florida. Here SF soldiers are taught the skills needed for SCUBA and other underwater breathing systems, as well as tactical insertion and underwater navigation techniques. Though the curriculum is very like the one used by the SEALs, it is focused on supporting the specific operations of the Special Forces.[34]

The next few years of a Special Forces soldier's life will be very busy. Barring the occasional major regional conflict, a typical SF soldier can expect to spend between ninety and 180 days a year downrange (that's Special Forces for overseas) and the rest of the time training. The only real break from this routine will be the occasional staff assignment at home base, or one of the many other training courses that he can attend if he is lucky enough to find the time. For example, 18Bs (weapons sergeants) can attend sniper school to refine their long-range shooting skills. 18Fs (intelligence sergeants) can attend advanced intelligence and technical courses.

But this is all icing on the cake. The *real* life in Special Forces is about being in the SF ODA teams and going on missions downrange. This is the reason soldiers join the Special Forces, and why most choose to stay in.

---

[34] I should mention that the Navy has some understandable complaints about the apparent duplication of efforts, but, in fact, the Combat Diver program maintains an important capability for the Special Forces.

Inside the Rucksack: Special Forces Stuff

What soldiers carry and don't carry says volumes about how they do their work. Military operations require tools—typically, complex tools, and a lot of them—weapons, gear, equipment, vehicles, clothing, electronics. They are, in some ways, the language of the military.

Lean and adaptive though they are, Special Forces soldiers partake of this abundance, as all soldiers do.

Yet does it follow that "special" forces require "special" tools for their "special" missions? Or, to put this another way, what kinds of stuff do SF soldiers carry with them when they go downrange?

There's no simple, uniform answer to either of these questions. Yes, SF guys have "special" equipment and weapons, but far fewer of such things than you might imagine. James Bonds they are not. And then, owing to the wide variety and range of SF missions, there are many and various loads they might take on a mission or assignment. On raids or reconnaissance missions, the load may be limited to what can be carried on soldiers' backs or thrown out of a helicopter or transport aircraft, while a large-scale training or humanitarian relief effort might see SF teams going in "heavy," with a C-17A Globemaster to carry the vehicles, equipment, and supply pallets.

On the other hand, SF soldiers do take with them a few standard items on almost *every* kind of mission they run.

While individual SF soldiers are talented and skilled technicians in their individual specialties (weapons, engineering, communications, etc.), all are still brutally effective warriors. The problem is that SF soldiers normally go into the field carrying only light and personal weapons, and a far from substantial ammunition load. Conventional Army units can look for ways to bring their heavy firepower to bear against an enemy; SF soldiers will usually try to outsmart their opponents. Special Forces teams must therefore choose their fights carefully, and always leave a back door to escape through, if things go south. This places a premium on careful selection of the gear they wear, and everything they carry.

Until very recently, virtually everything Special Forces troops used, wore, or carried was either normal military-issue weapons and gear or else was commercially available. Very little of it was purposefully designed for Special Forces use.

But this—finally—has begun to change.

Though SOCOM (the unified command that operates Special Forces Command and the other Special Operations Forces) has been in operation for better than a decade and has its own funding stream, separate from any parent command, it takes a specially trained staff of procurement professionals to buy anything in the U.S. government, and setting up such a staff takes time. The various SOCOM components have now done that, and their own procurement and developmental commands are up and running. (SFC's shop is known under the military staff designation of G7.)

Started up early in 1999, SFG's G7 shop is commanded by a seasoned SF officer, Lieutenant Colonel Dan Moore. Lieutenant Colonel Moore and his staff of procurement gurus face a dauntingly complex task. For openers, SF soldiers see the world (and their tools of trade) through different lenses from their "normal" infantry brethren. They can expect to visit places, face situations, and meet people "normal" soldiers would never expect to encounter. SF operations are hardly ever *like* normal Army operations. Thus, everything SF soldiers use must be viewed in a different context from that of a conventional Army or Marine unit.

On a "normal" mission, to use an obvious example, SF soldiers will *not* expect to fight. That is—if the mission is properly run and the breaks go right—an SF team should *never need* their weapons.

Or, to use another example, saving a pound or two on a rifle or backpack might seem trivial to most soldiers, who can usually just throw their stuff into the back of a truck or personnel carrier during the ride to the battlefield. But for SF personnel, who expect to carry *everything* they need for a mission on their backs, those two pounds might represent enough food for another day of operations, or another thirty rounds of 5.56mm ammunition. Like mountain climbers preparing for a climb, SF teams about to go downrange do a lot of trading off. The wrong choice can easily turn deadly, so they choose very carefully.

Meanwhile, SF units have often had to "make do" with weapons, equipment, and supplies that were hardly optimal to their kinds of operations. Even so, the Special Forces team has done their best to make maximum use of the existing military inventory of such items (for all the obvious reasons).

But now, SFC's G7 shop (paid for by SOCOM's independent line of funding) provides the SF team with the means to go outside the Army supply system to find *exactly* what *they* need (within obvious limits).[35]

To make all this work, Lieutenant Colonel Moore and his staff have to carefully choose the "special" items they want to buy or develop. That means they must carefully leverage their limited supply of SOCOM dollars and resist the temptation to do everything at once.

So far, they have had some exciting successes, most notably the modification of the relatively heavy and large M16 combat rifle into the very useful, small, and lightweight M4 carbine.

---

35 SF units are given a "Force Package One" status by the Department of Defense. Units with this priority status are normally kept at high alert levels, and thus will receive preference in the distribution of equipment and supplies. Thus SF units draw new gear and other Army inventory items ahead of all other units except the 82nd and 101st Airborne Divisions, the 75th Ranger Regiment, and a handful of armored units.

But SFC's G7 shop and the other SOCOM procurement agencies have not limited their creative attention to weapons. For example, SOF units have led the drive to develop new, lighter-weight rations that would be better suited to patrol operations than the Meals Ready to Eat (MREs) that have been the diet staple for American field units for over a decade. These "performance enhancing" foods are proving popular not only in SOF units, but in the entire Army.

Encouraged by achievements like these, Lieutenant Colonel Moore and his team expect to influence even bigger changes in the future. At the same time, they are happy to be making a difference in the operations of SF soldiers *today*. Lieutenant Colonel Moore and his team are now sending SF units downrange better equipped than at any time in their history.

One final addition: Earlier I said that as long as their mission is correctly executed, SF soldiers should never need their weapons. Does that mean that SF soldiers can safely travel unarmed? Hardly. No SF soldier goes anywhere without the ability to turn instantly into an armed warrior. No SF soldier would *ever* go downrange without his full fit of personal weaponry . . . even on what are called humanitarian or other "peaceful" missions. Too often, Special Forces personnel have found themselves thrown into the middle of a firefight (or a revolution) without warning. It is a sign of the growing maturity of the American military that we no longer send military personnel overseas naked of weapons, and the authorization to use them when threatened. How much force and when to apply should and usually is left to the professional warriors in the field, as it should be. Let us hope that our military and professional leaders continue to show the same kind of common sense.

And now—armed with these thoughts and paradoxes—let's look at the stuff SF troops use and carry.

Carrying Stuff: Rucksacks and Containers

No matter how skilled they are at reducing the weight and bulk of what they carry to missions, Special Forces soldiers still have a lot of things to carry there and back. How to carry it is a continually daunting task both for individual soldiers and for the teams.

Depending on the mission, a Special Forces soldier may be faced with lugging a load exceeding his own body weight. For example, his job might include carrying a heavy load of demolitions gear, such as C4 explosive, several hundred pounds of which may be needed to drop a heavy bridge or structure. Even with the explosive payload spread over ten men in a team, there's going to be a lot of stuff on everyone's back. Prior to the Desert Storm ground war, some members of the Special Reconnaissance teams that were inserted deep behind enemy lines carried loads of over 200 lb./91 kg. several miles/kilometers before they reached their hide sites. Impressive as such tasks of brute strength might be, they are blessedly rare.[36] All the same, Special

---

36 These loads were fairly extreme even by Special Forces standards, as the troops had to carry the building materials for their hide sites, along with all the other items required for their missions. A more "normal" load for an SF soldier on a mission might start out at around 110 lb./50 kg. This would allow for some mobility without literally tearing his body apart.

Classic ALICE pack systems on the backs of Special Forces candidates. The ALICE system is about to be replaced with a more modern system, with better load carriage characteristics and an internal hydration system.

JOHN D. GRESHAM

Forces soldiers still need containers to pack all their stuff into so they can lug it to where it is going to be used.

Packs and Belts: ALICE and MLS Gear

There are two long-standing Special Forces symbols—the Green Berets and the old rucksacks the men once carried.[37] Though this now-obsolete piece of field gear still occasionally shows up as a daypack, it has long since been replaced as a means of moving an SF soldier's load.

What has replaced it?

If you read the official fine print of every SF unit's designator, you find the word *Airborne* in parenthesis. This is not an empty word: It has consequences. It means, for example, that the primary load-carrying system of the SF soldier must not only hold stuff and have straps, it must be compatible with jumping out of an airplane doing up to 130 knots.

For more than a decade, the standard personal load-carrying system has been known by the long-winded name of All-purpose Lightweight Individual Carrying Equipment (ALICE). The ALICE system is composed of a large pack, aluminum frame with kidney pad and cargo shelf, and shoulder straps. It is designed to carry large loads and distribute the load across the back and shoulders; and it can be cus-

---

37 The "myth" of the rucksack derives from the way SOFs go into battle: That is, they carry with them everything they'll need. Today the old "rucks" are still used in training and qualification, not so much for their utility but because their use will remind trainees of their origins. *The Rucksack* magazine has been one of the more visible means of keeping old Special Forces traditions alive. *The Rucksack* is the product of the U.S. Army Special Operations Command Public Affairs office, and is dedicated to stories about SF personnel and their techniques of operating in the field.

tomized to fit a wide variety of personnel and roles. For airborne operations, the ALICE gear is attached to a tether, and is carried between the jumper's legs until after chute opening (after which the gear is allowed to hang down on the tether, thus reducing the weight the jumper must bear when he lands and allowing a better, injury-reducing landing position).[38]

Since carrying a heavily loaded ALICE pack is undesirable if you're expecting a firefight, SF soldiers also have a set of what is known as "Load Bearing Gear" (officially it is known as the "LC-2")—essentially oversized suspenders with a belt attached. Clipped onto this rig are a variety of pouches and holders. In the event of a sudden firefight or, say, a daylong trek, the ALICE pack can be dropped or cached, and retrieved later. A normal LC-2 load includes six 30-round M16/M4 ammunition magazines, four grenades, two one-quart canteens, a pistol with holster and two spare magazines, a radio, compass, and perhaps a couple of field dressings.

Using these systems, an SF soldier is expected to pack or hang off his body enough ammunition, explosives, weapons, food, water, and other assorted gear to run a three- to five-day mission in the field without resupply.

Meanwhile, there are plans to replace the ALICE system with a derivative of the new rucksack rig that is already going into service with the Marine Corps. Known as the MOdular Lightweight Load-carrying Equipment (MOLLE) system, it incorporates many new features that represent a significant improvement over the ALICE gear.

The Army's version of the MOLLE system starts with the LBV-88 load-bearing vest, which replaces the old LC-2 harness. Because the vest better spreads the load over the body, allowing more muscles to work at once, it should theoretically allow for carriage of greater weight with more agility for the wearer. To this is attached the pack/frame/pouch section, which can be configured a variety of ways. Each has a 2,300-cubic-inch main pack and frame, over which can be hung or attached a smaller "combat patrol pack" and all variety of pouches.

This section is attached to the vest with quick release fittings, which can be dropped with a single quick movement. The 1,200-cubic-inch combat patrol pack can also be detached and worn separately, providing enough room for a full day's worth of supplies for operations in the field. There is additionally a built-in water bladder, with a capacity of approximately two quarts/liters, feeding what is called a "hydration system." Instead of carrying water in a hard water bottle, it comes in a flexible, insulated bladder that lies against the wearer's back, and which feeds a small hose that allows easy access to the water, even on the move. The outside of the pack is covered with pockets and pouches that have been optimized for various weapons specialties; all have the ability to carry "pooled" equipment and munitions like claymore mines, explosives, electrical batteries, and spare ammunition magazines.

It will be several years before the Army completes its evaluation of the MOLLE system and begins procurement.[39] At the same time, the SFC G7 shop is evaluating

---

38 While it is an improvement over the backpacks used in Vietnam, the ALICE system is positively ancient compared with what can be bought out of any outdoors equipment catalog. More on its replacement shortly.

39 If you are wondering why fielding new personal equipment takes so long, the responsibility lies with the Army's equipment center at Natick, Massachusetts, near Boston. There every new piece of personal equipment from pocket-knives to boots is rigorously tested (sometimes to absurd standards). The good news is that gear issued to field units

their own versions of MOLLE, with two versions undergoing tests right now. Plans are to introduce this new system in 2001, though this may slip somewhat. Until that time, count on seeing SF soldiers using the ALICE system to carry their combat stuff in the field.

Pallets, Containers, and Ziploc Bags

Not every mission requires an SF soldier to carry all his stuff on his back. In fact, since most SF teams are assigned to peaceful missions in highly permissive environments, more often than not a Special Forces mission will not require a forced entry into the target area. This means the teams can usually carry many things to make their lot more comfortable. Unfortunately, a couple of pieces of Samsonite luggage will hardly do, even in these situations. Something tougher is needed.

In the old days, each SF soldier would have packed duffel bags or heavy and clumsy wooden and steel footlockers, hoping they would arrive intact and dry. Today, modern plastics have made this job much easier. Most Special Forces personnel now pack their nontactical gear in one of the new generation of lightweight and nearly indestructible molded plastic footlockers produced by companies like Rubbermaid. These come in a variety of shapes and sizes, and many can be sealed nearly airtight and locked. Some even have built-in wheels and handles.

Normally, SF soldiers purchase one or two of these plastic footlockers with their own funds, and keep them ready for deployment on a moment's notice. When deployed, the SF soldiers usually stow them in their team room. Each Operational Detachment Alpha (ODA) will also usually have a number of these plastic footlockers for all the stuff that does not have a Military Specifications (Mil-Spec) carrying container. These days, this can include digital cameras, laser printers, and the team's stash of junk food and compact disks.

Naturally, nobody expects that even the wonders of modern injection molded plastics are going to survive the tender mercies of Air Force or commercial baggage handlers. To make sure everything in these containers actually gets to its destination dry and intact, the Special Forces soldier has other tools at his disposal: Specifically, every SF trooper I know swears by zippered plastic bags and duct tape for keeping his stuff safe in transit. Everything they use—from CD-ROMs to candy bars—goes inside a zippered plastic bag . . . or sometimes two if an item is *really* valuable.

Items too large for a gallon-sized Ziploc bag are wrapped in sheets of thick plastic, and then each seam is sealed with layers of military-issue duct tape.[40] This green 2-in./5-cm.-wide tape is used in huge quantities by SF personnel.

---

is normally excellent. The bad news is that equally excellent gear has been commercially available to campers and sportsmen for years before soldiers see theirs. Meanwhile, the Marines have benefited both from their smaller size and the willpower of their 31st Commandant, General Charles "Chuck" Krulak, USMC. Krulak made it a personal goal to get new boots, packs, and other gear for his Marines, and went to Congress himself to obtain the funds and authorization for them.

40 This is not the silver tape that you buy at the hardware store. The military-issue "speed" tape is tougher with an adhesive surface that will stick to almost anything under virtually any condition, and is capable of standing up to wind loads of over 100 knots. For this reason, it is rated as an expedient airframe repair item. You can use it to patch bullet holes in the skin of helicopters so they can fly home for repairs.

When everything is loaded into the big plastic footlockers, these also get several layers of tape on the seams and corners. All the nonman-portable items are then loaded onto Air Force or commercially approved pallets, shrink-wrapped (if there is time), covered in a cargo net, and marked with an inventory control barcode. This way, there is a chance that the team will eventually see all of it when they arrive downrange.

Weapons

Like the Marine, every SF soldier is a trained rifleman, no matter what specialty code he may carry back in his personnel file. Believe me when I say they know exactly how to use all of them. The Special Forces provides their soldiers with a full array of light and infantry weapons.

M4 5.56mm Carbine

Few combat weapons are more easily recognized than the M16 combat rifle. Now in its fourth decade of U.S. military service, the current M16A2 version of this classic weapon is perhaps the best general-purpose infantry weapon in the world. Produced by Colts Manufacturing in Hartford, Connecticut, and licensed for production around the world, the M16 family of weapons is second only to the AK-series assault rifles (designed by Mikhail Kalashnikov of Russia) in numbers produced, sold, and issued.

Though the M16A2—with its unloaded weight of 7.9 lb./3.58 kg. and a length of 39.6 in./100.7 cm.—can hardly be considered light or compact, it remains a valuable and flexible weapon (it uses NATO-compatible 5.56mm ammunition and its basic working mechanism has long been appreciated for its fine qualities). In order to make what is already good even better, Colts began developing a lighter and shorter version of the M16A2 (technically a carbine[41]) in 1993. The original requirement for this new weapon came from the SOF community, including the Special Forces. The result was the M4, the first new carbine issued to U.S. forces since the Vietnam War.

The current SOF version (the M4A1) is essentially an M16A2 with a collapsible metal tube buttstock, shorter barrel, and modified sight deck. These modifications allow the M4 to weigh in (unloaded) at 5.65 lb./2.56 kg., and it is only 29.8 in./75.7 cm. long with the stock stowed. The M4 fires the same family of NATO-compatible 5.56mm-/.223-caliber ammunition as the M16 and the M249 SAW, which helps keep logistics simple. All the normal features of the M16A2 are present (selectable semi-automatic and automatic burst modes, thirty-round magazines, etc.), all in a more compact package.

The M4A1 in turn forms the basis for the Special Forces Modular Weapons System (MWS). Using the M4A1 as a foundation, any number of add-ons can be attached to give the weapon further capabilities. These range from the M203 40mm grenade launcher, to various low-light and thermal imager systems, as well as laser pointing and sighting devices. The current range of add-on systems is known as Spe-

---

41 Technically, a carbine is a light, short, shoulder firearm, originally created to provide cavalry troops with a weapon that would be easy to stow and carry when mounted, but would give them the firepower of infantry when dismounted.

An M4 5.56mm carbine equipped with an M203 40mm grenade launcher. Based on the classic M16 combat rifle, the M4 has become a worldwide favorite among light infantry forces.

JOHN D. GRESHAM

cial Operations Modification (SOPMOD) I, with a second upgrade (SOPMOD II) due early in the twenty-first century. SOPMOD II will take the various SOPMOD I components and repackage them into a smaller and lighter system.

Generally, the M4A1 fires about the same as an M16A2, though it does have a somewhat lighter "feel" and a more satisfying "crack" when fired (due to the acoustics of the shorter barrel). And unlike most short-barreled shoulder weapons, it still retains the accuracy of the M16 out to most ranges. This is due to the tight tolerances of the M4A1, combined with the excellent sights.

Aircrews like it for the small size and easy stowage in crammed cockpits. Officers like having a credible weapon without having to lug around a bulky and awkward fully loaded M16. The Special Forces like it for its light weight and for its ease of packing when they have to jump out of aircraft. Frankly, most infantrymen I know would rather carry an M4 than an M16, if given the choice.

Until the Army issues its new combat rifle sometime in the early twenty-first century, plan on seeing the M4A1 as the personal weapon of the Special Forces.[42] They may even keep it in service after that, since so many of the nations visited by ODAs and ODBs are unlikely to have weapons on a par with the M16 or M4. Showing up with an even more advanced system would likely embarrass the host nation military personnel, and slow up the process of building rapport and trust.

MP-5 9mm Submachine Gun

For some specific operations, SF soldiers can be issued with the Heckler & Koch (H&K) MP-5, a popular close-quarters weapon with the Army, Navy, Marines, and

42 Sometime around 2006, the Army and Marines will begin to field the new Objective Individual Combat Weapon (OICW) as a replacement for the M16A2 and M4. This new weapon is being developed and produced by a team headed by Alliant Techsystems, and is based upon a Heckler & Koch design. It will be controlled by a state-of-the-art sighting and fire control system, which will become the primary sensor systems for the user.

An M24 7.62mm sniper rifle with an attached sighting scope. The M24 is equipped with a bipod, and the sighting scope on the tripod is used by a spotter to coach the shooter onto the target.

law enforcement agencies (and one of my favorite firearms). Built with German precision and efficiency, the MP-5 fires NATO-standard 9mm pistol ammunition and is amazingly accurate, especially at close ranges. With a thirty-round magazine and both semi- and fully automatic firing modes, this weapon can spit out a lot of lead in a very short time. Normally it is issued to Special Forces personnel assigned to missions like raids, urban, and close-quarters combat, or perhaps underwater infiltrations. A nice weapon, I love the rare occasions when I get to fire one.

M24 Sniper Rifle

The Special Forces continue to support the tradition of marksmanship at long range. Imbedded within the 18B weapons specialty are the sniper skills necessary to provide the Special Forces with a credible sniper force, using the M24 Sniper Weapon System (SWS).[43] The M24 was introduced in 1988, as the replacement for the old M21 sniper rifle, built from the obsolete M14 semiautomatic rifle. Based on the excellent Remington 700 sniper rifle, the M24 is a solid weapon with some very forgiving features.

The M24 has an aluminum/fiberglass/Kevlar composite bed/buttstock, and fires the M118 Special Ball round. This round is matched to the M24 SWS, and is optimized for ranges out to 460 meters/500 yards. To provide an appropriate view of potential targets, the M24 SWS is equipped with a 10 × 24 Leopold M3 Ultra scope. While this hardly seems comparable to the 1,000+-yard/-meter ranges of Marine snipers firing the M40 SWS, remember that the SF 18B weapons sergeants are not full-time snipers. Maintaining that kind of range and accuracy is a full-time occupation, something the Special Forces do not try to match.

---

43 The U.S. Marine Corps maintains what may be the finest sniper capability among the world's armed forces. They are equipped with both the 7.62mm M40 sniper rifle, along with the incomparable Barrett M82A1 .50 caliber weapon. More important, Marine snipers are employed in their chosen specialty full-time, while most other military units maintain snipers as an add-on capability. For this reason, the Marine sniper retains a much higher level of tactical skill and accuracy, especially when working at long ranges and in denied territory.

The 5.56mm M249 Squad Automatic Weapon. Firing the same ammunition as the M16 and M4, the M249 is based on a Belgian design.

JOHN D. GRESHAM

Though the Special Forces are quite satisfied with their snipers, and the M24 SWS are well-matched to the job and personnel, there have been efforts to upgrade the SF sniper capability, and a few M82A1 Barretts have been procured and issued to deployed SF teams for field operations. There is also a planned modification to the M4A1, which will replace the short barrel with a longer unit from the M16, and may be able to replace the M24. This would eliminate the need to carry a dedicated sniper weapon on most missions, another lightening of the Special Forces soldier's load.

M249 5.56mm Squad Automatic Weapon (SAW)

Like the rest of the U.S. military, the Special Forces have adopted the M249 Squad Automatic Weapon (SAW) as their standard light machine gun. Based upon a Belgian design from Fabrique Nationale, the M249 weighs only 22 lb./10 kg., and fires the same 5.56mm-/.223-caliber ammunition as the M16A2 and M4. It can fire the ammunition from belts or the M16/M4 thirty-round magazine. Normally, an M249 gunner feeds the weapon from a 200-round plastic box magazine, which can be fed from either the left or right side. Because of its light weight, a single gunner can easily operate the M249, firing either from the prone position (using a built-in bipod) or standing (using a shoulder strap). A mounting point allows the M249 to be mounted on the pintle and ring machine gun mounts on vehicles like the High Mobility Multi-Wheeled Vehicle (HMMWV). If the M249 has a shortcoming, it is that the 5.56mm round it fires is too light for some targets. The 5.56mm-/.223-caliber round has little stopping or penetration power against light (nonarmored) vehicles or sandbagged strongpoints. One possible solution for this weakness may lie in the new generation of armor-piercing, discarding sabot, 5.56mm rounds, which can penetrate over an inch of armor plate. But for now, the M249 is limited to firing the standard ball and tracer rounds issued to line units.

M9 Baretta 9mm Pistol

The Special Forces *really* need a good semiautomatic pistol. As weapons go, a pistol is not only the least aggressive firearm one can show, but it can be easily concealed, allowing for even more discretion should the situation warrant. For these reasons, virtually every member of the Special Forces is issued an M9 Baretta Model 92F 9mm pistol, and is encouraged to be skilled in using it. By comparison, conventional Army units normally issue pistols only to officers and sergeants, who only need qualify with the M9 periodically.

In service for more than a decade (long enough to overcome early teething problems), the M9 is equipped with a fifteen-round magazine and utilizes a double-action trigger mechanism. Given practice, shooters can go into combat with the M9 and stand a good chance of survival and victory.

While I personally prefer other pistols for their various virtues, the M9 has proven to be an excellent general-purpose firearm for the U.S. military.[44]

M240G 7.62mm Light Machine Gun

Though Special Forces units must generally limit their weapons to man-portable systems, this does not mean they have no uses for heavier weapons. In particular, the need for enhanced force protection at forward bases has meant that weapons like the M240G 7.62mm machine gun have enjoyed a renewed appreciation within Special Forces groups. Normally mounted on a HMMWV or at a security strongpoint, the M240G fires the 7.62mm cartridge, which has a great deal more range and penetration power than the far lighter 5.56mm round. On the downside, the M240G is large (47.5 in./120.6 cm. long) and heavy (24.2 lb./11 kg.), and usually requires two soldiers to fire and serve it effectively.

M203 40mm Grenade Launcher

With the possible exception of the combat/assault rifle, probably the most powerful infantry weapon adopted in the last century has been the direct-fire grenade launcher. An outgrowth of the old World War II rifle grenade, the modern grenade launcher is actually a short-barreled projector for shells that may contain a variety of useful payloads. These range from high explosive and incendiary rounds to shells containing illumination payloads, and even "beanbags" for nonlethal incapacitation.

The first such grenade launcher was the M79, a single-shot 40mm weapon issued

---

44 There are efforts to field a new offensive handgun using either 9mm or .45-caliber ammunition, but this is years from fielding.

The Mk. 19 40mm automatic grenade launcher mounted on a tripod. This weapon is normally used for base defense or mounted on vehicles.

in the early 1960s and still used around the world by law enforcement agencies. Today, the Special Forces use a more practical weapon, the M203 (ODAs usually have two of them). The M203 is a 40mm breach-loading grenade launcher that can be "clipped" under the barrel of a normal combat rifle. Since the M203 only weighs 3 lb./1.36 kg., it is easy to carry and does not greatly affect the performance of the weapon it is attached to. The advantage of the M203 is that it provides a twelve-man ODA with a pair of grenade launchers without any reduction in the number of M4s. As an added bonus, the M203 is quite accurate out to ranges approaching 330 ft./100 m., and is able to fire the same family of 40mm rounds as the fully-automatic Mk. 19 machine gun.

Mk. 19 40mm Grenade Launcher

Another heavy weapon used for base security and force protection, the Navy originally developed the Mk. 19 for use on patrol boats. Today, because of the incredible firepower it can deliver, this "machine gun" (it's actually a fully-automatic, rapid-fire grenade launcher) is used by all the U.S. military services. Able to spit out sixty rounds a minute, the Mk. 19 is certified to fire high explosive (HE) and high explosive, dual purpose (HEDP) rounds, which can literally blanket a target with 40mm grenades. Like the M240G, the Mk. 19 is normally used on vehicles and at strongpoints, where its firepower can be applied to force and base protection roles.

Eventually, the Special Forces may adopt the new 25mm Objective Crew Served Weapon being designed to replace the Mk. 19, though this is beyond the event horizon of most current SF soldiers.

Hand Grenades

The modern hand grenade is a far cry from the "pineapple" weapons of World War II.[45] Today the U.S. issues almost a dozen types of these weapons, the most common being the M67 fragmentation model. There are also smoke, incendiary, concussion, tear gas, and concussion/stun grenades, which can be carried and used as required. Because of their simplicity and utility, Special Forces units make a point of taking along a supply of hand grenades wherever they deploy. Normally each SF soldier would carry a pair of M67s, along with a couple of colored smoke units for signaling and marking targets. Hardly a high-tech weapon, grenades can be used in a variety of combat and emergency situations, for everything from signaling a rescue helicopter to assembling an improvised booby trap.

Land Mines

The modern land mine is a mixed blessing. On the one hand, mines are valuable because they are simple and cheap weapons that can deny critical ground to an enemy without having to be monitored or tended, and when they are properly laid and primed, the locations of the minefields are known, which means the mines can be removed later. On the other hand, they are (with good reason) hated, because they don't necessarily go away once a conflict is over. All too often they are forgotten until some unfortunate child or farmer walks over one.

In theory, the recent international land mine accord has banned the production, sale, and use of such weapons, and the United States has committed itself to the elimination of land mines from its military inventory (with the exception of the mine belts along the 38th Parallel/Demilitarized Zone between North and South Korea).

But in practice, the land mine convention is a wasted effort, which will very probably create more practical problems than it solves. Because they are simple and cheap, land mines can be built in large numbers by even the most backward nations. And it's not hard for troops in the field to improvise homemade versions.

Given a choice between being overrun and killed, or building homemade land mines to protect your position, what would you do? Improvised munitions are by their nature going to be less safe than military specification land mines—a fact that the bleeding hearts who pushed the international land mine convention in the first place fail to understand. While it cannot be denied that unexploded land mines, bombs, and other munitions are a major worldwide health hazard, banning an entire class of conventional weapons as basic as land mines is foolish.

So, where does this situation leave Special Forces or other units charged with protecting a forward base or compound? In point of fact, the land mine ban has proved to be more of a nuisance than a major threat to force security, mainly because the mine ban does not cover aboveground antipersonnel weapons like the M18A1 claymore.

Though it is often called a "mine," that is not *exactly* what it is. A mine is

---

45 American World War II–era grenades were designed to fragment for maximum antipersonnel effect. This was achieved by serriating the external case of the weapon, which gave it the famous "pineapple" look.

technically a mine when it is detonated by a tripwire or other passive detonation device. Thus it is possible to use a claymore in an internationally "acceptable" manner by detonating it by remote control.

The M18A1 itself is a shallow, curved metal plate filled with steel balls embedded in plastic explosive. When fired, the 1.5 lb./.68 kg. C4 charge fires a 60° fan-shaped pattern of fragments, each the size of a ball bearing, which are lethal out to a range of around 328 ft./100 m. Normally it is mounted on a small stand or rock, some distance in front of an ambush site or defended position.

Multi-Purpose Infantry Munition (MPIM)

Though their combat use is mostly reserved for force protection and raids, "heavy" weapons systems, such as rocket launchers and antiarmor missiles, are also part of the SF capabilities.

Designed to replace obsolete infantry antiarmor/bunker systems like AT-4 and the old M72 LAWS rocket, the Multi-Purpose Infantry Munition (MPIM) will be introduced into the Army and Marine Corps inventory in 2002. (The Marines will call it the Short Range Antiarmor Weapon—SRAW.) The MPIM is being developed and produced by Lockheed Martin, and consists of an inertially guided rocket in a disposable launch tube. Though it is somewhat heavy by the standards of such weapons (at 20 lb./9.1 kg.), MPIM will be able to defeat both heavy bunkers and any known or planned armored vehicle. As an added bonus, MPIM will have an extremely useful range band (from 55 to 1,640 ft./17 to 500m.), and will be able to be fired in urban and enclosed conditions.

Javelin Antitank Missile

The Special Forces are also taking delivery of an extremely useful guided missile system known as Javelin. Designed to replace the old Dragon Antitank missile system, Javelin has an advanced "fire-and-forget" seeker that locks onto the thermal signature of a target and guides onto only that target out to a range of 8,200 ft./2,500 m. Thanks to an extremely energetic rocket motor and powerful warhead, Javelin can engage armored and wheeled vehicles, bunkers, buildings, and even low-flying aircraft like helicopters and spotting aircraft. Javelin also has an advanced thermal imaging sight, allowing the command-and-launch system to be used as a surveillance system as well. Moreover, it is extremely mobile: The Javelin system can be lugged around by two soldiers.

The military has not yet explored this extremely powerful system's full range of capabilities.

Foreign Weapons

One aim of Special Forces training is to make troops proficient in operating foreign weaponry, especially those weapons that may be in use by a host nation. For

Two soldiers firing a Javelin antitank missile. Guided by an imaging infrared seeker, the Javelin can also be fired against vehicles, bunkers, and even low-flying aircraft.

RAYTHEON CORPORATION

that reason, SF soldiers are quite capable of using all variety of personal and heavy weapons, from pistols to antitank rockets.

These, of course, include systems like Russian AK-47/74 assault rifles, Israeli Uzi submachine guns, and even foreign-made rocket-propelled grenades. Naturally, the desire is for Special Forces soldiers to effectively use captured or stolen weapons in the field, should theirs become inoperable or run out of ammunition. But there is an even greater need for expertise when training or working with foreign national forces. A big part of establishing rapport with host nation soldiers is proficiency (or even expertise) with the weapons used locally. As a minimum, an SF soldier must be able to assemble, clean, and field strip, zero sights, choose employment tactics, and display marksmanship on the range. Even rudimentary skills with foreign weapons can save lives in the field by allowing a Special Forces soldier to know how such armaments will be used against *him*! For example, if you know a Kalashnikov's distinctive sounds and its limitations (barrel rise and poor accuracy when fired from standing positions), you just may survive an ambush and turn the situation around.

Explosives

> *There is no situation in the human condition that cannot be solved through a properly sized, shaped, packed, placed, timed, and detonated charge of high explosive!*

Military Engineering Axiom

Blowing things up has long been a primary tool of the warrior. First there was the mysterious Greek Fire. Later there was gunpowder. Later still there was Alfred Nobel, who just before the start of the twentieth century discovered and marketed commercial high explosives. (His dismay at the use of his products in war impelled him to create the prizes given in his name.) And later still the variety of explosive pyrotechnics has grown to the point where they are viewed by professionals not as blunt instruments but as precision tools.

Consider if you will that skilled use of conventional explosives (in shaping initial shock waves) is the key to producing a nuclear detonation. A very different kind of shaped charge, using a differently formulated explosive, will "carefully" drop a single obsolete building without harming the structures on either side, while precision-guided munitions, armed with another explosive formulation and dropped by a stealth bomber, will find their way unerringly into an enemy's headquarters.

Special Forces soldiers are skilled with a variety of explosives (though they normally carry only a couple of types at any one time).

Explosives can be generally classed into two types—"slow" (or "push") and "fast" (or "burning"). TNT (Trinitrotoluene) is a "slow" explosive.[46] That is, its primary destruction mechanism is the shock wave or "front" of explosive gases created during detonation. TNT destroys or disassembles targets by structurally blowing them over or apart.

This is in contrast to "fast" explosives like C4 (Composite Explosive Four—better known as "plastique"), which detonate very quickly and can actually burn (i.e., break the molecular bonds) through structural materials like steel. C4 tends to be more useful to SF soldiers than TNT, since it is quite safe to handle; has a higher explosive yield per measure; and, because of its "plastic" character, it can be cut and shaped into more efficient charges. At normal temperatures (50° F/10° C to 120° F/49° C) C4 has the same consistency of molding clay or frozen ice cream. Usually issued in one-pound blocks, you can cut and shape it and even burn the stuff without causing a high-order detonation. (In a high-order detonation, the entire charge goes off all at once, as opposed to a low-order or "string" series of explosions.) This kind of explosive requires an electrical detonator, blasting cap, or other precision igniter (a burning fuse will not usually cause a detonation in fast explosives).

By way of example, a two-lane steel-girder bridge that might require a TNT charge of up to 300 lb./136 kg. to "push" it over can be dropped by "burning" the steel structural beams with less than 100 lb./45 kg. of C4. When you are asking a twelve-man Special Forces ODA team to carry on their backs for most of a week the explosive "payload" to destroy a target, it is easy to see which they prefer to use, the target allowing.

Of course, it is important to pay attention to that last point. *Every* target is unique, requiring a tailored approach to take it down. Special Forces weapons (18B) and engineering (18C) sergeants are skilled in assessing the quantities and types of explosives needed to "drop" a particular target. In making that assessment, these men use

---

46 TNT is also the measure of all other explosive pyrotechnics. Thus nuclear weapons are measured in kilo- and megatons of TNT.

Special Forces engineering sergeants practice the use of plastic explosives on a steel I-beam. They are using C4 to "cut" the beam, much as they would to destroy the structural members of a bridge.

JOHN D. GRESHAM

many of the same techniques that Air Force planners have developed to plan air strikes with precision weapons. They use builder's blueprints, satellite reconnaissance photos, and any other available information. Nobody wants to have to hit a target twice. This is especially true of SF soldiers, for whom a failed raid or strike means a target sure to be better protected the next time around.

One final consideration: While precision air strikes sometimes fail to be "precise" (as in the time a B-2 strike hit the Chinese Embassy in Belgrade[47]), SF teams can destroy their targets with absolute certainty. There are just some targets that are better destroyed by men on the ground than satellite-guided bombs. For one thing, they can eyeball a building to make sure the target is not a foreign embassy or babyfood factory.

Not all explosive jobs are as heavyweight as dropping a bridge or building. There are other times, for example, when you're only called upon to create an opening or breach in a wall. For this kind of job, very small explosive charges can be used with greater safety and reliability than mechanical cutters or battering rams. In fact, such breaches can frequently be cut with Detonation Cord (called "Det Cord" in the field). Det Cord is a synthetic rope impregnated with explosive and has a burning speed measured in thousands of feet per second and a temperature high enough to burn through thin metal. Det Cord can cut breaches and burn thin metal, and it is frequently

---

47 In all fairness, we should not forget that the bomb hit the point where it was aimed (it went to the right address), but it turned out that Intelligence was wrong about what was at that address.

used as a flying fuse (i.e., an old-fashioned burning fuse such as you've seen in movies and cartoons) for larger explosive charges. A deployed ODA even on a "noncombat" mission will usually carry a supply of explosives and detonation gear, just in case a real-world contingency develops in their neighborhood.

Special Forces soldiers are not only skilled with conventional explosives, they are equally skilled in improvising where the situation calls for it. That is to say, they can take commonly available materials and turn them into a useful explosive charge. For example, fertilizers and diesel fuel are quite effective if mixed and placed properly (this mixture was used against the World Trade Center in New York and Federal Building in Oklahoma City). And many other explosive concoctions are possible in the field.

Nonlethal Weapons

We've all heard much noise in recent years about the development and deployment of nonlethal weapons systems—weapons whose effects are so precise and focused that they are capable of rendering a person or piece of equipment nonfunctional without actually destroying and/or killing them. Bleeding heart types are fond of nonlethals because they seem to make wars nicer, and they do have their uses in certain so-called "peacekeeping" missions.

As it happens, Special Forces are hardly ever involved in that kind of peacekeeping, and so nonlethals have only limited utility with Special Forces units. The commitment of an SF team to a mission—combat or just training—is a serious statement by the National Command Authorities or regional CINC. That means the only nonlethal weapons likely to be carried by Special Forces units are 40mm riot and tear gas grenades, which can be fired by the M203.

Sometime in the future this class of weapon may become useful to SF soldiers (and Special Forces Command continues to evaluate new varieties), but right now they lack the utility to make them worth packing in a rucksack.

Clothing/Body Armor

What does the well-dressed Special Forces soldier wear in the field?

The answer to this question depends on the mission and the conditions to be encountered. Because these vary far more for SF units than for other soldiers, the Special Forces are sartorially the most variable of American military forces (you'll even find them now and again using makeup and other props to blend into a street or countryside). A core objective of SF personnel on missions is to avoid being noticed, and they work hard at maintaining their stealthy, low profile.

Battle Dress Uniforms

At home base or in the field (when the situation does not demand otherwise), the Special Forces normally wear the standard family of Battle Dress Uniforms (BDUs) worn by the rest of the U.S. military. These come in several weights and fabrics (all cotton and a cotton-polyester blend), and are produced with a variety of camouflage patterns—most frequently the green, brown, beige, and black "woodland" pattern. There are also three- and six-colored desert patterns (the choice depends on the ground cover in an operating area). And finally, there are two types of urban camouflage patterns—one in black, white, and gray (for operations around light-colored buildings), and the other in shades of blue (useful around dark-painted objects or in shadows). Each set of BDUs—whatever the pattern and weight—will have pants and a blouse shirt, each festooned with an impressive array of pockets.

Along with the basic BDU come appropriate caps and boots, again the type being dependent upon the environment where they are worn. Normally, Special Forces soldiers prefer a good airborne jump boot, which can stand up to all manner of situations.

Cold Weather Garments

Given a choice, most SF soldiers that I know prefer hot to cold climates. Wet clothing that has been exposed to cold wind is a wick for body heat, and hypothermia is just about the deadliest environmental condition soldiers deal with. For this reason, the Army has devoted considerable money and resources to providing troops with cold-weather gear, which they call the Extended Cold Weather Clothing System (ECWCS). This family of cold weather clothing is based on basic BDU patterns, but uses Gor-Tex to provide the insulation and water-resistant qualities needed for operating in extremely cold climates.

Like basic BDUs, ECWCS clothing comes in two weights, depending on the conditions, and normally a pair of heavy BDUs is worn under the ECWCS pants and jacket, which has a hood sized to allow a helmet to be worn underneath. ECWCS pants and parkas are extremely fine and well-designed garments, and have become quite popular around the world. The ECWCS jacket is particularly prized by sportsmen, who treasure its excellent Gor-Tex insulation and waterproofing.

Helmet/Body Armor

Helmets and body armor are hot and heavy, and so Special Forces soldiers hate to wear them, preferring that their training provide them with the protection needed to get in and out of tough situations. (But they will drop such inhibitions when facing a significant threat of return fire.)

In spite of their reluctance, the Army makes sure they are given an appropriate issue of Kevlar helmets and flak jackets to protect against small arms fire and artillery fragments. The Personal Armor System, Ground Troops (PASGT) provides protection for the head and torso against enemy fire up to 7.62mm. While admittedly heavy and hot (Kevlar is a superior insulator, especially in hot and humid conditions), the PASGT family of body armor and helmets is among the best in the world; and in recent years improved Kevlar formulations have considerably reduced weight and bulk. The basic PASGT helmet now only weighs 3 lb./1.36 kg., a significant reduction from the early PASGT helmets of the 1980s.

Meanwhile, a whole family of new body armor is on the way, with new battlefield and lightweight flak jackets and helmets due for introduction early in the twenty-first century.

Mufti

Most professional soldiers would tell you that the best camouflage in the world is to dress in native garb ("Mufti") and behave like the locals, and very often you'll find Special Forces guys (armed with their excellent language skills and cultural sensitivities) doing just that, even when they are visiting friendly host nations. When "going native" proves impossible, SF guys might then buy European or other foreign-made clothes, so they can pose as *anything* but American. Given the risks for military personnel of overseas exposure these days, this makes a lot of sense. As always, flexibility is the key to their actions.

Sleeping Gear

A sleeping bag is not always a necessary item in an SF rucksack, for many reconnaissance and raid missions require neither shelter nor sleeping gear. But there are times that you just can't survive without them. This kind of gear is constantly being improved (check the REI or L. L. Bean Web sites for commercial examples), and the U.S. military (not to be outdone) has introduced a new family of Gor-Tex-lined intermediate and extreme cold weather sleeping bags, along with several water-resistant "bivy" covers (which eliminate the need to carry a tent or ground cover— *and their weight*).

Food and Water

An army travels on its stomach.

Napoleon Bonaparte

Except for the actual "payloads" (weapons, explosives, radio gear, sensors, etc.) needed for their mission, SF soldiers carry in their rucksacks nothing more impor-tant—or heavier and bulkier—than the food and drink that keeps them going. And it is here, more than in any other logistical area, that the Army fails to provide for the unique requirements of the Special Forces.

The Army tends to view all soldiers alike. But the requirements of the Special Forces are vastly different from those of "normal" soldiers. Because Army units can usually expect daily resupplies of food and water, weight, volume, and the waste generated are only minor concerns. Such issues are far from minor to Special Forces.

The good news is that the Army has finally taken the complaints of field units to heart, and is about to issue more new kinds of packaged field rations than at any time since World War II.

Meals Ready to Eat (MREs)

It's hard to find lovers of Meals Ready to Eat (MREs—the Army's standard field rations). Despite improvements in quality and variety during the past decade, they still represent a notable compromise solution to the problem of giving soldiers a nutritious, tasty meal in the field.

For those not familiar with them, MREs are heavy—about 1.2 lb./.54 kg. each, most of which is water and packaging. Each MRE is packaged in a nearly indestructible plastic bag (bring a knife or multitool to get it open), enclosing yet more plastic foil packaging for the food (an entrée, starch, drinks, dessert, and some form of bread or biscuit). These foods are stabilized or sterilized either by heat or radiation, giving them a long shelf life.

What remains when soldiers are done with them also has a long life. That is to say there's a lot of "wet" trash, and thus used packaging must be buried or carried to avoid leaving evidence behind (wet trash is quite "noseable" to bloodhounds and other tracking canines).

Special Forces guys, always improvising, have done what they can to adapt MREs to Special Forces operations. They start by taking their loads of MREs apart, and removing every piece of nonessential packaging. They then select only the foods they need and want to eat, and stuff them back into the original heavy plastic bags. In this way, a discriminating eater can pack three meals into the volume usually required by one, and reduce the weight by half. By carefully rationing their stripped-down MREs, a week's worth of food can weigh no more than just 12 lb./5.4 kg. Still, this is a lot of weight and bulk to have to lug around in a rucksack, and not an optimal food source while out on patrols and missions. For instance, the high caloric and vitamin content of MREs tends to make for pungent urine discharges (attractive to dogs and electronic "sniffer" sensors).[48]

As a final shortcoming, each MRE carton contains twelve different meals (there are over two dozen varieties of MREs), making it difficult to use MREs for community eating or sharing. This limits their utility in coalition or insurgency operations like those demonstrated during Robin Sage.

If the Special Forces have anything good to say about MREs, it is that they are relatively cheap and easily available worldwide. They cost only a few dollars per meal, millions are produced every year, and the U.S. not only sells them to allies but also pre-positions them in mass depots and aboard ships stationed around the globe.

Meal Cold Weather (MCW)/Long Range Patrol (LRP) Rations

While MREs have their virtues, the cons outweigh the pros in the minds of SF units, and you hear a lot of wishes for a "patrol" ration, which would be lighter and more concentrated, and would not generate so much trash.

Interestingly, the Army has had such a ration in its inventory for some years, though its issue has been limited to units with cold weather and mountain warfare

---

[48] There is, however, a hope that the Army will produce foods to "spice" the urine to make it mimic a "local" cuisine and thus foil tracking (stealthy urine).

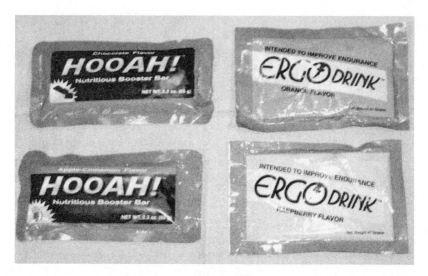

Prototypes of the Army's new Performance-Enhancing Ration Components. The ERGO Drink is designed to support long marches and operations in high-temperature environments, while the HOOAH! Bars provide a march ration for between-meal energy boosting.

JOHN D. GRESHAM

missions. The Meal Cold Weather (MCW)/Long Range Patrol (LRP) family of rations is essentially the same high-quality freeze-dried food you can buy at any camping supplier or outfitter. Though MCW/LRP rations are packaged in the same kind of plastic bags as MREs, because they are totally freeze-dried, they are much lighter (by half) than MREs, are immune to freezing, and are considered much better tasting (twelve different menus are now available). Each package contains two meals, water-free and vacuum packed.

To eat, add water. No problem . . . except that for years the Army only contracted for a small number of cold weather rations, compared with the tens of millions of MREs it procures every year. However, production is being increased to accommodate the growing demand of SOF units and other U.S. military formations. The one downside is cost, which is about three times that of an MRE per meal.

Performance-Enhancing Ration Components (PERCs)

For years, athletes and other physically active people have known the benefits of performance-enhancement products, like sports drinks (Gatorade, Powerade, etc.) and so-called "sports nutrition" bars (like PowerBars and Clif Bars).

SF soldiers (who certainly qualify as physically active) have long used such commercial products as "patrol rations" (frequently bought at personal expense).

The Army, recognizing this need, has developed what are known as Performance-Enhancing Ration Components (PERCs). But the Army PERCs will have real differences from their commercial counterparts. The PERCs are not only formulated to provide energy and delay fatigue, they will also improve situational awareness and other mental facilities during times of high stress. To this end, much of the sugar, starch, coloring, and other flavor-oriented ingredients found in commercial products are being deleted and replaced with more useful components.

The first two PERC products are hitting the inventory right now, and include:

- **ERGO Drink**—Mixed with water, the ERGO Drink will provide replacement of minerals, vitamins, and other needed nutrients. Sized in packets that make a quart/liter of drink at a time (fitting a standard canteen), ERGO has proved very popular with soldiers in early tests.
- **HOOAH! Bar**—HOOAH! is a bar-sized ration, packaged like a commercial nutrition bar, and can be consumed on the run to give a burst of energy and nutrition under tactical situations.

   Both ERGO and HOOAH! are being formulated in a variety of flavors, and will have mass distribution in 2000.

Shelf Stable Pouch Bread

Although fresh bread is one of the most perfect foods, leavened bread products rapidly deteriorate. Scientists have for a long time tried to discover ways to remedy this situation; and in fact attempts to sterilize bread with radiation have shown promise (though yielding shelf lives that only marginally improve on what is currently normal).

Army labs and food contractors have spent considerable time and money developing bread and pastry products that can stay fresh for up to three years; and with the Shelf Stable Pouch Bread product, they seem to have found a winner. (They accomplish this feat by carefully monitoring water content during production and oxygen level during packaging.) They will soon issue a bun-sized loaf of fresh bread in MREs and other field rations.

Mobility-Enhancing Ration Components (MERCs)

The Mobility-Enhancing Ration Components (MERCs) family of food products is an outgrowth of the Shelf Stable Pouch Bread program. MERCs are designed to fulfill the Special Forces dream of a small, lightweight ration with the characteristics of a sandwich, but packaged in the form of a large candy bar or pastry. Indeed, MERCs look very much like "pocket pastries" filled with meat, cheese, vegetables, and other foods, but are jammed with nutrients to help keep a SF soldier on the go during a mission. Early fillings ranged from barbecue beef to ham and eggs.

Each MERC will have a three-year shelf life, making it compatible not only with carriage in a rucksack but overseas pre-positioning requirements.

T-Rations/Fresh Food

Not everything a Special Forces soldier eats in the field is a "tactical" ration. At forward bases or training sites, there are frequently kitchen facilities that allow for cooking of "normal" meals. At such times, SF units tap into the Army supply system for what are called T-series rations—a decided step up from MREs. T-Rations are precooked meals packaged into aluminum trays, then sealed, irradiated, and shipped (usually refrigerated, though they can survive room temperature for days if necessary). Each T-Ration contains meat, starch, and vegetable selections, along with two large and treasured bottles of McIlhenny's Tabasco sauce (SF soldiers *never* leave home without it!). The results are actually surprisingly tasty, especially the special meals laid out for holidays like Christmas and Thanksgiving. All that's needed to make T-Rations ready to eat is to heat them in buffet-style hot-water heaters, and then serve them up.

Another option is to procure and cook fresh food locally. Even in the Third World, most fresh foods are perfectly safe to eat. The trick is simply careful preparation, proper cooking, and care with the water (impure water is the source of most travelers' nasty gastric problems). As an added bonus, eating local food gives SF soldiers a chance to shop at local stores and markets, and so develop friendships and build relationships that have real value when they are operating downrange.

Water and Hydration Systems

While most healthy people (depending on body fat and other factors) might last a month or more without food, none of us can survive more than a few days without fresh water. Since they tend to spend a lot of time where water is rare, Special Forces pay a lot of attention to making sure they have enough of it. In line with current physiological thinking, which maintains that a body under stress should be given as much water as it needs, current U.S. military thinking about water consumption is to provide soldiers with as much of it as they can drink. This helps maintain strength and energy levels, and avoids dehydration, digestive, and renal problems. The difficulty is that water is extremely heavy and bulky, with a gallon weighing around 8 lb./3.6 kg. When you consider that a soldier resting in shade in dry heat needs at least two gallons a day, the water supply problem makes itself obvious. Put that same soldier into the Persian Gulf heat and humidity during high summer, and you can actually quadruple that amount.

The Special Forces deal with this problem in several ways.

In parts of the world where water supplies are plentiful, but their purity is questionable, SF soldiers follow the rule of only drinking water that comes out of sealed bottles. In some areas, they use water filters and purification chemicals, and establish a regular water resupply schedule, so that every soldier always has at least two quarts/liters available.

In places where water is scarce (deserts, high altitudes, etc.), Special Forces teams tend to bring in enough water to complete their entire mission, cache it around their operating area, and then make runs to retrieve the cached water (and other consumable supplies as required). Though doing this can be dangerous in areas patrolled by enemy forces, sometimes it's the only way to survive.

Sometimes just getting fresh water into an area is dangerous. Because it's about as subtle as a circus train, the least desirable water resupply method is by air, either

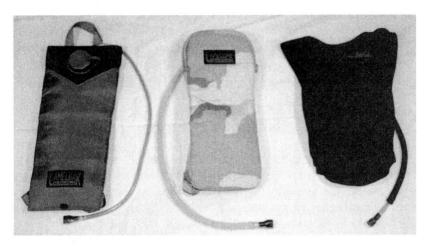

Three examples of Camelbak hydration systems. From left to right: the Storm is being issued to install in existing pack systems, the Thermobak for high-temperature/desert operations, while the Stealth is for aircrews and vehicle drivers.

JOHN D. GRESHAM

from helicopters or parachute drop, and SF soldiers try to avoid it whenever possible. In their view, if aircraft are used on missions, they should only be used twice. Once on the way in, and then on the way out.

Meanwhile, the carrying and delivering of potable liquids has recently been going through significant changes. For several hundred years, soldiers on the move have carried a day's ration of water in canteens. Early models were carved from wood or made from gourds. Now, lightweight plastics and space-age engineering have made traditional canteens virtually obsolete.

Their replacement, known as hydration systems, were pioneered by the Camelbak Company, and were originally developed to deliver fluids to astronauts and aircrews sealed in space or full-pressure suits. The idea was to provide a ready supply of water, which a person could consume gradually. The Camelbak designers placed a canteen-sized plastic bladder inside a small nylon bag, which was hung on the back of the user. Water was fed through a small hose over the shoulder. This system allows the wearer to take fluids while moving. That is, he or she does not have to stop and open an unwieldy canteen.

Camelbak and other hydration systems have proved so popular with soldiers and sportsmen that there is now a hydration system industry. Though in the past, soldiers have had to buy their own hydration gear (or try to slip a commercial purchase through their local G7 shop), starting in 2000, the Army has selected the Camelbak Company to supply their hydration system gear (including the one scheduled to go into the MOLLE derivative system when it arrives).

That unit, known as a Storm Maximum Gear, is a 100 fl. oz./3.0 liter bladder with a ballistic nylon cover and feed tube. It is designed to be dropped into an existing backpack system (such as the MOLLE), and will be bought in large numbers in the coming years. By the middle of the next decade, every soldier in the U.S. Army will have one.

Another new design, known as the Stealth, is specifically designed for aircrews (who often suffer from dehydration and fatigue on long flights). This unit is built to fit between the wearer's back and his or her aircraft seat (it's actually very comfortable).

Navigation Equipment

Despite their low-tech beginnings, the Special Forces have not been immune to the flow of high technology into their rucksacks. This means that SF soldiers are more frequently making use of electronics and advanced technology products to better accomplish their missions. Right now, a mix of old and cutting-edge equipment is being used in the field by SF units. But in ten years you may find the Special Forces as dependent as Wall Street stockbrokers on wireless phone, data, and information services.

Global Position System Receivers

In the few years since the NAVISTAR GPS system went online, its impact has been truly remarkable. This system of twenty-four satellites in Earth orbit sends signals to relatively inexpensive receivers that are translated into amazingly accurate three-dimensional position and timing data.

Even though the first practical use of GPS came only as recently as the 1991 Gulf War, millions of GPS receivers have been built and sold in the years since. Some civilian models can be bought for less than a hundred dollars; others will likely be standard equipment in the next new car you buy. Military models are certified as accurate to within 20 ft./6 m. (with the new Block IIR satellites), and can be made small enough to guide missiles and bombs.

The standard GPS receiver issued to the Special Forces is the Rockwell Collins AN/PSN-11 Portable Lightweight GPS Receiver (PLGR—called the "plugger"). The PLGR is a handheld device about the size of a brick, and weighs less than 3 lb./1.5 kg. Two are normally carried in each ODA, so that one will always be available during split-team operations. A number of the older Trimble Navigation Small Lightweight GPS Receivers (SLGR—"slugger") are also still in use, frequently mounted on vehicles. Both provide absolutely accurate position and timing data.

Compasses

While GPS is the preferred means of navigation, sometimes technology fails. Batteries go dead; equipment gets dropped and breaks. In such circumstances, SF soldiers are still expected to reach their objectives, and if they have to do it the old-fashioned way, using their maps and compasses, they can do that.

The standard U.S. Army model of compass is little changed since the Second World War. Based upon a folding circular design (which compacts down to smaller than a hockey puck), it has a luminescent bezel and needle, and is set up to take sightings along a bearing line. High-tech it is not, but it will always work as long as the Earth has a magnetic field.

Sensors and Communications Equipment

Many other electronic devices have found their way into SF rucksacks. You might find there, for instance, low-light goggles, palmtop computers, and digital cameras, and there will likely be more as we move further into the twenty-first century, saddling SF soldiers with an even greater load to tote.

Night Vision Goggles

American military forces own the night; they can fight round the clock.

A far remove from the primitive Starlight amplification scopes of the Vietnam War, Night Vision Goggles (NVGs) have now become so sensitive and accurate that pilots of helicopters and fixed-wing aircraft wear them at night to attack ground targets.

On the ground, the NVG being issued to the Special Forces is the PVS-7D—a marvelous little device that can be worn on a helmet or harness, or, if need be, used handheld like a pair of binoculars. By amplifying ambient light from stars and other available light millions of times, a clear (albeit monochrome green) picture is presented to the eyes of the user. Should there be no celestial lighting or if the user goes indoors, a small infrared light on the front of the NVGs can be activated to provide illumination. The PVS-7D has been procured in sufficient numbers to provide a set to every SF soldier on missions.

In the near future, the Special Forces will receive a new series of night sights known as the PVS-13 (a small thermal sight for weapons) and PVS-14 (a monocular helmet-mounted NVG unit). These will be evolutionary developments of the PVS-7D, but with much higher resolution and a better depth of field.

Eventually these systems and their successors (which will include small, lightweight, forward-looking infrared—FLIR—thermal imagers, the first of which are now being used on M16A2s) will be integrated into the "Digital Soldier" ensembles being prepared for Army service in the early twenty-first century.[49]

The SFC G7 shop also has a number of programs in the works to develop their own family of sensors, and should begin to field these new systems sometime around 2005.

---

[49] "Digital Soldier" is an Army marketing term used to describe the new ensemble of gear that will be carried by the infantry in the early twenty-first century. This will include a central processor/communications/navigation package to keep the soldier in touch and oriented at all times. There will additionally be a new helmet-mounted heads-up display to show digital maps, sensor readouts, and other data, and will leave the soldier's hands free for weapons. Though "Digital Soldier" promises to be an impressive array of systems, it is unlikely that Special Forces will choose to adopt it anytime soon. The complexity and weight will likely keep them using more "basic" but dependable systems until the second (and hopefully bug-free) generation of "Digital Soldier" technology arrives.

Radios

A traditional strong point of Special Forces units has been their ability to communicate reliably from anywhere in the world. For more than five decades, SF soldiers have stayed on the leading edge of communications technology. To that end, they will use in the field whatever works—old or new. And so the communications gear a team might take downrange will often be a mix of the tried-and-true and the advanced.

To provide short-range tactical communications, SF teams are equipped with the Motorola PRC-126 Saber-series radios, which are a marvel of clarity of transmission, and have become a favorite of military and police forces throughout the world. Built in a small "brick" configuration, the Saber is normally worn on a soldier's LC-2 harness; a headset keeps hands free. Range is around 6 miles/10 km. under good conditions without repeaters.

However, technology is moving rapidly, and the Saber is about to be replaced by the Multiband, Intra-Team Radio (MBITR) systems. The advantage of MBITR is that it will communicate across a much wider band of frequencies, including VHF-FM, VHF-AM, and UHF-AM/FM. SF soldiers are also being equipped with the new PRQ-7 Combat Survivor Evader Locator System (CSEL), which combines a GPS receiver and remote tracking beacon. CSEL allows combat search-and-rescue units to remotely track a soldier or team with GPS precision and without the need for voice transmissions from the operator. Expect to see every SF unit get several of these "911" radio/navigating systems starting in 2001.

Long-range communications are normally based around one of several lightweight satellite communications (SATCOM) systems. Most often used is the PRC-5, though the new PRC-137F Special Mission Radio (SMRS) is rapidly being introduced. Unlike the PRC-5, the PRC-137 SMRS has a built-in encryption device (the PRC-5 needs a separate encryption system, like the KY-99A, to send secure messages). It can also be easily hooked up to a Morse keypad, a microphone, or a laptop/palmtop computer (for e-mail messages). This last can also take advantage of commercially available software to send along other files such as digital photos and text messages.

The major problem with SATCOM systems is that they are not always available (i.e., when there is no available satellite transponder overhead—a situation that will gradually improve as more satellites are lofted into place). Until that day, SF teams will have to work within SATCOM access "windows" scheduled to the minute by the U.S. Space Command. Atmospheric conditions and solar activity will also occasionally "blank" out SATCOM channels. To protect against these possibilities, extra radio gear has to be carried.

When everything else fails, the communications sergeants (18E) turn to old reliable—their TRQ-43 High Frequency radio sets, which bounce their HF signals on the upper atmosphere (like skipping a stone on a pond). When equipped with a KL-43 encryption device, the "Turkey-43" (as it is called) can reliably fire off secure HF radio "shots" to just about anywhere in the world. The trick is the skill of the 18E communications sergeants in cutting and stringing the special wire antennas that optimize the "bounce" off the upper atmosphere—an arcane science.

Finally, there are cellular phones. On training missions, SF teams will rent cell

A Special Forces soldier using a lightweight satellite communications terminal. Mounted on an HMMWV, the antenna is the small cross-shaped object just to the left of the soldier.

phones from local utilities, and use them as a backup system for the encrypted radio systems. They are also useful for talking with locals who have their own cell phones.

Ground Laser Target Designator

A key SF wartime mission is known as Terminal Guidance (TG). TG missions require SF teams to locate specific targets as part of a Special Reconnaissance (SR) mission, then designate it for attack by supporting aircraft, artillery, or missiles. Because TG targets are most often high-payoff enemy assets, like headquarters units or SCUD missile launchers, SFC is willing to risk placing an ODA within range of a heavily defended target site.

For many years, SF soldiers have lugged a lot of gear around to help them plot and designate their TG targets (never with completely satisfactory results). There was a particular need for a lightweight means of pointing out to aircraft exactly where to place their weapons. That need has recently been met in the form of the Litton PAQ-10 Ground Laser Target Designator (GLTD).

The GLTD is a moderate-sized system, about the size of two shoeboxes taped together, weighing in at just under 12 lb./5.5 kg. It is equipped with a set of 10X sighting optics and a laser rangefinder/designator, with which it can sight, range, and designate targets up to 6.1 miles/10 km. away for aircraft equipped with laser spot trackers. An aircraft or helicopter that's so equipped can track in on the laser spot

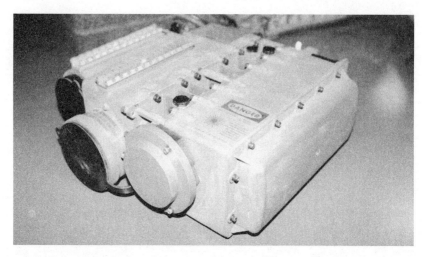

A PAQ-10 Ground Laser Target Designator. The PAQ-10 is a combination thermal imager, rangefinder, and laser designator that can be attached to a GPS receiver and radio to provide precision targeting coordinates for attacking aircraft.

JOHN D. GRESHAM

and use it to aim unguided ordnance with amazing accuracy. GLTD also provides guidance for laser-guided weapons like Paveway-guided bombs and AGM-114 Hellfire antitank missiles. Finally, interface ports can be used to connect the GLTD with other systems like the PLGR GPS receiver and various radio systems. When so configured, accurate target coordinates can be passed automatically to other systems, like the Army's Advanced Field Artillery Tactical Data System (a component of the "Digital Battlefield" fire systems that are coming online).

Lightweight Video Reconnaissance System (LVRS)

Special Reconnaissance/Terminal Guidance missions are among the riskiest of SF tasks. All too often SF ODAs have found more excitement than they wished when they had to be extracted from a "blown" SR hide site under enemy fire. During Desert Storm, several ODAs were very nearly destroyed while on SR missions deep inside Iraqi territory.

To take some of the risk and confusion out of the SR process, SFC has developed the Lightweight Video Reconnaissance System (LVRS). LVRS consists of small still-frame video cameras, which are networked via wireless radio links to a small portable "out" PHV-1 workstation assigned to a deployed ODA.

The base station can be located up to 6 miles/10 km. from the cameras, and except to site and retrieve the units, no men are needed to handle them. The cameras can be augmented by adding NVG or thermal imaging equipment, giving the LVRS a day and night capability. Should a camera "see" a target of interest, the imagery can be rapidly sent from the "out" station to a PVH-2 base station back at a mission support center or forward operating base. The imagery can also be transmitted via

SATCOM or other radio link, providing nearly real-time monitoring of critical road junctions, buildings, or other sites.

An improved version, LVRS II, with improved cameras and smaller packaging, should be fielded in 2001. There are also plans to field a fully automated, remotely controlled robot surveillance station, as well as small unmanned aerial vehicles. SF planners hope to "seed" these robot sensor stations around an area, and then feed the surveillance data through the ODA's "out" workstation back to higher headquarters.

In years to come, a single SF soldier may be able to task an earth-orbiting photo-reconnaissance satellite to photograph a target, which will then be transmitted in real time to a strike aircraft or artillery unit for immediate action.

Computers

Computers have become as necessary to Special Forces units as they are to all other trained professionals. Laptop machines are found in abundance on training missions and at forward bases, while palmtop units often go on missions with ODAs. The most popular are the small and rugged Hewlett-Packard 300- and 600-series machines, which can be hooked up directly to SATCOM transmitters to send files and reports. But these will surely give way to newer palmtop computers and personal data assistants as they become smaller, more powerful, and more rugged.

Digital Cameras

Digital photography, which can send nearly real-time reconnaissance data back to command authorities, is a fairly recent (but *very* exciting) development. Digital cameras take photos with a photo-sensitive computer chip, which converts the image into a computer file (normally into JPEG format). This can then be loaded onto a computer and uploaded by a SATCOM system to virtually anywhere in the world. Right now, Special Forces teams use a mix of commercial digital camera gear—both high-end Kodak/Nikon units and cheaper Casio devices.

During a recent exercise at Fort Polk, I saw a photo of an Opposing Force aircraft being displayed just minutes after it was taken over two hundred miles away in Mississippi. This is exactly the kind of timely and high-quality data that customers of Special Forces services want.

Plan on seeing digital cameras in *every* SF soldier's kit bag soon.

Transportation

Once a Special Forces soldier is properly clothed, armed, equipped, and packed, a way has to be found to get him to where he is needed—one of the most expensive elements, it turns out, of Special Forces operations, and an enormous and complex planning issue for the SFC leadership. As long as missions continue to be sent to every part of the world except Antarctica, transportation will remain a difficult challenge for SFC.

Transportation can be looked at in three phases: First, you have to get forces out of the U.S. and into the general vicinity of their target. Then you have to get to the actual operating area and onto the ground. And finally, you have to be able to move around on the ground.

Airlift from the U.S. Transportation Command generally handles transport to the general vicinity of the target, while the 160th Special Operations Aviation Regiment (SOAR) or Air Force Special Operations can get you into the operating area. Getting onto the ground and to the targets is more complicated, though.

Parachutes

Unlike the troopers of the 82nd Airborne Division and 75th Ranger Regiment (who enter a target area in relatively large numbers), Special Forces soldiers need to have a high degree of precision and control when they jump from aircraft. To accomplish this goal, they use the MC-4 steerable parachute system, which can be "jumped" up to altitudes of over 30,000 ft./9,150 m. These High Altitude, High Opening (HAHO) jumps can take place up to 25 miles/40 km. from a target area, providing covert entry into high-threat areas.

All-Terrain Vehicles (ATVs)

Though SF soldiers are used to walking, and prefer it for most occasions that call for a stealthy approach to a target, there are times when they need help moving their gear and supplies to hide sites or cache sites. To provide this muscle, SFC has procured a number of lightweight, compact, and powerful four-wheeled All-Terrain Vehicles (ATVs). These can be carried on aircraft, including helicopters. (A number of them can be carried on a C-130 Hercules transport or MH-47 Chinook helicopter.) They can also be dropped by cargo parachute. Small trailers towed by ATVs can then tote heavy loads of water, ammunition, and other critical material quietly and quickly to where these are needed.

Ground Mobility Vehicle

Long-range mounted patrol and reconnaissance operations have long been the specialty of the British Special Air Service (SAS), which began such rides in North Africa during World War II. Later, during the 1991 Persian Gulf War, SAS teams mounted aboard specially configured Land Rovers ranged across the Iraqi desert, hunting SCUD missile launchers, blowing up critical targets, and generally raising merry hell wherever they went.

Though the Special Forces have lacked a tradition of these operations, they have in recent times taken notice of this valuable capability and have decided to procure their own long-range patrol vehicle.

The Ground Mobility Vehicle (GMV), a heavily modified variant of the M1097 "Heavy Hummer" version of the HMMWV, is well suited to operations in all kinds of environments around the globe. Each GMV, which is modified at an Army depot, is equipped with a modified suspension system, which can be compressed to allow

A Ground Mobility Vehicle assigned to the 5th Special Forces Group in Kuwait. This vehicle is rigged on a pallet to be dropped from a cargo aircraft, and is used to support Kuwaiti Army operations.

stowage aboard the MC-47 Chinook helicopters of the 160th SOAR. They can also be carried by C-130s, and even parachuted into an area, if that is required. Best of all, they are no larger than a normal HMMWV, meaning they pose no special problems for handling and carriage during deployments.

Once on the ground, the GMV can carry enough fuel, food, and water to support three SF soldiers for up to a week of mounted operations. Though GMVs are each the size of a large sports utility vehicle, they are surprisingly difficult to spot when properly painted or camouflaged; and since most GMV movement would be at night, they are very stealthy vehicles. Equipment includes a mount for heavy weapons (M249, M240G, Mk. 19, etc.), a full radio suite, and a GPS receiver (allowing it to move quietly with pinpoint precision even at night, while hiding under built-in camouflage netting during the day).

The first units were delivered to forward-deployed elements of the 5th Special Forces Group in Kuwait, who used them to provide close air support to Kuwaiti Army units. The 3rd Special Forces Group will get theirs over the next few years, and other groups may obtain GMVs down the road, depending upon their future needs and responsibilities.

Rental Vehicles

Very often, SFC will authorize the rental of commercial vehicles and cars to support training missions and transportation requirements in permissive environments. This is normally done through rental companies like Hertz and Avis, much as you would on any normal business trip. The vehicles most in demand by Special Forces personnel are, of course, sports utility vehicles and trucks, which give them the off-

INSIDE THE RUCKSACK ■ 125

road capabilities they treasure without requiring the movement of a HMMWV from the U.S.

When it was first issued back in 1952, the SF soldier's rucksack was a pretty basic piece of gear. Since then, it has gotten a great deal larger, it carries vastly more, and has even become "techier." Despite all these changes, the rucksack remains the symbol of Special Forces mobility, and it will continue to be that into the new century—a link back to SF roots to a time when computers were only found in laboratories and "digital" referred to your fingers. What the next generation of rucksack will look like I cannot say. What I do know is that whatever form it takes, SF soldiers will still be carefully packing it before going downrange on missions.

U.S. Army Special Forces Command

De Oppresso Liber

"To Free the Oppressed"

Official Motto of the U.S. Army Special Forces Command

El Salvador is a nation named for "The Savior" . . . where, until scarcely a decade ago, the Savior seemed far, far away. For its citizens, the tragic little Central American country was hell. Year after year during the 1960s and '70s, its doom was to tear itself apart in an ugly, vicious, and seemingly endless civil war. Thousands of lives were lost, many in combat, but many also in massacres and acts of vengeance.

On one side was the right-wing (thus anticommunist, thus U.S-backed) government, derived from the ranks of the old land-owning families who had formed the ruling elite for generations, and supported by the National Police and the Army (derived from the ranks of the small middle classes), who backed the government in the hope of themselves climbing into the power elite. On the other side was an irregular army of Marxist guerrillas, operating in the countryside and supported by Fidel Castro's Cuba and the Nicaraguan Sandinistas. In between was the (more or less) 80% of the population who simply wanted a good, secure life, with jobs and health and education for their children—and including moderate politicians, members of the clergy, peasants, and Indians.

The government forces—every bit as vicious and repressive as the Serbs in Kosovo—were intent on crushing the rebellion, no matter who stood in their way (or were perceived to stand in their way), or how many lifeless bodies were scattered across the countryside. Army and National Police "Death Squads" roamed the country, killing even clergy members and relief workers trying to spread the word of peace across the troubled land.

The rebels were no less vicious and violent.

Following the inauguration of President Ronald Reagan in 1981, the new administration (under an initiative headed by Secretary of State Haig and Director of Central Intelligence Casey) decided to do something about the mess in El Salvador

... specifically, to send Special Forces personnel there to provide training and advice to the Army and National Police Forces.

Sending military assistance missions to El Salvador and other Central American countries was one of the few actions available to the administration that did not require congressional approval ... unlikely to come from the then Democrat-controlled Congress. (Military deployments of less than 180 days require no congressional oversight or approval, an administrative loophole that still continues.)

The official goal of these ODAs was to help the military forces of El Salvador become more professional and better able to defend themselves against the leftist threats. *Their* mission, in other words, was *not* to defeat the rebels. Thus, the Green Berets in El Salvador had no authority or rules of engagement that allowed them to take offensive action (though of course they could defend themselves). Neither were the ODAs there to prop up the Salvadoran government against the legitimate political opposition of that country.

At this point, things began to get interesting.

Though the Reagan people were of course hardly friendly to the left-wing insurgents, the government in place could hardly be called a benevolent, representative democracy, either. What was needed was a potentially positive *third force*. And to this end, the Reagan administration made an inspired choice. It seems that they viewed the Army and National Police as "centers of gravity," which, if reformed, could change the course of the national leadership.

Therefore, the job of the SF ODAs was to teach Salvadoran government forces both the military skills needed to better prosecute the war, *and* the ethical and moral lessons that would inspire them to operate according to civilized standards. Members of the 7th Special Forces Group—(Airborne) (7th SFG [A]) carried on this work for almost a dozen years ... and paid a high price for it, in lives and in blood.

Their blood and their labors bore fruit.

Sometime during the late 1980s, the Salvadoran Army tried acting in other than brutal and repressive ways toward their fellow countrymen; they began to halt activities of their death squads[50] and to actually show respect for basic human rights. These actions resulted in pleasant side effects.

First, support for the rebels eroded, and the Army started having a real effect against the rebels in the countryside. (The cities and towns, it seems, were never especially vulnerable to them, since the Army and National Police always had "home court advantage" there.)

Then, when the tide turned against them, the rebels asked for—and were promptly granted—peace talks ... to good result. By the end of the Cold War, the peace treaty was a done deal, the civil war had ended, and today there is a coalition government, with elements of the entire political spectrum (including a moderate middle) sharing power.

Though it would be on the far side of realistic to claim that the ODAs on their

---

50 It should be noted that not all death squads came from right-wing sources. Recent evidence shows that the left had their death squads, too, the best known of their actions being the massacre of a Catholic priest and several nuns. This raised up a serious stir when it happened.

own changed the course of a nation (the greater part of the credit must go to the Salvadoran people themselves), the Special Forces detachments in El Salvador surely had a major effect. These special men did their jobs . . . even when they had to somehow teach the right path to thugs and just this side of genocidal madmen; even at the cost of the lives of companions and friends, and even after clergy massacres in El Salvador had turned U.S public opinion against our involvement in that country, and Congress was within an inch of pulling the funding and authorization plug on SF missions there. (Congress has only one control over such missions, which is funding.)

In the face of all that—and worse—they trained an Army . . . and redirected the moral path of a nation. (This, by the way, is standard policy for SF soldiers. They try to teach good lessons, even to bad people!)

There's an interesting corollary to all this:

In the light of the above, you'd think American Special Forces troops would be far from welcome to the Salvadoran guerrillas. In fact, that's not quite the case.

Starting with the initial peace talks, and continuing with the follow-up negotiations that are still going on, the *rebel* opposition forces have insisted that each meeting include U.S. Special Forces soldiers as part of the mediation team. The reason? The rebels only trust the government representatives to negotiate in good faith when SF soldiers are present.

It's hard to imagine a greater compliment for the Special Forces soldiers who went to fight in that dirty little war.

El Salvador is not the only Special Forces success story. America's "quiet professionals" continue to take on seemingly impossible missions and bring them off . . . not by overwhelming the "ignorant, good-for-nothing natives" with the mindless, violent, macho, "Ramboid" trash you see in movies or television. Instead, they do the job more often with concrete acts of kindness, aid, conciliation, cooperation, and compassion than with guns.

That most of us know little of their exploits is primarily due to the desire of Special Forces personnel to practice their trade discreetly. Let's lift the veils of discretion and take a look at some of the vital tasks that Special Forces Command and their supporting units do around the world.

But first, it's worth examining how the guys in Special Forces came into that very special spirit—that esprit—that distinguishes them from every other military force in the world.

Touchstones: Traditions and Heritage

All elite military units are clannish . . . tribal. But few are more clannish and tribal than the U.S Special Forces (their reticence is a function of this).

They will, however, talk to one another.

Special Forces revere their achievements. They live and breathe their history and their traditions. These provide the "glue" that holds them together in the field. But they revere especially those extraordinary individuals who've given everything they have in behalf of their fellow SF soldiers, their mission, and their personal honor.

Of course, it would be hard for SF personnel to avoid the inspiration of those who came before them, who sacrificed their lives to save a hopeless situation, another SF soldier, or sometimes an innocent bystander who just got in the way. But the physical presence of equally heroic Special Forces personnel who lived to tell the story is what truly gives life and spirit to the organization. These people have become almost mystical touchstones to SF soldiers in the teams; and their stories provide the common language for experienced SF hands.

Thus, the many-times decorated warrior heroes from earlier years are often invited to spend time with the new SF recruits at Camp MacKall in North Carolina, and to observe their training. To meet and touch a living legend or Medal of Honor winner has a powerful effect on "Q" Course students.

Knowledge of the heritage of the Special Forces allows you to measure current soldiers against the great troopers of the past. Similarly, knowledge of the achievements of past units allows you to more accurately judge the actions of today. For that reason, let's take a quick excursion down the path that brought the Special Forces Community to its present eminence.

Roots

The crucible of World War II made America see the wisdom of creating Special Operations units, and it is from the units that first saw the light of day in that conflict that the SOF communities draw their historic lineage.

Thus the 75th Ranger Regiment traces its roots back to "Darby's Rangers," who scaled the Norman cliffs of Pointe du Hoc on D-Day, and later fought across Western Europe. The SEALs look back to the exploits of the early Underwater Demolition Teams that led the way for amphibious operations in every theater of war. The roots of the Special Forces spring from the rich ground of the Devil's Brigade and the OSS.

The 1st Special Service Force, better known as the "Devil's Brigade," was a joint U.S.-Canadian unit whose specialty was deep reconnaissance and close-quarters fighting. The brigade was formed at Fort William Henry Harrison in Montana in 1942, and it was originally tasked to take part in an airborne raid into Norway (which was cancelled). Later, they were assigned to combat operations in Italy (such as the famous assault on Mount La Difensa) and southern France, where they discharged their deep reconnaissance and close-quarters fighting specialties with unparalleled violence. Their training and raw combat power allowed them to defeat enemy units much larger than their own . . . though frequently at a high cost. They suffered 2,314 casualties, representing 134% of their original strength, in five separate campaigns. By the time of their last battle in France in late 1944, the Brigade was a shadow of its original strength. Their casualties had been so high and their OpTempo so vigorous that rebuilding the units with replacements was no longer practical. The unit was "played out," as they used to say in the Civil War.

Today, each Special Forces Group traces a spiritual lineage to one of the companies of the 1st Special Service Force, and they celebrate this lineage every December 5th, which is known as Menton Day, the date on which the original Brigade was stood down at the French village of Menton. It is from this tradition of close combat against superior odds that the fearsome combat reputation of the Special Forces would be born.

From General "Wild Bill" Donovan's Office of Strategic Services, the Special Forces derived their more unusual roles and missions: reconnaissance, intelligence gathering, unconventional warfare, and humanitarian assistance. During World War II, the OSS conducted many valuable operations in all parts of the world. Examples abound. Here are a few: In Burma, they led tribesmen against the Japanese. In Vietnam, they supported a young nationalist (who we know as Ho Chi Minh). At the end of the war, they located German weapons scientists and brought them to the West. The OSS was, in short, a magnet for enthusiastic young men and women searching for high adventure. Many paid for their enthusiasm with their lives.

One of the more adventurous OSS exploits was to drop clandestine teams behind enemy lines to gather intelligence and support resistance groups:

Three-man Jedburgh Teams were dropped into France and Belgium, where they linked up with resistance forces and then helped train and equip the various partisan units. After the Allied landing in June 1944, they joined the partisans on raids behind the lines.

The OSS also formed what were known as Operational Groups (OGs), thirty-four-man teams that were the direct ancestors of all of today's SF detachments. The OGs normally fought as split teams of fifteen to seventeen personnel, and were used for operations in Italy, France, Greece, Yugoslavia, and Norway. Like the Jedburghs, they not only conducted their own raids, but also worked to train and equip partisan and resistance units. And they are commemorated today by the signature OSS dagger on the shoulder patch of the Special Forces.

Though the OSS and the Devil's Brigade made important contributions to the eventual Allied victory in World War II, neither survived into the postwar period. Nevertheless, their contributions would pave the way for the eventual creation of the Special Forces.

Aaron Bank: The Father of the Special Forces

CIA and SOF failures during and after the Korean War eventually pointed up the Special Operations gaps in American military capabilities. It was within these gaps that the Army Special Forces would eventually find their niche.

Even before the signing of the Korean armistice in 1953, it was clear that if the United States wanted to revive the Special Operations capabilities available during World War II, someone outside of the CIA would have to make it happen.

As luck would have it, a small band of OSS veterans within the U.S. Army believed in the value of guerrilla warfare in the Cold War world. Since it was obvious that major powers would never resort to nuclear weapons (unless they went mad), the OSS vets were convinced that other modes of warfare would have to be developed and perfected. They were looking specifically at ways of fighting "small wars."

Led by Brigadier General Robert McClure, a former OSS operative, and a pair of talented colonels, Aaron Bank and Russell Volckmann, the group fought to find support for their concepts within the Army. The target of their thinking was Eastern

Colonel Aaron Bank, USA. Colonel Bank is considered the founding father of the modern Special Forces, and commanded the 10th Special Forces Group.

OFFICIAL U.S. ARMY PHOTO

Europe, where, in their view, guerrilla and unconventional warfare could provide a new weapon against the growing threat of communist aggression. In the event of a Soviet invasion of Western Europe, special units could be used as "stay behind" forces. Once the main Soviet effort had passed by, the teams of Special Operations units could conduct raids, gather intelligence, and generally harass the communist forces. Much like Colonel John S. Mosby's rebel raiders during the American Civil War, they would make the Eastern European plains their "briar patch," and draw off front-line forces to chase them down.[51]

Though these ideas were clearly outside the realm of normal Army doctrine, the leadership saw merit in their madness. Since fighting a nuclear war to the death in Europe had obvious negatives, a clandestine Plan B made sense . . . especially if things were to go bad for NATO. Moreover, the new force would be cheap to form and operate, and involved very little risk.

In early 1952, Colonel Bank went down to Fort Bragg, North Carolina (the long-standing center of quick reaction warfare, with the necessary personnel base and Airborne training equipment and facilities), with orders to form 2,300 men into the first of the unconventional warfare units. At Fort Bragg, Bank selected a site on what was called Smoke Bomb Hill to build what was called at that time, "a physiological/special

---

51 John Singleton Mosby was the famous Southern cavalry officer who established a force of rebel raiders (primarily composed of civilian irregulars) in the northwestern counties of Virginia. For several years they struck at Union supply and transportation lines and provided superb reconnaissance for Robert E. Lee's Army of Northern Virginia. So effective were Mosby's raiders that the areas of Loudoun and Prince William counties west of Washington, D.C., became known as "Mosby's Country."

132 ■ SPECIAL FORCES

center." Once the physical facilities were in place, Bank then set about the task of finding the men for his unit.

Predictably, many who were attracted to Bank's unit had once been OSS operatives, longing for the adventure and comradeship that the regular Army had never provided them. Others were refugees from Eastern Europe, seeking a means to liberate their former homes from communist domination. (Many still had family members on the other side of the Iron Curtain; for them the East–West conflict was more than a political struggle.)[52] All were volunteers. All had to be jump qualified in Airborne operations, with a heavy dose of infantry experience, and most spoke two or more languages. Most enlisted personnel were sergeants with years of service in the Army.

They all joined knowing full well that if they were captured behind enemy lines, they would likely be executed as spies. (I've talked with some of Colonel Bank's early recruits. They could have cared less about that.) These were highly motivated and skilled personnel, thrilled at the chance to fight the Cold War on terms of their own choosing. For them, it was an irresistible challenge.

After months of recruiting, training, and organizing, Bank's unit was stood up on June 19th, 1952. Designated the 10th Special Forces Group—Airborne, it was specifically designed to work in the European theater. Though the unit had only ten men (including Colonel Bank) when stood up, that number grew quickly in the months that followed into the 2,300 originally envisaged.

Their training covered a variety of skills, from radio and medical skills to language and parachute jump training. Their planned missions included intelligence gathering, deep-penetration raids, counterinsurgency operations, and a variety of other tasks, including especially the ability to operate and survive in enemy-controlled territory, perhaps for months or years.

In 1953, even before the training was completed, a series of labor-related riots in East Germany created enough concern about possible Soviet operations in Europe to send the 10th SFG into the field. But first the unit was split in two, with half being sent to Bad Tölz in West Germany (near Stuttgart). The remaining SF soldiers were reflagged as the 77th SFG, which remained Stateside for a few years, until ordered to send a series of small detachments to the Far East (in the face of the growing threat of the People's Republic of China in that region).

In 1957 these detachments were designated as the 1st SFG (A), and their focus was on East Asia, since it was believed that this region required a similar capability to the one the 10th SFG gave to Europe.

Meanwhile, the Stateside 77th itself became a full group in 1960, when it was flagged as the 7th SFG (A), with a Latin American focus.

In less than a decade, the Special Forces had become a permanent part of the Army force structure, and were sending operational detachments into the field all over the world.

---

52 Most of the immigrants who became early Special Forces soldiers were given American citizenship under what was known as the Lodge Act. Named for its sponsor, Senator Henry Cabot Lodge, the bill gave the U.S. government the right to grant immediate citizenship to personnel from politically persecuted countries if they chose to serve in the U.S. military.

As for the man who started it all, Colonel Bank is still alive and living in the Los Angeles area. A few years ago, a new building (which incidentally contains the USASOC archives) was built as part of the Special Forces school. Senior leaders at USASOC make no secret that when Colonel Bank passes on, they will proudly flag the building with his name, so that the father of the Special Forces will be properly remembered by the new SF soldiers being trained there.

The Green Beret

Berets have long been approved headgear for military units in countries like Britain and (of course) France, but *not* (until recently) in the United States. The ban on berets, however, did not stop the Special Forces from wearing them.

For a number of years before the headgear was officially approved by the Department of the Army, Special Forces soldiers had worn a green beret (designed by Major Herb Brucker, a World War II OSS veteran) during field and deployed operations. They liked the style and swagger it represented. It became a symbol of the Special Forces esprit and professionalism . . . And the ban only made SF soldiers wear it more often around their home bases.

In 1961, the ban was lifted. And therein lies a tale.

John Kennedy—himself a man of style and swagger—came to the presidency with the goal of actively engaging communism . . . of taking on the communists mano a mano, especially in what he characterized, "so-called wars of national liberation"—small wars of communist insurrection. (Crises in Berlin and Cuba swiftly put a cautious lid on his early swagger, but that's another tale.)

It will come as no surprise that his chosen weapon in the "small wars" would be the newly created SFGs.

In 1961, the new president flew down to Fort Bragg to tour the 82nd Airborne Division and the other units of XVIII Airborne Corps. While there, he also paid a visit to the Special Forces soldiers. Having previously been briefed on their capabilities, he wanted to see them for himself. He also wanted to see them wearing green berets (which he had somehow heard about). The caps were the kind of thing he *liked*.

Seeing the way the wind was blowing, the Army did a very quick about-face, and before Kennedy arrived at Fort Bragg the beret had been authorized as an official uniform item for the Special Forces.

At Bragg, Kennedy gave the SF troops one of his signature speeches, complete with rousing promises that they would be on the front lines in upcoming battles with communism. Prophetic words!

Within months, a vast expansion of the Special Forces was ordered, and no less than four new SFGs were activated, effectively doubling the size of the Special Forces. The 5th SFG (A) was formed on September 21st, 1961, and was quickly committed as the primary SF unit in Southeast Asia (it would become a legendary force in Vietnam). The 3rd, 6th, and 8th SFGs followed in 1963.

So important was John Kennedy to the SF community that when he was assassinated in 1963, the SF training center was named after him—the JFK Special Warfare Center at Fort Bragg.

But it was the young president's love of the stylish SF headgear that had a more wide-ranging effect. Like John Kennedy, the American people took a shining to the good-looking green berets of the SF troops, so much so that the troops, by metonymy, came to be associated with their caps—they came to be called the "Green Berets." The name spawned a blockbuster John Wayne movie and a 1960s hit song.

All of this did not actually sit well with SF soldiers. Though they are fiercely proud of their classic headgear, they cringe when you call them Green Berets.

"We're *not* hats!" they insist.

Roger Donlon: The Ultimate Icon

To most of us who remember the Vietnam War at all, American involvement began sometime in the mid-1960s, with the Gulf of Tonkin Incident and the subsequent American intervention by Marines and air cavalry. But for the Special Forces, the war in Southeast Asia started much earlier. In fact, the first American soldier to die in Vietnam was killed on October 21st, 1956. He was Captain Harry G. Cramer, Jr., of the 14th Special Forces Operational Detachment (SFOD) of the 77th SFG, the first active-duty personnel America committed to the war in Vietnam.

Cramer's name heads the list on the Vietnam Veterans' Memorial in the Mall in Washington.

Year after year, SF personnel remained in Vietnam and other Southeast Asian countries, teaching the skills critical for surviving the growing communist aggression. This advisory period continued until August 1964, when an attack in the Tonkin Gulf of a U.S. Navy destroyer led to the deployment of division-sized units from the Army and Marine Corps to Vietnam.

After the Tonkin Gulf attack, the SF mission to train ARVN units remained unchanged, but that became only one mission among many. Thus the entire 5th SFG (A) was moved to Vietnam, with its headquarters in Nha Trang. SF units were then sent out to provide eyes, ears, and security for the larger conventional units and, from a series of joint U.S./ARVN camps, to provide "tripwire" patrols, looking for North Vietnamese units filtering in from Laos and Cambodia. At these joint camps occurred some of the most vicious firefights of the war.

One of these attacks came on the night of July 6, 1964, when two full Viet Cong battalions tried to overrun a critical outpost near Nam Dong in the Central Highlands, which was defended by SF Detachment A-726 and a mixed force of ARVN, native, and Australian soldiers.

As the attack raged on, many of the camps' defensive positions began to run short of ammunition. Though wounded numerous times from enemy grenades and mortar fire, Captain Roger Donlon led the defense, helped move ammunition from a burning building and carry it to forward positions, and then helped drag wounded comrades to the rear. Wounded himself several times, his actions continued until Donlon was sure the camp was safe and all his men had been taken care of.

The dawn brought relief: Donlon's force still held Nam Dong; the surviving Viet

Cong headed back into the countryside, and Roger Donlon's heroism had caused him to earn the first Medal of Honor awarded in Vietnam.[53]

Donlon recovered from his wounds and quietly lives today in Kansas.

Colonel Roger Donlon's gallantry was not unique. Over the next decade, 5th SFG personnel would win 17 Medals of Honor, 60 Distinguished Service Crosses, 814 Silver Stars, 13,234 Bronze Stars, 235 Legions of Merit, 46 Distinguished Flying Crosses, and 2,658 Purple Hearts. They were by far the most decorated unit of the Vietnam War.

Though SF guys are justifiably proud of all these honors, it was that first Medal of Honor that set the standard for SF performance in combat. And to this day, pictures of this quiet, modest man hang on many SF office and team room walls. I'm told that when the days get tough, many SF guys will swing their eyes up to a photo of Donlon, and instantly remember why they're there.

Operation Kingpin: Bull Simons and the Son Tay Raid

Colonel Arthur "Bull" Simons, a veteran of World War II with the Rangers, became an SF soldier in the 1950s. By the time he arrived in Vietnam, he had a well-deserved reputation for leadership and toughness. Other men wanted to serve with him and follow him.

Simons's first major exploit in Vietnam occurred during the 1960s, as part of what was known as Operation White Star. Simons took 107 SF soldiers into Laos, where they recruited thousands of Meo tribesmen and led them on raids and ambushes against the Pathet Lao forces. After six months in the bush, he brought every one of his 107 SF soldiers safely home, an achievement that only added to an already impressive list of accomplishments.

And then in 1970, a truly special opportunity presented itself.

Let me fill in some background:

At that time, most American POWs in North Vietnam were held in the infamous "Hanoi Hilton" (its actual name was Hoa Lo). Conditions there—simply—were inhuman. There was little food (the staples were pumpkin soup and tainted bread), little opportunity for exercise of body or mind, and worst of all, except for interrogations and beatings, prisoners were kept in virtually total isolation. POWs depend on socializing with other POWs to keep their spirits up. Without this contact you can forget about morale. It was hard to maintain much faith or hope under the Hanoi Hilton regime.

Early in 1970, an unmanned reconnaissance drone snapped pictures of a new North Vietnamese POW camp west of Hanoi, at a bend in the Red River. The camp, known as Son Tay, was an overflow facility for the Hanoi Hilton, which by then was bursting at the seams with captured Americans. When the pictures were analyzed, the

---

53 The assault on Nam Dong became the basis for the John Wayne film *The Green Berets*. Though fictionalized, the situation presented in the film was accurate, as was the level of force the North Vietnamese used to attack the camp.

photo-interpreters found messages from the POWs: The more than fifty prisoners at Son Tay—not unsurprisingly—wanted to be rescued.[54]

Very soon, word went around Fort Bragg that Simons was looking for volunteers for a special mission. Before anyone knew its nature, more than five hundred SF soldiers had offered their services for it.

The mission, of course, was to rescue the Son Tay POWs.

It was called Operation Kingpin, and it was to be led by Simons. Operation Kingpin centered on a handpicked team of a hundred-plus volunteer SF soldiers, all SF veterans with experience in Southeast Asia.

In preparation for the mission, the volunteers went through months of specialized training at Eglin AFB in Florida; and by the time the raid was ready to go, they knew the Son Tay prison compound better than their own homes.[55] To insert the team into the camp, the Air Force provided a task force of long-range helicopters. To maximize surprise, the lead helicopter, carrying a special assault team, would be intentionally crashed into the center of the camp compound (there's more to this story, as we'll see shortly). Cover for the raid would be provided by decoy Air Force and Navy air strikes on Hanoi and Haiphong (Kingpin was a true joint operation, long before that term became fashionable).

President Richard Nixon authorized the Son Tay raid early in November 1970. The personnel and aircraft were immediately moved into place, and the raid was launched on November 21, 1970.

The raid was executed to near perfection. The lead helicopter crashed into the compound right on time, the guards were quickly killed, and the team swarmed over the compound looking for the prisoners. Meanwhile, the helicopter carrying Bull Simons and his part of the raiding force mistakenly landed a few kilometers from the camp, near what intelligence analysts had called "a secondary school." What they found was a barracks filled with several hundred enemy soldiers. The enemy put up a fight, and were all promptly killed.

When that job was finished, Simons and his guys loaded back on their helicopter and moved to the POW camp to finish the raid.

Unfortunately, as things turned out, they'd hit a dry hole. No POWs were in the camp. Some weeks earlier, they had been moved to another camp several miles away. Bitterly disappointed, Simons and his raiders loaded back aboard the helicopters and headed home.

Publicly, the raid looked like a failure. In actuality, the results were surprisingly positive. For one thing, the cost turned out to be very low (due partly to the excellent training and partly to luck)—total cost was an F-105G Wild Weasel aircraft shot down

---

54 It should be noted that the prisoners at Son Tay were treated somewhat better than they would have been at Hoa Lo. They were allowed to socialize and were expected to work in the local fields, which helped keep them more fit and sane.

55 To assist the Son Tay raiders in familiarizing themselves with the POW camp and its surroundings, a large-scale model was constructed (at a cost of $60,000, code-named "Barbara") by a special shop at the CIA. In addition, a collapsible full-scale model was built at Eglin AFB for dress rehearsals. Because the full-scale model could be dismantled, Soviet photo-reconnaissance satellites were unable to detect the training area or infer the mission's target. Today, visitors can view "Barbara" at the Special Forces museum at Fort Bragg. (The museum itself, I should note, was recently renamed for Colonel "Bull" Simons.)

The Arthur "Bull" Simons Memorial on the day of its dedication at Fort Bragg, North Carolina. A legendary Special Forces soldier, he led the Son Tay Raid into North Vietnam in 1970.

JOHN D. GRESHAM

during the decoy raids (both crewmen ejected and were rescued), and a single SF soldier with an injured leg.

Far more important, however, the raid taught the North Vietnamese some important lessons:

First, with the threat of further raids hanging over their heads, the North Vietnamese pulled all the POWs back to Hoa Lo in Hanoi. Now they were kept eight and ten to a cell . . . not exactly an ideal way to live, but if you're a POW, contact with fellow POWs is a heap better than isolation. Morale skyrocketed.

Second, the North Vietnamese began to cast a cold eye in the direction of world opinion. What would happen, they wondered, if tortured and emaciated POWs were rescued and put before TV cameras?

The result was better treatment for the Americans. Vicious interrogation sessions ended, food got better and more plentiful, and conditions in general improved. The prisoners, they realized, were more useful as pawns than as scapegoats.

As for the prisoners themselves, the Son Tay raid gave them hope that up to then had eluded them. For the first time during the Vietnam War, they realized that their country had showed it still cared about the POWs. It had proved, at least, that it still at least had "the guts to try."[56]

An SF failure, in other words, had turned into another legendary SF victory.

---

[56] After the war, Texas computer magnate Ross Perot threw a party for the Son Tay raiders and the men they'd tried to rescue. Even as most of their fellow countrymen were turning their backs on Vietnam veterans, Perot wanted the raiders to understand how much the POWs and their loved ones treasured what they'd tried to do . . . Flash forward to Iran, where several of Perot's employees are held hostage during the Islamic Revolution. Who does Perot turn to for help? Bull Simons. Simons then led a force of Perot's executives into Iran and, without loss or casualty, successfully retrieved the hostages.

Dick Meadows: The Eternal Warrior

Who is the all-time greatest Special Forces soldier?

Don't ask that question around the SF world unless you want a hot argument. The guys who've completed the SF "Q" Course are a special breed of human to begin with, and then many of these go on to extraordinary careers, filled with incredible accomplishments. Trying to choose the best is like choosing the all-time most beautiful woman. The vast number and variety of top contenders makes the choice hopeless.

And yet, mention one name among SF soldiers and you're sure to get a warm smile and a gentle nodding of heads—Major Richard "Dick" Meadows. Dick Meadows is the quintessential Special Forces soldier, seemingly sprung directly from the brow of the god of Special Forces.

Dick Meadows came to the Army early, enlisting at age fifteen, and soon became the youngest master sergeant in the Army. In 1953, he joined the 10th SFG. Though he would eventually serve in groups around the world (including an exchange tour with the elite British Special Air Service), it was in Southeast Asia that Meadows performed the exploits that would make his name legendary.

Eventually Meadows would serve three tours with the 5th SFG in Vietnam. He was, for example, a member of Simon's White Star team. As one of Simon's patrol leaders, he led native Meo warriors against the Pathet Lao. His skills as a jungle fighter and patrol leader so impressed the leadership in Saigon that he was given a field commission to captain personally by General William Westmoreland, the first such commission of the war for an enlisted man.

But it was the Son Tay raid that took him into the history books. It was Meadows who conceived the idea of intentionally crashing a helicopter loaded with SF raiders into the prison compound courtyard (he'd correctly judged that that was the quickest way to insert them), and he personally led the team. During the mission, when it became obvious that the camp was empty, he got his team back to the main raiding force helicopters. Every man came home safely.

In the years following Vietnam, Dick Meadows spent his remaining time in the Army as an instructor.

In theory, he retired in 1977 after thirty years of service. In actuality, even though his official connection with the U.S. Army had been severed, he just kept on being an SF soldier.

Thus in the late 1970s, Colonel Chargin' Charlie Beckwith hired him as a training consultant for the Delta Force. Shortly after that, in 1980, the CIA realized there were no on-the-ground personnel to support the Iranian hostage rescue mission. Meadows was therefore tapped to go to Tehran to do the job.

Given cover as an Irish businessman, he personally reconnoitered the Embassy complex, recruited and trained support operatives, bought and prepared trucks and other transportation assets, and made ready for Beckwith's and the Delta Force's arrival.

And then, when the rescue mission at Desert One was aborted (and in chaos), he was left hanging. The CIA had somehow neglected to let him know that the rescue

The memorial to Major Dick Meadows next to the U.S. Special Operations Command building at Fort Bragg, North Carolina. Meadows was an indestructible Special Forces soldier, whose exploits ranged from Vietnam and Laos to Iran.

JOHN D. GRESHAM

force had been recalled (he read about it in the Iranian press), and had left him in Tehran on his own.

Not to worry. He conducted his own escape and evasion, and made it safely home yet again.

During the 1980s, Meadows continued to train counterterrorist professionals throughout the world, and would still be at it but for the single battle he lost. In 1995, he was struck down by leukemia, which was discovered less than two months before he died.

Dick Meadows died amid a flood of citations, accolades, decorations, and medals. Whatever decoration it was possible to get, he got . . . *except* the Medal of Honor. (Though as one close friend remarked, "If the record of his classified missions is ever made public, he'll get that one, too!")

Today three reminders of Dick Meadows enduringly remain in the Special Forces: his son Mark, now an Army Ranger officer; a bronze statue in the courtyard of USASOC headquarters; and finally a special SOCOM award, in his name, given each year to an outstanding young processional officer in the command.

For all this, I proudly nominate Dick Meadows as the Special Forces eternal warrior. Meadows represents everything that is good, smart, and professional about this unique breed of men.

I somehow feel that most SF professionals will drink to this without too much dissent.

The Lean Years

Like the rest of the American military establishment, the Special Forces were punished in the 1970s for the failure in Vietnam. This translated into the disestablishment of the 1st, 3rd, 6th, and 8th SFGs, fully half the community. There were, in fact, proposals to completely eliminate SOF capabilities, and only the determined efforts of a few visionaries kept the Special Forces alive. I could go on for pages about the misery SF soldiers and other SOF units suffered during this period, but one story will suffice.

At some point during the dark years of the Carter administration, some people in the Army came up with an initiative that would allow the Army to hold on to the remaining SF capability (the 5th and 7th SFGs). The program was called Special Proficiency at Rugged Training and Nation Building (SPARTAN); and on the face of it, it was a dumb idea—not because the work proposed was a waste, but it was a waste to use SFGs (some with years of field experience) to do it. On the other hand, the make-work may have saved the SFGs.

In any event, SPARTAN sent SF soldiers into depressed areas of the United States, where they were assigned jobs much like those of the Depression-era Civil Conservation Corps. They built roads and bridges, provided medical treatment, and performed other worthwhile services, primarily among impoverished inhabitants of North Carolina's Hoke and Anson counties, and Indian tribes in Florida, Arizona, and Montana.

Noble though these services were, they were hardly what SF soldiers had joined up to do. All the same, Project SPARTAN demonstrated what they were willing to put up with to keep their community alive.

I hang my head that professional warriors had to do such things . . . yet take pride that they were willing to do them. Thanks, guys!

Fighting Back

The administration of President Ronald Reagan changed all that. And during the 1980s, Special Forces, along with the rest of the U.S. military community, rebuilt. Now the largest component of the new SOCOM, they not only restored much of their lost community (the 1st and 3rd SFGs were reactivated) but helped to expand American influence and power (as for example, in El Salvador).

More important, the renewed Special Forces proved themselves yet again in the crucible of battle.

In December 1989, Operation Just Cause was executed against Panamanian strongman Manuel Noriega. General Maxwell Thurman, the U.S. Southern Command commander in chief, made SOF units the spearhead of the invasion, with SF soldiers a crucial component of that spearhead. SF teams conducted the full spectrum of Special Forces missions. They raided command-and-control facilities, fought a number of vicious firefights with Panamanian defense units, and took large numbers of prisoners.

And then, just months after Just Cause, SF troops were operating in the deserts of the Persian Gulf.

Despite General Schwarzkopf's shortsighted attitude toward Special Forces (see the first chapter), the SF deployment in Desert Shield/Storm was the largest since Vietnam. Both the 3rd and 5th SFGs moved their full strength to Saudi Arabia in support of the allied coalition, and immediately found useful work . . . though not what they wanted to do most. Because they had the largest group of Arabic speakers in the military, they were in the best position to set up an underground rebel movement in Kuwait. (Schwarzkopf nixed this plan. He didn't want people he couldn't control in situations that could jumpstart the war before he was ready to begin it.)

Failing that, SF soldiers became liaison officers to the many Arab and Muslim allied units in the coalition (a job they would have had even if the Kuwait mission had been okayed). SF soldiers rode into battle with their allies as advisors and observers, and were among the first troops to enter the liberated Kuwait City in February 1991.

Meanwhile, as soon as the decision was made to conduct a ground offensive against Iraq, several dozen SF teams were inserted deep into enemy territory, where they gathered critical intelligence on Iraqi troop movements that greatly helped the ground commanders during the 100 Hour War. (Though a couple of the teams were compromised when Bedouin civilians stumbled over their hide sites, all managed to escape back to friendly lines.)

During the decade following the Gulf War, Special Forces soldiers have played a major part in every important U.S. military operation, including those in Haiti, Rwanda, and the Balkans, even as Special Forces Command continues the more "normal" missions, quietly training and assisting our allies to better manage and protect their interests.

Right now, the soldiers of the SFC are among the most trusted of America's warriors by the national leadership . . . a situation they both value and regret. Though it's nice to be trusted, that has a downside: It means they're given more missions than they can handle.

Special Forces Command: The Green Berets

Special Forces Command, which is commanded by an Army major (two-star) general, is not only the largest community within SOCOM (with over half the 30,000 SOF personnel billets), it is also the most operationally active. At any given moment, forty to sixty SF detachments are conducting missions around the world, giving them an OpTempo even higher than the Navy's aircraft carrier battle groups (CVBGs) or the USMC Marine Expeditionary Units—Special Operations Capable (MEU [SOC]s). In fact, according to the usual measure of such things—man-days per year out of area (i.e., overseas)—the Special Forces are America's busiest warriors.

They are also probably the most "joint" of American units. That is, SF detachments in the field work with a wider variety of units and personnel from other services and nations than any other military community in the U.S. They regularly accept transportation from the U.S. Air Force or Navy, frequently exercise with the USMC,

and every year conduct field operations overseas (downrange) in up to a hundred countries. Clearly, this places a heavy burden on SFC.

SFC, itself only created in 1989 in the wake of Goldwater-Nichols, has cradle-to-grave responsibility for every facet of Special Forces life: SFC keeps a direct watch over the JFK training center, which recruits and trains new SF soldiers; it controls the various SF groups, their organization, equipment, and training; and it is the clearing-house for SF operations, and must be consulted before *any* deployment or mission is authorized.

Like the other major components within SOCOM (Rangers, SEALs, etc.), SFC has almost total control over how their units are structured, trained, equipped, and tasked. Such control can be frustrating to those wishing to task SFC for missions, yet it ensures that the Special Forces troops actually have the wherewithal to do the job. Every request for a mission or tasking gets a hard, professional scrub by people who understand the special needs and limitations of SF soldiers and units. The power to carefully review, and even delay, unrealistic requests is just good sense in the long term.

There is much more to SFC than its control function. Let's take a closer look at this, and at the units it operates.

The Fortress: Special Forces Command Headquarters

Fort Bragg, North Carolina, is among America's largest and busiest military bases. Located between the sand hills and coastal plains of North Carolina, it has been the center of America's rapid reaction forces since the Second World War. On the

The U.S. Army Special Operations Command headquarters at Fort Bragg, North Carolina. This massive building contains the command elements for the Special Forces, along with other Army Special Operations components.

eastern side of this massive base are the headquarters, barracks, and other facilities for the 82nd Airborne Division and XVIII Airborne Corps.

But it is on the southeastern side of the base where our interest lies. Near the original SF training site on Smoke Bomb Hill is situated the fortresslike headquarters of both U.S. Army Special Operations Command and Special Forces Command—a massive red brick monument to the present-day military obsession with force protection. It has all the charm and warmth of a medieval castle, which was surely the intent when it was designed in the mid-1990s.[57] All it lacks is a moat. Except for the carefully groomed lawns, shrubbery, and walks, the place screams, "Keep Away! The stuff inside's too serious for the likes of you!" Even the parking lot is carefully secured: concrete barriers separate the building from the lot, and there are no "Visitor" spaces. (I had to park almost 200 yards from the main door, across a steaming, mind-frying parking lot.) Inside, security is even tighter, with computer-controlled turnstiles and armed guards.

Special Forces Command Leadership

The leadership of Special Forces Command traditionally keeps a low profile. Most heads of the various communities and component commands have spent their professional lives behind a curtain of security. Few have any desire to come out. And yet—despite the organization's instinctive clannishness and reticence—when I needed them to be open to me, they were as open as they could be. I'm very grateful for the access they allowed me.

At the top of the SFC chain of command is Major General William G. Boykin, a quiet, deeply religious, almost reclusive career SOF professional, with extensive

---

[57] I should note that U.S. government buildings around the world have been getting "harder" as a result of the plague of terrorist bombings over the past two decades. Poor security and force protection have cost lives, and no military commander wants to be found negligent in such matters.

experience in Special Forces and other USASOC units (he previously commanded the Delta Force and was a staff officer within Joint Special Operations Command, two of America's darkest and most secretive units).

General Boykin has a number of key objectives. These include:

- **Operations Tempo**—Over the last decade, the pace of overseas SF operations has approached the breaking point. Consider the table below, which shows the number of countries and missions run by SF personnel in the mid-1990s, as well as the number of personnel involved overall and on each mission:

	FY92	FY93	FY94	FY95	FY96	FY97
Countries Involved	72	121	150	184	167	131
Missions Run	495	554	1,066	1,593	2,325	2,183
Personnel Deployed	14,678	15,192	16,012	17,022	20,642	21,951
Personnel Per Mission	29.65	27.42	15.02	10.69	8.88	10.06

The trends are disturbing: During the past decade, the number of countries receiving missions has roughly doubled; the total number of missions has risen a mind-numbing 400%; the number of personnel deployed has grown fully 50%; and the number of personnel involved in each mission has dropped by almost two thirds.

How does this translate into real terms? It means, first, that every SF soldier must spend up to 180 days downrange per year. Second, because the number of personnel per mission has dropped, each mission must now be staffed with *less* than a full twelve-man A-Team.

In other words: the U.S. government is dangerously overworking the Special Forces; and as we've already seen, many SF soldiers are voting with their feet. High OpTempos are causing SF soldiers to leave the service . . . which of course puts even more strain on the teams that are deployed.

General Boykin has worked hard to provide his troops relief, as did General Bowra before him (General Bowra went on to command SWC). Even before 1998, when General Boykin took command, there were minor improvements, as the Fiscal Year 1997 figures reveal. General Boykin, continuing the trend, has pushed the State Department to reduce the number of overseas missions, mandated minimum "down" time back at home base, and provided better forward-deployed facilities and services.

- **Combat Skills**—In General Boykin's view, the emphasis on peacekeeping, humanitarian, and other noncombat operations may have caused the combat skills of the Special Forces to decline. Therefore, a greater training focus is now being placed on combat drills and exercises. He has also increased SF participation at large-scale training exercises, such as those at the Joint Readiness Training Center (JRTC—located at Fort Polk, Louisiana), the National Training Center (NTC—at Fort Irwin, California), and the big Joint Task Force Exercises (JTFEXs).

- **Quality of Life**—Nobody doubts that the SF lifestyle is hard on personal relationships, and that the kinds of people who are attracted to SF can be difficult to live with. (The joke that anyone who survives more than five years of service on the teams without a divorce is not working hard enough contains more than a little truth.) In order to provide his SF troops and their families with something better, General Boykin has done what he could to lessen the intrusions upon his people's private time, by, for example, reducing OpTempos, by allowing soldiers to fully use their accumulated leave, and by giving more time off in general—where possible.

- **Modernization**—The Special Forces have spent the majority of their history using equipment and supplies developed for conventional military units. Now that much of this gear has become worn out or obsolete, SFC has stood up its own procurement shop (G7) to help develop and procure the "stuff" that SF soldiers will need into the early twenty-first century.

- **Infrastructure**—The rebirth of Special Forces in the 1980s did not change the condition of the places they call home (usually the poorest and least desirable real estate on Army posts). Most of these were falling apart. Some groups had headquarters and barracks buildings that dated back to the Second World War. Though change has been slow, that situation *has* changed, and with the exception of the 5th SFG (at Fort Campbell, Kentucky), who are still waiting for new buildings and facilities, all the SF units are getting new purpose-built headquarters, barracks, and training facilities.

Supporting General Boykin is a compact command staff, reflecting the lean character of the Special Forces: His command sergeant major is Mike Bishop, while the deputy commanding general is Brigadier General John Scales (who is actually assigned to the National Guard). There is a chief of staff, along with the usual staff officers for intelligence (G-2), operations (G-3), and so on, as well as a chaplain. All told, SFC has only about a hundred military and twenty civilian staff assigned to run a command of more than 10,000 personnel with a worldwide mission . . . a tiny number compared with other military units of comparable size. This says a lot about the no-nonsense nature of the Special Forces.

One measure of combat units is called the "nose-to-tail" ratio, referring to the number of combat troops compared to support personnel. In a typical Army combat unit, this runs about one out of three. By comparison, SF units typically have two out of every three personnel assigned to combat roles. In other words, every SF unit, from the office of the commanding general to the smallest detachment, is lean and combat-oriented.

The Groups: The Sharp Edge

The twelve-man Operational Detachment Alpha, as we've seen, is the basic SF unit. But these units do not go on missions alone. Every ODA is part of a larger parent unit, called a Special Force Group—Airborne,[58] of which there are a total of seven. Though all seven share a similar organization and structure, each carries its own history, missions, and cultures (and two of them are part of the Army National Guard, meaning that they are manned by part-time "weekend warriors"). A few small units are also assigned to SFC, which need to be looked at because of their growing relevance in the current world climate.

One quick caution: I will be introducing you to a number of real-world personnel. Since it's in the job description that military personnel are moved around a lot, what you will see is a "snapshot" that reflects the status of the various groups around March 1st, 1999. And since I will be describing men whose regular trips downrange place them at a relatively high risk of hostile action, I will only give a few names.

Structure: Makeup of a Special Forces Group

When Colonel Aaron Bank set up the 10th SFG in 1952, he was surely unaware that he was designing a template that would survive for half a century (with no sign of wearing out). Today, seven SFGs make up the fighting power of the SFC. Except for the 75th Ranger Regiment at Fort Benning, Georgia, they are the largest SOF units in the U.S. military. And with apologies to the fine fighting qualities of the Rangers, I defy any other combat unit in the world to conduct a wider variety of tasks than a deployed SFG.

Let's review the complement of a fully manned ODA:

- **Command**—The command of an ODA is given to an SF captain (18A), and his executive officer, a warrant officer (180A).
- **Operations/Planning**—The jobs of operations planning and intelligence are split between two senior sergeants. A master sergeant acts as the team sergeant and the operations non-commissioned officer (NCO—18Z). He is assisted by another more junior NCO, with specialization in intelligence and operations (18F).
- **Weapons**—The A-Team has two NCOs assigned as weapons specialists (18B). Again, one is senior to the other, with both carrying the same specialty code.
- **Engineering**—As with the weapons section, two engineering (18C) NCOs are assigned to each A-Team.
- **Medical**—Two of the SF's superb medical specialists (18D) are assigned to each A-Team. They are among the busiest and most valuable personnel in the SFC.
- **Communications**—Each A-Team has two communications (18E) NCOs.

As is normal with SF personnel, the team members are cross-trained in other skills, in the event of casualties, split-team operations, or a shortage of personnel prior to a mission deployment. All have regionally relevant language skills and training to deal with local cultural sensitivities, traditions, and mores.

---

58 While all SF units are "Airborne" units (every SF soldier must be fully jump qualified while on operational status), and properly so called, I'll use the shorter version and refer to them simply as SFGs.

Special Forces Company Headquarters
Operational Detachment Alpha
A-Team

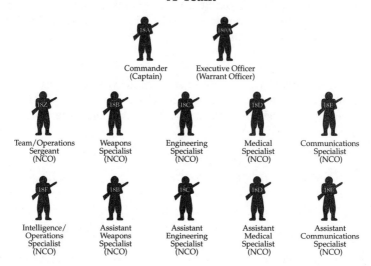

The structure and personnel of a Special Forces Operational Detachment Alpha (ODA), or A-Team.

RUBICON, INC., BY LAURA DeNINNO

To build an SFG, you start by grouping six ODAs into a company. To these are added an Operational Detachment Bravo (ODB), which acts as the company headquarters. There are communications (18E) and engineering (18C) specialists. A company warrant (180A) provides operational expertise and leadership, with an SF major (18A) and sergeant major (18Z) commanding.

This SF company then provides the core units for the next piece in the SFG: the SF battalion.

Each SF battalion is composed of three SF companies, a support company (logistics, transportation, etc.), and a headquarters and headquarters detachment (HHD). The SF battalion HHD is composed of thirty-seven personnel, including a lieutenant colonel (18A) commander, a major (18A) executive officer, and a command sergeant major (1800Z). Officially called an Operational Detachment Charlie, the battalion headquarters has a full operations staff, as well as medical, communications, engineering, intelligence, and even civil personnel.

The three SF companies—labeled Alpha (A), Bravo (B), and Charlie (C)—are each marked for particular specialty tasks. Thus for example, A-Company is assigned to maintain on ODA capable of military free-fall (MFF) parachute operations, while B-Company has an A-Team qualified for underwater operations (UWO).

All told, the SF battalion has a total of 383 personnel, which makes the SF battalion a self-contained SOF force, requiring only intelligence, logistic, and transportation support from higher headquarters and agencies to begin operations. In fact, when a major regional contingency (MRC . . . a nice way of saying that the shit is

Special Forces Company Headquarters
Operational Detachment Bravo
B-Team

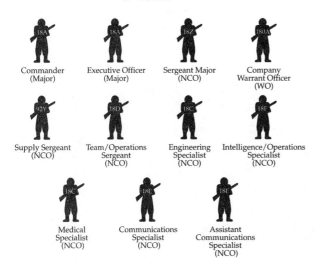

Commander (Major)	Executive Officer (Major)	Sergeant Major (NCO)	Company Warrant Officer (WO)
Supply Sergeant (NCO)	Team/Operations Sergeant (NCO)	Engineering Specialist (NCO)	Intelligence/Operations Specialist (NCO)
Medical Specialist (NCO)	Communications Specialist (NCO)	Assistant Communications Specialist (NCO)	

The structure and personnel of a Special Forces Company Headquarters, Operational Detachment Bravo (ODB), or B-Team.

RUBICON, INC., BY LAURA DeNINNO

hitting the fan[59]) breaks out somewhere, the first response from SOCOM is frequently an SF battalion sending in its lead company.

The final step is to group three SF battalions together with another HHC/ODC (89 personnel—about twice the size of the battalion HHD) and a group support company (144 troops). This creates a complete group, which is roughly the strength of a traditional Army infantry brigade, and has a total of 1,382 personnel, two thirds of which are in the teams as deployable, mission-ready SF soldiers.

Each SFG (including the two ANG—Army National Guard—groups) has been assigned to conduct and support operations in particular parts of the world. This means that the personnel all have appropriate language and cultural training, and the group HHC constantly monitors the political and military situation in their assigned region. This means that some portion of the group may actually be forward deployed or based, so that transit times to a crisis zone can be reduced. Thus 10th SFG still maintains a battalion based in Germany. 1st SFG has one in Okinawa and 7th SFG has a company in Puerto Rico.

The regional orientation has a number of interesting consequences. For example, the assigned region frequently defines the culture and lifestyle of a particular group. There is a standing joke in the 7th SFG (which covers Latin America) that an unmarried SF soldier will bring home a Latino wife before he's been deployed downrange twice. And in 1st SFG (assigned to the Far East), oriental food and spouses are the norm.

More to the point, the noncombat missions overseas ensure a likelihood there'll be an ODA near a breaking crisis. A quick change of orders and clothing can instantly transform a team conducting humanitarian or training operations into a special recon-

---

59 The "c" in MRC will at times also stand for "crisis" or "conflict." Contingency, crisis, or conflict, it's all the same—BIG trouble.

**Special Forces Battalion Headquarters
Operational Detachment Charlie
C-Team**

Executive Officer
(Major)

Commander
(Lieutenant Colonel)

Command Sergeant
Major (NCO)

Medical
Section

Battalion
Staff

Communications
Section

The structure and personnel of a Special Forces Battalion Headquarters, Operational Detachment Charlie (ODC), or C-Team.

RUBICON, INC., BY LAURA DeNINNO

naissance team ready to be inserted into the trouble spot. This has often put reliable eyes on a situation just hours or minutes after the outbreak of trouble. To say that politicians and diplomats find such capabilities useful is an understatement.

1st Special Forces Group

We'll start our tour at what is arguably the prettiest spot in the SF world: Fort Lewis, Washington, near Tacoma at the southern end of Puget Sound, and within sight (on a clear day) of Mount Rainier. Fort Lewis is a hub for all variety of Pacific coast

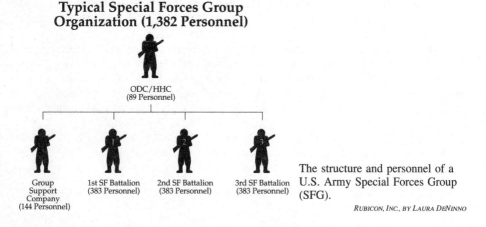

**Typical Special Forces Group
Organization (1,382 Personnel)**

ODC/HHC
(89 Personnel)

Group
Support
Company
(144 Personnel)

1st SF Battalion
(383 Personnel)

2nd SF Battalion
(383 Personnel)

3rd SF Battalion
(383 Personnel)

The structure and personnel of a U.S. Army Special Forces Group (SFG).

RUBICON, INC., BY LAURA DeNINNO

U.S. Army Special Forces Command Structure

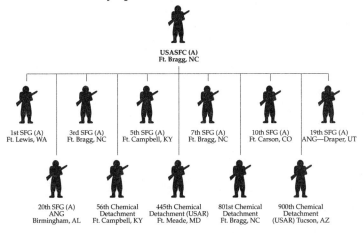

The units and organization of the U.S. Army Special Force Command.

RUBICON, INC., BY LAURA DENINNO

military operations; and nearby McCord AFB will soon be home to the second operational wing of C-17A Globemaster III heavy-lift cargo jets, the choice carrier of logistics professionals everywhere. Also based at Fort Lewis is the U.S. Army's I Corps, commanded by an old friend, Lieutenant General George Crocker.[60]

Over on the north side of the post is the new home of the 1st SFG. Built in the same style as the other new SF headquarters complexes, it is low to the ground and recessed into a hill. All around the headquarters are barracks, training facilities, and other buildings, as well as the requisite security fences and surveillance cameras.

A trip inside the 1st SFG headquarters (after a quick ID check) got me a surprisingly good cup of Army coffee and an informative visit with the commanding officer, Colonel Thomas R. Csrnko (pronounced Chernko) and his command sergeant major (SGM) James McDaniel.

The 1st provides SF services to the U.S. Pacific Command (whose CINC is Admiral Dennis Blair). PACOM covers an area from the West Coast of the U.S. to the India/Pakistani border (and includes Korea, whose U.S. commander is General John H. Tilleli, Jr.). In between is an area covering almost half the known world. Or, as Colonel Csrnko proudly likes to point out, the 1st SFG's area of responsibility covers more square miles, people, cultures, and languages than that of the rest of the groups combined. In fact, the region contains over three billion people, as much as the rest of the world combined.

This can stretch the personnel thin. Luckily, they get help from one of the ANG groups.

Like the other groups within SFC, 1st SFG is composed of three SF battalions, but only two of these are actually based at Fort Lewis, the 2/1 SFG and the 3/1 SFG.

---

60 We last saw General Crocker as commander of the 82nd Airborne Division in *Airborne* (Berkley Books, 1997). He has since been promoted to lieutenant general, and given command of I Corps.

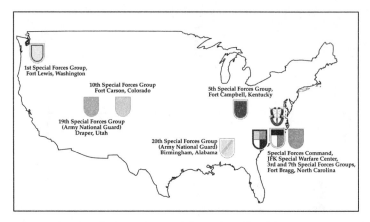

A map showing the home bases of the various Special Forces Command units in the continental United States.

RUBICON, INC., BY LAURA DeNINNO

Because of the time and distances involved in rapidly moving personnel and gear across the Pacific, the 1st Battalion of the 1st SFG (1/1 SFG) is forward-based on Okinawa, and commanded by a lieutenant colonel. 1/1 SFG provides a rapid response capability in the event of a conflict in Korea, Taiwan, the Philippines, or other Far East hot spot.[61]

Originally formed in 1960 to support the Vietnam War, the 1st SFG traces its spiritual lineage back to the 2nd Company of the 1st Battalion, 1st Regiment, 1st Special Service Force (the Devil's Brigade). In 1974, following Vietnam, they were disestablished at Fort Bragg, and the group colors were cased and preserved for almost a decade, in anticipation of the day that they might be needed again.

That happened in the 1980s, during the Reagan expansion of the Special Forces, and the group now provides SFC and the nation a solid base of skills in jungle, winter, and mountain warfare, along with skills in countermine operations.

So what exactly is 1st SFG doing out there in Asia these days? Quite a bit actually.

Their missions break down into four distinct areas. They include:

- **Contingencies**—Without question, the single biggest worry for 1st SFG continues to be the threat from North Korea. Thus the group has a continuing presence in South Korea, as well as a significant place in operations plans in the event of a communist invasion. 1st SFG also stands ready to support U.S. interests in Taiwan, Thailand, and other allied nations in the area, in the event of conflict.[62] As for

---

61 1st SFG also maintains a single ODA in Korea, to support operations along the DMZ.

62 Officially, Taiwan is not part of the regional 1st SFG operations plan. Because of the "One China" policy, which has since 1973 recognized the People's Republic of China as the sole government of China, Taiwan (officially known as the Republic of China) is something of a "nonnation." Even so, the U.S. maintains extremely close military ties with the nationalist Chinese.

The official shoulder flash (emblem) of the 1st Special Forces Group (Airborne)

emerging threats, the group is watching closely the growth of China's military, and the ethnic and economic chaos along the Java barrier.

• **Operations**—Over the past few years, 1st SFG has been involved in two kinds of ongoing operations. The first is the effort to support demining and unexploded ordnance (UXO) disposal in Southeast Asia. Worldwide, disposal of mines and UXO is a major problem, and has become a significant public health hazard. Areas containing mines and UXO are obviously hazardous, and thus unusable for cultivation or raising livestock. 1st SFG has been involved in ninety-day rotations into Thailand, Cambodia, and Laos, to support the training of personnel to remove these hazardous war relics. The Laotian effort has been particularly successful, with the program due to come to a close within a year or two. The other ongoing 1st SFG operation has included support of counterdrug efforts in PACOM. Each year, the group sends eight ODAs on thirty-day overseas rotations to selected nations, where they conduct training with law enforcement and military units to improve their skills at slowing the flow of narcotics.

• **JCS Exercises**—When an SFG sends an ODA overseas for a particular job or mission, it is always at the direction of the Joint Chiefs of Staff, and has the support of the State Department, the host nation, and a number of other coordinating agencies. For our purposes, these missions come under the heading of "JCS exercises." These cover a variety of tasks, most have code names (which can tell you where they take place and what they are about), and most fall under the heading of the Joint Combined Exercise Training (JCET) program. JCETs normally involve only one or two ODAs, possibly with an ODB to provide command and control. JCET missions are designed primarily to conduct ODA training, though sometimes they are conducted in support of humanitarian or civil engineering projects. (SF *training* is, of course, always the primary goal of *any* JCET mission.) This is a sampling of the JCET missions being run by 1st SFG:

—**Ulchi Focus Lens/Foal Eagle**—In Korea, 1st SFG has been running a pair of large-scale (battalion-sized) headquarters defense exercises that run for weeks at a time.

—**Cobra Gold**—Held annually in Thailand, a 1st SFG battalion acts as the Joint Special Operations Task Force (JSOTF) headquarters for a large force of I Corps troops and Marines doing force-on-force training with regional military forces.

—**Balikatan**—A somewhat smaller (company-sized) operation held in the Philippines, Balikatan is a force-on-force training exercise. It allows the Philippine military to practice critical low-intensity conflict skills.

—**Balance-series JCETs**[63]—Every year, PACOM schedules 1st SFG to run nearly forty JCET missions, of which about 80% are actually run. (The other 20% are not run because there can be as much as eighteen months between planning for missions and their execution. During that time, governments and economies fall, wars occur, and politics change.)

1/1st SFG runs approximately twelve, while the other two battalions usually execute around nine each. In FY99, 1st SFG planned to run Balance (B.) Iron (Indonesia), B. Mint (Malaysia), B. Saber (Singapore), B. Magic (Mongolia), B. Nail (Nepal), B. Tiger (Tonga), and B. Passion (Papua New Guinea), among others.

• **CONUS Training**—Along with their overseas missions, the 1st SFG conducted a full array of training in the continental United States (CONUS). This included a pair of JRTC rotations for the 2nd and 3rd battalions (1st is excluded because of its forward basing), as well as support for counterdrug training and proficiency training for live-fire, winter war, and mountain operations.

3rd Special Forces Group

Once you're at USASOC headquarters at Fort Bragg, getting to the 3rd SFG is easy. All you have to do is walk out the front door, go two hundred yards across the parking lot, jog over a small road, and you are there. The 3rd SFG is housed in a new buff-colored headquarters building much like the 1st SFG's at Fort Lewis. Here you will run into Colonel Gary Jones and his CSM David Farmer.

The 3rd, like the 1st, was stood up as an SFG in 1960, served during the 1960s, was disestablished (in 1969), and was reactivated in the 1980s. The 3rd also traces its lineage back to the Devil's Brigade—in their case, the HHC detachment of the 1st Battalion, 2nd Regiment.

Their area of responsibility is a new one for SFC. For the first time, an SFG's primary orientation is toward Africa. With the exception of the nations along the horn of Africa (Sudan, Egypt, Eritrea, Djibouti, Somalia, Ethiopia, and Kenya), which, because of the Muslim connection, lie within the AOR of CENTCOM and the 5th

---

63 "Balance" is the Department of Defense code word used to denote 1st SFG operations in PACOM. Every 1st SFG operation has a two-word designator, the first word of which is always "Balance."

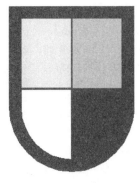

The official shoulder flash (emblem) of the 3rd Special Forces Group (Airborne)

SFG, the entire continent is now within the AOR of the 3rd SFG (under the overall command of the CINC of EUCOM). Before the change, they had to share North Africa with 10th SFG (under EUCOM) and East Africa with 5th SFG. This AOR unity should allow the group to develop better long-term relationships within the AOR, and maintain a better focus.

During the Cold War, the U.S. viewed Africa mainly as a provider of natural resources. Since the chief threat to the obtaining of these resources was seen as left-wing revolutions, U.S. policy toward Africa was aimed at stability—in other words, it was a policy of connivance with the status quo, which explains the decades-long tolerance of South Africa's policy of apartheid, and dictators like Nigeria's General Sani Abacha. The status did not, however, remain quo, and by the end of the Cold War, Africa was racked by war, insurrection, ethnic and racial tension, environmental and ecological troubles, and the alarming spread of the HIV virus.

A decade after the end of the Cold War, much has changed in Africa. South Africa has a strong, multiracial democracy, the wars of insurrection seem to be playing themselves out (though the civil war in Angola is still a serious problem), and the region generally seems to be sorting itself out.

Though significant problems still exist, so do vast opportunities, and the 3rd SFG is trying to exploit these.

All three battalions of the 3rd SFG are based at Fort Bragg, and there is no permanent forward-based presence on the African continent.

As might be imagined, this has both advantages and disadvantages. The major advantage is that the group can train and work together. The downside is that most deployments are "expeditionary" in nature, involving air travel of up to 6,000 miles, and teams then must operate on the least-developed continent on earth. All of this places a premium on field, cultural, and language skills.

Like the other groups, 3rd SFG has a full plate of training, exercise, and other activities, the full group was deployed to Saudi Arabia for Desert Storm in 1990–1991 and to Haiti for Uphold Democracy in 1995.

Does that mean there's not enough work for them in Africa? Hardly.

Their regular missions these days include:

- **Contingencies**—The soldiers of the 3rd SFG have been greatly relieved at the decline in serious contingency situations in Africa: South Africa seems to be making real progress; the nasty little West African civil wars have apparently been resolved; and a democratic turnover of power seems to have occurred in Nigeria. On the other hand, the civil war continues in Angola; Congo is a mess; the tribal problems in central Africa remain ugly; and there seems to be no lessening of the HIV crisis. Still, there exists very little potential for an MRC within the AOR.

- **Operations**—The most important long-term 3rd SFG operation is called the African Crisis Response Initiative. ACRI is among the most exciting ideas in recent diplomatic/military history . . . and it is quite possibly a model for programs in other regions, such as Southeast Asia and Latin America. Both the end of the Cold War and the French government's relinquishing of its traditional colonial-era responses to African instability have left a significant power vacuum on the African continent. Though Africa is a far less chaotic place than it has been, the seeds of further conflict still remain. In order to deal with such contingencies, the U.S. Department of State, in 1996, initiated ACRI, a program designed to build a powerful and rapidly deployable force of peacekeepers, manned entirely by troops from selected African nations (with the 3rd SFG as the operational control and training agency). The force will be highly interoperable (standard ammunition, communications, and logistics chains, etc.) and able to rapidly move into a war zone to bring it under control. So far, 3rd SFG has trained over two thousand African troops from six nations (Ghana, Malawi, Mali, Senegal, Uganda, and Benin), with others waiting to join.

- **JCS Exercises**—ACRI missions have all been four or five ODAs backed up by an ODB for command and control and CA specialists to work with local cultures. Approximately seventy SF soldiers are dispatched overseas for up to seventy days at a time. In addition to ACRI, the 3rd SFG sends out dozens of JCETs, conducting the same kinds of missions that 1st SFG and the other groups run. And, as previously mentioned, it periodically runs missions to augment groups in other AORs.

- **CONUS Training**—Like other SFGs, the 3rd makes regular rotations to JRTC, NTC, and the usual litany of specialty and refresher training programs. These include desert warfare training, advanced parachute jumping, AMOUT, and other skills necessary for working in their vast AOR.

5th Special Forces Group

If there is a SFG which stands out as "tough," it has to be the 5th.

For starters: They are the primary SOF unit within the Special Operations Command of U.S. Central Command (SOCCENT). This means they have the almost impossible task of covering the Muslim areas of the Middle East, the Persian Gulf, the Horn of Africa, and central Asia (about as far away from America as you can go and

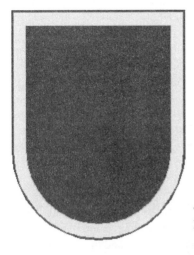

The official shoulder flash (emblem) of the 5th Special Forces Group (Airborne)

still stand on dry land), a region that is the most restrictive in the world . . . and the least tolerant toward Western culture. During recent years, more than a dozen major wars have erupted in the region, terrorist incidents number in the hundreds, and there have been too many skirmishes involving exchange of fire to count. And don't ever forget that all this is happening on top of the majority of the world's known oil and gas reserves.

Add to this: Their AOR has grown to include a new CENTCOM responsibility—the former Soviet republics of Kazakhstan, Uzbekistan, Turkmenistan, Tajikistan, and Kyrgyzstan, known familiarly as the "Stans." The Stans are fiercely Islamic, deeply distrustful of the states on their borders, and potentially great petrochemical powers. Since they border such bastions of stability as Iran, Afghanistan, and Pakistan, the 5th's new responsibility is already looking like a prescription for high adventure.

The 5th SFG's AOR makes everything they do, from transporting men and equipment to just coordinating phone calls home with a time zone difference of nine or ten hours a major hassle.

Commanding this unit is Colonel Daniel Brownlee, and he is assisted by CSM Denzil Ames.

The group's personnel range over a region three times the size of the continental U.S., with almost 430 million people. There are seventeen major ethnic groups, further complicated by the abundance of (often mutually unfriendly) Islamic, Christian, and Jewish religious groups. To cover all this, 5th SFG personnel are trained in five different languages—Arabic, Farsi, Pushtu (an Iranian dialect), Russian (for the Stans), and Urdu (for Muslims in Western Pakistan)—and they must be close to angelically sensitive to the many cultural differences of the region.

As if they don't have enough challenges, the 5th is not allowed by any of our regional allies to permanently base units in the region, which means all missions and deployments must be made from CONUS. In other words, they get lots of frequent flyer miles! Most 5th SFG NCOs travel more than the president, which is really saying something.

All this stretches the 5th about as far as you can stretch a military unit.

And, to make things even more interesting, they have seen more real combat in the last decade than any other group in SFC.

In short, the 5th's OpTempo is the busiest in SFC, and there is no indication that this will change. Life in the 5th is tough. Very tough!

Of course, life was never easy for the 5th.

During Vietnam, as decoration and casualty figures demonstrate, they bore the brunt of the fighting and dying in SFC. And when the war ended, they had to carry on after four other groups were disestablished . . . and after their own ranks had been gutted to support other units, such as Special Forces Operational Detachment Delta (the famous Delta Force). Later, when the 1st and 3rd SFGs were reactivated, 5th SFG was banished from Fort Bragg and sent to a set of fifties-era facilities on the rump end of Fort Campbell (just about the shabbiest of the SF headquarters). There they struggle along, sucking hind tit to Campbell's other occupants, the mighty 101st Airborne Division (Air Assault—the famous Screaming Eagles) and the 160th Special Operations Aviation Regiment (SOAR—the Nightstalkers), in priority and funding.

Simply put, it's business as usual for the 5th SFG, and they probably would not want it any other way!

The 5th SFG was formally stood up in 1960, and have not had to case their colors since.[64] They are, of course, justifiably proud of their long record (second only to the 10th SFG in continuous service). Here are a few additional highlights:

- **Contingencies**—The two really *big* problems in the 5th SFG AOR are of course Iran and Iraq. On those occasions when the Persian Gulf bullies have not been making war on each other or on their own ethnic minorities, they have been invading their smaller neighbors, disrupting maritime traffic, and trying to acquire weapons of mass destruction. In 1998 alone, three major battalion-sized deployments were made in support of operations against Iraq, and are likely to continue until Saddam Hussein leaves power.

  Add to that the new crises erupting in the AOR, ranging from the war between Ethiopia and Eritrea (currently the world's largest armed conflict) to the presence in Afghanistan of the Isama bin Laden terrorist group. In between are several dozen slow-burning disputes, any one of which could require a major deployment of 5th SFG units and personnel.

- **Operations**—While it is technically true that none of our allies in the region allow permanent forward basing of SOF units and personnel, what is allowed (and asked for) is regular rotations of SOF units into the AOR. This effectively gives SOC-CENT a regular force level there. The 5th SFG's operational activities center on Camp Doha, north of Kuwait City. Here the U.S. Army maintains a vast pre-positioning base, filled with enough armor, vehicles, aircraft, and weapons to equip a full-sized armored brigade, a Patriot missile battalion, and a complete SF battal-

---

64 Like the other groups, they trace their spiritual lineage back to the Devil's Brigade; specifically, the HHC of the 1st Battalion of the brigade's 1st Regiment.

The official shoulder flash (emblem) of the 7th Special Forces Group (Airborne)

ion. The Army rotates about a third of the 5th's capacity into Camp Doha, effectively keeping a minimum force in Kuwait to deter Iraqi and Iranian aggression. In the event of a crisis, additional units can fall onto the pre-positioned gear at Camp Doha, and be ready to fight in a matter of days.

The primary continuing exercise in Kuwait is known as Iris Gold, which is a special liaison operation with the Kuwaiti military. Three-man SF teams in specially built vehicles operate with the four brigades of the Kuwait Army, providing liaison and spotting services for American airpower to support the Kuwaitis in the event of an invasion.

In the event of a crisis, two additional companies of SF soldiers can be quickly deployed to Kuwait, to be followed by a battalion ODC to support combat search and rescue of downed Allied aircrews and deep reconnaissance/strike missions.

In addition to support operations in Kuwait, 5th SFG also contributes to ACRI and several peacekeeping efforts.

- **JCS Exercises**—Despite the 5th's high OpTempo for continuing and contingency operations, there is still a requirement for JCET training in the region. While the 5th does less of this than the other groups (and sometimes gets help from other groups), a large quota of such missions remains. These range from firearms training for national police forces to establishing a military specialty like sniping in an Army without these skills.

- **CONUS Training**—The 5th SFG, like every other military force, must train to keep sharp. Though the OpTempos make these deployments increasingly rare, whenever possible, they try to get each battalion into NTC every two years. More critical are maintenance of perishable skills such as MFF, AMOUT, UWO, and maritime operations. These are being kept up, but just barely.

7th Special Forces Group

Is there an SFG where life is "fun"?

Well, yes . . . after a fashion.

If there's an AOR that's fun, it's the 7th SFG's—Latin America and the Caribbean. And the men of the 7th SFG know more about having "fun" downrange than any other soldiers in the command. I might also say that you'd be hard-pressed to find a better group of representatives for our nation in Latin America and the Caribbean.

You can find the 7th SFG right across the street from USASOC headquarters at Fort Bragg in an almost identical buff-colored building complex as the 3rd SFG's. It is tasked with providing SOF services and units to the U.S. Southern Command (SOUTHCOM).

In recent years SOUTHCOM and Special Operations Command, SOUTHCOM (SOCSOUTH), have been kept busy: First, they've had to move from their former bases in Panama to new centers in Miami, Florida, and Puerto Rico.[65] And then the recent regional boundary shuffle has given them additional territory—the Caribbean region (formerly part of Atlantic Command). Now everything south of the U.S. border, with the exception of Mexico, falls under the responsibility of SOUTHCOM.

The 7th SFG traces its roots back to the 1st Company of the 1st Battalion, 1st Regiment of the Devil's Brigade. They were reborn in 1960 when the 77th SFG was split. Since then, they have had a primarily Latin American mission, which usually meant dirty little conflicts like the one in El Salvador.

But times are changing. Today the 7th SFG operates in a region emerging from centuries of economic exploitation and political repression to economic growth and democracy.

As I said, the 7th SFG operates in an AOR you could almost call fun.

On top of that, the language requirements are modest (Spanish, Portuguese), nowhere in the AOR is more than a few hours' flying time from Fort Bragg, and the missions take place no more than a time zone or two away from ours. Such things ease the strains on 7th SFG personnel, and allow them more discretionary time for training and other development projects. They also tend to get more time at home base (which improves quality of life within the command, and therefore retention).

The personality of 7th's commander also helps.[66] Colonel Ed Phillips is a tall and joyous man, clearly in love with both his life in SF and with his soldiers. He is backed by CSM Richard Tudor, and a staff of dedicated SF professionals. The 7th SFG may have a good time at their chosen profession, but don't think they have it easy. They are as dedicated as anyone in SFC; and they run as many downrange missions as any group:

- **Contingencies**—Now that the great dictatorships (in Argentina, Chile, Brazil, and Panama) are history, and the Marxist governments (in Nicaragua and Cuba) have either gone away or have been neutralized by events, Latin America has become a much kinder, gentler place. For now, the only significant risks of conflict in the region center on Cuba (What happens when Fidel Castro dies?) and Colombia

---

65 The move from Panama is a consequence of the U.S. turnover of the Canal Zone under the treaty negotiated in the 1970s by the Carter Administration.
66 After writing this, I learned that Phillips has retired from the Army.

The official shoulder flash (emblem) of the 10th Special Forces Group (Airborne)

(Will the government collapse under the pressure from narcotics traffickers/terrorists?).

To prepare for this second eventuality (which could cause serious problems), the 7th has been heavily involved in Colombia in counternarcotics and counterterrorist training through the JCET program, and has been preparing other governments' militaries, in case the shoe drops in Colombia.

- **Operations**—The end of the Cold War has *not* seen a decline in the number of continuing 7th SFG operations. One of recent note was the world's smallest and most successful peacekeeping operation: Once upon a time Ecuador and Peru were at war over a border. The 7th SFG was sent down to deal with the problem. And after several years of hands-on engagement with the two combatants, there is now a legally established and recognized border between the two nations. (The operation terminated in the winter of 1998–1999.)

- **JCS Exercises**—Though the 7th SFG has few real-world operations and contingencies, they are not sitting at home cutting the grass and waiting for happy hour. On the contrary, after two centuries of bad memories of American interventions, Latin America offers a full slate of real-world challenges. We clearly need to clean up our past messes. To this end, the 7th SFG is one of the most heavily tasked units in the JCET program, with several hundred downrange missions run per year. Many of these are humanitarian, such as building infrastructure like clinics and public utilities, as well as the more usual military, paramilitary, and police force training.

- **CONUS Training**—Because of the relatively relaxed security situation in SOUTHCOM, the 7th can train more than other SFGs back in the U.S. The group not only attends more JRTC and NTC rotations than the other groups, they also dedicate a large portion of their time to experimental projects and exercises (these benefit all the groups).

10th Special Forces Group

The headquarters of the 10th SFG sits in Fort Carson, Colorado, on a mountain prairie that looks like a scene from *High Plains Drifter*. As you stare at it, you can have a hard time remembering that the 10th is the SF unit assigned to the European mission within SOCEUR.

Located in a mountain valley near Colorado Springs, Fort Carson is home to a variety of Army units, including the 7th Infantry Division and 3rd Armored Cavalry

Regiment.[67] It is a far cry from their old barracks in Bad Tölz, West Germany, and their one-time home at Fort Devens, Massachusetts. Now they have state-of-the-art facilities at Fort Carson, and at Panzer Kasern, Germany (near Stuttgart), they have a new home for their forward-deployed 1st Battalion.

The 10th SFG, established back in 1952 by Colonel Aaron Bank, is the longest-lived of all of the groups. And like all the other groups, the 10th traces its spiritual lineage to the Devil's Brigade, where it claims the 4th Company of the 2nd Battalion, 1st Regiment as its parent unit. Today it is headed by Colonel Richard Mills and his CSM, Henry Ramirez.

Though the group retains its European focus, the collapse of the Soviet Union and the Warsaw Pact has removed Colonel Bank's original reason for creating the 10th. Yet in its place has come a far more challenging set of problems. The group is forward deployed and fully engaged, second only to the 5th SFG for its OpTempo and number of real-world contingency operations. They are fully involved in the effort to expand NATO, and in the peacekeeping efforts in the Balkans. They are also working hard to bring professionalism and a respect for democracy to the militaries of the former communist nations of Europe.

The 10th SFG has been given some relief from their busy pace by the recent redrawing of regional boundary lines. In 1998, they gave up responsibility for the Stans and North Africa, retaining only Israel, Lebanon, and Turkey in the Middle East. Nevertheless, they still retain responsibility for SF operations in Eastern Europe, including Russia, most of the old Soviet Union, and all the former Warsaw Pact nations.

Because of the need for a quick response capability,[68] the 10th SFG still maintains their 1st Battalion forward based in Germany. The 2nd and 3rd Battalions are based back at Fort Carson.

Here is a look at some of what they're up to:

- **Contingencies**—Unless you have been on the dark side of the moon, you probably already know what kinds of contingency operations are at the core of the 10th SFG's missions. Key are those in the Balkans, the Middle East, and Russia. Operations like Allied Force, Deliberate Force, and the various Balkan relief efforts have been key examples of quick responses by the 10th SFG.

- **Operations**—Most of the 10th SFG's ongoing operations in recent years have supported Balkan operations. The biggest have been peacekeeping and demining support for Operations Joint Forge in Bosnia, and Joint Guardian and Noble Anvil in Kosovo.

- **JCS Exercises**—In 1999, 10th SFG was heavily involved in JCS exercises, including more than two dozen JCETs, mobile training teams (MTTs) sent to the Baltic states, counterdrug, and demining operations.

---

67 Fort Carson is located on the south side of Colorado Springs. The city is also home to the Air Force Academy, Cheyenne Mountain/NORAD, and is the headquarters of U.S. Space Command.

68 This is based upon the likelihood of a fast-breaking crisis in a relatively small theater. In addition, politics dictate that (as in Korea) we maintain a high level of readiness and posture in places like Europe that we really care about.

The official shoulder flash (emblem) of the 19th Special Forces Group (Airborne)

OFFICIAL U.S. ARMY GRAPHIC

- **CONUS Training**—Recent years have seen a heavy level of CONUS training operations for the 10th SFG, including exercises to help qualify former Warsaw Pact nations for NATO membership. The 10th also has a heavy schedule of refresher and requalification training, especially for mountain and cold-weather operations.

19th Special Forces Group (Army National Guard)

In addition to the five active-duty SFGs, there are two Army National Guard (ANG) SFGs under SFC. These units are staffed by former active-duty SF personnel, can be tasked with the same kinds of missions, and are composed of a mixed group of ANG formations from dozens of states. These are, in other words, not just weekend warriors, but highly skilled SF professionals who just happen to have other jobs during the week.

This is not a novelty for Special Forces. Long before the development of the "Total Force" concept of operations,[69] the Special Forces had formed and operated nonactive duty SF units. During the 1950s, the 77th SFG provided personnel and assistance to reserve and ANG operational detachments in North Carolina, New Jersey, Illinois, and a number of Western states. By 1960 the first Army Reserve group, the 11th SFG, was formed in Boston, Massachusetts. Eventually, a total of nine AR and ANG SFGs were formed, though all but two have since been inactivated.

According to the SFC leadership, their two ANG groups are the best bargains in the whole command. On the one hand, personnel costs are extremely low, since the soldiers are only paid for monthly weekend duty and their yearly two-week active-duty tour. On the other hand, a number of highly experienced senior SF soldiers are not lost to the organization. In fact, the ANG groups allow these men to have the best of both worlds—a useful career after their active-duty SF tour and the opportunity to take part in very challenging missions and operations.

Naturally, it would be unrealistic to expect part-time soldiers to maintain the

---

69 "Total Force" is the U.S. military's core-operating concept today: According to the "Total Force" concept, active-duty, reserve, and national guard units are equipped with the same equipment, given the same training, and able to fight together as a complete team.

physical condition and combat skills of active-duty SF troopers. While they do a credible job of keeping in shape, the ANG personnel are not expected to be fearsome in combat but to use their greater experience and skills base. Thus, SFC tends to task the ANG groups with the less intense missions, such as JCETs and other training-oriented operations.

But don't think they can't fight. They are smart and very qualified soldiers, and are well respected by their active-duty counterparts. A few weeks back on operations will reveal few differences between active-duty and ANG SF soldiers.

The 19th SFG is headquartered in Draper, Utah (near Salt Lake City), in a large office building, and it is commanded by Colonel Jordan Hughes and his CSM, Owen Quarnberg. Like the active-duty groups, they have a spiritual lineage that traces back to the Devil's Brigade, in their case, the 1st Company of the 1st Battalion, 3rd Regiment.

The 19th is structured exactly like the active-duty groups, with the only difference being that the component units are scattered across the country. Its units are spread throughout seven states—California, Washington, Utah, Colorado, Ohio, Rhode Island, and West Virginia. These units are normally housed at ANG posts and armories. Since these are owned and operated by the governments of their home states, unit costs are spread across a wider base of public finance. It further means that in the event of a natural disaster or state emergency, the units are available to support relief operations.

When it comes to mission tasking, there are a few general rules for the ANG SFGs. First, while they are fully capable of combat and other contingency operations, ANG units are mainly used to backfill less difficult or arduous missions. This has the effect of enabling an active-duty SF unit to go somewhere that's more critical or timely.

The 19th has a broad geographic focus. Thus its overseas operations are conducted in Africa, the Middle East, Asia, and the Far East. The 19th SFG's recent tasking is shown below:

- **Contingencies**—Though the 19th SFG is not generally involved with standing contingency operations, this may change in the future. ANG SF units may soon take on full-time counterdrug, counterterrorism, and counterWMD missions. (This could be done practically in two ways: First, presidential orders could activate the units. Or, various ANG ODAs could hand a duty off from one team to another.)

- **Operations**—As stated above, the 19th SFG has no responsibility for standing operations.

- **JCS Exercises**—Here the ANG SFGs earn their keep. They take over missions that normally would require the services of an active-duty SF unit. In 1999, the 19th ran missions to Kenya, Jordan, and Oman, with one or two ODAs teaching reconnaissance, patrol, and strike skills. The 19th also ran several command post exercises in South Korea, with company-sized deployments downrange. Their largest series of missions were a series of JCETs in support of the 1st SFG in Asia. These included almost a dozen ODA-sized missions to Micronesia, Papua New

The official shoulder flash (emblem) of the 20th Special Forces Group (Airborne)

OFFICIAL U.S. ARMY GRAPHIC

Guinea, South Korea, the Java Barrier, and the Maldives. There the 19th taught a variety of skills to local military and police units, ranging from medical lifesaving to sniping.

- **CONUS Training**—The 19th ran a full array of Stateside refresher training in 1999, including MFF, UWO, and various specialty requalifications.

20th Special Forces Group (Army National Guard)

Headed by Colonel James Yarbrough and CSM Joe Riley, the 20th SFG is based in eight eastern states (Alabama, Mississippi, Florida, Kentucky, Virginia, Maryland, Illinois, and Massachussetts), and headquartered in Birmingham, Alabama. Their spiritual roots in the Devil's Brigade go back to the 2nd Company of the 1st Battalion, 3rd Regiment.

The 20th SFG has a primary Latin American–Caribbean mission focus, being tasked mainly by SOCSOUTH. This makes them a useful augment to the 7th SFG. In 1999, their jobs included:

- **Contingencies**—Like the 7th and 19th SFGs, the 20th SFG has no serious potential contingencies to deal with. While they do have the capability to support crisis situations, it is likely they will continue to support mainly JCS and CONUS training missions.
- **Operations**—The 20th has no ongoing operations, though they have had to deal with some natural disaster relief (Hurricane Mitch, etc.) in 1998 and 1999.
- **JCS Exercises**—In 1998 and 1999, the 20th had a busy schedule of JCS exercises, particularly JCETs. They ran two small exercises in Guyana and Panama, and over twenty JCETs. These included JCETs to Honduras, El Salvador, Ecuador, Costa Rica, Suriname, Panama, Trinidad, Venezuela, Barbados, Antigua, and Puerto Rico. These operations covered a variety of mission skills, including humanitarian

assistance, combat search and rescue, counterdrug and countermine training, and peacekeeping.

- **CONUS Training**—Like the 19th, the 20th SFG ran a full array of Stateside refresher training in 1999, including MFF, UWO, and various specialty requalifications.

The two ANG groups are an important augment to the five active-duty SFGs. In fact, it would surely be wise to activate additional ANG groups to support SF missions to more permissive environments, reserving the high-end operations for the active-duty groups. Given their high OpTempos, this may well happen soon.

Other SFC Units

SFC is also responsible for four chemical reconnaissance detachments (CRDs). Two of these, the 56th and 801st CRDs are active-duty units based at Fort Campbell and Fort Bragg respectively. There are also two U.S. Army Reserve CRDs, the 445th and 900th at Fort Meade, Maryland, and Fort Carson, Colorado, These are small, specialized detachments with special training and equipment whose function is to detect, map, and assess threats and actual usage of chemical weapons for SOF commanders; and they are the only Army units qualified to provide chemical warfare services in the SOF arena.

Supporting Units

SFC are limited in their abilities to go places and do things without external help. Key among these necessary services are transportation resources, communications services, intelligence support, and weather data. Luckily, many of these services are available within USASOC and SOCOM, and are available for tasking by SF units.

- **160th Special Operations Aviation Regiment (SOAR—the Nightstalkers)**— The most secret and technologically advanced unit in USASOC, the Nightstalkers provide the rest of the command with the aviation support that was lacking during the Iranian hostage rescue in 1980. Based at Fort Campbell, Kentucky, the 160th flies a mix of helicopters, all heavily modified and specialized. These include:

  —**MH-47D/E Chinook**—The long-range, heavy-lift component of the 160th, the MH-47 is a heavily modified variant of the Army's famous twin-engine/rotor Boeing Chinook helicopter. Equipped with a specially engineered mission equipment package—terrain following radar (TFR), forward-looking infrared (FLIR) scanner, electronics countermeasures (ECM), an in-flight refueling probe, etc.— and computer system, the MH-47 is able to accomplish the kinds of nonstop missions that were impossible in Iran back in 1980. A single MH-47 can carry up to twenty fully equipped special operations personnel or a rubber boat with a dozen men.

An MH-47 transport helicopter from the 160th Special Operations Aviation Regiment kicks up dust and debris as it lands. The 160th provides the Army Special Operations community with its own airborne insertion capability.

—**MH-60K/L Pave Hawk**—Based on the familiar UH-60 Blackhawk, the MH-60 is the little brother to the MH-47 Chinook. Equipped with a similar mission equipment package, the Pave Hawk is designed to conduct similar missions of shorter duration and with smaller payloads. The MH-60K model is, however, equipped with an in-flight refueling probe, so that longer missions can be flown, as well as air-to-ground rockets and machine guns. There are also unconfirmed reports of an attack version of the MH-60K, known as the AH-60, which reportedly has a laser designator, in addition to the normal mission equipment package, and a pair of 30mm chain guns. This gives it firepower similar to that of the AH-64 Apache attack helicopter, which includes both Hellfire and Stinger missiles for attacking ground and air targets respectively.

—**A/M/TH-6 "Little Bird"**—The most secret of the 160th's livery, the Little Bird is actually a family of light attack, assault, and surveillance helicopters based upon the familiar H-6/MD-500-series helicopter now built by Boeing (formerly McDonnell Douglas and Hughes). Though many of the details surrounding these birds are highly classified, most are equipped with a lightweight FLIR system, and can be armed with 7.62mm six-barreled miniguns and air-to-ground rockets. The Little Bird can also be used as an urban assault transport helicopter, equipped to "fast rope" as many as six special operations personnel into built-up environments like cities and industrial zones.

The Nightstalkers specialize in night operations, where their advantages in sensors, navigational equipment, weapons, and crew skills can translate into a significant edge in combat. They have seen their share of action since they were formed in the early 1980s, and have become one of the busiest units in the U.S. military. If they have a shortcoming, it is their small numbers and their need for infrastructure and support (basing, logistics, etc.), which can limit their usefulness in expeditionary environments.

Air Force Special Operations (AFSOC)

Along with the 160th SOAR, SOCOM also maintains a significant SOF transport capability within the Air Force Special Operations Command (AFSOC) at Hurlbert Field, Florida. These include specially equipped MC-130 Hercules turboprop transports, with a package of satellite communications and navigation systems. The 130s can be used for both airborne and air delivery operations for SOF units. There is also a squadron of C-141B Starlifter heavy-lift transports, which are capable of similar services.[70] Heavy fire support can also be provided by the AFSOC force of AC-130 Spectre gunships. These can deliver pinpoint fire from 105mm, 25mm, 20mm, and 7.62mm cannon and machine guns in almost any weather or visibility. Finally, AFSOC also maintains a small fleet of special operations helicopters—MH-53J Pave Lows. The Pave Lows are heavily armed, and equipped to operate in almost any weather, visibility, or air defense environment and are currently the world's most capable SOF transport aircraft.

In just a few years, AFSOC will take delivery of an SOF version of the new V-22 Osprey tilt-rotor transport aircraft. The Osprey will replace the Pave Lows and some of the MC-130s, providing a vast improvement in range, payload, and other capabilities.

The Navy: Subs and Special Boats

The Special Forces also retain a significant capability for maritime and riverine insertion into denied areas (that is, areas occupied by people who don't want them there). SF units have long had the ability to operate rubber boats, and they can deploy these from a variety of platforms. Thus, the Navy can be tasked to provide transport services in the form of SOF-capable submarines and boats. To this end, the Navy has designated two former nuclear ballistic missile submarines, the *Kamehameha* (SSN-642) and *James K. Polk* (SSN-645), as well as the Special Operations boat, *Parche* (SSN-683). (*Parche* and the now-retired *Richard Russell* were based upon long-hulled Sturgeon (SSN-637)-class attack boats, and there appear to be plans to make the *Jimmy Carter* (SSN-23) the replacement for *Parche*.) These boats have lock-out chambers for divers, as well as external hangers for powered delivery vehicles or rubber boats. The Navy can also be tasked for a loan from one of their special boat squadrons. The Special Forces especially like the new *Cyclone* (PC-1)-class boats, since they can carry several ODAs and their gear into water as shallow as small rivers. The Navy also operates smaller craft, including the new Mark V-series boats, which can move upriver into creeks and streams, or make high-speed movements through coastal waters.

75th Ranger Regiment

Though the Special Forces have an impressive ability to conduct small-unit operations against specific targets, sometimes you need to attack, capture, or wreck

---

70 While the SOF heavy-lift capability is currently based with the 437th Airlift Wing at Charleston AFB, South Carolina, it will shortly move to McGuire AFB, New Jersey. And there is a good possibility that when the SOF-capable C-141Bs are retired in a few years, a squadron of C-17 Globemaster IIIs will be modified to take over the SOF mission.

something *really* BIG! When this need comes up, SOCOM calls the 75th Ranger Regiment at Fort Benning, Georgia. Composed of three Ranger battalions (two at Fort Benning and one at Fort Lewis), the 75th provides the national command authorities with a quick-reaction force that is airborne qualified, and large enough to handle a variety of tasks. This includes missions like airfield assaults and takeovers (as was done in Grenada and Panama) and large-scale urban combat (in Somalia).

The 75th has a fearsome combat reputation, which is in line with their traditions going back to World War II. The Rangers are America's own reverse fire brigade. That is, they scare their opponents like a maniac with a flame thrower.

I try not to get them mad.

U.S. Space Command (SPACECOM)

No external service is more important to SF units than the U.S. Space Command. Based at Peterson AFB near Colorado Springs, Colorado, SPACECOM is the clearinghouse for satellite communications services, as well as weather and intelligence data—all vital to any SF mission. SPACECOM keeps these necessary services available and reliable, making possible the wide range of SFC global missions.

Roles and Missions: The Special Forces Way

Now it's time to get into what these folks do.

SFC has carved out a special niche in the SOF world; there are well-established roles and missions that they call their own. While it goes without saying that no military unit can possibly do everything, the Special Forces can cover quite a lot. The key is knowing their limits.

For example, instead of parachuting a whole battalion of SF soldiers onto an airfield in order to take it, better to use one or two ODAs to scout the place, and let a Ranger battalion do the job.

Another major SF strength is planning.

This might surprise lovers of adventure movies, but SOF personnel are *not* mindless killers. SF soldiers know better. That's *not* the way things really get done. Mindless killers tend to get killed downrange. In truth, SF soldiers are among the brightest folks you will ever meet. They will spend hours considering every detail of even the simplest training class, looking for better ways to accomplish their mission. Many carry into the field state-of-the-art laptop computers and digital cameras, and often use them to create operational planning documents with enough substance to interest the JCS.

Of course, every SF soldier always has at the ready "stubby pencil" planning tools—a notebook, pen or pencil, compass, map, and protractor—just in case.

Special Forces Missions

- **Foreign Internal Defense (FID)**—The most frequent SF mission, FID involves teaching the military, paramilitary, and police forces of other nations to better

A Special Forces soldier (kneeling) instructs Venezuelan soldiers in marksmanship. This training is conducted as a "Foreign Internal Defense" mission, one of several deployed Special Forces teams can execute in the field.

defend themselves against subversion, insurgency, and high-end criminal activity. This mission can be run anywhere in the warfare spectrum, from prewar peacetime, to wartime resistance efforts, and even post-war military reconstruction.

- **Antiterrorism Training**—That is, the training of other nations' forces in the basics of the counterterrorism art. This includes surveillance techniques, close-combat weapons and tactics training, and special planning procedures.

- **Special Reconnaissance (SR)**—Perhaps the most common and vital SF combat mission, SR is an intelligence-gathering mission that involves obtaining or collecting information regarding the capabilities, intentions, activities, or equipment of an enemy force.

- **Unconventional Warfare (UW)**—UW was the core mission of the original members of the 10th SFG back in 1952, and it now covers a broad spectrum of warfare skills, both military and paramilitary. It is mainly practiced by indigenous, militia, or native units, which are organized, trained, equipped, and supported by SF personnel operating under a national policy finding or decision.

- **Direct Action (DA)**—DA covers short-duration operations . . . in other words, raids—small offensive actions of limited size, scope, and duration, designed to seize, damage, or destroy specific targets. Targets by the way, cover a variety of items, including military equipment, bases, personnel, or other materials designated by higher command or the national command authorities.

- **Collateral Activities**—In addition to their primary mission activities, SF ODAs frequently are tasked with any of a number of peripheral jobs. These include:

  —**Humanitarian Assistance**—When deployed downrange, ODA medical personnel (18D) are frequently asked to use their considerable talents to improve the health of and treat local, native, or host nation personnel.

  —**Security Assistance/Mobile Training Teams (SA/MTT)**—Occasionally during missions, ODAs will form MTTs to teach local military, paramilitary, and police force personnel particular skills, procedures, or orientation on new equipment. In addition, SF personnel are also sometimes assigned to provide local security for political leaders and other VIPs.

  —**Counter-Mine Activities**—SF soldiers are frequently tasked to instruct host nation personnel in the necessary skills and procedures to demine an area. In many cases, this takes on the form of a "train-the-trainer" course, where SF soldiers teach others their own teaching techniques, so that the "tribal" knowledge of countermining is preserved locally.

  —**Counterdrug Activities**—To help the military, paramilitary, and police forces of host nations combat narcotics growth, processing, and trafficking, SF soldiers are occasionally tasked to train local personnel in the techniques and tactics of counternarcotics warfare. This includes training in intelligence gathering, raid planning and execution, and proper law enforcement techniques.

  —**Peacekeeping**—SF personnel have recently become deeply involved with peacekeeping missions. Following the conclusion of their successful Ecuador operations, they are now involved in the Balkans missions in Bosnia and Kosovo.

  —**Combat Search and Rescue (CSAR)**—SF units sometimes are tasked to provide the ground security element of a CSAR mission to recover downed aircrews or other personnel. The SF soldiers are teamed with helicopters and other support aircraft to assist in the recovery.

  —**Coalition Support**—Because of their unique combination of language skills, regional orientation, and cultural sensitivity, SF soldiers are often tasked to provide liaison services between U.S. and coalition allied forces.

The knowledge and skills required of these missions are all part of the "Q" Course core curriculum, and subsequent specialty school training. An SF ODA can normally accomplish any of these, and probably do a pretty good job.

Slices of the Pie: Areas of Responsibility (AORs)

Under the Goldwater-Nichols and Nunn-Cohen bills, each regional command has various subcomponents, including one specifically to coordinate SOF activities. These component commanders actually control the major collections of units (Army, Air Force, Marine, Naval, SOF, etc.) assigned in the event of a crisis. For example, during Desert Storm the Central Command Air Force (CENTAF) boss was my old friend

General Charles "Chuck" Horner, USAF (Ret.). In that capacity, he controlled just about everything that flew. As might be imagined, such control has caused more than a few personal disagreements. But until someone comes up with a better system, the current unified command operations structure is the best there is.

The Special Operations Command (SOC) components for each unified command have the same regional orientation as the SFGs themselves. A senior SOF officer who reports directly to the four-star theater commander (CINC) heads each. Currently, these are the active regional SOC commands, and the officers who command them:

- **Special Operations Command, Central (SOCCENT)**—Commanded by Brigadier General Frank J. Toney, Jr. USA, SOCCENT is based at MacDill AFB, Florida, with a forward headquarters located in Bahrain. General Toney commands the SOC forces in today's most active theater. The SF contingent in these forces is the 5th SFG. CENTCOM is responsible for U.S. military operations from the Horn of Africa to the Stans, as well as all the Persian Gulf states, Afghanistan, and Pakistan.

- **Special Operations Command, Europe (SOCEUR)**—The largest SOC component by the number and size of units assigned, SOCEUR has two full groups (3rd and 10th SFGs) and part of the 19th SFG available for SOF operations. EUCOM's territory covers everything between the North Cape and the Cape of Good Hope, and extends as far inland as Russia and Israel. SOCEUR is commanded by Brigadier General Eldon A. Bargewell, USA.

- **Special Operations Command, South (SOCSOUTH)**—Like the rest of SOUTHCOM, SOCSOUTH has acquired new responsibilities with the handover of the Caribbean region from USACOM. SOCSOUTH has recently moved its headquarters from the Canal Zone in Panama to Puerto Rico. A longtime SF soldier, Brigadier General James W. Parker commands SOCSOUTH, and controls both the 7th and 20th SFGs.

- **Special Operations Command, Atlantic (SOCLANT)**—Following the recent handover of its remaining regional responsibility to SOUTHCOM, no dedicated SFG is assigned. SOCLANT is commanded by an O-6, Colonel Hayward S. Florer, USA.

- **Special Operations Command, Pacific (SOCPAC)**—Based in Hawaii, SOCPAC is commanded by Brigadier General Jack R. Holbien, USAF. He has two SFGs dedicated to his region; the 1st SFG and most of the 19th SFG, if needed.

- **Special Operations Command, Korea (SOCKOR)**—While technically not a major regional command, U.S. Forces, Korea, is commanded by a four-star Army general with his own dedicated SOC commander. SOCKOR is headed by Colonel Robert C. Leicht, USA, who has a Special Forces Detachment in country the forward-deployed 1/1st SFG on Okinawa and other on-call SOF forces as assigned from other commands.

Special Forces CONOPS: A Few Examples

Let's look now at the ways Special Forces groups are packaged and sent on their missions. Be aware that SF leaders approach this subject with a certain minimalist

A map showing the current areas covered by each of the active-duty Special Forces Groups, and their assigned unified command.

1st Special Forces Group/ U.S. Pacific Command (PACOM)

5th Special Forces Group/U.S. Central Command (CENTCOM)

3rd Special Forces Group/ U.S. European Command (EUCOM)

10th Special Forces Group/ U.S. European Command (EUCOM)

7th Special Forces Group/ U.S. Southern Command (SOUTHCOM)

RUBICON, INC. BY LAURA DeNINNO

attitude. They know that a few SF ODAs are not going to win a war, campaign, or even a battle. Special Forces understand that they are an enabling force that—if all goes as planned—will allow larger, more powerful forces to prevail.

We'll look at three representative SF deployment force packages. While there is no "standard" SF deployment force, these represent the kinds of units that SFC likes to mix together for the jobs they're likely to be assigned.

Example #1: Low-Intensity, Permissive Operations

The vast majority of Special Forces missions are relatively small deployments, usually composed of one to three ODAs, and backed up by an ODB for command-and-control purposes. Such a package is ideally suited to enter a friendly host nation to conduct training. Let's say that a friendly Latin American host nation has requested and been granted a ninety-day JCET mission by the Department of State and the JCS. SFC then tasks 7th SFG at Fort Bragg with a requirement for a package of two ODAs and an ODB that will be deployed downrange in approximately six to nine months. This gives the group command staff the necessary lead time to select the teams to be sent, assign a mission commander, and conduct the necessary premission site surveys in the host nation.

The next phase of the JCET begins approximately three months prior to the actual mission deployment, when the selected teams begin to train. The teams are "selected" from teams in what is called "Amber" status. That is, these teams have been home for a few months, have had some leave and/or training, and are ready to be tasked.[71]

Around this time, a site survey team (one or two personnel) will deploy to the host nation to visit the U.S. embassy, coordinate activities and plans, and select the necessary billeting and training facilities. They will also arrange for any special logistical, communications, transportation, or infrastructure purchases/leases that may be needed. For example, most Latin American countries have a well-developed cellular phone system. This is an invaluable coordination and emergency communications tool. Back home, their notes and ideas will be used by the teams in their training.

Approximately four weeks before deployment, the SF team training will still be on-going, and premission packing will begin. At this point, transportation becomes the critical issue. The amount of personnel, gear, and supplies to be taken determines how it will be shipped. For example, the SF soldiers might fly to a Caribbean Island, while their heavy gear and supplies are placed in cargo containers to be transported via truck and ship.

Obviously, SF personnel love to use heavy-lift transports like C-17A Globemaster IIIs, which can carry most everything in one big lift, but such operations are costly, and TRANSCOM (Air Force Transportation Command) doesn't have many of them.

During the weeks just prior to the deployment there are *lots* of briefings for the mission and team leaders, so they will fully understand the world they'll be moving into. These leaders will meanwhile also brief their own training, deployment, force

---

71 The Special Forces grade the operational readiness status of a unit by the Green/Amber/Red scale. Green means mission ready, Amber means the unit is in training and getting ready to deploy, and Red signifies that the unit is just back from a deployment and needs leave and training.

protection, communications, and emergency procedures plans to the group and SFC command staffs, and to State Department representatives. Only when everyone agrees that they are ready is the mission approved and the deployment order signed.

While this is going on, the individual SF soldiers are getting their shots, updating wills, and preparing for the separation from family, friends, and loved ones.

On deployment day, the teams are packed and ready to move. In the event that TRANSCOM has supplied a military aircraft, they will launch out of Pope AFB (next to Fort Bragg). Otherwise, everyone will dress in civilian clothing and take commercial flights to the host nation.

Once the teams have arrived, they will initially be put up in a hotel near the U.S. embassy, and their first few days will be spent in embassy briefings and getting to know their host nation unit personnel. Rental vehicles and cell phones will also be picked up and issued. Only after everyone has been properly introduced and briefed will the teams be allowed to move downrange to their deployment sites near the host nation units they will be training.

Once downrange, each team will have a site selected for use as a team house—frequently a private residence that the team leases for a period of months. At other times the team might use an empty barracks, or even deploy tents (though this is now rare).

A team house must be easily defended in the event of a terrorist incident or riot, and have several escape and evasion (E&E) routes available. Some level of comfort is also desirable (air-conditioning and a satellite TV dish are a big advantage). Finally, since teams may actually be hundreds of miles apart, the prime selection criterion for a team house is its utility.

From this last, the leap is not far to command, control, and communications. Just what radios and other communications systems does an SF major need to run his three teams and keep SOCSOUTH, SFC, and the national command authorities informed of his progress and situation? Again, a minimalist attitude is best. For starters, team communications sergeants have a variety of radios and cryptographic systems to choose from when equipping a team for a mission. The ODAs would normally establish a communications center (actually a bench) in a corner of the team house. Here they would normally set up at least three secure communications systems—a satellite communications (SATCOM) transceiver, a high-frequency (HF) radio system, and SABRE frequency modulated (FM) radio network. A cellular telephone (if available) is usually included as a further backup.

The SATCOM system will be rigged to operate with both a voice and data capability, which allows communication anywhere in the world on a moment's notice.[72] The HF radio is more limited, being restricted to Morse key transmissions. However, with the Morse limitations comes greater reliability and availability than the SATCOM systems. This is due to the legendary HF antenna-cutting skills of the 18Es and the limited number of SATCOM channels and transponders that SPACE-

---

72 The data device is usually nothing more than a laptop computer or personal digital assistant, with the data stream going to the radio through a digital encryption device. This allows the sending of e-mail messages using commercially available software, a real benefit for the team members.

COM can dedicate to these missions at any one time.[73] The FM SABRE radio system is normally used for local and tactical voice and data communications. Cellular telephone systems can also be useful, but, of course, lack the cryptographic security of the radio systems.

The ODB communications setup uses the same gear, but because they need to communicate regularly with the outside world, and especially back to Fort Bragg, they normally have twice as much of it. Thus, they will normally establish two sets of SATCOM and HF radio systems, one for working with the ODAs locally, and the other for reporting back to "the world."

Once all these systems are set up, a routine reporting schedule is established, usually several times daily, with additional checks during critical periods or events. The radio traffic back to the U.S. is sent to the SFC communications center on Chicken Road at Fort Bragg, where it is then distributed to the various interested parties. While radio brevity is appreciated as an Operations Security (OpSec) issue, I've never heard of anyone on an FID mission being called out for checking in too often. Bitter lessons over four decades downrange have taught SF soldiers to be cautious, even in the most pleasant host nation. (I might add that every SF mission takes along a full array of weapons, including M16s, M249 SAW, M230 40mm grenade launchers, and other systems as required.) More than once, a peaceful FID mission has changed into a fast-breaking combat assignment. SF soldiers have to be ready.

A mission force protection plan can also include security obstacles and armed guards (if necessary). But normally, the best force protection involves imbedding the teams into the local community, and making friends with ordinary folks. When they eat at local restaurants, buy food and other supplies from local vendors, and—in general—help the local population (like sending the 18D medical sergeant on house calls), the teams become friends and not the rich, overbearing American cousins. Friendly behavior has regularly proved to be far more effective than body armor and fortress walls at keeping team members safe.

(Remember that a big part of FID missions involves selling America to the host nationals; heavily armed soldiers make for a hard sell.)

For that reason, team members usually wear uniforms and BDUs during their training classes and civilian clothes when outside the team house.

Now that the teams are bedded down, their communications established, and security set up, the actual purpose of the FID mission can begin: training of host nation units. Normally, the two ODAs would be tasked to train company- or battalion-sized military, paramilitary, or police units in various tactical, operational, and equipment techniques. These classes follow an exact lesson plan, which always includes indoctrination in human rights policies as well as more belligerent skills. Even the ODB gets into the training act, usually delivering lectures and technical skills training in land navigation, radio communications, mission planning, and the like. These train-

---

73 SPACECOM is understandably frugal with the limited SATCOM resources available. Thus several SF missions in various parts of a region may have to share a single satellite channel or transponder, depending upon the urgency and importance of their tasking.

ing plans are also followed to the letter, with regular evaluations for the students and lots of reports home to group headquarters and SFC.

Toward the end of the three-month deployment, the classes end and the teams begin packing up. Back at home base, a few steps remain. Once gear has been cleaned and turned in, reports must be written, debriefings held, and a total mission assessment made. This assessment will determine the success of the operation and whether or not future FID missions will be scheduled to the host nation.

Once all these tasks have been completed, the teams are declared to be in the "Red" cycle, and sent on leave.

Meanwhile, future missions are already being prepared for the teams, and will soon be assigned. The cycle never ends.

Example #2: Fast-Breaking Crisis

Our next example of SF is a response to an actual crisis or conflict. As you might expect, this kind of mission requires a somewhat larger response.

Suppose an ally somewhere—or simply some nation we care about—is threatened. Clearly, a U.S. response is called for, and is quickly put into gear. The regional CINC establishes a Joint Task Force (JTF), and begins to assemble his forces for deployment to the crisis area. An order goes to the theater SOC commander, and a decision is made to deploy an SOF force to support the JTF. Included is an order to move a full SF battalion into the theater to establish a forward-operating base (FOB) for SOF units.

Since all SF units have rapid-response deployment plans, and packages ready to go at a moment's notice, things then begin to move very quickly.

First, a full SF battalion is assembled and made ready to deploy to their FOB site. Meanwhile, other units from USASOC and SFC have been working hard to support them.

Almost as soon as the deployment order for the battalion arrives, the group commander authorizes the movement of the ODC (battalion command team), and makes a request for certain USASOC and support units. Among these is a battalion "slice" package of communications personnel and equipment from the 112th Signal Battalion, USASOC's own unit for keeping in touch. There will also be a team of support and logistics personnel from USASOC's 528th Special Operations Support Battalion. The USASOC leadership will also probably arrange for a package of helicopters from the 160th SOAR, and perhaps a contingent of military police and/or engineers from XVIII Airborne Corps.

Because these units are needed to build the bare FOB prior to the arrival of the battalion's three SF companies, all of them will be dispatched to the FOB site via USAF transport aircraft before the first SF team member is sent.

Once the lead units arrive in the host nation, things get very busy. The real challenge is to prepare the FOB for the three companies that will probably arrive in just a few days. The first problem is to find a site. Permanent facilities like barracks or aircraft hangars make ideal FOBs, but the groups are ready to resort to tents if necessary. Whatever the accommodations, the lead elements of the SOF task force has to work *fast*, if they are to get into the fight in time.

The next few days are a frenzy of activity, as each unit exercises its own special talents: The MPs and engineers establish a perimeter and begin to work on the force protection plan; the 112th Signals Battalion team starts setting up a communications center, wiring the FOB for phones, and setting up the computer network; and the 528th Special Operations Support Battalion force sets up their logistical and support functions, including mess arrangements, sanitation facilities, and suitable sleeping quarters for all that will be coming.

The FOB begins to come to life when the communications center is activated . . . normally within hours. Because of the need to support mission planning, receive intelligence data, and control teams on missions the number of SATCOM and HF radio circuits is much larger than we saw in Example #1. The FOB usually has between eight and twelve circuits of each type, which creates a farm of antennas outside the communications center. As might be imagined, supplies of good electrical power are as important as food and water, and the engineers have to work hard to supply it.

Once they're in-country, the individual SF companies set up their own facilities, including the ODB company headquarters and ODA teams. Their communications packages will probably be at least as large as those from the FID mission, and can operate alongside the FOB's comms setup.

The idea in general is to rapidly build up a base from which missions supporting the needs of the JTF commander can rapidly be generated. To help the JTF staff in their tasking, a small SF cell known as a Special Operation Command and Control Element (SOCCE) is established at JTF headquarters to act as a conduit for orders and information to and from the FOB.

If everything has been properly done, the SF battalion will be installed in its FOB and ready to go within two to three days. By this time, the FOB will probably have begun planning their initial missions in support of the JTF. Normally these will be SR missions, designed to put trained eyes onto priority intelligence targets for the JTF commander.

The first SR missions are usually launched within ninety-six hours of the arrival of the first ODAs. If possible, mission rehearsals will be run, and then the teams will be dispatched via the SOAR aircraft or other available transport. At the same time, more SR missions will be planned, as well as the first Direct Action operations in support of the JTF commander's overall engagement strategy. By this time—if the influx of American units has not deterred the hostile forces—there may be open conflict in the theater.

Meanwhile, as they get eyes onto the targets of interest, the SR teams are sending in data from behind enemy lines. These data—combined with intelligence from satellites, reconnaissance aircraft, radio intercepts, and other sources—allow the JTF commander to decide how he will react to the intentions of the enemy.

If the hostile forces have not yet initiated combat operations, then the JTF commander will probably order the SR teams to continue to watch and report (the SR teams will rotate out periodically).

If the enemy has started shooting, the SF battalion switches into high gear. DA missions will be deployed to destroy enemy infrastructure (bridges, communications, etc.), to hunt down WMDs and the personnel qualified to employ them, and possibly to initiate UW operations behind enemy lines (contact will be made with opposition groups that will be supported in a guerrilla campaign). This can, of course, take quite some time to accomplish.

These operations will continue until a resolution to the conflict occurs and both sides come to a peace agreement. Even then, the SF mission will probably continue long after other conventional units have gone home. For example, the JTF commander will probably want to use the SF teams to monitor compliance with an armistice or cease-fire agreement. The SF teams might also be called upon to set up relief efforts for refugees, or to begin training demining teams. Even after the FOB is torn down and the battalion rotated back to home base, it is likely that the JTF commander will still want some SF muscle in his theater, and a company-sized deployment might be sent.

Example #3: Major Regional Conflict

This is a worst-case scenario, where a major crisis has escalated into a full-blown war, or as they call it inside the Beltway, an MRC. Such a conflict requires a minimum deployment of a full group and the establishment of an additional level of SOF command and control. This is called a Joint Special Operations Task Force (JSOTF) headquarters, which is tied to the theater commander's own HQ (and is normally located in a friendly neighboring country). The JSOTF looks a lot like an FOB, and has similar facilities, communications resources, and personnel. The difference is that the JSOTF is designed to coordinate SOF units on a theater level. It would not only task and command an entire SFG, but might also handle operations planning and support for the Ranger Regiment, SEAL Teams and Special Boat Squadrons, or USAF SOC aircraft.

Normally, the JSOTF will be commanded by a colonel or brigadier general, with the theater SOC or SFG commander in charge. Very few people know how to command and control such large, mixed formations of SOF units, and the JSOTF job is not taken lightly.

Meanwhile, the deployment of the SF battalions will move forward as in the preceding scenario, except that each will be located separately (clustering such units makes a too tempting target). Missions will also be run as in that scenario, except that there must be greater coordination with the other component commanders to avoid unpleasant situations and "blue-on-blue" incidents.

The communications requirements, especially for SATCOM resources, will be enormous. In fact, some commercial SATCOM time may have to be bought to handle housekeeping traffic that does not have to be classified or encrypted.

The rest of the scenario will depend on the nature of the contingency and the requirements of the JTF/theater commander (though in many respects it will follow the pattern of Example #2 writ larger and with higher stakes). However it proceeds, you can count on the SF/SOF units to be deeply engaged throughout the process from start to finish.

Getting Ready:
Training for the "Big" One

If you think education is expensive . . . try ignorance!

Unknown Schoolteacher

In the U.S government, the new year begins on the first day of October, which is the first day of the new fiscal year. On this day the financial books of the old year are closed, and new funds begin to flow. On this day also most new military operations and missions officially begin (usually designated with the fiscal year and a code number).

It is not coincidental that October happens to be the month when major training exercises are launched. (The negative coincidence has to do with the flow of money. Because training tends to get cancelled to pay for "contingencies" that can break out anytime, it makes sense to schedule training as early as possible during the fiscal year.)

The largest exercises take place at the Joint Readiness Training Center (JRTC) at Fort Polk, Louisiana, and the National Training Center (NTC) at Fort Irwin, California. Most SFGs will get a rotation to one or the other, though not to both. The 3rd and 5th SFGs (with their African, Mideast, and Persian Gulf missions) tend to take part in NTC, while the 1st, 7th, 10th, 19th, and 20th tend toward JRTC. (Interestingly, SFGs participate in few overseas exercises, since real-world missions take up all their overseas time . . . and help keep them sharp.)

Because the point is to mimic as closely as possible real situations our military men and women might expect to face, exercises tend to be large and complex. Meaning: I won't be able to give you more than a taste of the world of Special Forces training. I did, however, spend quality time with soldiers from the SFGs during some of their more important training events. And I trust that the taste will fairly represent the whole meal.

A note: Army unit commanders and personnel build their entire yearly schedules around preparing for their major training rotations (the occasional real-world contingency is almost an afterthought . . . though *not* entirely). They're the "final exams" for a command tour, and can make or break a career. . . . Even so—paradoxically—commanders love them!

And a caution: In order to protect SF soldiers during their downrange missions, I must be careful about revealing their identities. Thus, with the exception of commanders of SF battalions or groups, SF soldiers will be identified by pseudonyms.

JRTC 99-1: The Odyssey of ODA 745

For over a decade, the Army's Joint Readiness Training Center has been training units and soldiers in the art of infantry warfare. Originally located at Fort Chaffee, Arkansas, it was relocated in 1993 to Fort Polk, Louisiana (where there is far more room). Here amid pine forests and swamps, units from all over the Army receive the finest force-on-force training in the world.

This is not idle talk. Many of the best new ideas and concepts for training military personnel have come out of Fort Polk. To name two: the use of third-party personnel (neutral, civilian, nongovernmental, and peacekeeper) and of what are called "adaptive scenario methods" (nonscripted random events, variable threat levels, and the like). These have been applied by other services and commands in their own exercises. Already U.S. Atlantic Command has used many of the JRTC's adaptive scenario methods to improve the quality of their own Joint Task Force Exercises (JTFEXs)[74]—the huge wargames that are run to certify the deployment readiness of Navy carrier battle groups (CVBGs), amphibious ready groups (ARGs), and Marine Expeditionary Units—Special Operations Capable (MEU [SOC]s).

The JRTC staff have additionally developed training scenarios in preparation for such operations as peacekeeping in Bosnia and humanitarian relief in Haiti; they have set up exercises that were used to demonstrate which former Warsaw Pact nations were ready for NATO membership under the Partnership for Peace (PFP) Program;[75] and they have increased the number and visibility of SOF operations during training rotations (so conventional force leaders and units can better understand the capabilities of SOF units and learn how to work better with them). Finally, they have developed a greater focus on public—and therefore media—visibility.

As little as three years ago, SOF operations in support of conventional units during JRTC rotations were not openly discussed with the public or media personnel. This has changed. U.S. Army Special Operations Command and Special Forces Command (with no little urging from the JRTC/Fort Polk commanding officer, Brigadier General Sam Thompson) have come to realize that a little openness can't hurt.

It is in this context that I headed down to Fort Polk in October 1998. Here I would experience the SOF operations of a JRTC rotation, the first of FY99 (JRTC 99-1).

This was the first major exercise of the year for Special Forces, and a major force-on-force training event by the 2nd Battalion of the 7th Special Forces Group (2/

---

74 For more on the JTFEX series, see *Marine; Airborne;* and *Carrier* (Berkley Books, 1996, 1997, and 1999 respectively).

75 These exercises (known as Cooperative Nugget-95 and -97) provided NATO with an opportunity to look over the forces of various PFP nations, and evaluate their worthiness for membership within the Atlantic alliance. In 1999, three former PFP nations, Poland, Hungary, and the Czech Republic, became the latest additions to NATO.

7th SFG). The 2/7th SFG would be the major SOF component supporting a larger conventional unit exercise by the 1st Brigade of the 10th (1/10th) Mountain Division. According to the exercise scenario, the 2/7th SFG would establish a forward operating base (FOB) on the Fort Polk reservation, then train, package, and deliver executable SF missions in support of the 1/10th Mountain. These would involve a wide range of SF capabilities, including Special Reconnaissance (SR), Direct Action (DA), and Civil Affairs (CA), and their outcome would directly affect the conditions encountered by the 1/10th Mountain. This direct linkage between conventional and SOF operations is designed to better reflect the real-world synergism of the two forces.

Tuesday, October 6th—Fort Polk, Louisiana

I flew commercially into the England Municipal Airpark, in Alexandria, Louisiana, about fifty miles from the town of Leesville and Fort Polk.

As I headed my rental car west on Louisiana Route 28[76] out of the airpark, I could see the marshalling area for the 1/10th Mountain, already filled with vehicles, tents, and personnel, while helicopters from a nearby pad buzzed around and about. All were getting ready for their movement in a few days into the JRTC "box" (the Fort Polk force-on-force exercise area).

On arriving at the Fort, I checked in with old friends Paula Schlag and Dan Nance at the Public Affairs Office (PAO), then made a short office call on Brigadier General Samuel S. Thompson III (the JRTC/Fort Polk commanding officer and a Vietnam-era Special Forces soldier).

Sam Thompson is a major reason for the recent success of JRTC, and he works hard to improve on that record, as well as keep his post healthy and busy. All over the base you can see the fruits of his work, from improved base housing to new roads and other infrastructure.

Fort Polk has changed and grown a great deal since the 1993 move down from Fort Chaffee. Though the central Louisiana locale is nothing if not off-putting. (It's fifty miles from anything like civilization; until last year there was not even a Wal-Mart in the town of Leesville. There are no AOL access numbers there, the weather runs the gamut from uncomfortable to miserable, and the countryside is crowded with alligators and four types of poisonous snakes.) Yet this is one of the most advanced and exciting classrooms in the world.

Following my chat with General Thompson, I drove over to the headquarters of the Special Operations Training Detachment on the north side of the post. SOTD, which is headed by Lieutenant Colonel Mike Rozsypal, is the control-and-observation element that watches over the SOF parts of JRTC exercises. Staffed by a highly experienced team of observer/controller personnel (they used to be known as referees), SOTD supervises and evaluates SOF units at both JRTC and NTC, and makes possible

---

76 This facility was once the old England AFB, which had been home to a wing of A-10A Thunderbolts (Warthogs) that fought during Desert Storm. It was closed during one of the rounds of base closings of the early 1990s. Today, the base facilities have been commercialized, but the government still maintains some limited facilities (such as the JRTC marshalling yard) on the property.

Lieutenant Colonel Mike Rozsypal, USA. As head of the Special Operations Training Division at the Army's Joint Readiness Training Center (located at Fort Polk, Louisiana), Rozsypal is charged with supervising the execution of Special Operations exercises during training rotations.

JOHN D. GRESHAM

the smooth interface between SOF and conventional units and operations in force-on-force training exercises.

The SOTD team has the toughest job in the entire JRTC O/C pool. Unlike conventional units, SOFs do not necessarily stay in the "box"—or even on the Fort Polk reservation—during rotations.

Though the reservation devotes over 100,000 acres of usable land to its exercise space (the total post acreage measures almost 200,000 acres) this sandbox is too small for SOF units to play on. To fully accommodate the variety of targets, terrain, and scenarios necessary to make full use of SOF units, SOTD has made arrangements to use other facilities as far away as California and the Carolinas, thus providing SOF participants with the elbowroom they would find in a real-world military theater of operations. This diversity of facilities and locations is a wonderful thing for the SOF units, but it places a huge burden on SOTD and the JRTC range support personnel.

During an exercise, SOTD O/Cs might start the day before dawn in coordination meetings at Fort Polk, travel all day to a distant field site, and then work all night supporting an SOF unit conducting SR or DA missions hundreds of miles away from Fort Polk. It's tough work for Lieutenant Colonel Rozsypal and his troops, but it has greatly improved the readiness of SOF units for large-scale contingency operations.

Lieutenant Colonel Rozsypal himself is a tall, thin, soft-spoken Texan, with a gravelly voice. When I arrived at SOTD, he introduced me to his staff, then led me into the conference room in order to lay out the ground rules he expected me to follow during the coming operation.

Since I was to be flagged as both "press" and an SOTD O/C, I was, as far as

The imaginary Aragon Island, which is used for operations at the U.S. Army's Joint Readiness Training Center (JRTC). Though JRTC is based at Fort Polk, Louisiana, operations can run over the entire Aragon area.

RUBICON, INC., BY LAURA DENINNO

Mike Rozsypal and his crew were concerned, an O/C in every way but the paycheck . . . as long as I followed the O/C rules.

The downside to all this: I had to be careful about what I said and did around the various SOF and Opposing Force (OpFor) personnel while they were in "play." The upside: I'd have access to unique knowledge about scheduled training events, and be able to observe specific missions and events of my own choosing.

After my meeting with Lieutenant Colonel Rozsypal, I was handed over to his capable executive officer, Major Bill Shaw, an experienced 10th SFG soldier, with extensive time in Europe (especially Bosnia-Herzegovina). Bill instructed me in more practical matters concerning the exercise.

His first task was to pass over to me the small red-and-black notebook that was the JRTC bible. It contained information on every scheduled SOF mission and event for JRTC 99-1, and, he explained, it was exactly like the ones his SOTD O/Cs used during each JRTC rotation. I should therefore consider it "exercise classified" for the duration of the current rotation and was not to share it with *anyone* I did not personally recognize as an O/C.

Meanwhile, he continued, I was expected to be properly dressed for field operations, which meant full battle dress uniform (BDU), soft field cap, and camouflage paint for my face (when ordered).

Once he'd spelled out the rules and regulations, Major Shaw laid out the exercise scenario for JRTC 99-1:

The overall scenario had the 2/7th SFG supporting movement of the 1/10th Mountain into what Army nomenclature calls "a slow-developing international crisis." This was to take place on the imaginary island of Aragon—which was theoretically located in the middle of the Atlantic Ocean some 2,000 miles/3,200 km east of Washington, D.C. (and which, for the sake of the exercise, was made up of parts of Louisiana, Arkansas, Mississippi, Alabama, Oklahoma, Texas, and Tennessee). Aragon was divided into three hypothetical countries—Cortina (the "good guys"), Atlantica (the "bad guys"), and Victoria (nonspecific neutrals, which is to say, they could be allies with the "good" guys or the "bad" guys, depending upon the scenario). In JRTC 99-1, the Victorians allowed the basing of U.S. units and aircraft on their soil, and were essentially pro-U.S./Cortina. Aragon is assumed to be divided among English-, Spanish-, and French-speaking peoples. They are multiethnic and religiously Christian.

The JRTC 99-1 scenario assumed that the Atlantican Forces (called the People's Revolutionary Army) was preparing to invade Cortina, where it would be assisted by insurgent forces in Cortina itself (the Cortinian Liberation Front). The U.S. was then assumed to have pre-emptively moved its military forces into the region to stop the Atlantican aggression, and would operate from bases both in Victoria and Cortina. The 1/10th was the largest of these forces, and would bear the brunt of the conventional fighting against the PRA and the CLF. The mission would be to stabilize the situation on Cortina, neutralize the CLF insurgents, and defeat the expected Atlantican invasion.

Since my focus was on the SOF end of JRTC 99-1, Major Shaw rapidly filled in the details about this part of the rotation. Special Forces personnel, together with elements of the 160th Special Operations Aviation Regiment (SOAR—the Nightstalkers) would provide the 1/10th Mountain brigade commander (acting as the Joint Task Force—Cortina commander) with the necessary SOF muscle to accomplish his assigned missions. The SOF units would support the conventional forces, and conduct missions to interdict the combat potential of enemy forces. A number of USASOC SOF units had been to JRTC 99-1. These broke down this way:

- **Joint Special Operations Task Force Cortina (JSOTF [Cortina])**—A JSOTF commander and headquarters are normally atop any theater-level SOF chain of command, but for JRTC rotations, this role is played by part of the Operations Group staff. These personnel script the SOF scenario and control events in real-time during operations. The JSOTF Cortina was actually located at a site near the port of Beaumont, Texas.

- **Special Operations Command and Control Element Cortina (SOCCE [Cortina])**—This is the most significant link between SOF and conventional units . . . and a major reason why operational relations between the two have significantly improved. The SOCCE concept places a coordination element of about a dozen SOF personnel (usually commanded by a major) at a higher command—brigade or division—Tactical Operations Center. In JRTC 99-1, SOCCE (Cortina) would provide the 1/10th Mountain commander with the ability to send tasking data to 2/7th SFG, in addition to providing him with controls on missions in the field. For JRTC 99-1, the SOCCE (Cortina) personnel were drawn from 2/7th SFG, but would remain colocated with the TOC of the 1/10th Mountain. Initially, this was at the England Airpark marshalling area. They moved into the Fort Polk "box" when the 10th Mountain deployed there.

- **2/7th SFG**—For JRTC 99-1, 2/7th SFG brought along most of their command element (ODC), but only about a single company of SF teams and supporting units. These included:

  —**Forward Operating Base 72 (FOB 72)/Operational Detachment Charlie**—Led by the 2/7th SFG commander, Lieutenant Colonel Joe Smith, FOB 72 would be tasked with planning, preparing, and controlling the various missions being run for JSOTF (Cortina) and SOCCE (Cortina).

  —**Operational Detachment Alphas (ODAs)**—For JRTC 99-1, 2/7th SFG brought along five ODAs. These were drawn mainly from 2/7th SFG (including some coming off downrange missions that had returned only hours prior to the end of FY98).

  —**Support Operations Team Bravo (SOT-B)**—Along with the five ODAs, 2/7th SFG brought along some serious military intelligence (MI) collection capability in the form of an SOT-B element. The SOT-B team provided intelligence coordination for the staff of FOB 72 and command and control for the two SOT-A collection teams described below.

  —**Support Operations Team Alpha (SOT-A)**—2/7th SFG brought along a pair of SOT-A teams to provide downrange signals and electronic collection capability for the FOB. Usually composed of four specially trained communications sergeants, an SOT-A is equipped with lightweight interception gear suitable for field use. Normally, an SOT-A would be attached to an ODA during actual mission operations.

  Though Lieutenant Colonel Smith had only brought along a few hundred SF soldiers, they would simulate the operations of a full battalion. Along with planning and executing actual missions, they would lay out a number of others, which would never be run. This would provide the FOB staff with the experience of a wartime workload.

- **478th Civil Affairs Battalion**—Also assigned to FOB 72 was a small but important civil affairs (CA) detachment. Composed of just six Army Reserve personnel from the Miami-based 478th Civil Affairs Battalion, this detachment would be a critical resource in helping deal with CA challenges in the "box."

- **3rd Battalion/160th SOAR (the Nightstalkers)**—At USASOC's direction, the 160th SOAR sent four MH-60 Special Operations transport helicopters to provide long-range transportation for the various missions of 2/7th SFG. Assigned to the regiment's 3rd Battalion at Hunter Army Airfield near Fort Stewart, Georgia, the MH-60s are earlier model helicopters and lack some of the latest avionics, though they are equipped for in-flight refueling. For the duration of JRTC 99-1, the 160th helicopters would form their own forward-deployment location at Barksdale AFB near Shreveport, Louisiana.

- **4th Marine Air Wing (MAW)**—To fulfill the aerial refueling needs of the 160th's MH-60s, the USMC provided a KC-130T tanker aircraft from the 4th MAW. Based at Naval Air Station Fort Worth Joint Reserve Base (formerly Carswell AFB) in Fort Worth, Texas, the KC-130T was assigned to Marine Aerial Refueler Transport

An MH-60L Blackhawk helicopter assigned to the 160th Special Operations Regiment. A pair of these helicopters were used to transport ODA 745 from Fort Polk, Louisiana, to Camp Shelby in Mississippi.

OFFICIAL U.S. ARMY PHOTO

Squadron 234 (VNGR-234). Unlike most USAF tanker aircraft, which are jet powered, turboprops power the KC-130s, which means they can fly at much slower speeds. Also, the KC-130s carry the NATO-standard "drogue and probe" refueling rig (used by the 160th's MH-47s and MH-60s), rather than the USAF "flying boom" system. As an added bonus, the KC-130s can also be used as a conventional medium transport aircraft, and can carry airborne troops.

- **16th Special Operations Wing**—To provide additional aerial refueling, transport, and airdrop support for 2/7th SFG, a USAF MC-130 Combat Talon Special Operations aircraft was sent over from Air Force Special Operations Command. Assigned to the 16th Special Operations Wing at Hurlbert Field, Florida, the MC-130 can conduct covert penetrations of denied airspace, precision parachute drops of supplies and personnel, and refueling of Special Operations or Marine helicopters. Combat Talon can also be used as a bomber to deliver the huge 15,000-lb./6,800-kg. BLU-82. Officially known as Commando Vault, it is better known by the nicknames "Big Blue 82" or the "Daisy Cutter."[77]

This was a considerable amount of SOF muscle, though Major Shaw made it clear that every bit of it would be busy during the upcoming rotation.

---

77 The BLU-82 was used during the Vietnam War to knock down tree and plant structures, creating an instant helicopter landing pad. During the 1991 Persian Gulf War, BLU-82s were used to clear Iraqi minefields and terrorize enemy troops in conjunction with leaflet drops.

Forward Operating Base 72 during JRTC 99-1. This was the headquarters for the 2nd Battalion of the 7th Special Forces Group during the rotation.

JOHN D. GRESHAM

After Major Shaw's JRTC 99-1 SOF briefing, I headed over to the post motor lodge for the night. In the morning I would get a look inside FOB 72 and the missions they were planning for the coming rotation.

Wednesday, October 7th—Fort Polk

The morning dawned dark and overcast, promising storms. Up early in order to take in as many of the FOB 72 operations as I could, I met Major Bill Shaw at the SOTD headquarters at 0600. After handing me a security badge to clip to my pocket, he walked me across the street to the O/C entrance to the FOB 72 compound—mostly World War II–era barracks buildings that a strong wind might blow over. Given the rough-looking weather, that seemed a strong possibility!

The ground was already sodden from several days of heavy rain, and sheets of plywood had been laid down to provide a stable walking surface between buildings.

Our destination was the 2/7th mess hall, where we were joined by our USASOC project officer, Major Tom McCollum, the Special Forces PAO (he would act in the same role within the exercise). Tom would be "in play" during JRTC 99-1 as part of the Army's "Media on the Battlefield" program, running a hypothetical public affairs effort for FOB 72. Like all the other participants (Allied, OpFor, neutral civilians, etc.), he would be wearing a Multiple Integrated Laser Exercise System (MILES) harness, which would "score" him as a casualty if he were "shot" or otherwise wounded during the exercise.[78]

SF soldiers love a good, hot meal. The leadership of SFC, 7th SFG, and 2/7th SFG is aware of this, and was pulling out all stops to make sure that the soldiers at FOB 72 were well-fed and cared for. There was fresh fruit and/or a salad bar at the

---

[78] For more on MILES and its use in force-on-force training, see *Armored Cav* and *Airborne* (Berkley Books, 1994 and 1998 respectively).

served meals (breakfast and dinner), and lots of down-home American food. Breakfast was a full country affair, with eggs-to-order, pancakes, biscuits and gravy, and an array of morning meats.

After filling my plate, I headed to a table to meet my host for the next few days, Lieutenant Colonel Joseph M. Smith. Joe Smith is one of the new generation of SF leaders—long in downrange experience, yet savvy in the new technologies that are revolutionizing the trade. As a 7th SFG battalion commander, he is at the forefront in bringing new computer, communications, and other technologies into Special Forces units and missions.

I would get my fill of such things shortly, but first came a more human, real-world issue.

Major McCollum and Lieutenant Colonel Smith called over a young Hispanic SF soldier, who they introduced as Captain Carlos. Carlos had just returned from a mission downrange in Ecuador, where several ODAs had been conducting peace-keeping, humanitarian, and other duties. He and his team were assigned to work out in the mountainous countryside, mostly inhabited by various Indian tribes.

Here he was introduced to a little boy I'll call Juan, a lad of perhaps four years when Carlos and his ODA arrived in the mountain village where he lived. When Juan was perhaps two years old, he fell into a wood cooking fire (his village had no electricity, gas, sewers, or phones) and was horribly disfigured: From just below his chin down to midchest was a massive scar. Eating, talking, and even moving were all difficult. Clearly, fate had cast a very cold eye on this little boy.

Despite his misfortune, Juan was a happy, delightful child, the darling of the villagers. He instantly won Captain Carlos's heart as well. "What can be done for the little guy?" he asked himself.

On a visit back to the American embassy in Quito, Carlos phoned his father in Miami. A little homework uncovered a Shriners' program for children like Juan. This would not only pay for the boy's plastic surgery, but contribute to his father's living expenses during the recovery period.

Captain Carlos personally took care of the paper work (including photos) for submission to the Shriners' Foundation, and within weeks, word arrived that Juan could go to the U.S. for the operation.

Arrangements were made with the Texas Children's Hospital in Houston and everything looked ready to go . . . Except for one small problem: Someone had to arrange for Juan and his dad to travel to the U.S.

Undaunted, Captain Carlos again swung into action, and personally asked the American Ambassador in Ecuador if he could arrange something. It turned out he could, and Juan and his father were given seats on a business jet owned by the Drug Enforcement Agency for the flight to Miami. (Though the flight was going up empty anyway, carrying civilian foreign nationals was officially not permitted. The ambassador waived the technicality.)

Within weeks, Juan and his father were at the Miami airport. They were met by Captain Carlos's dad, who got them headed for Houston. (Though not before

Lieutenant Colonel Joe Smith, USA. Smith was the commander of the 2nd Battalion of the 7th Special Forces Group during JRTC 99-1.

JOHN D. GRESHAM

Juan's father had discovered the airport's automatic flush toilets. He was enchanted by them.)

Juan's surgeries went well, and he was headed home a few weeks later—a little boy whose life was forever changed for the better by an SF soldier who saw he could help. (It's easy to imagine also the reaction of Juan's fellow villagers. No rebel movement will get a toehold there!)

His story finished, the young captain headed back to his team room to plan his ODA's assigned mission.

After breakfast, I followed Lieutenant Colonel Smith and Major McCollum across the compound to the FOB 72 operations center.

As we walked across the soggy courtyard between barracks, Lieutenant Colonel Smith pointed out the force protection measures his unit had put into effect. The compound—almost a city block long and a hundred yards wide—was ringed with antipersonnel wire and obstacles; guard towers had been built and floodlights rigged; motion/infrared sensors had been installed; and roving patrols were running continuously.

These precautions were far from idle: The previous evening, a sniper had shot an SF soldier in the compound, sending him to the JRTC casualty evacuation collection point, where he was assessed as "dead"—the first 2/7th casualty.[79]

FOB 72 personnel avenged this attack when they caught another CLF team trying

---

[79] At JRTC, the casualty/evacuation system sends each person judged as wounded by his or her MILES harness to a central receiving station near the post's Army airfield. Here they are randomly given a card that assesses their wounds. Some can be "treated;" others are judged "dead." The JRTC replacement system allows some of the "dead" to go back to their units and get back into the action . . . but only if they are properly handled in the system by their home unit.

to enter the compound through an apparent blind spot in the wire. The CLF insurgents "died" in a hail of SF automatic weapons fire. Though other vicious little firefights were fought over the next two weeks, the security of the FOB held up.

The command center was located in a two-story barracks building, itself protected by another layer of barbed wire and security fencing. The staff and command elements had each established a desk or work area on the first floor, arranged much like a mission control center in Houston and manned around the clock. They were equipped with an array of desktop and laptop computers, printers, phones, SABER radios, and laminated maps. The computers, like all of those around the FOB, were linked into a large local area network (LAN), which would allow users to access everything from e-mail off the Internet to secure data from classified databases on a large file server in another barracks building.

Upstairs was a briefing room, equipped with a large-screen projection system for electronic briefing slides. This was my current destination, as Lieutenant Colonel Smith had invited me to the morning shift change briefing at 0700. The FOB staff is split into two sections. Twice a day, the entire staff meets to brief each other and hand off the duty for another twelve hours. It is during these briefings that you can typically get the best feeling for how SF operations are being organized and run.

Following briefings by intelligence, weather, logistics, and public affairs personnel, the operations officer (S-3) began to lay out the missions that FOB 72 would run during JRTC 99-1. As tasked by JSOTF (Cortina), a total of six SF missions were planned for actual execution—three SRs, two DAs, and a single CA. The missions laid out like this:

- **CA001**—CA001 was designed to assess the morale and political leanings of civilians (contract roleplayers in this case) in the Carnis Village area (an artificial training town located in the Northwest corner of the exercise area). Carnis, known as Joint Special Operations Area (JSOA) "Acorn," was important to the 1/10th Mountain/JTF (Cortina) commander, because it stood astride his planned entry route into the "box." The CA001 personnel included a small CA detachment (two members of the 478th CA Battalion) and an ODA to provide security. These had been infiltrated into the Fort Polk "box" by a pair of 160th SOAR MH-60L helicopters. Though CA001 was originally scheduled for completion the previous day, it had been extended (and was still going on) due to the high quality and quantity of information it had developed.

- **SR001**—To better assess the logistical capabilities of the CLF to sustain operations in the field, an ODA and an SOT-A were to be inserted into an area in the southwest part of the "box," where they would gather information and transmit it back to the FOB. The combined ODA/SOT-A team would be parachuted in, and eventually extracted, following a link-up with the 1/10th Mountain after their scheduled entry into the area on October 9th.

- **SR002**—SR002 was to be tasked with locating a suspected CLF psychological operations broadcast site in the southeastern end of the "box," known as "Paint." Like SR001, SR002 would be composed of a combined ODA/SOT-A team, which would then listen in on the enemy broadcasts and hopefully provide targeting data back to JSOTF (Cortina). SR002 would also be extracted following a link-up with the 1/10th Mountain.

- **SR003**—A major part of the overall JRTC 99-1 scenario was the suppression of enemy weapons of mass destruction capabilities. SR003 was planned as a reconnaissance to assess the CLF's ability to employ chemical mines (filled with faux mustard gas). Composed of a single ODA, the mission would be inserted into Crosby Airfield (part of the Humochitto National Forest southeast of Natchez, Mississippi, known as JSOA "Gator") by a pair of 160th SOAR MH-60Ls. The ODA planned to set up several observation posts there to monitor the suspected transshipment site, and send targeting data back to JSOTF (Cortina).

- **DA001**—The DA001 mission was a rare one these days: They were to perform an assassination. The target was a notional Atlantican-trained CLF officer, who was the only person trained and equipped to supervise the arming and deployment of chemical mines . . . Federal laws place considerable restrictions on assassination missions, even in wartime. This, as we'll see, was an exceptional situation, and a justifiable killing. Here is what made the "hit" legal: He was a uniformed member of a known military service. For this reason, JSOTF (Cortina) had authorized his elimination, and 2/7th SFG was tasked to do the job with a specially formed sniper ODA. The ODA would be inserted into and extracted from Camp Shelby, Mississippi (JSOA "Snake") via a pair of 160th SOAR MH-60L helicopters.

- **DA003**—Another WMD-related mission, DA003 was designed to eliminate another chemical weapons technician from the CLF roster. This one would not be killed, however, for this particular specialist had passed the word that he would like to "defect." The ODA assigned to DA003 would therefore conduct a "snatch and grab" operation to effect that. The ODA would be inserted into the abandoned Stennis Space Center (at one time the primary assembly facility for the various stages of Saturn 5 moon rockets) in Mississippi (JSOA "Magic") on a pair of 160th SOAR MH-60Ls. Once there, they planned to link up with the defector, establish their bonafides, and then exfiltrate on another pair of MH-60s.

Though these missions would be executed by 2/7th SFG, several others were planned and rehearsed, but not actually run. Each ODA would plan two missions, but only execute one. These planning missions included:

- **SR004**—Designed to deny the CLF use of a new antitank weapon (the Russian-built AT-7), SR004 would have inserted an ODA into Camp McCain, Mississippi (JSOA "Gold"). Once on the ground, the team would have to locate and target the AT-7 missile supply facility for allied air assets.

- **DA004**—An extremely large and complex mission, DA004 would have inserted two ODAs into the Peason Ridge (JSOA "Nerve") and Horses Head (JSOA "Horse") areas on the Fort Polk live-fire ranges to attack and destroy a pair of CLF command-and-control targets. The teams would have located and destroyed a pair of caches for cryptographic machines and materials. By denying the CLF secure communications, allied conventional forces could better anticipate and defeat future CLF operations.

All of these operations, both planned and executed, were designed by JSOTF (Cortina) to directly support the needs and desires of the 1/10th Mountain. Depending upon the results, the 1/10th Mountain might or might not face the threat of WMDs or enhanced antitank weapons.

To better understand the process of planning, preparation, and execution of SF missions in general, I decided to follow one from start to finish. As you might imagine, the one that caught my eyes was DA001. Following ten very intriguing young men on a classic sniper mission all the way to the hit was not only genuinely exciting, it would display some of the most interesting aspects of SOF operations.

Once the shift change briefing was over, I continued on my tour of FOB 72. Despite the decrepit look of the buildings, 2/7th SFG had done an excellent job of turning it into their home away from home. All around the FOB compound there was a sense of gathering momentum. Already, CA001 was in the "box," generating important data for JSOTF (Cortina) and 1/10th Mountain, while SR001, SR002, and DA001 were due to launch within the next twenty-four hours.

But there was a looming—and growing—problem: the weather. Over the past few days, a number of nasty thunderstorms had moved through the area, and more were expected. The sky continued to threaten as we headed toward the building where ODA 745 was located, another two-story barracks.

ODA 745 occupied the entire first floor, with their team room in the front, and sleeping quarters in the rear. This morning was a busy time for them, as they were preparing to launch DA001 that evening. Even so, they greeted me warmly, offered a cup of coffee, and then gave me a good look at what they were doing.

All around were more than a dozen SF soldiers working away. Some were members of the team that would carry out DA001, others belonged to other ODAs and were helping "push" the mission out into the world. In a corner a sergeant was "stripping" down packages of Meals Ready to Eat of their excess packaging (cardboard boxes). By taking only the sealed pouches of prepared food, three complete meals can be packed in just one of the tough brown plastic MRE bags. These were then resealed with duct tape and put into another zippered plastic bag for protection. Each member of ODA 745 would carry six of these packages, along with enough water for several days. The team could then stay hidden in JSOA "Snake" (Camp Shelby) if necessary, without having to look for water every day.

After a few moments to get the feel of the place, I was introduced to the members of ODA 745 who would carry out DA001.[80] ODA 745 was a "pickup team" for JRTC

---

80 While seemingly random, the ODA numbering system does have logic behind it: The first digit refers to the number of the ODA's SFG. The second references its assigned company (there are nine per SFG). The last numbers the ODA within its company, from one to six. Therefore, the designation ODA 745 tells you that the team is assigned to the 7th SFG, 2nd Battalion/Company "A," 5th ODA.

99-1. That is, several of the SF soldiers assigned to the team normally worked in other ODAs; their specific talents would be needed for DA001.

Let me introduce you to the nine young men of ODA 745:

- **Commander**—The ODA would be led by Captain Greg, who would command the mission in the field and act as part of the security force during the "hit."
- **Team Sergeant**—Actual running of the day-to-day operations of ODA 745 would be left to Sergeant Charlie, a long-time 7th SFG soldier. Once in the target area at Camp Shelby, Charlie would run the Mission Support Site (MSS or base camp) for the team.
- **Communications**—DA001 would place a heavy burden on communications, both within the team and back to FOB 72. For this mission only a single 18E would go along, Staff Sergeant John.
- **Medic**—All SF missions take along at least one medic (18D). For DA001, ODA 745 ODA 745 had an experienced 18D in Staff Sergeant Brandon.
- **Snipers**—Two sniper teams would conduct the actual "hit." Each would be composed of a sniper armed with an M24 sniper rifle and a spotter with a high-powered spotting scope. The two snipers for DA001 would be Sergeants Sean and Shannon.
- **Spotters**—For this mission the snipers were not actually certified for that role; it was the spotters on the scopes who were sniper qualified. That is, the men assigned to shoot Major Benitiz, while qualified weapons sergeants, had not taken the sniper course. Captain Greg and Sergeant Jim had taken the advice of their two certified snipers, who'd argued that the toughest part of this hit would be spotting the target and coaching the shooters onto it. We'll call the spotters Sergeants Jim and Glenn.
- **SAW Gunner**—To provide the two sniper teams cover after taking their shots at the target, the team took along a gunner armed with an M249 SAW light machine gun. Captain Greg and Sergeant Louis (the M249 gunner) would man this "blocking position."

While this ODA was short several vital personnel—an 18C (engineering), 18D (medical), and 18E (communications)—they were well able to carry out the mission. ODAs these days frequently go downrange short critical personnel; DA001 reflected this real-world trend.

Already, the team was into what they call their "isolation phase," a period of time where they work out final mission plans, equipment, schedules, and other details. The isolation is not total, and is broken for briefings, inspections, and a mission rehearsal (if that is possible).

The mission rehearsal had in fact already taken place at a local range on Fort Polk, and the shooter teams were proudly showing off their paper witness targets (big paper targets with silhouettes of people on them). Both had scored in the "ten ring" (kill zone). Now all they needed before they were totally ready was time to finish their preparations, and then there'd be a "briefback" and inspection by Lieutenant Colonel Smith.[81]

After accepting an invitation to join ODA 745 during their briefback at 1600 that afternoon, I headed off to visit other teams. As I moved between buildings, the storm that had been threatening finally broke—followed by several hours of heavy rain, severe thunder and lightning, and high winds. This storm was headed east, into the drop and infiltration zones for SR001, SR002, and DA001. Clearly the chances for a weather delay were high.

I arrived back in the ODA 745 team room at 1600. In attendance were Lieutenant Colonel Smith, his command sergeant major, several other 2/7th SFG staff officers, and Major McCollum (acting as a "press" escort). At the front of the room was the entire ODA 745 team, with numerous charts, maps, and satellite photos mounted on briefing boards behind them. What they had put together was part "stubby pencil" and part laptop computer/color inkjet printer, with some butcher paper and marker charts thrown in. It wasn't elegant, but you had to be impressed with what the team had generated in only a few days.

When everyone was ready, the team presented the details of their mission. Some of the major topics included:

- **Target**—The target for DA001, Major Raul Benitiz, a hypothetical CLF officer, trained in chemical weapons employment by the PRA in Atlantica, was presumed to be the only member of the CLF with the technical knowledge and skills to arm and place land mines and artillery shells filled with nerve and mustard agents. Benitiz's mission during JRTC 99-1 was to train a cadre of CLF technicians to handle and deliver chemical mines and shells, which could prove disastrous to JTF (Cortina). His elimination would almost surely eliminate the chance that the 1/10th Mountain would face a WMD threat when they entered the JRTC "box." Allied intelligence had not only located Benitiz at Camp Shelby, deep within Atlantica, but had established a pattern to his daily schedule.

- **Timeline**—DA001 was scheduled to start at 2100 hours that evening. Should a weather delay occur, a twenty-four-hour "push" pad had been built into the plan. Two windows of opportunity had been projected for the actual hit—one on the evening of the 8th, and the other on the 9th. That meant ODA 745 had to be in the target area before dawn on the day of the hit. Once the teams had taken their shots, the team would rapidly leave the target area, move to the exfiltration area, and wait for pickup on either the 8th or 9th.

- **Transportation**—The entire infiltration flight on 160th SOAR MH-60L Black-hawk helicopters would be nonstop (except for the team infiltration in to the landing zone), with an in-flight refueling from an airborne tanker on the way back to their FOB at Barksdale AFB. Once on the ground, the team would travel by foot only (there'd be no motor transportation). In the event that the helicopter exfiltra-

---

81 Briefbacks are the final briefings just prior to mission execution. Frequently these will be used to hammer out final problems, set Rules of Engagement (ROEs), and other last-minute items.

tion could not take place, ODA 745 was prepared to conduct a highly classified escape and evasion evolution, and work their way back to friendly lines.[82]

- **Logistics**—For DA001, logistics would be a minimal concern. Thanks to the short duration of the mission, there would be no attempt to supply the team while they were on the ground. Team members would carry their allotment of stripped-down MREs and several days' supply of water. The only real sustenance issue was to locate a good hiding place for the MSS close to potable water. The FOB 72 intelligence staff had suggested several possible MSSs, and the team had determined march routes to each.

- **Communications**—While ODA 745 did not have to carry a lot of food and water, they were going to lug around a heavy load of communications gear. Along with a man-portable SATCOM set, the team would also have the standard HF radio and a cell phone, in the event of a real-world emergency situation (such as a severe medical problem or personnel injury). For team communications, each team member would be equipped with a Motorola Saber FM radio set. Much of the mission plan depended upon the Saber radios working well, since coordination between the sniper, blocking, and MSS teams would be essential.

- **Expected Threat Forces**—DA001 was going *deep* into enemy territory. The flight to Camp Shelby would run over 250 miles/400 km., and the threat of OpFor action was quite real. On the other hand, the terrain was fairly good for the ODA—rolling hills and swampy, stream-laced low areas. These areas were generally overgrown, though there were numerous trails and roads in the target area. Major Benitiz was expected to be found in a small bungalow in a meadow. The bungalow would be surrounded by a personal security force of three to five CLF/PRA soldiers armed with light machine guns and automatic weapons. There was also a platoon (twenty-plus personnel) of enemy soldiers patrolling the area, equipped with mortars and machine guns. Additional troops (sixty-plus) in the area included local forest rangers and Atlantican law enforcement personnel.

- **Objectives**—The key objective for DA001 would be the elimination (i.e., killing) of Major Benitiz in his bungalow. If possible, the team would assess his condition following the hit, though this was a secondary priority to getting the team to the exfiltration area. ODA 745 was also to assess the progress of Benitiz's training of the CLF, based on any equipment (KHF-2 chemical mines or chemical warfare garments) that they might encounter during the mission.

- **Risk Assessment**—Because military operations hardly ever work as planned, planners need to figure out what might go wrong, and then provide appropriate remedies. This is called "risk assessment." To this end, Captain Greg's team had evaluated the major mission risks DA001 might encounter. The downside possibilities included events like a helicopter dropping out during the infiltration (in which case a reduced seven-man team would attempt the hit), and "friendly fire"

---

82 Special Forces E&Es are among the most classified of their many operational procedures. Even during exercises like JRTC 99-1, I was asked not to ask questions or obtain information about E&E procedures. I can say that SF E&E skills are an important part of their training, and are regularly practiced.

casualties (best avoided by figuring the optimum shoot angles on the target). The bottom line was fairly obvious: DA001 was a high-risk, high-payoff mission, but with good planning, an excellent rehearsal, and the established skills of the team members, it would likely succeed.

It was a solid plan, and Lieutenant Colonel Smith and his staff quickly approved it.

Now the time had come for the team to get some rest, finish packing, and take care of private business.

For me it meant a wait of a day or two until I could observe the hit at Camp Shelby (this would mean a six-hour drive to Mississippi). Until then, I would observe other aspects of the JRTC 99-1 operations.

Wednesday, October 7th—England Airpark, Alexandria, Louisiana

When I arrived at the FOB 72 compound, it was obvious that yesterday's storms had sent things into the toilet. The weather had forced "pushes" on the launch of DA001 and the parachute infiltrations of SR001 and SR002. (When a delay occurs, the planned operation is "pushed" later in the schedule. Most missions have pre-arranged "push" points built into the plan in case of weather delays or other uncontrollable events.) These would all be rescheduled to start again that evening.

The morning shift change briefing laid out the new launch plans. To my surprise, the mood in the team rooms continued to be optimistic. For ODA 745, the day's wait meant extra sleep and a chance to fine-tune the operations plan—though it also meant they would have to move faster than they'd like when they got to Camp Shelby. It took more than bad weather to upset experienced SF soldiers.

After the 0700 briefing, Major McCollum and Lieutenant Colonel Smith made me an offer I couldn't refuse. There was room on the helicopters for me to accompany ODA 745 on that evening's infiltration mission. My *yes* did not come hard.

Meanwhile, Major McCollum and I drove back to the England Airpark where we'd visit the SOCCE (Cortina) coordination team working with the 1/10th Mountain. An hour later, we were at the 1/10th Mountain staging area. The brigade was at this point setting off for the JRTC "box," and the lead elements of truck convoys could be seen heading west toward Fort Polk.

On the way into the staging area, Major McCollum and I had to show our passes several times; the force protection security cordon was extremely tight.

The JTF (Cortina) 1/10th Mountain headquarters were inside a large warehouse at one end of the compound; SOCCE (Cortina) was located at a corner of the warehouse, with plywood walls separating them from the rest of the 1/10th headquarters TOC. The SOCCE (Cortina) team was composed of an ODB/company headquarters team, which had been drawn from 7th SFG. Major David, a 7th SFG company commander, supervised the team with cool efficiency.

As I looked around and asked questions here and there, things seemed pretty quiet. The CA001 mission was still running near Carnis Village, and Major David came and went several times with updates and information for the JTF commander and his staff, but nothing much else seemed to be happening. All around us, the dozen or so SF soldiers assigned to the SOCCE went about their work in near silence.

But an hour later, during a briefing on SOCCE tasking and coordination procedures, things got interesting. At 1430 hours, a message arrived from FOB 72 that the CLF had ambushed the team running CA001 in Carnis Village at 0100 hours. The SF troops had taken heavy casualties and desperately needed relief.

Soon after that, other reports from the Carnis Village constable and World Relief (a team of roleplayers simulating a nongovernmental organization providing civilian relief services) filled in details: The ambush had left seven SF and CA soldiers down; some, it seems, were "dead," though no one knew how many.

Major David gathered the early fragmentary reports up and headed through the door to the 1/10th TOC to talk to the brigade commander.

Meanwhile, one of the major's SOCCE staff members, a SOCCE staff sergeant, who was also an 18D (medical sergeant), began to put together his gear. Outside soldiers from the 1/10th Mountain could be heard gathering.

Over the next hour, the reports became less fragmentary. This, it turns out, is what had happened:

Some days earlier, a portion of the CA001 security detachment had been pulled back in order to get ready for another mission later in the rotation. This left just four CA troops from the 478th and a four-man security team of SF soldiers. They had been generating an extremely valuable flow of intelligence information on the civil situation in the village of Carnis for several days . . . so valuable that JSOTF (Cortina) had planned to leave them there until the 1/10th Mountain's arrived late the next day.[83] Now the team had been wiped out, and a seemingly successful CA mission had turned very bad indeed.

Almost instantly, Major David's team put together a rescue force. A platoon of troops from the 1/10th Mountain assembled with their weapons and supplies outside the SOCCE, where they were briefed by the warrant officer who would act as the medic for the force. A few hundred yards away, a pair of UH-60L Blackhawks and another pair of OH-58D Kiowa Warrior scout/attack helicopters were made ready for launch. The first Blackhawk would carry the troops and evacuate the wounded; the other would act as a command-and-control platform, while the Kiowa Warriors would act as escort/cover.

While all this was going on, Major David was making a quick risk assessment. He didn't like the "feel" of the situation he was sending his rescue force into. What if the enemy had larger ambush plans? What if he was sending more guys into a bigger trap? Carnis Village was scarcely more than a few buildings at a fork in the road at the northern end of the Fort Polk "box." The one clearing large enough to act as an LZ (landing zone) for the UH-60s was several hundred yards/meters from the village. It wouldn't take much effort for the CLF to set up an ambush with a couple of mortars, man-portable SAMs, or rocket-propelled grenade teams there.[84] . . . A messy situation.

---

83 The plan called for the 1/10th Mountain forward reconnaissance elements to enter the "box" at 1900 hours on the 7th, while the main elements planned to arrive at Carnis at 1300 hours on the 8th.

84 During Vietnam, Viet Cong often used wounded American soldiers and Marines as "bait" to draw other forces into an ambush zone.

And things could get worse.

For starters, countering it would require dispatching an even larger relief force to rescue the first team of rescuers . . . Opening up even worse possibilities of worse ambushes . . . It was beginning to sound like a recipe for chaos that might endanger the entire entry plan of 1/10th Mountain into JRTC 99-1. The major was beginning to wonder if he should risk sending the rescue force to Carnis.

This is why command ain't easy.

On the other hand, there are occasions when time makes command less hard.

That's what happened this day. After an hour of working the problem, it resolved itself. At 1530 Hours, word arrived that a doctor from World Relief had picked up the wounded CA/SF soldiers and driven them to a local clinic, and they were expected to survive. That meant the rescue mission could be terminated, and everyone at the SOCCE could stand down.

This was my cue to leave.

As Major McCollum and I drove back to Fort Polk, we couldn't help wondering if CA001 should have even been out there in the first place. According to the original plan, CA001 would work in Carnis for just a couple of days, and they'd have a security detail to watch out for bad guys. In the event, they'd spent the better part of a week there, and most of the security detail had pulled back to FOB 72. That this had been done at the orders of JSOTF (Cortina) made little difference. Seven SF and CA soldiers had been taken out of play, and the CA casualties represented two-thirds of the tiny CA detachment of the 478th. The two surviving representatives would have a very hard time managing until replacements arrived.

Did commanders make the wrong decisions? It's hard to say. Certainly Major McCollum and I had no good answers to that question. But, as might be imagined, the "Carnis Massacre" was discussed for days around FOB 72.

Meanwhile, I had to get ready for my ride with ODA 745 later that evening.

Wednesday, October 7th—Fort Polk

At 2130 hours, Major McCollum and I were at the FOB 72 compound waiting for the two 160th SOAR MH-60Ls. I was dressed in a fire-resistant NOMEX flight suit and carried a helmet, gloves, flight jacket, some food and water, a notebook, and a green nylon bag.

According to my agreement with SFC and the 160th SOAR, there would be no photos that night, nor would I make note of the names of the crews and their call signs. In exchange for these (sensible) restrictions, I was about to get a taste of something that few civilians have experienced: a ride with the 160th SOAR (the Night-stalkers) on one of their Special Operations helicopters.

These particular birds were MH-60Ls, early model Special Operations helicopters now being superceded by the newer MH-60K version. Based upon the Sikorsky Black-hawk airframe, the "L" model MH-60 was an interim version procured while the regiment waited for the more capable "K" model (equipped with in-flight refueling probes and terrain following radars). Two "K" models had been scheduled to fly ODA

745 the previous evening, but they weren't available tonight. Thus, a pair of MH-60Ls were on their way down from their FOB at Barksdale AFB near Shreveport to carry the team to Camp Shelby.

Though they lacked the in-flight refueling and TFR capability, the "Ls" were equipped with AAQ-16 forward-looking infrared (FLIR) thermal imagers and night vision goggles (NVGs), and each had a complete SATCOM communication suite, a pair of 7.62mm six-barreled miniguns, an onboard ARN-148 navigation system with a global positioning satellite receiver tied to the avionics, and extra fuel tanks on the external stores systems racks outboard. Each MH-60 carries a crew of four—a pilot, copilot, and two gunners (one is also the crew chief). When fully loaded with fuel, personnel (up to six loaded passengers), and gear, these birds are truly jammed.

It would be a busy night of flying for the teams of 2/7th SFG. The 160th SOAR had flown additional aircraft into JRTC 99-1, including several of the larger MH-47K Chinook twin-rotor transport helicopters, which would be used later in the rotation. In addition to the delivery of ODA 745 into Camp Shelby, SR001 and SR002 would be parachuted into the "box" by the USAF MC-130. As its initial task, SR002 would link up with the survivors of CA001 and debrief them.

Just outside the north perimeter fence of FOB 72 a pair of landing pads had been laid out. Here I met with the SOAR coordination officer, who gave me a quick safety briefing and instructions on using NVGs (PVS-7Bs, which gave excellent resolution when properly adjusted).

Promptly at 2100 hours, the two MH-60s swept in from the north and landed on the twin pads of the LZ. After shutting them down, the crews exited the helicopters, while a ground crew refueled them from a fuel truck. While this was going on, Captain Greg and his team marched down from their team room, accompanied by Lieutenant Colonel Smith and a couple of staff officers. Pulling everyone into a circle, the crews of the two SOAR helicopters gave everyone their preflight briefing and explained the load plan:

Five of the ODA 745 soldiers (A-Team) would fly in the lead aircraft (where I would be), while the other four (B-Team) would go in the second. Each man would carry a roughly 90 lb./41 kg. rucksack, along with their load-bearing gear and weapons. It was going to be tight, and legroom would be scarce.[85] I was shoehorned in a tiny jumpseat behind the cockpit for almost four hours, the duration of the flight to Camp Shelby and then back to their refueling field. It wasn't comfortable, but it wasn't boring either.

By 2200 hours, the birds were fully fueled, everyone and their gear had been packed aboard, and the engines were turning. After a short wait for clearance from the Fort Polk Army Airfield, the two heavily laden helicopters lifted off and headed east into the night sky.

---

85 The Blackhawk's seats are designed to provide passengers with protection in the event of a crash landing; for that they work quite well. But during combat operations, SOF personnel usually like to remove them so they'll have more room and can get rest on long infiltration flights. For JRTC 99-1, the 160th SOAR left the seats in as a safety measure (their usual practice during Stateside training).

Major McCollum, meanwhile, drove the rental car north to Barksdale AFB to meet me at the completion of the mission.

Aboard the lead MH-60, the first few minutes were spent setting up the instruments, radios, displays, and other avionics so the flight crew would be comfortable. The five soldiers of the A-Team were behind me, trying to get some sleep.

It was a marvelous evening for flying—cool, crisp, and bright. A big harvest moon was rising in the windshield ahead, and stars and ground lights were everywhere. The flight crews had settled onto their base course to the east at around 1,500 ft./457 m. aboveground and a speed of 120 knots.

The Nightstalkers have a truly impressive ability to fly low-level penetrations at night and in bad weather; their cockpit and crew management procedures for night flying work incredibly well. Though the flying conditions this evening were in fact splendid, everyone aboard acted as if they were flying through a pea-soup fog . . . keeping sharp.

Up front, the two flight crewmen took turns actually flying the aircraft. One would handle the controls for fifteen to twenty minutes, then hand the flying off to the other. The nonflying aviator managed the flight systems, checked the navigational systems, and monitored the formation spacing between the two helicopters. This routine was designed to prevent fatigue and vertigo, which can hit without warning if not looked out for.

When he was on the controls, the flying crewman wore a pair of special NVGs, which are matched to the specially illuminated cockpit displays. These provide surprising resolution, even under poor illumination conditions. But ambient light outside was so bright that evening, it was washing out the NVGs, and the two pilots had to raise them up frequently to check visual cues on the ground.

Meanwhile, everyone aboard (not only the pilots) was tasked with watching for phone and power lines, perhaps the most hazardous obstacles to low-level night helicopter flying. Though these are marked on the flying charts, we all had the responsibility to call *"Wire!"* if we saw them.

After an hour, I could see the bright lights of Baton Rouge just to the south, and off the right side were some of the many chemical plants and oil refineries that line the Mississippi River. Thirty minutes later, we passed over the Louisiana–Mississippi border and into "denied territory." From an exercise standpoint, the U.S. had just violated Atlantican airspace. Meaning: The war had just begun.

The crews now doused their lights and reduced their altitude to 500 ft./167 m. aboveground. They were now flying under real-world conditions, exactly simulating a combat infiltration into a "hot" LZ. Occasionally, we climbed to clear a power or phone line, but then down we went again. We flew that way for another thirty minutes, at which point we entered JSOA "Snake" (Camp Shelby) and dropped even lower.

Now the flight crews were using hills and other terrain to mask them from detection and possible enemy action. That lasted another fifteen minutes.

At 0013 hours on October 8th, the infiltration LZ came into sight—a half mile/ km. in length, and a hundred yds./m. wide. Moments later, the side doors were open, and the soldiers ready to go. The gunners manned their miniguns, ready to spray (simulated) 7.62mm ammunition at anyone unfortunate enough to detect us. The crew chief called "Thirty seconds" to the A-Team, and then the Blackhawk flared and rapidly slowed.

The LZ (named "Angus") was filled with tall grass, and was soggy from the recent rains. Wisely, the pilots of the two Blackhawks decided to avoid a touch down (lest they get caught in the mud). They hovered for less than twenty seconds while the soldiers tossed out their bundles of gear and then jumped. I heard splashes as the rucksacks hit, followed by the curses of Captain Greg and his men as they dropped into the ankle-deep water. And then we were off, headed west toward Louisiana.

Because the side doors had been left open, the crew compartment got downright cold, and there wasn't room enough for me to put on my leather flight jacket. For the next forty-five minutes, while the helicopters got out of Mississippi and located their refueling site, I shivered. The refueling site was a small civil airfield near Hammond, Louisiana, and we landed at around 0100 hours. Three hours of continuous flight meant a stampede to the restrooms and coffee machines. By 0200 hours, both birds were fueled, and everyone was back aboard for the two-hour flight back to Barksdale AFB.

The huge bomber base (home to the 8th Air Force and the 2nd Bombardment Wing, which flies the B-52H Stratofortress) came into view at 0400 hours. The 160th's spot on the ramp was between two squadrons of B-52s. One of these was working late this evening. Tensions with Iraq had risen again, and six of the huge bombers armed with air-launched cruise missiles were scheduled to leave shortly for Diego Garcia in the Indian Ocean. (These bombers and crews took part in Operation Desert Fox against Iraq less than three months later.)

For now, it was time to rest. As the rotors spun down, I collected my helmet and bag, and spotted Major McCollum waiting at the edge of the ramp.

The major had found rooms at the Barksdale AFB motor lodge. We slept until noon, and then drove back to Fort Polk that afternoon.

By then, ODA 745 had made contact with the FOB, confirmed that they had found a suitable MSS location, and had made their first water resupply. DA001 was off to a good start.

The hit was now scheduled for the evening of the next day, October 9th.

Friday, October 9th—Fort Polk

The day again dawned bright and clear, perfect for the three-hundred-mile drive that Major McCollum and I would make to Camp Shelby. Before we left, we stopped at the FOB operations center to check on DA001 and the other active missions. After the massacre of CA001, the group had grown more intense than ever; the lesson of two days earlier was still fresh in all their minds. On the way to see Lieutenant Colonel Smith, we stopped at the Civil Affairs desk to talk to the sole survivor of the "carnage" at Carnis, a female CA soldier. She confirmed what I had suspected: Getting stranded out in the "box" for so long had left the team pretty jittery . . . yet there had been no signs of CLF or PRA activity until the first rounds of automatic weapons fire. Meanwhile, she said, the 1/10th Mountain reconnaissance elements had entered the "box" and things seemed to be under control. However, the survivors from the CA detachment were staying close to the FOB, having essentially shut down operations until the JRTC casualty/evacuation system returned their "dead" and "wounded" comrades to action.

Looking at DA001: ODA 745 had moved in position to make the "hit" that evening, and were scouting for good firing positions. That meant it was time for Major McCollum and me to head out to watch. After changing into BDUs and gathering our field gear, we hopped into the car and settled in for the six-hour trip.

By midafternoon we had crossed the Mississippi River at Natchez, and were headed toward Hattiesburg (where there's the campus of the University of Southern Mississippi). It is also the "outside the gate" town for Camp Shelby.

This post was one of many "realigned" in the early 1990s as a result of the Base Reduction and Closing Commission (BRAC) program. Under BRAC, Camp Shelby had become a base to Mississippi National Guard and Army Reserve units, and was also used for other training tasks. One of these was to act as a satellite training facility for JRTC, which makes use of its large ranges and varying terrain for many types of missions.

We arrived at around 1800 hours and made our way to the Range Control Group headquarters on the south side of the post. From here we were directed to a small Quonset hut nearby, where a team of SOTD and JRTC range group personnel were preparing to move out to the live-fire range to finish setting up the target arrays for the night's activity. Leading the group was Major Tim Fitzgerald, known as "Fitz" to his friends.

For the planned "hit" by ODA 745, the ammunition would be real, with all the hazards that involves. Putting actual "steel on target" is the best measure of a sniper mission; it cannot be disputed later. Besides, blanks never feel the same as real rounds to the men who would sight the rifles and pull the triggers.

Major Fitzgerald ran us out to the target area in a HMMWV. Here his range operations troops had taken an old shack and turned it into a highly sophisticated target array. Inside, a mannequin had been rigged to act as the target—Major Raul Benitiz. The Benitiz dummy was mounted on a device that would sense the impact of a bullet, and then swing it backwards and to the ground if rounds impacted (the way a real body would behave). To provide the sniper teams with a reasonable target, a 60-watt lightbulb was hung in the ceiling. It would appear that Benitiz was sitting and reading.

Meanwhile, another mannequin had been hung on a trolley system, which ran to a "mortar pit" a few yards away. There were simulated machine gun nests as well, to represent Benitiz's bodyguards.

All of these simulators had been rigged with remote-controlled pyrotechnic de-

A rigger from JRTC sets up the target mannequin for ODA 745 at Camp Shelby, Mississippi, designed to simulate an enemy chemical weapons specialist named Major Benitiz.

JOHN D. GRESHAM

vices (fireworks). When the snipers took their shots, they would get a rousing response.

As darkness fell, we rode the HMMWV a few hundred yards to the northeast, parked behind an abandoned ammunitions bunker, and then climbed the grass-covered sides and sat next to the operator of the remote-controlled pyrotechnics. A two-hour wait followed.

As we munched MREs, Fitz and his crew of O/Cs and range workers showed us a map of the area and pointed out the MSSs and infiltration routes to the target area. The team that would carry out the hit had been in the area for several hours, invisible to us in their hide sites. In fact, while we had been poking around the target shack, Captain Greg and his soldiers had probably been watching us—one reason why each of us flagged as O/Cs wore soft field caps and face camouflage paint. That way those "in play" could differentiate us from OpFor soldiers that were patrolling the area.

It was dark by 2030 hours.

As he passed over to us PVS-7B NVGs, Major Fitzgerald asked for quiet during the rest of the operation; he would notify us when something was about to happen.

The first sign that ODA 745 was closing in for the kill came when Captain Greg and Sergeant Louis (his M249 SAW gunner) silently moved past us on the bunker and set up the blocking position, about 75 yds./m. in front of us. Moments later, the sniper teams moved out of the treeline to our northwest and into position.

Before I go further, let's break down the organization of ODA 745 for the "hit" mission. The following chart shows where each member of the team was assigned:

ODA 745 Element	Personnel Assigned
Blocking Position	Captain Greg (C/O) and Sergeant Louis (M249 Gunner)
Sniper Team #1	Sergeant Sean (Sniper) and Sergeant Jim (Spotter)
Sniper Team #2	Sergeant Shannon (Sniper) and Sergeant Glenn (Spotter)
MSS Team	Sergeant Charlie (Team Sergeant), Sergeant John (Communications), and Sergeant Brandon (Medic)

The four elements were task organized, with the two sniper teams and the blocking position elements out front to conduct the "hit," while the three MSS personnel were in the rear. The MSS element was tasked with maintaining communications with the FOB, and providing security for the exfiltration route from the killing zone. While there was little redundancy in this plan, only six men would be working in an area of several hundred wooded and grassy acres. Darkness and ground cover should allow the forward elements of ODA 745 to avoid detection by the OpFor patrols.[86] And besides, it was assumed that the OpFor did not have NVGs.

The window of opportunity for the shoot opened at 2030 hours and closed at 2130 hours. As the deadline neared, Major Fitzgerald worked the radio circuits hard to make sure the team had an open range and a clear shot. By 2015 hours, all three teams were in position.

The bunker and the road ahead of us dropped off into a large meadow, with the shack about 500 yds./m. directly in front of us. Captain Greg's blocking position was concealed by brush, perhaps 300 yds./m. from the target. Meanwhile, the sniper teams had moved into the meadow from the woods on our right, maintaining a minimum of 15° of separation from the target between each team. This meant that Sniper Team #1 would be firing into the window of the shack from an angle of around 45° from the front. Sniper Team #2 had a better shot, with only about 30° from the optimum front shot.

Visibility was good (no ground fog or mist), there was almost no crosswind, and the cover in front of the shack actually got thicker than what was on the slope down from the road. This meant that Sniper Team #1 had cover and a good shot from only 298 yds./273 m. to the target,[87] and Sniper Team #2 would fire from a similar range. While the high graze angles would increase the difficulty of the shots, the short range would offset the bad geometry.

But then, as luck would have it, just as the shoot window was opening, the range control officers put the range on a "hold;" a civilian emergency rescue helicopter was flying over in response to an automobile accident a few miles away, and it was feared

---

[86] During planning, ODA 745 considered wearing what are known as "Gilly Suits" during the "hit." These are camouflaged overgarments, designed to blend the wearer into local vegetation. Though later analysis indicated they might have proved useful, it was decided not to take them because of their weight and bulk (they can get very warm).

[87] It's important in sniping to accurately assess ranges without using laser or other active rangefinding equipment. The techniques involve a lot of fieldcraft, and the result is normally accurate.

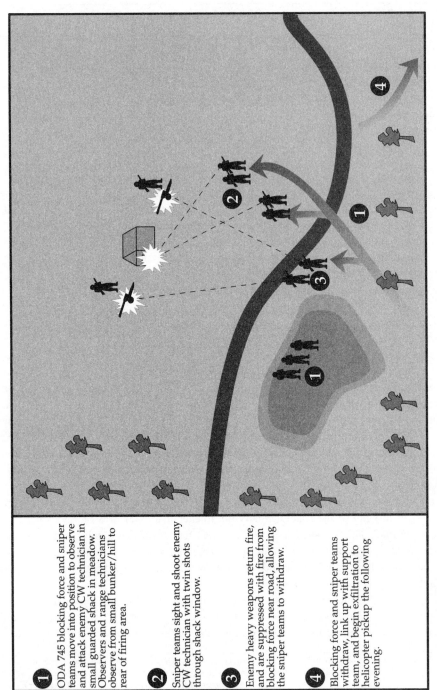

1. ODA 745 blocking force and sniper teams move into position to observe and attack enemy CW technician in small guarded shack in meadow. Observers and range technicians observe from small bunker/hill to rear of firing area.

2. Sniper teams sight and shoot enemy CW technician with twin shots through shack window.

3. Enemy heavy weapons return fire, and are suppressed with fire from blocking force near road, allowing the sniper teams to withdraw.

4. Blocking force and sniper teams withdraw, link up with support team, and begin exfiltration to helicopter pickup the following evening.

A map of ODA 745's "hit" on Major Benitiz at Camp Shelby, Mississippi.

that a live round might ricochet upwards and hit the helicopter (this is not as farfetched as it sounds).

During the hold, Captain Greg used the extra time to get a firm handle on the exact locations of his sniper teams. Each man in ODA 745 had been equipped with a multifunction strobe light, which could be set to pulse only directional infrared signals. These light pulses are invisible to the unaided human eye, but to users of NVGs or FLIRs they stand out brightly. Greg had each team show their positions with their IR strobes, so there would be no chance of a stray round from his position hitting anyone on the sniper teams.

At 2045 hours, the range control group cleared the hold, and the hard part of DA001 was underway: shooting the target and getting away with it. Sergeants Jim and Glenn began to work their spotting scopes, taking their time to line up Major Benitiz in the dimly lit shack window.

It is an axiom of the sniper trade that a shot of less than 500 yards is a fairly simple task. Now don't get me wrong, hitting a man-sized target at quarter-mile range is not *easy*. But it can be easily learned by a skilled rifleman. The hard part, as the two rated snipers were well aware, was not hitting the target, but acquiring it visually. This is why they had chosen to be the spotters, the better to coach Sergeants Shannon and Sean with their M24s onto the target.

Major Fitzgerald and Captain Greg gave the sniper teams the green light. At that moment time slowed to a crawl. The radio circuit went silent, and we could see and hear nothing. After what seemed like hours (actually four minutes), the spotters came up on the circuit signaling their readiness. Captain Greg gave the word that the hit was a "go." And then things moved fast.

Though the target was not actually visible through Sergeants Shannon's and Sean's scopes (the light pickup was not adequate), the spotters carefully coached them onto the target. They were to aim at a point on the dark blur in the window that represented Major Benitiz.

Back on the bunker, we heard the dual cracks of the M24 7.62mm sniper rifles firing fractions of a second apart.

Using two guns to go through a window to hit a target was an old sniper's trick. The first round smashes the glass, and perhaps hits the target. The second round, without the glass to deflect it, flies true to the target. That was what Shannon and Sean were doing. The first round from Sniper Team #1 flew toward the six-paned window, smashed the lower right pane, took a turn after the impact, and punched into Major Benitiz's lower abdomen (into his liver if he had been real). The second 7.62mm round flew truer. After passing through the hole made by the first round, it impacted the major in the lower left chest. If he had been real, it would have ripped apart the blood vessels just below his heart. Both rounds would have killed a human victim.

Major Raul Benitiz of the CLF was officially judged "dead."

Both sniper teams had done a perfect job. Now it was time to get the hell out of there.

This was not going to be easy.

As soon as the sniper rounds impacted, the range control operator who controlled the pyrotechnics hit his buttons, and within seconds the two (simulated) machine gun nests opened up. At the same time, mortar round simulators began to go off near the treeline to our right, well back from the sniper teams but still in the area they would have to soon transit. This was exactly the reason for the blocking position. Sergeant Louis opened up with the M249 SAW on the enemy positions, and Captain Greg added rounds from his own M4 carbine. In all, the two of them poured some 860 rounds of 5.56mm ammunition onto the machine gun nests and mortar pit. This gave the sniper teams time to gather their gear and get moving to their escape routes.

Once they were moving, Greg and Louis abandoned the blocking position and set off after them toward the rally point—the corner of an antenna behind the bunker.

Here the rest of us on the bunker gathered about thirty minutes later, during an artificial training hold to allow the team members to "safe" their weapons and turn in any remaining live ammunition. Everyone was still wearing PVS-7B NVGs, so the heat from the M249 SAW barrel glowed bright green through what the guys call "nods."

Though the six ODA 745 members were still coming down from their adrenaline rush and wanted to talk, time was short, and as soon as they had reloaded with blank ammunition, they were headed back to the MSS. They blended silently into the night, and were gone.

Then Major Fitzgerald collected Major McCollum and me, and we headed back to the rental car for the six-hour run back to Fort Polk.

Saturday, October 10th—Fort Polk

I slept until noon.

It was midafternoon before I got over to FOB 72 to get the word about how ODA 745 was doing.

After the hit, everyone had made it safely back to the hide site. As soon as it got dark, they would move to the exfiltration site—another meadow LZ like the one where they had landed two nights earlier. Here they would be picked up about 2230 hours by two 160th SOAR MH-60Ls and flown directly to the FOB 72 LZ, where there would be an immediate debriefing (which I was invited to sit in on).

Meanwhile, the rest of the missions seemed to be running well.

The big news was the substantial reinforcement of the SOAR aviation contingent at Barksdale AFB, which had grown to four MH-60Ls, two MH-60Ks, and an MH-47K. These aviation assets were being heavily utilized during JRTC 99-1. (This would be noted when future SOAR tasking was considered for field operations.)

Following dinner with the JRTC PAO staff in Leesville, I returned with Major Bill Shaw to the FOB 72 compound for an update on the progress of ODA 745:

When the two MH-60Ls had arrived at the exfiltration LZ, an OpFor machine gun team had been ready to ambush the choppers. But the door gunners on the Blackhawks had opened up with their six-barreled 7.62mm miniguns, instantly killing the three members of the CLF team. Quickly loading up ODA 745, they turned west, and exited Atlantican airspace. The rest of the flight went smoothly, and the two choppers landed at the FOB 72 LZ at 0140 hours. Lieutenant Colonel Smith and much of the 2/7th SFG staff were there to greet ODA 745 and escort them back to their team room.

The men were given a few minutes to safe their weapons and stow rucksacks, and then they sat down for a debriefing.

Sunday, October 11th—Fort Polk

Ever since the lies of Vietnam, the after-action debriefing and After Action Review (AAR)—honest assessments of the success or failure of an operation—have become Army absolutes.

Naturally, the Special Forces have their own traditions and procedures for handling such things.

As soon as the tired but happy ODA 745 had unshouldered their rucksacks, they sat down in a semicircle in front of the FOB 72 leaders and staff. Pulling out notepads and maps, they began to lay out their activities over the past few days, to give Lieutenant Colonel Smith and his staff a "quick look" report which would be the basis of an initial report to JSOTF (Cortina) and SOCCE (Cortina). (The AAR later would be a more formal review of the entire mission, where all aspects of the mission would be discussed.)

Captain Greg and his troops ran through the basic facts of the hit on Major Benitiz and their exfiltration back to the MSS, including observations about the higher-than-expected level of OpFor activity at Camp Shelby. They even thought the OpFor had tried to use bloodhounds to track them down.

This last made the rest of us break into smiles. The team had not been told that the local raccoon-hunting season had opened the previous week (the fact had not made it into the premission intelligence briefing). During DA001 dozens of hunters and their coon dogs had been hunting at the open post of Camp Shelby. It seemed to ODA 745 that the whole state of Mississippi was out looking for them.

The team went on to discuss other issues, such as OpFor WMD activity (the team had discovered no sign of chemical or other WMD munitions), the use of IR and laser illumination for coordination during the hit, and problems with the exfiltration at the primary LZ. The entire mission had involved slogging through swampy country, and many areas thought to be clear had turned out to be overgrown. Thus, the exfiltration LZ had turned out to be large enough to land only one MH-60 at a time, instead of the planned two.

The absence of WMD activity in DA001's operational area made the mission a complete success from the JTF (Cortina) point of view. 1/10th Mountain could finish their entry into the "box" with little worry about chemical munitions.

After the debriefing, Lieutenant Colonel Smith and the staff had a few more questions for the team, and then he turned the men loose for chow and rest.

At this point it was time to head back to my hotel. On the way out, Smith gave me still another invitation I couldn't refuse. The AAR was scheduled for 1800 hours that evening in the SOTD theater on the edge of the FOB 72 compound. Would I like to attend? (SF AARs are almost always kept private.)

"Absolutely," I answered.

The AAR would be my final JRTC 99-1 activity. After that it was time to go home.

A few minutes before 1800, Paula Schlag of the JRTC/Fort Polk PAO escorted me to the SOTD theater facility. It turned out that I was not to be allowed in the AAR itself (where I might be a disruption), but would watch the live feed in the video control room.

The issues brought up during the AAR were varied—and somewhat scattered. Here is a sample:

The discussion opened with comments on the twenty-four-hour delay in starting the mission. This, it turned out, had not caused a disruption, but had helped the team in route planning, terrain familiarization, and a number of other ways. The delay also allowed the team to get needed rest, which reduced fatigue levels in the field, and gave ODA 745 (which was composed of personnel from five separate teams) greater opportunity to bond and establish working relationships.

On the other hand, the compression of the mission schedule affected the availability of the SOAR helicopters during both infiltration and exfiltration, and meant the team had to rush more than they would have liked. For instance, more time to observe the target area would have been desirable. And while the firefight in the pickup LZ had gone their way, it might have been avoided if they could have moved slower or had had additional pickup LZ options.

Next came comments on the planning cycle. On the one hand, there were problems: The software used to plan movement rates over various types of ground surface had proved unable to deal with the actual muddy, swampy terrain they'd encountered. On the other hand, accurate GPS coordinates made the location planning easy (e.g., locating the MSS/hide site and the shooting positions for the sniper teams).

They turned next to the sardine-can packing of the MH-60s. Four loaded SF soldiers and a four-man crew made the helicopter crowded and uncomfortable. The seats were the problem, and the guys wanted them out. Then they could sit on their rucksacks and exit the bird more quickly.

In short, in spite of a few limiting factors and "artificialities,"[88] DA001 had turned out to be an excellent training event. The guys on ODA 745 had clearly enjoyed their experiences and would take good lessons back to their teams.

Some of these included:

- **MSS Site**—A strong point of DA001 was the choice of the MSS/hide site, deep in the heart of the Camp Shelby swamps. Easy to defend, with a good supply of fresh water, the site also proved excellent for radio transmissions, and was even comfortable (considering the location). Its weakness was no "back door." (There

---

88 An "artificiality" is a situation inherent in a model or a wargame that generates a result, but would never happen in real life. (Examples are range safety or limits on time when a range can be used.) The result can be good or positive and teach important lessons. Still, the end state created is artificial, and this must be understood by the participants and creators so as not to bias the final assessment and lessons learned.

The members of ODA 745 and their target mannequin following their successful mission and After Action Review at JRTC 99-1. The mannequin was hit by two sniper rounds, both assessed to have "killed" the target.

JOHN D. GRESHAM

was only one way in or out.) Still, despite the hunters and dogs running around (they should not have been there; they were a safety hazard), it was a snug and secure place to do business.

- **Rehearsals**—Many of the critical decisions that made DA001 successful—such as the use of the certified snipers as spotters—were a direct result of rehearsals and tests prior to the mission. Clearly, a mission as complex as DA001 required as many tests and rehearsals as could be crammed in.

- **Communications**—The DA001 communications plan was excellent, as was the suite of gear selected for the various phases of the mission. This included SAT-COM and HF sets to talk back to FOB 72, Saber FM sets for the "walkaround" phases of the mission, and the IR-/laser-signaling devices.

- **Feedback**—To a man, the ODA 745 team members considered DA001 to be one of the most stressful and realistic training missions they had participated in. Real-world feelings of haste, isolation, and stress were all there.

After the AAR, I headed back to the FOB 72 operations center for one last look at the other 2/7th SFG's missions. Nothing much to report: SR001, SR002, SR003, and DA003 were all underway, and all seemed to be going well. There is a rule of thumb in the SOF business that if you get more than a 50% success or positive information flow from your mission matrix, then things are going pretty good. Except for the massacre of CA001, the various missions seem to have done better than that;

and this was reflected in the relative ease of 1/10th Mountain's entry into the JRTC "box."

This is not to say that anyone had it easy at the JRTC. Units come there to be tested and exercised, not just to go through the motions. Before long, the OpFor began to hit back at 1/10th. They made several effective and vicious attacks on the 1/10th brigade TOC.

But that is another story.

For now, it was time to fly home.

Going West: NTC 99-02

In October, a few weeks after the JRTC, I was once again observing an SF battalion in a force-on-force rotation . . . but a very different kind of force-on-force rotation from the one at Fort Polk.

The western desert of the U.S. is about as different from the lush low country of Louisiana as terrain can be. Though the landscape seems more like Mars than a place where Americans might fight, here the Army and Marines learned important lessons that helped them win the 1991 Persian Gulf War on the ground. Scattered across the desert are facilities like the National Training Center at Fort Irwin and the Marine Desert Training Center at Twenty-Nine Palms in California, and the Yuma Proving Grounds in Arizona. These offer enough real estate to maneuver entire brigades against similar-sized OpFor formations without disturbing their neighbors in Barstow and Palm Springs.

Here also, as at JRTC, SOF troops round out the training scenarios.

My first destination on this trip was the desert town of Yuma, Arizona, about 300 miles southeast of Fort Irwin on the Mexico/California/Arizona border. The 1st Battalion, 3rd Special Forces Group (1/3rd SFG) had come to Yuma to support the 3rd Brigade of the 3rd Infantry Division (Mechanized) in their NTC rotation at Fort Irwin.[89]

NTCs differ from JRTCs in a number of ways. For starters, NTCs focus on traditional large-unit operations by armored and mechanized forces; and at NTCs, operations tend to be more decentralized. Thus, there is greater emphasis on deep operations behind enemy lines for SOF units; CA missions are usually not required; but there are more SR and DA operations. For the same reason, 1/3rd SFG would establish their FOB hundreds of miles/kilometers from the AOR where the conventional unit would deploy.

Because SOF units participate in only a few NTC rotations every year, they are administrated and adjudicated by the same SOTD staff that handles the duty at JRTC. This meant for me another visit in the field with my friends, Lieutenant Colonel Mike Rozsypal, Major Bill Shaw, and Major Tim Fitzgerald.

The town of Yuma is an eclectic mix of old Mexican charm, forced irrigation

---

[89] While it is technically part of the 3rd Infantry Division (Mechanized), which is based at Fort Stewart, Georgia, the 3rd/3rd Infantry (Mech.) calls Fort Benning, Georgia, home. Such distinctions are common in today's Army, where various parts of larger units can be located literally thousands of miles/kilometers from each other.

agriculture, military functionality, and fast food. Because of its location near the Colorado River, the town has a long history as a center of transportation and farming, but its huge nearby training and testing ranges have also proved invaluable to the American military. To the east of the city is Chocolate Mountain, where the Navy and Marine Corps maintain instrumented and live-fire ranges for bombing and air-to-air training. Closer in is a large U-shaped Army tract known as the Yuma Proving Ground, or YPG.

YPG is the desert equipment testing center for the Army and other services, with more than 1,300 square miles/3,400 square km. of desert terrain to work with. Here fighting vehicles are tested in high, hot, and dusty conditions. (The M-1 Abrams main battle tanks proved themselves here in the 1980s . . . in conditions very like those of the Persian Gulf, where they proved themselves again in 1991.[90]) Here also is an artillery range large enough to test systems like the Block 1A (extended-range) versions of the Army Tactical Missile System (ATACMS). And here also is home to the JFK Special Warfare Center and School's Military Free Fall School, where SOF personnel learn exotic forms of parachute infiltration. All in all, YPG is a huge sandbox where all variety of training and testing can be conducted . . . *without* unduly disturbing the desert environment.[91]

You have to work to get to Yuma. For me, there was a transcontinental ride to Los Angeles, followed by a commuter flight to the Yuma Airport, a dual civilian/Marine Corps facility. As I stepped out of the aircraft, the desert heat hit like an oven. In Yuma, you need an air-conditioner for much of the year, and you don't go anywhere without a cold drink.

There to greet me was my USASOC project officer, Major Tom McCollum, who would guide me through NTC 99-02.

After dinner at the motel on the edge of town that would be my base for the next few days, he and I sat down for an information session. Since I was again to be flagged as an SOTD member, Tom repeated the O/C rules from several weeks before.

"Drink plenty of water," he advised, before he left me for the night.

Wednesday, October 28th—Yuma Proving Ground, Arizona

My first day at FOB 31 (1/3rd SFG used the same naming convention as 2/7th SFG had at JRTC) opened sunny, clear, and hot . . . exactly as advertised.

On the drive east to the YPG post was a rare sight for an easterner like me—a radar-equipped, tethered aerostat (a small, blimp-shaped balloon), designed to look for drug-smuggling aircraft coming in from Mexico. A number of these airborne sensors are used along America's southern border (except during bad weather, when

---

90 Before Operation Desert Storm, critics of American made weapons prophesied that the heat and dust of the Persian Gulf would cause our weapons to fail. In fact, every military specified system in service—tanks, helicopters and trucks; radios, rifles, and computers—had been tested at YPG and other test facilities. They *all worked* in the desert. Part of the high cost of military systems is due to the process of "ruggedizing" and testing to make them function anywhere, from the Arctic to the Sahara.

91 YPG has an exceptional record of protecting the acreage under its control. So effective has been its stewardship that the facility recently won the Department of the Army Environmental Award as the post with the finest environmental record in the service.

Forward Operating Base 31 during NTC 99-02 at the Yuma Proving Ground in Arizona. This was headquarters for the 1st Battalion of the 3rd Special Forces Group during their rotation to the National Training Center.

drug smugglers don't like to fly anyway). They have done good service in the drug war.

Sometime later, and some distance farther east, lies an Army airfield. Just past the Free Fall School and the Army Aviation Test Directorate buildings was an encampment of tents and trailers. This was my objective: FOB 31—a far more sparse, expeditionary, and impermanent establishment than FOB 72. Here the shelters were a mix of construction site–type trailers and large Army tents. Everywhere was the sound of generators and air-conditioners. Even the tents had air-conditioners, as the teams and other personnel lived and did the bulk of their work in them. FOB 31 was, of course, surrounded by the same kinds of barricades, wire, and antipersonnel defense I saw at FOB 72.

The 1/3rd SFG headquarters and operations center was located in one of the trailers—a much more Spartan and less "high-tech"-looking place than the 7th SFG's, reflecting the 3rd SFG's more "stubby pencil" approach to going to war. Naturally, 3rd SFG personnel *do* take laptops, SARCOM links, and GPS receivers downrange. It's just that they are not as dependent upon these tools as other groups—more use is made of paper briefing charts and maps, and their electronic briefing slides are decidedly "unsexy." This simplicity comes partly from their own style, and partly from the requirements of their African AOR, the least technologically advanced in the SF world. The 3rd SFG soldiers are *hugely* sensitive to the native peoples of their AOR. It would not do for them to come on like "ugly Americans."

Though cramped, FOB 31 Op Center was completely functional; and there was a no-nonsense atmosphere about the entire compound. SF soldiers moved between the tents and trailers with measured haste and purpose, clearly with mission launch deadlines on their minds.

The NTC 99-02 scenario was very like other force-on-force scenarios I've encountered: The brigade from the 3rd/3rd Infantry (Mech.) would move into Fort Ir-

The cartoon of ODA 745's debriefing.

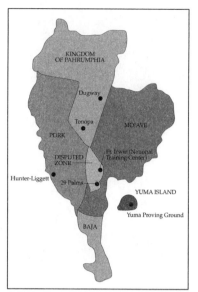

The imaginary Tierra Del Diablo, which is used for operations at the U.S. Army's National Training Center (NTC). Though NTC is based at Fort Irwin, California, operations can run over the entire Tierra Del Diablo area.

RUBICON, INC., BY LAURA DeNINNO

win's maneuver area to do battle with the OpFor of the 11th Armored Cavalry Regiment (ACR).[92] NTC 99-02 would (again) take place on a hypothetical island. This one was known as Tierra Del Diablo ("Land of the Devil"), and was spread out over (real) California, Nevada, Oregon, Baja California, and parts of Arizona and Utah. Tierra Del Diablo was (again) divided into three imaginary nations—Mojave (our friends), the Kingdom of Pahrumphia (enemies of Mojave), and the People's Democratic Republic of Krasnovia (PDRK—everyone's enemy!).[93]

For NTC 99-02, the Krasnovians and Pahrumphians had formed an alliance, and were in a natural resources dispute with Mojave. Large uranium deposits had been found, and the new Krasnovia–Pahrumphia Confederation (KPC) wanted to take over the mines to support their own WMD program (for nuclear weapons). The forces of the KPC were invading the resource areas of Mojave—the area around Fort Irwin. The 11th Cavalry would play the part of the KPC 11th Motor Rifle Division (MRD), which would face down the brigade from the 3rd Infantry.[94] 1/3rd SFG's mission would be to support the U.S. brigade's entry into Fort Irwin and to help allied air units.

For the duration of NTC 99-02, the units assigned to FOB 72 would operate from the imaginary Island of Yuma, which was defined to be part of Mojave. These units included:

---

[92] The 11th ACR is the famous "Blackhorse Cav," which spent the Cold War watching over the critical Fulda Gap in Germany. After the end of that conflict, they were for a time disestablished; but were later reflagged as the NTC OpFor. They also retain a wartime mission as a normal ACR. For more Blackhorse lore, see *Into the Storm*, written with my good friend General (Ret.) Fred Franks (Berkley Books, 1997).

[93] The idea is to create names that participants will *never* run into again, but are easily remembered.

[94] For more on NTC, see *Armored Cav* (Berkley Books, 1994).

- **FOB 31**—Assigned to FOB 31, 1/3rd SFG would undertake the missions assigned during the rotation. Like 2/7th SFG at JRTC, 1/3rd SFG brought a battalion headquarters with a company (approximately) of ODAs and other supporting units. They broke down this way.

  —**HHC/Operational Detachment Charlie**—Led by the 1/3rd SFG commander, Lieutenant Colonel James L. (Roy) Dunn, FOB 31 would be tasked with planning, preparing, and controlling the various missions being run for JSOTF (Mojave) and SOCCE (Mojave).

  —**Support Operations Team, Bravo (SOT-B)**—1/3rd SFG also brought a SOT-B element to provide a military intelligence command, control, and analysis for FOB 31.

  —**SOCCE 31**—To provide a liaison with the 3rd/3rd Infantry Division, a SOCCE element was established at the larger unit's TOC.

  —**Operational Detachment, Alphas (ODAs)**—1/3rd SFG brought along five ODAs to run actual missions.

  —**Support Operations Team, Alpha (SOT-A)**—To provide signals and electronic collection capabilities for FOB 31, 1/3rd SFG brought a pair of SOT-A teams to NTC 99-02.

  —**112th Chemical Reconnaissance Detachment (CRD)**—This was a five-man element to provide chemical weapons talent to the units at FOB 31.

  —**2nd Platoon/108th Military Police Company (2/108th MP)**—Due to the expeditionary nature of the FOB 31 deployment, 1/3rd SFG took along a platoon of military police drawn from the 16th MP Brigades/503rd MP Battalion/108th Company. The MP platoon would patrol the FOB 31 perimeter, relieving 1/3rd SFG personnel from security duty.

  With the exception of the MPs, 1/3rd SFG's array of SF units was almost identical to 2/7th's at JRTC, and would attempt to simulate the same kinds of mission workloads.

- **3rd Marine Air Wing (3rd MAW)**—Based at MCAS Miramar (near San Diego, California) and Yuma, 3rd MAW provided two types of aircraft to support SOF operations during NTC 99-02. These included:

  —**Marine Attack Squadron 513 (VMA-513—the Nightmares)**—A primary training objective for 1/3rd SFG was to demonstrate their ability to call in joint airstrikes and artillery fire. The Marines were tasked to support them with four AV-8B Harrier II bombing sorties, which would be supplied by the Nightmares of VMA-513 from MCAS Yuma. AV-8B Harrier IIs are equipped with the Angle Rate Bombing System (ARBS), an electro-optical weapons delivery system, equipped with a laser spot tracker. The ARBS gives Harrier pilots the ability to locate ground targets that are illuminated by a laser designator. There are several types of designators available—e.g., units like the AAQ-14 LANTIRN carried by Air Force and Navy aircraft, and also lightweight man-portable units, such as the PAQ-10 Ground Target Laser Designator. Once the ARBS locks onto a laser spot from a designator, it calculates an optimum ballistic solution for the weapons and drops them automatically. Used properly, ARBS can put down a stick of unguided "iron" bombs with accuracy approaching Precision Guided Munitions (PGMs). The actual process, known as "Terminal Guidance" (TG), would be practiced several times by 1/3rd SFG during NTC 99-02.

—**Marine Aerial Refueler Transport Squadron 352 (VMGR-352—the Raiders)**—Even though none of the aircraft flown on SOF support missions during NTC 99-02 would require in-flight refueling, there was still a need to transport teams to distant locations and to conduct parachute infiltrations. The Marines were tasked to supply a pair of KC-130 Hercules tanker/transport aircraft, this time from the Raiders of VMGR-352 based at MCAS Miramar.

- **Nevada Army National Guard**—To assist with covert infiltrations and retrievals of ODAs, the Nevada Army National Guard contributed a CH-47 Chinook heavy lift helicopter to the SOF effort.

    You may have noticed that the 160th SOAR had assigned no aircraft or personnel to MTC 99-02. They were busy preparing for possible real-world operations in Iraq and the Balkans.

As I waited for Lieutenant Colonel Dunn to finish a staff meeting, Major Bill Shaw from the JRTC SOTD gave me an exercise briefing notebook and led me through the planned missions. These included:

- **SR001**—SR001 would conduct reconnaissance upon a suspected WMD (chemical weapons) production plant at a site in Pahrumphia, to be known as JSOA "Tiger" (on the old Dugway Proving Ground in Utah). The ODA with the five-man CRD would infiltrate the area via a low-level parachute insertion (static line jump from a Marine KC-130), then move to an overwatch position on the site (that is, a position on high ground with good cover, from which a constant surveillance of a particular piece of ground can be maintained). In addition to monitoring the site, the ODA and CRD would collect actual evidence of the WMD production (chemical and soil samples). When this was accomplished, the team would link up with a Mojavian agent, and then move to a site where another Marine KC-130 could land and retrieve them.

- **SR002**—The most ambitious of the SR missions, SR002 would insert a combined ODA/SOT-A team into Fort Irwin (JSOA "Otter") to provide early warning of KPC forces moving toward Irwin Military City (IMC—the Fort Irwin post complex). The team would fly to IMC on one of the MC-130s, then be inserted into JSOA "Otter" by the Nevada ANG CH-47. Once the team had occupied a position overlooking a critical crossroads, they would monitor enemy vehicle traffic and report back to FOB 31. This was planned to go on for several days, after which the team could be extracted by a UH-60 Blackhawk from the aviation brigade of the 3rd Infantry (Mech.) and return to Yuma on an MC-130. The team would also provide terminal guidance for one of the two Marine Harrier strikes (though they would not be told this until after their insertion). This would place considerable responsibility—as well as extreme stress—on the personnel assigned to the task.

- **SR003**—SR003, like SR002, was designed to cover a potential KPC infiltration route (JSOA "Gator") into the Irwin Military City complex. This would be a mounted mission, using GMVs. The team would be a duplicate of the ODA/SOT-A unit used in SR002, and would be tasked with the same basic tasks. They'd be infiltrated by an MC-130, which would make a combat assault landing. The exfiltration would be handled the same way.[95]

- **DA001**—DA001 would be a raid upon a suspected WMD (chemical weapons) cache in Pahrumphia, and known as JSOA "Horse" (also at the old Dugway Proving Ground in Utah). The ODA would conduct its infiltration using a High Altitude, High Opening (HAHO) parachute technique. Once the targets were destroyed, the ODA would contact a Mojavian agent (a roleplayer simulating a member of a local resistance cell) on the ground, and move to an exfiltration airfield where they would be picked up by a Marine KC-130 Hercules.

- **DA002**—This mission was designed to destroy a cache of KPC surface-to-surface rockets and their operating crews. To accomplish this, a GMV-mounted ODA would be infiltrated into Twenty-Nine Palms—JSOA "Bison" (near Palm Springs in California)—onboard a Marine KC-130 conducting a combat assault landing. On the ground, the ODA would infiltrate overland to a site overlooking the target area to conduct prestrike reconnaissance. When the targets were properly fixed, the team would move in, destroy the sites with explosives, and then exfiltrate aboard another Marine KC-130.

- **DA003 (Planning)**—A planning mission only, DA003 was designed to recover an injured Mojavian agent, trapped behind the lines in Krasnovia, who had special knowledge of the Krasnovian WMD program. The ODA planned to infiltrate via Marine KC-130 into Fort Hunter-Ligget—JSOA "Eagle" (near Monterey, California)—and then make contact with the Krasnovian resistance who were sheltering the Mojavian agent.

- **DA004 (Planning)**—Another planning mission, DA004 was tasked to disable a Pahrumphian rocket fuel plant located at the Tonapah Test Range—JSOA "Snake" (in northern Nevada, formerly home to the F-117 Nighthawk wing). The area was assumed to be so heavily defended that a ground team would have a better chance against the target than even a large airstrike with PGMs.

- **UW001**—One of the more intriguing missions assigned to FOB 31 was an Unconventional Warfare (UW) operation flagged as UW001. This mission had personnel from FOB 31 rigging supply bundles for airdrop to insurgents in

---

95 The assault landing is a specialty of the C-130 Hercules transport: A fully loaded C-130, with all its flaps down, comes in to land literally hanging on its props. Once the aircraft hits the ground, the turboprops are reversed, and the Hercules stops after a rollout as short as 1,000 ft./305 m. The aircraft is then rapidly offloaded (sometimes it does not even stop), and then takes off in much the same way as it landed. Though the C-17A Globemaster III can make similar landings, the wisdom of using a jet transport costing $250 million a copy in a high-threat area is questionable.

The command center for Forward Operating Base 31 during JRTC 99-02.
JOHN D. GRESHAM

Pahrumphia, and it would be run late in NTC 99-02. The bundles would be dropped from a KC-130 at the Dugway Proving Grounds up in Utah.

Most professional soldiers will tell you that given a choice between desert and forest, they will pick cover and water. The SF deploying on missions during NTC 99-02 would have to deal with a number of desert-related problems. For obvious starters, they would carry every drop of water they used, endure extremes of heat and cold, and face an absolute absence of overhead cover. The geology of the region posed less obvious, but equally serious, challenges. At the higher elevations, where they would frequently be conducting missions, the land is mostly basalt—rock with an extremely high iron content. This tends to make compass navigation difficult and radio communications extremely dicey. The communications sergeants (18E) had to plan carefully to ensure reliable radio links back to FOB 31.

About the time Bill Shaw was finishing up his briefing, Lieutenant Colonel Dunn emerged from his staff meeting and introduced himself. A stately and charming Southerner, Roy Dunn made me instantly welcome. He specifically invited me to observe a number of events, among them a "Media on the Battlefield" exercise to be held the next afternoon—a simulated press conference where he would face a "cable news crew" from the JRTC PAO shop. The JRTC Media on the Battlefield crew have a fierce reputation. It promised to be a good show.

After meeting the commander, I was given a tour of the encampment.

In each tent, teams were preparing for their missions, conducting briefbacks, running rehearsals, and packing their rucksacks up to the 140 lb./91 kg. maximum allowed on operations. Much of what they would carry would be water, gallons of which would be required for survival.[96] The rest of the load would be food, ammunition, weapons and explosives, communications and navigation gear, and sensor equipment (if needed). There would also be camouflage netting, Gilly Suits, and hide site materials for those teams that would have to stay in one place for any length of time.

That night SR001, SR002, and SR003 would all launch on their missions. And on Monday, I would drive the 350 miles/565 km. up to Fort Irwin to observe the terminal guidance phase of SR002.

Thursday, October 29th—Yuma Proving Ground

It was a quiet day, with nothing much on my schedule until the Media on the Battlefield event in the afternoon. I passed the time in the operations center, listening to the progress of the three SR teams after their insertions. All of them had gotten into their hide positions and set up their surveillance systems; and good data on enemy troop and vehicle movements had started coming in. This was immediately passed along to the SOCCE (Mojave), located with the 3rd/3rd Infantry (Mech.) moving into IMC and the JSOTF (Mojave). So far enemy action north of IMC had been light.

As expected, SR002 had a tough time getting into position.

After insertion by the Nevada ANG CH-47, their team had split into three smaller elements and moved into hide positions north of IMC on a mountain overlooking a critical crossroads. The three team elements were spread over a pair of peaks and a small saddle, which allowed them to observe the crossroads and gave them enough angular separation so the two SOT-A intercept receivers could generate cross-bearings off of radio transmissions. The good news was that they were in good positions to observe the KPC ground and helicopter traffic, which was heavy. The bad news was that the KPC ground and helicopter traffic was heavy, which made their own positions hazardous. Further bad news came in the form of a large basalt formation on which ODA 324/SOT-A 301 had set up their positions, which made a mess of SATCOM radio frequencies. This meant they had to communicate by means of an old-fashioned HF radio set with a Morse key until they could get the SATCOM and other sets working reliably (it took two days).

Media on the Battlefield is an Army-wide program designed to prepare soldiers in field situations to deal with the media. The preparation can take several forms. It can be as simple as providing soldiers with cards that spell out procedures for handling unplanned media events, and it can be as elaborate as formal classroom training (such as PAOs receive).

The JRTC Media on the Battlefield Program places a unit commander in a press conference situation with a simulated television news crew trained to give the officer a grueling workout under the lights and cameras (all of which is taped for later as-

---

96 Each gallon of water weighs about 8 lb. Even with a consumption of just a gallon per day, on a six-day mission, each SF soldier would have to carry almost 50 lb. of water . . . and containers. In fact, the Army standard for soldiers in a desert environment is a minimum consumption of two gallons per day.

Lieutenant Colonel Roy Dunn, USA, following a simulated press conference during NTC 99-02. The woman next to him is a roleplayer from Fort Polk, Louisiana, who simulates a "challenging" member of the media on the battlefield.

JOHN D. GRESHAM

sessment and scoring). Led by a female roleplayer, who goes by the name "Maggie LaLouch," the three-person team throws *tough* questions. Not a few officers would choose combat before an hour with Maggie and her crew.[97]

Handling a skilled reporter may not be up there with combat in the soldier's hierarchy, but the military must still face the consequences of the "CNN Effect" (when the shoe drops, everyone in the world will be watching what they are doing). Reporters are not *always* hostile. But they *often* are. Screwups can be costly. Maggie came on as tough and hostile.

The press conference started promptly at 1600 hours. Lieutenant Colonel Dunn opened with a short command briefing about FOB 31 and its job on the Island of Yuma, with emphasis on efforts to reach out to the local population. He looked good, he was well-prepared, and had a nice, relaxed presence before the camera.

Maggie's first questions were lobs, and Dunn's answers were charming. It was all pretty easygoing . . . for a while.

She came on tougher when she slipped in a question about chemical warfare training (implying that chemical weapons might be used in the "Tierra Del Diablo War"). But Dunn handled that one as smoothly as the lobs (chemical warfare training is necessary insurance, but the U.S. would never be the first to use WMDs).

About twenty minutes into the interview she fired her "bomb": "What about the soldier who went AWOL?" ("AWOL" or "Absent Without Leave" is the military term for desertion, and is a very serious crime.)

A few days earlier, a *pair* of MPs from the 108th MP Company had gone AWOL

---

97 "Maggie LaLouch" (her real name is Margaret) is a civilian JRTC employee on the Fort Polk Public Affairs staff, and the wife of a JRTC range operator. She is a bright, talented lady who takes seriously her role as the "Media OpFor," and works hard to teach officers how not to give reporters openings they don't deserve.

for real, and were still missing. Maggie was hitting him with questions about a real-world event and not a contrived exercise situation. In other words, the question was totally unexpected, and totally unprepared for. Even worse, from Dunn's point of view, AWOLs are an extremely sensitive subject among our military. On the one hand, they are extremely rare. On the other, they cast doubt on the leadership of the unit deserted—a subject other commanders don't relish getting into in public.

Dunn took the high road. "No, Maggie, we do not have one AWOL, we have two," he acknowledged, "but we've been making a serious and ongoing effort to find and return the two soldiers." And he went on: "I do hope the young men are safe and will come in before the charges they face get more serious." He added: "And if their families have any idea about where they are, I would ask them for their help in getting the two safely back to their units."

Almost as an afterthought—a *smart* afterthought—he offered to bring the female captain commanding the MP detachment to the briefing theater for an interview. This was in fact done (and she did okay). After which the conference came to a friendly end.

In the AAR that followed, Maggie and her crew gave Lieutenant Colonel Dunn a big thumb's-up. His obvious compassion, tact, and openness, together with the artfulness of his responses, had proved a winning combination.

Friday, October 30th—Yuma Proving Ground

On October 30th, the 3rd/3rd Infantry (Mech.) entered the fight up at Fort Irwin, and (not specifically related to that event) change-of-mission orders went out to the SR teams in the field. (In real combat, where events are fluid—not to say chaotic—plans must constantly be changed. So also in simulated combat.)

For ODA 324/SOT-A 301 working on SR002, their new orders meant big changes: Their mission would now be extended several days (they would be resupplied over the weekend); the team would be conducting a TG (Terminal Guidance) mission on Monday (their assigned target would be an enemy camp just north of the crossroads, approximately 1.5 miles/2,500 m. from their current position); and instead of an exfiltration by a UH-60 Blackhawk, they would link up with elements of the conventional forces sometime the following week. The mission change—from observation and signals interception to a DA assignment—brought with it extra hazards.

All in a day's work.

The team immediately began to consider where to site their PAQ-10 Ground Laser Target Designator (GLTD) to maximize the probability of a successful and precise strike on the target.

Since the target was well within the range of their battery-powered GLTD, and the Harrier drivers would use their ARBS to handle the delivery, in theory, all the team had to do was punch in a digital pulse code into the GLTD, "paint" the target with the laser spot just prior to the strike, and the ARBS would handle the rest. In fact, the mission was more complicated than that. For the team would also be responsible for the Harriers' final approach route to the target. That is, they would have to find the best way for the two Marine aircraft to thread through probable antiaircraft defenses, while at the same time placing them on a course that maximized their chances for a successful weapons delivery.

To this end, the team captain made several reconnaissance trips on foot to map out the area, and then transmitted the results back to FOB 31. This information went up to the SOCCE (Mojave) element at IMC, which handed it off to the air-tasking cell of JTF (Mojave).

On Monday, I would ride up to Fort Irwin and observe the outcome of all this activity.

Monday, November 2nd—National Training Center, Fort Irwin, California

Because of the ever present possibility of discovery by the bad guys, it was an anxious weekend for the members of the ODA 324/SOT-A 301 team. The change of mission was not exactly welcome, either, but the team, of course, accepted it with typical SF stoicism. Meanwhile, SATCOM communications were still spotty, though the HF systems continued to work reliably.

On the brighter side, the resupply mission that weekend could almost be called a blessing. More MREs. And fresh water.

The airstrike was scheduled for 2200 hours Pacific Standard Time that evening, which meant that Major McCollum and I had some serious travel ahead of us. The run to Fort Irwin would take a supremely boring six hours.

We arrived around 1800 hours PST, and linked up with the post PAO. After a quick run to the local Burger King, we loaded into a HMMWV and headed north for the two-hour drive into the Fort Irwin "box."

During this nighttime action, we would once again be using PVS-7B NVGs, and all the O/C rules (wearing BDUs, full-face camouflage, etc.) were in effect. Since this would technically be a "live-fire" event (the Harriers would be dropping live Mk. 82 500 lb./227 kg. bombs), we would have to observe it from a sandbagged position laid out by the Fort Irwin range control personnel. Per the rules, this site was uprange and to the side of the planned flight/weapons delivery path of the Marine jets. Also present at the safe site were a number of other personnel from the NTC staff.

Darkness fell about 2000 hours, and we stayed in the HMMWVs until just thirty minutes prior to the planned Time-on-Target (TOT). Moving about in the dark at Fort Irwin is not recommended. Rattlesnakes and other unpleasant critters are common.

At the sandbagged bunker, range control personnel handed out Kevlar helmets and flak jackets, in case a Harrier dropped "short." And then we listened to the chatter of the range control and O/C radio circuits. The two VMA-513 AV-8Bs had launched successfully from Yuma, and were holding near the main post until they were cleared to make their run. At about fifteen minutes to TOT (2200 hours), the range was cleared as green, and we listened to the ODA 324/SOT-A 301 team coach the Marine pilots in. Final instructions were transmitted, along with authentication codes and laser code. At five minutes to TOT, the jets were cleared "hot," and they began their run onto the target. Meanwhile, the PAQ-10 GLTD was turned on, and the target was illuminated by the laser designator.

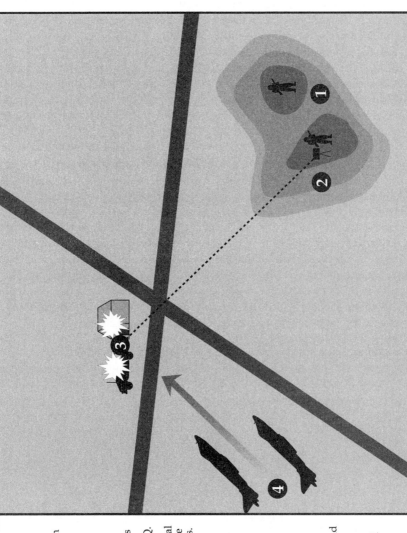

1 ODA 324 infiltrates into enemy territory, and sets up a split-team observation site on a mountain overlooking a crossroads on the NTC range complex.

2 ODA 324 observes enemy troops and vehicles establish a camp at the crossroads, and contacts HQ. JTF commander orders FOB to have ODA 324 conduct a terminal guidance mission for two Marine AV-8B Harrier II fighter bombers.

3 ODA 324 personnel "paint" the target with a PAQ-10 laser spot designator, so that the ARBS systems on the Harriers can automatically deliver their load of bombs.

4 Two VMA-513 AV-8B Harrier II fighter bombers deliver their load of six Mk. 82 general-purpose bombs (each) onto the target. ODA 324 then exfiltrates to the southeast, linking up with allied forces the following day.

A map of ODA 324's Terminal Guidance mission during NTC 99-02.

RUBICON, INC., BY LAURA DENINNO

Since the jets were making their run at over 500 knots, we only heard them a few seconds before they arrived. In the cockpits, the pilots tuned their ARBS to "look" for the LLDR laser spot, and successfully "saw" it.

"The target is locked," they announced, and the final run started.

The first Harrier roared over the mountain to our south, making a low-level "laydown" run to the target tents north of the crossroads. When the onboard computer decided the time was right, it released the bombs from the racks. Once released, the weapons were retarded by high-drag "ballute" fittings so the Harrier could escape from shrapnel after the bombs detonated.

From our position more than two miles away, we stared through our NVGs as the bombs crashed directly on the target. The second Harrier, a few seconds later, had little to do but "make the rubble bounce."

And that was it.

The range control personnel headed out to the target area to make sure all the bombs had detonated safely. And we headed back to Fort Irwin—a brief stop for me, to be followed by a drive to Las Vegas, an overnight stay, and a flight home.

The next day ODA 324/SOT-A 301 abandoned their surveillance positions and exfiltrated successfully to the lines of the 3rd/3rd Infantry (Mech.). In fact, as it turned out, all the FOB 31 missions had good outcomes; every major objective was attained, and every target hit as planned. As a result, the 3rd/3rd Infantry (Mech.) went into their rotation free of worry from enemy WMD and missile attack.

The close, professional coordination between the conventional and SOF forces had greatly contributed to the eventual success of NTC 99-02.

Downrange:
Special Forces in the Field

It's Metric Monday in Kuwait!

Army Special Forces Chief Warrant Officer

Military forces don't earn their keep perfecting their skills, but in operations in other countries . . . downrange. Training is obviously essential, and observing training can tell us a great deal about a military organization, but there is no substitute for the real thing. For that reason, SFC wanted me to spend as much "downrange" time as possible. There I could best observe how Special Forces play their unique part within the national security system.

Specifically, SFC wanted me to experience the day-to-day activities of SF soldiers doing JCET-type missions (which comprise the majority of SF field missions), as well as to sample a broad cross-section of other SF operations.

Almost There: Bosnia

To that end, on our journey east after NTC 99-02, Major McCollum and I made a stop at Fort Carson, Colorado, one of the many military facilities scattered around Colorado Springs (others: the Air Force Academy, Peterson AFB and Shriever AFB, and Cheyenne Mountain—home to the North American Aerospace Defense Command, NORAD). Fort Carson is home to the 7th Infantry Division (an Army National Guard formation), 3rd Armored Cavalry Regiment, and numerous other units, including the 10th Special Forces Group (a newly built compound houses its two continental U.S.–based battalions).

This trip had a double purpose: First, I would talk with the 2/10th SFG command staff about their unit and its capabilities. But second, a plan was afoot to have me experience 10th SFG operations downrange in Bosnia-Herzegovina (I was to observe SF teams carrying out actual peacekeeping mission tasks), and I was to receive initial briefings and other instructions in preparation for that trip.

Three 10th SFG ODAs were scheduled to deploy to Bosnia-Herzegovina shortly after New Year's 1999, where they would be working as part of the United Nations peacekeeping force. This force, working under Operation Joint Forge (the NATO name for the operation), was responsible for implementing the terms of the 1995 Dayton Accords.[98] So far, the peace plan had held up without a major breach—but only *just*. The Bosnian Serbs didn't like it: The Accords meant they would lose the regional dominance that had been theirs prior to the summer of 1995. They had made their distaste evident mostly by "foot dragging" on full implementation of the agreement, and more openly by the occasional protest or riot, or by harassment of NATO personnel. The U.S.-led peacekeeping force had had to come down on them hard.

Meanwhile, the dogs of war were barking again in what was left of Yugoslavia, and NATO was butting heads with Slobodan Milosevic over the fate of Kosovo's ethnic Albanians.

Practically, that meant the units headed into the next rotation had to prepare for a wide range of contingencies—from simple conflict resolution to full-scale civil war. It was against this backdrop that Major McCollum and I tugged our coats against a light falling snow, and headed over to the headquarters of the 2/10th SFG.

Wednesday, November 4th, 1998—2/10th SFG Headquarters, Fort Carson, Colorado

The 2/10th's commanding officer, Lieutenant Colonel Tom Rendall, met us in the 2/10th SFG headquarter's lobby. After introductions, he guided us to the battalion's briefing room. Tacked to all the walls were maps, photos, and charts, outlining missions SF teams would run into Bosnia-Herzegovina. Earlier, Major McCollum had made initial arrangements for my own Bosnia trip. Now things began to get serious. Today I was to be given operational sensitive material about dates, locations, personnel, and intent of several key missions being executed by 2/10th SFG. If I blabbed, real people—including me—could be at risk.

As I took a seat, the commander explained this and other ground rules. Then the lights were doused and the briefings began.

Here is the situation at the time: The peacekeeping operation in Bosnia-Herzegovina (Operation Joint Forge) is in its fourth year. The peacekeeping force, known as the Stabilization Force (SFOR), is composed of heavy and conventional forces from more than two dozen nations, most of which are members either of NATO or the associated Partnership for Peace program (the NATO program that helps qualify former Warsaw Pact and other nations for NATO membership). SFOR works missions in the three primary control zones—American, French, and British. The American force, known as Task Force Eagle, is based at a huge, heavily defended fortress compound near Tuzla in the northern part of the American zone (most of the center

---

98 In late 1995, following Operation Deliberate Force (a short bombing campaign against the Bosnian Serbs), the various warring factions in the ongoing Bosnian civil war met at Wright-Patterson AFB in Dayton to craft an agreement to settle the war. The terms of the agreement included a withdrawal of military support by the Serbs and the Croats, a partition of Bosnia-Herzegovina into ethnic/religious zones, and a multinational peacekeeping force to enforce the whole arrangement. The three primary nations in the peacekeeping force are the U.S., Britain, and France, though dozens of others—including Russia—have contributed units.

The new headquarters of the 10th Special Forces Group at Fort Carson, Colorado. Located in a high mountain valley, this is the home for the group assigned to support European Special Operations.

JOHN D. GRESHAM

portion of Bosnia). Because of its ethnically mixed population, the peace is not easy to keep here. Thus brigade-sized units rotate in and out.

What do they do? Quite a bit: patrolling and reconnaissance; evaluating possible future "hot" spots; settling property and access disputes; and suppressing any insurgent activity.

Originally, the American brigade came from units based in Europe, but more recently the mission has been handled by units based in the continental U.S. During the early part of 1999, a brigade from the 1st Armored Cavalry Division at Fort Hood, Texas, was operating out of Tuzla. They would be replaced by a brigade from the 10th Mountain Division (who had been training for that at JRTC).

Peacekeeping is never easy: Because people with a mind to hatred, revenge, and violence are not easily persuaded to calm down, a peacekeeping *force* is close to an oxymoron—yet a necessary oxymoron. The "force" must behave peacefully, yet carry a big stick. If there's no stick, warring factions will simply resume fighting . . . and everyone in the force becomes a potential hostage and target for extortion—or bullets. These truths glare especially bright in what was once Yugoslavia, where the wounds have been open for centuries, and only the heavy hand of Marshal Tito kept something like order in that tragic land. A good case can be made that diplomacy is wasted here.

For these reasons, SFOR has traditionally maintained a "big dog" posture. This means lots of Bradley fighting vehicles and heavily armed HMMWVs, with soldiers in full body armor and their weapons locked and loaded. Such a concept of operations, of course, where the unit resembles an occupation force more than a flock of Mother Teresa's nuns, does very little to persuade the locals that peace is in their near-term future. On the other hand, peace has hardly been part of their near- or long-term past. Perhaps here is an instance where we have to give force a chance.

So far, in fact, the SFOR approach to their mission has worked. Perhaps keeping the lid on the pressure cooker will give the various factions a chance to make some kind of workable—and peaceful—arrangements with one another. There is no reason why the two kinds of Christians—Orthodox and Roman—can't get along with each other and with their Muslim neighbors. Someday it may come home to all of them that they all worship the same God.

Meanwhile, the heavy, conventional forces—the lid on the cooker—would be blind without good on-the-ground intelligence. Along with superb air and logistics support and a high level of intelligence surveillance, SFOR has placed a small contingent of Special Forces teams out in the countryside. These teams, drawn from the 10th SFG, and 3rd SFG, are sent into problem areas, putting down eyes and ears where they will be needed most . . . for example, inside a town near a partition line where they expect tension. The teams are also used as liaison elements with nonU.S. peacekeeping units.

My hope was to visit some of these teams in Bosnia-Herzegovina.

The briefing I was about to witness covered the mission plans being presented to the 2/10th operations staff for critique and consideration:

Beginning in January 1999, 2/10th SFG would deploy three teams into Bosnia-Herzegovina, to provide support for Operation Joint Forge. The following units were assigned to the missions:

- **AOB 060**—Coordinating forward activities for the SF missions would be an ODB, which would provide command, control, and communications for the other two missions in the American peacekeeping zone.

- **ODA 040**—One of the toughest challenges for Americans in SFOR is maintaining communications and coordination with peacekeeping units from other participating nations. Of these challenges, the toughest of all has been working with the Russians, who have committed a full brigade of paratroops for Joint Forge (the armored column that later raced down to the Pristina Airport in Kosovo at the end of the NATO air campaign against Yugoslavia came from this unit). Since the Russian Army's communications equipment is several generations of technology behind the U.S. military's, the Russians have a hard time staying in touch with our guys . . . a potentially dangerous problem in multinational military operations. Even sending a fax is difficult. Thus the need for a reliable liaison. To that end, ODA 040 would be stationed with the Russian brigade and act as a Liaison Coordination Element (LCE), providing a direct connection with the rest of SFOR and Task Force Eagle at Tuzla. ODA 040 would also provide a necessary but unstated benefit. They'd get an unrestricted view of Russian behavior in the field. The Russians' long-standing close connection to their brother Slavs, the Serbs, has resulted in actions whose even-handedness is at best doubtful. SF watchers would not necessarily make the Russians behave, but they could document misbehavior.

- **ODA 062**—The other 2/10th SFG mission would act as a Joint Coordination Observer (JCO) team in the crucial town of Doboj, which lies at the meeting point of three ethnic zones (Serb, Muslim, and Croat) in the American Zone, and was expected to be a trouble spot. ODA 062 would move into the town and establish a team house. That is, they would rent a private home, flesh it out with an appropriate array of communications gear, and then use it as a base to patrol the area in rented—and unmarked—sports utility vehicles. The team members would operate in civilian clothes or soft BDUs, with a minimum of armament or body armor showing. They would make the rounds of the area, get to know the local inhabitants, try to make friends, and keep an eye on the mood of the people . . . in the hope that they would solve problems before they reached a stage requiring an Apache gunship or Bradley fighting vehicle.

After this part of the briefing, the commander asked me to step outside, while the more classified aspects of the mission plans were discussed.

Sometime later, when I was back in the briefing room, the discussion had turned to general topics like the murky and convoluted history and politics of the Balkans—areas of ignorance where I was concerned. Surely, I thought, the SF staff recommends reading for SF soldiers about to deploy there (SF soldiers are voracious readers—they always have a stash in their bags or at the team house). Since it would be exceedingly useful if I could bone up on these books, I asked the 2/10th SFG staff for their suggestions.

Their list was insightful (it wasn't actually a list; they had the books on hand and tossed them one by one on a table):

- *Peacekeeper: The Road to Sarajevo* by **Major General Louis MacKenzie**—Written by a former commander of the UN peacekeeping force, this is a critical analysis of the entire NATO policy in the Balkans up to the signing and implementation of the Dayton Accords.

- *To End a War* by **Richard Holbrooke**—The standard work on the brokering of the deal that currently holds Bosnia-Herzegovina together. Because it is a book about diplomacy by a diplomat (the current UN ambassador and a man of famously large ego), its focus is limited.

- *Bosnia: A Short History* by **Noel Malcomb**—This tells the story of how Bosnia-Herzegovina decayed in the 1990s into the danger spot it is today. An excellent work for those who want a recent perspective on the region.

- *Yugoslavia: Death of a Nation* by **Laura Silber and Allan Little**—This is the companion book to an excellent but controversial five-hour documentary series run on the Discovery Channel and BBC in 1996. The series and the companion book take the "long" view that the conflict has roots hundreds of years deep; yet they also presume that the leaderships of the various modern factions (much like Hitler and the Nazis) have made use of the ancient ethnic symbols to validate recent hatreds and their own self-serving policies.

- *Endgame: The Betrayal and Fall of Srebrenica* by **David Rhode**—The Srebrenica crisis was one of the really "nasty" incidents of the civil war. There—in full view of western observers and the press—the Serbs murdered thousands of Croats and Muslims and threw them into mass graves. Though out of print and hard to find, David Rhodes's fine examination of the crisis and the mass murder is compelling, and important to those trying to understand the dynamic of hatred and revenge in the Balkans.

- *The Ugly American* by Eugene Burdick and William J. Lederer—This 1950s classic still rings true today, and is required reading for *all* SF soldiers. The novel (based on the adventures of an actual CIA agent in Vietnam, whose story also formed the basis for Graham Greene's *The Quiet American*) remains the standard work on what Americans should *not* do overseas, and how *not* to do it.

- *Eastern Approaches* by Fitzroy MacLean—A memoir of the author's travels in eastern Europe in the 1930s and '40s (as a British diplomat), *Eastern Approaches* is a clear look at how Marshal Tito and his partisans created the Yugoslav state.

- *Low-Intensity Operations: Subversion, Insurgency, Peacekeeping* by Frank Kitson—A surprisingly clear and easy-to-read "how-to" for low-intensity warfare, this is *the* handbook for running a revolution, and covers all the major political and military actions necessary for a populist rebellion, including the indicators of success or failure. Unlike other books on the subject, which tend to idolize guerrilla leaders and ignore positive possibilities (such as peacekeeping operations), this book covers the full spectrum, and is thus a useful volume for SF soldiers learning the trade.

- *FM 100-20*—U.S. Army Training and Doctrine Command—*The* Bible for SF soldiers. Field Manual (FM) 100-20 is the standard U.S. training guide on low-intensity conflict.

- *How to Win Friends and Influence People* by Dale Carnegie—Perhaps a surprising inclusion, but consider for a moment its core principles: The whole point of the book is to persuade folks who do not know you or your motives how to look at you and what you are doing in the most positive light possible. It lays out a plan of approach to other people that emphasizes learning what is valuable to them, then winning their admiration and trust, and then showing them how what you are selling can be useful and important to them. It works in sales, it works downrange. People are people around the world, and usually less sophisticated than Americans about recognizing the marketing techniques favored by Dale Carnegie. The basics of listening to people and winning their trust and admiration are keys to any mission that SF runs.

The last book to be dropped on the table clearly held a special place in SF hearts:

- *Fielding's The World's Most Dangerous Places, Third Edition* by Robert Young Pelton—If you are a fan of quirky, farcical adventures, you will love *Dangerous Places* (known as *DP* to loyal followers). DP is a compact compendium of personal notes, travel logs, and tongue-in-cheek ramblings on travel to planet Earth's most dangerous places, and surviving the visit. Though the book doubtless contains much that is hearsay, or is of otherwise doubtful accuracy, it has become a rucksack regular for SF personnel deploying downrange.

After the briefing, I listened to a few final words from the commander in his office. His main point was that at the moment, the situation in Bosnia was fairly stable, and so I could expect little physical danger in the American zone—especially given the high level of U.S. presence, and the excellent command-and-control arrangements. He did advise me to dress warmly (if possible in one of the new Gor-Tex parkas now keeping his men warm and dry).

On a more serious note, he was concerned about developments in the Southern Balkans. Already, the Serbs in Belgrade were making noises about ethnically cleansing Kosovo of ethnic Albanians. The crisis, he felt, could pop at any time, and was likely to draw NATO into a shooting war.

Suitably warned, I excused myself.

In early January, I was scheduled to meet Major McCollum at Eagle Base in Tuzla to head downrange. The plan was to fly to Hungary and then on to Tuzla. There Tom McCollum and the folks from 2/10th SFG 2 would pick me up for overnight visits to all three of the teams. I was especially looking forward to visiting the Russian paratroops in their lager, and enjoying hospitality from "the Bear."

Sadly, none of this came off.

Just days before my planned departure on a USAF C-5 Galaxy transport out of Dover AFB in Delaware, I was told there were "delays." Further excuses came from the public affairs folks in Tuzla, soon followed by the cancellation message that I had begun to expect: Until further notice, General Montgomery Meigs, the commander of U.S. Army Forces, Europe, was barring writers and journalists from the theater, no excuse given.[99]

I watched the news wires for the next days, and got my own answer. Two days after the cancellation, NATO SOF forces captured a Serbian general suspected of war crimes in Bosnia, a major "snatch" for the legal folks up at the Hague.

Almost immediately, the Serbs hit the fan. Within hours, NATO patrols all over Bosnia were harassed, and armored relief units had to be dispatched to save a few of them. The uproar continued for several weeks.

In other words, rather than risk civilians in a "hot" situation, General Meigs had taken them out of harm's way.

As it was, things were plenty tense around Eagle Base for the next month, and I eventually decided to skip the Bosnian trip entirely. I'm sorry it didn't come off, but I'm grateful to General Meigs for keeping my butt safe. Thanks, Monty!

The Persian Gulf

The Balkans was hardly the only worthwhile downrange location.

The Persian Gulf, for instance, had a lot to offer the curious observer . . . even

---

[99] General Montgomery Meigs is the latest in a string of Army general officers from one of the first families of the Army. His namesake, Abraham Lincoln's quartermaster general during the Civil War, commandeered Robert E. Lee's Virginia home to create the current-day Arlington National Cemetery. The present General Meigs, a veteran of the 1991 Gulf War, where he commanded an armored brigade against the Republican Guard, is a specialist in the arcane science of operations research and an excellent historian and writer.

though at the time I ended up going there (a month after my visit to Fort Carson), it looked like I might be headed into a real shooting war.

The difference between my failed trip to Bosnia and my successful trip to the Gulf was in the level of perceived danger to civilians. In Bosnia, it was thought that terrorist or other reprisals were likely. In the Gulf, it was judged that even in the event of a shooting war, there was little likelihood that people like me would be at risk. That does not mean that I wasn't looked after. There *were* dangers in the Gulf, and my SF friends did their best to avoid them. In this they were successful, thank God.

Meanwhile, Saddam Hussein was his normal, tiresome nuisance self, and America and her allies were pushing back hard. The long-simmering crisis over UN inspectors' access to his WMD and missile production sites had reached yet another impasse, and military action seemed imminent. The USS *Eisenhower* (CVN-69) carrier battle group (CVBG) had been moved into the Persian Gulf, accompanied by a stream of air and ground reinforcements. On both sides there was snorting, heavy breathing, and posturing. Who would call the other's bluff? And was it a bluff?

On November 14th, the posturing stopped, and an execution order for air strikes on Iraq went out to the Central Command commander, General Tony Zini. Aircraft (which could be recalled) were launched, and cruise missiles (which couldn't) were minutes from being fired when the Iraqis blinked and announced they would again accept UN inspectors.

The diplomats sat down again to try to figure things out. (In the event, they failed. But that's *another* story.)

During this breaking situation (*despite* this breaking situation), Special Forces Command arranged for me to visit elements of the 5th SFG in the Persian Gulf. After the experience of my abortive trip to Bosnia, I could be forgiven for doubting the Gulf trip. I was wrong to worry. It all came off fine.

The over 8,000-mile journey began at National Airport, where I met my guide for the expedition, an operations officer on the 5th SFG staff, who I'll call Major Neil. Neil was an experienced SF team and company commander, who had been assigned to me because of his language and cultural skills, and his experience watching over the security of VIPs. (Though Major McCollum was also due to accompany me, a last-minute visa problem left him back home.) So Neil became my sole guide, bodyguard, and the guarantor of my *bona fides* in the Gulf states.

The plan was to fly to Amsterdam, change planes, and continue on to Bahrain, the tiny island nation located in the bay between the great Saudi port of Dhahran and the peninsula occupied by Qatar (pronounced locally as "Gutter"). Here I would visit the forward headquarters for SOF units in CENTCOM—SOCCENT and a 5th SFG detachment that was finishing up a training mission. From there, we would fly to Kuwait and visit several more 5th SFG teams, including those involved in the ongoing deployment against Iraq.

Just to make things interesting, I had been alerted (through Major Neil) that the crisis with Iraq had sparked upwards of six terrorist groups in the region into an active mode. That meant he had *very* specific security instructions for me, and watched over me like a mother hen. Under the circumstances, I didn't mind the attention.

The flight from the U.S. to the international airport outside Bahrain's capital,

Manama, took close to twenty hours and three different flights, and I arrived pretty well wiped out. Once there, Major Neil got me quickly through customs and loaded into a rental car for the drive to our hotel, a Best Western (you expected something exotic?). His superior skills in the latest antiterrorist driving techniques were not wasted in Arab traffic (the real threat!).

At the hotel I managed to focus through my exhaustion long enough to take in from him a couple of basic cautions. One, keep the windows closed and the doors locked. And two, only drink what comes out of a bottle or is served to you. (Though desalinization plants along the coastline produce water, as precious as oil in this part of the world, the water that is pumped into homes and businesses is still more than a little salty. It's perfectly fine to wash or bathe in, but it's not really potable. For that reason, people tend to drink bottled water almost exclusively.)

Moments later, I was in my room doing what I could to recover from the Mother of All Jet Lags.

Thursday, November 19th—Camp Kalid, Sheik Isa, Bahrain

Next morning, over breakfast in the hotel's dining room (surprisingly good, with eggs and breakfast meats, and all variety of pastries, fruits, and cereals), Neil gave me a heads-up on the local situation. Bahrain, he explained, was the most liberal and tolerant of the Gulf States, the place where folks from stricter Arab nations came to "play." The island is connected to the Saudi mainland by a long causeway. At the Saudi end are all the normal Islamic restrictions on food, drink, and social behavior. But Manama comes at you in a bright, neon-lit rush, like Las Vegas.

Still—despite the KFCs and Dairy Queens—you know exactly where you are. Early in the morning, and on the appointed times throughout the day, you can hear the muezzins' cries—both from minaret tops and over all the local television channels. And when you step out onto the streets, you'll find a National Guardsman standing in front of the hotel with a fully automatic MP-5 machine pistol.[100] These guys are a major reason why street crime is rare in this part of the world.

After breakfast, I gathered my daypack, purchased several cold liter bottles of water, and climbed into the rental car for a run down to the southern end of the island and my first taste of SF life downrange.

I couldn't help but notice on the way a number of industrial sites in addition to the expected petrochemical plants. The ruling emir and his family are trying hard to build an industrial base that will survive the inevitable drying up of the oil wells.

About 31 miles/50 km. south of Manama, we entered a large military reservation, which does not appear on the local maps or travel guides. This is Sheik Isa (also called "Shakey's Pizza" by the U.S airmen who fly from there), a huge airbase capable of operating the heaviest aircraft. Right now, it was home to a USAF Air Expeditionary Force that included F-15 Eagles and Strike Eagles, F-16 Fighting Falcons,

---

100 Many nations maintain a National Guard—really, a National Police Force—which functions as a combination of the U.S. F.B.I., Treasury Department, State Police/Militia, and military reserve.

tankers, and even a detachment of four big B-1B Lancer bombers. A substantial flock of aircraft were visible to the south, in the traffic pattern.

Heading east toward the Gulf, we drove along a limestone escarpment; then Neil took a left turn toward a bunker complex and a few tents, and we were at our destination—Camp Kalid.

Camp Kalid was a small tent city, roughly ten acres in size, built among concrete bunkers on the northern end of the Sheik Isa reservation. Hot and dusty (the temperature was well over 90° F/32° C in late November), the camp was sparse and barren, except for the tents and a scattering of vehicles . . . and the tents were in the process of being dismantled. Here five SF teams (four ODAs and an ODB) from 5th SFG had set up a training center for military personnel from Bahrain and Qatar, placed here as part of the Joint combined Exercise Training (JCET) program, which helps SF soldiers on how to train foreign soldiers. The teams had been in Bahrain for the last seven weeks, and were planning to leave for home the next day (to be back in time for Thanksgiving).

I say "planning," because there was some question whether they would actually leave as planned, as a result of the Iraqi alert—a reminder of the constant reality 5th SFG has to face: *Everything* is always up in the air. As the group assigned to the most distant area of responsibility (AOR) covered by the U.S. military, the 5th SFG personnel often feel their hell is to wait for planes.

Major Neil smiled when I remarked on this. "Last year," he said, "I traveled well over 100,000 miles. You can't imagine how many frequent flyer miles I've got."

Though nothing much of interest was going on—unless you like to watch people packing—the conversation was stimulating, and the Camp commander, also a major, invited us to join his men for lunch, which was served buffet-style in a large tent. The food, prepared by a local caterer, was chicken, lamb, rice, vegetables, and some traditional American fare.

As we ate, the commander briefed us on his mission and on life as an SOF unit in the CENTCOM AOR.

Since it takes so much effort and such a long time to transport people to and from the Persian Gulf, the local SOCCENT commander works hard to keep his troops in theater as long as possible. This requirement has inspired what is called "Hub and Spoke" concept: Once they're in the AOR, SF teams move from one mission (out on a "spoke") to another somewhere else in the region (out on another spoke). The "Hub" is CENTSOC Forward headquarters in Bahrain. Hub and Spoke lets one team do several missions in theater before returning home, a benefit for limited transport resources, and it keeps more SF units in the region, which is good in case of a fast-breaking crisis. Its downside is it wastes the most valuable SF resource (personnel) on missions that sometimes resemble "make work," and badly burns out 5th SFG personnel, who are already the busiest SF soldiers in the Army.

It was clear that the SF soldiers felt they had spent too much time at Camp Kalid doing make work. Though they had been engaged in solid training with the local armed forces, that had taken up only about seven of the fifty days of their deployment. For the other forty-three days, they sat frustrated in their tents staying out of the sun and waiting for the Bahrainis to show up. Poor U.S. State and DoD coordination with Bahrain had, in their view, messed things up badly.

Under the circumstances, they were understandably eager to go home. And in fact, they did make it home in time for the holidays.

After lunch, I grabbed a bottle of cold water and was given a tour of what was left of Camp Kalid (much of the facility had already been taken down and packed up).

The bunkers, I learned, had been used as security and communications shacks, while the men themselves had lived in the tents. Nearby, the 2/5th SFG soldiers had laid out marksmanship ranges and navigation courses for the JCET training.

As we walked around, the commander gave me his views on his soldiers' main complaints—and conceded that much of their frustration was valid, but he was quick to point out that good training had been run, his men had gotten useful interaction with their allied counterparts, and all had learned valuable lessons for future JCET missions.

He also pointed out that the crisis with Iraq had put strains on relations between the U.S. and its allies in the Persian Gulf, and this called for patience. Few non-Iraqi Arabs are fond of Saddam Hussein, and most are grateful to the U.S. for standing up to him. But the Iraqis *are* their Arab brothers. And most Arabs—while the best of hosts during a short stay—are very nervous at the thought of a long-term foreign (read U.S.) presence in their lands. Best for all—in their view—would be for everyone involved to end their differences, and get back to pumping oil.

In short, most Arabs would like the Iraqi problem to simply go away.

About midafternoon, we completed the tour and headed back for Manama. On the way, Major Neil pointed out one of Bahrain's more interesting tourist sights, the "Tree of Life," a gnarled and ugly Joshua tree in the middle of nowhere, the only living thing of any size in a desolate tract of desert, and arguably the oldest living thing on the planet (it has been dated at thousands of years old). Here, some Muslims believe, the Garden of Eden may have been located.

Farther along, we passed burial mounds, for which Bahrain is famous (the national museum has a fascinating display devoted to them). Thousands were scattered around the island, varying in size from small mounds for individuals to elaborate structures for many people.

Not long after that, we were back in the Las Vegas of the Gulf and our hotel . . . soon followed by a shower, a nap, and a good dinner at the Hotel Diplomat, a local landmark.

Friday, November 20th—SOCCENT Headquarters (Forward), Bahrain

While Bahrain is more relaxed about Islamic rules than other Arab states, Fridays—the Muslim Sabbath—are still slow and quiet (though shops are allowed to open for a few hours in the middle of the day).

Since there was a few hours to kill before my next scheduled events—a visit with the commander of the forward element of the U.S. Special Operations Command

(SOCCENT), followed by my flight to Kuwait—I spent some time exploring the local *Souk*, the Arab market place, and well worth the visit.

Then it was a run over to the American naval compound and a visit with the local SOCCENT commander.

Because Bahrain is one of the few Arab nations that has allowed the development of permanent foreign bases on its soil, it has become an important lynchpin for U.S. interests in the Persian Gulf.

The harbor showed a substantial number of U.S., British, and Bahraini warships. And beside the harbor was growing one of the largest construction sites I've ever seen. Dozens of buildings were under construction behind a solid block wall perimeter. This was the Naval Forces, Central Command (NAVCENT) Forward complex, which had been in the works for several years.

Previously, NAVCENT had been based on a converted amphibious ship, the USS *LaSalle* (AGF-3). But now that the region had been given its own fleet designator (U.S. 5th Fleet), more permanent facilities had become necessary.

All of it, predictably, was being built like a fortress, fully self-contained, with billeting just outside the gate for personnel with families.

After a close check of our credentials, Major Neil and I entered the compound and walked a half-mile to the air-conditioned trailers that house the SOCCENT Forward headquarters, where Neil introduced me to Colonel James B. Conners, USAF, a veteran of the USAF SOC community, with a specialty in gunship operations.

Inside his office, the colonel took me through a varied and detailed rundown of SOF operations in the Persian Gulf.

He began by pointing out on a map the operations then running. Then he shared his thoughts on the near-war alert of the previous weekend. "We came *this* close to actual combat," he confirmed.

The alert had caused many other headaches, and led to his most immediately pressing problem: A lot of troops had started deploying to the Gulf, and for now they weren't needed. Worse, many units were stacked up in Europe and the Azores, with only the vaguest idea where they would end up. Worse still, deployments are hugely expensive (they're paid for out of various contingency funds, but it's still a zero sum game—somebody would lose; somebody's ox would be gored). So the colonel was doing his best to work with his superiors to sort things out and reverse the flow of personnel into his AOR.

Moving on to broader issues, Colonel Conners is very eager to see a dedicated SOF forward headquarters in the region, away from Army, Navy, and Air Force facilities[101] where SOF units are feeling squeezed. This would also please the local host nations, who would like to spread the American presence thinner. That is, they'd like the American presence to be less visibly present.

One idea is to build a dedicated SOF facility in Qatar, where the government has expressed willingness to allow it. But the key limiting factor right now is money, which, as always, is in short supply. Lawmakers in Washington much prefer to spend

---

101 The Army facility is Camp Doha, north of Kuwait City. The Navy facility is in Bahrain. And the Air Force is now at Al Karj (Prince Sultan Airbase, home of the 4th Wing during the war) in Saudi Arabia (it was once at Dhahran).

A change of command at the U.S. Navy compound in Bahrain. This compound supports operations by Navy SEALs and special warfare craft, along with Air Force and Army Special Operations units around the Persian Gulf.

construction funds in their own states than in foreign lands. Nevertheless, SOCOM is convinced a forward headquarters is necessary, and will probably be funded once the naval construction in Bahrain is completed.

When the briefing was over, I accepted the colonel's invitation to accompany him to the other side of the compound to witness a small joint ceremony—a change of command for the local Navy Sea-Air-Land (SEAL) team commander.

After a short walk, we entered what could have passed for a town square in Arizona or some other southwestern community. Bordering the square were ranch-style buildings (one housed an Internet café complete with coffee bar), with palm trees and grassy lawns. Young American military personnel wandered about . . . it could have been a pleasant, relaxed American weekend in the States.

Meanwhile, several hundred SOF personnel from all the services had gathered, with a large contingent of Navy SEALs in their formal whites. What followed was one of the more agreeable of military traditions: a formal change of command in the field. The outgoing commander's achievements were noted—including the establishment of the forward SEAL presence in the Persian Gulf. And there were sly comments about how the SEALs had recently used a small Mark V patrol boat to survey the vital Strait of Hormuz between Iran and Oman. In fact, that very night another Mark V would lead the USS *Enterprise* (CVN-65) CVBG into the Persian Gulf, where it would replace the group headed by the USS *Eisenhower* (CVN-69). It was a busy time in the Gulf.

An hour later, Major Neil and I were back at the airport for the hour-long flight to Kuwait. The flight was quick and comfortable, though full: Many Kuwaitis were returning home to start the Islamic workweek the next morning.

Kuwait International Airport was a shock after the almost casual security in Bahrain. The war scare may have been over, but you'd have had a hard time believing that here. Thousands of people were arriving this evening—allied military personnel, civilian contractors, and the usual flow of businessmen and civilians; and the Kuwaiti Ministry of the Interior Police (who handle local security, customs, border patrols, and antiterrorist functions) were out in force, each with his black uniform and MP-5 machine pistol.

After we passed through customs, Neil led me to the airport exit, where we were met by a burly man in civilian clothes—obviously a senior SF soldier. His name was Chief Warrant Officer Wade, and he was assigned to provide security and protective services during my visit. Wade directed us to a large Chevy Suburban in the parking lot.

On the twenty-minute drive that followed, I was shotgunned with security information and rules, in effect because of the Iraqi situation and concerns about reportedly active Islamic terrorist groups. That meant a full-fledged escape and evasion (E&E) plan had been worked out. Simply put, any time I was away from my hotel, I would be riding in this tank of an automobile surrounded by men with enough firepower to take out a shopping mall. In the back were several cans of fuel, a carton of MREs, and a couple of cases of bottled water just in case we had to run for Saudi Arabia.

The fact that I had entered a potential—and recent—war zone really hit home when I arrived at the Sheraton Kuwait. Its walls were splattered with the plastered-over bullet holes from the fighting in 1991. A sobering thought as I checked in for the night.

Saturday, November 21st—Camp Doha, Kuwait

Chief Wade arrived with the Suburban early the next morning. Today we were to check in at Camp Doha west of Kuwait City; and we were soon headed down a congested, four-lane boulevard beside the harbor. Noting the traffic, Chief Wade commented, "Metric Monday." Meaning: the Islamic workweek started on Saturday.

After about twenty minutes, the huge white walls of Camp Doha became visible, and we turned in to the security headquarters.

Camp Doha is the Army's forward headquarters in the Persian Gulf, and has been since the U.S. Army took it over from the UN back in the early 1990s; enough equipment is pre-positioned here for an entire armored or mechanized brigade, along with the support infrastructure for up to a division of follow-on troops. At any given time, under what is called Operation Intrinsic Action, there is usually a battalion from the 3rd Infantry Division (Mechanized) operating in Kuwait.

Though they are not technically based there (in deference to Kuwaiti sensitivities), Camp Doha is normally home to several thousand U.S. Army personnel. But the recent excitement had greatly swelled that number. An entire armored brigade and a Patriot missile battalion had fallen onto the equipment stockpiles . . . and were now putting everything back into storage and hoping to find transportation home for the holidays.

Our business was on the eastern end of the base, in one of the many warehouses that had been converted into barracks and operations buildings. After obtaining security badges and passing through a *tough* security checkpoint, Major Neil and I entered Advanced Operating Base (AOB) 590, the home of U.S. Special Forces in Kuwait. Here I would get briefed on SF operations in the region, prior to going out to the field.

The first briefing came from the Special Operations Command and Control Element—Kuwait (SOCCE-K) commander, a lieutenant colonel, who very quickly made clear the mission of SOF units in Kuwait: While a few JCET Foreign Internal Defense (FID) missions were underway, and SF maritime units support the ongoing maritime embargo of Iraq, supplying personnel and boats for the blockade, the SOF presence in Kuwait was primarily aimed at the threat of Iraqi (and also potentially Iranian) aggression . . . and specifically to stop any Iraqi or Iranian invasion short of Kuwait City. If war breaks out, U.S. SOF personnel are charged with helping the Kuwaiti Army gather intelligence, conduct artillery and close air support (CAS) missions, and support combat search-and-rescue of downed allied aircrews.

At the heart of the SOCCE-K mission is an operation, called Iris Gold, that takes up most of the SF muscle in the area.

At this point, AOB 590's commander, Major Wes, took over the briefing. Iris Gold, he explained, was a continuous company-sized JCS deployment from 5th SFG to Camp Doha—six ODAs, an ODB, and other supporting elements. The ODAs further break into a total of twenty-one three-man teams (called Coalition Support Teams—CSTs), each of which is equipped with a Ground Mobility Vehicle packed with fuel, ammunition, food, and radio gear. CSTs are highly skilled at operating with their Kuwait counterparts in the field; and under normal conditions, each can operate for a week with resupply only of water and diesel fuel.

The purpose of Iris Gold is to bolster the four Kuwait Land Forces (KLF) brigades (each with four armored/mechanized battalions) with enough airpower to hold on until follow-on allied land forces can arrive.[102] Since the four KLF brigades are now upgrading to new M1 Abrams tanks and Warrior infantry fighting vehicles, this is not a bad bet.

To implement that purpose, a mounted CST is assigned to every Kuwaiti brigade and battalion headquarters, with another stationed with the Kuwait Land Forces (KLF) mobile headquarters when deployed. In an invasion, the CSTs would provide a ground coordination element to call in artillery and allied CAS missions. (I should also say that a CST presence at every Kuwait TOC is an excellent way to determine Kuwaiti morale and to get the "ground truth" in a combat situation.)

Every four months, a new company from 5th SFG rotates in. A company from

---

[102] The four KLF brigades are laid out as follows: The 35th Armored covers the western border with Iraq; the 26th Cavalry holds the north. The 15th Armored Brigade is assigned the central region of the country; and the 6th Infantry (Mech.) defends Kuwait City.

A map showing how the Iris Gold Special Forces teams would be deployed in time of war.

RUBICON, INC., BY LAURA DENINNO

3rd/5th SFG was currently handling the duty. They had arrived in early October, and were due to rotate out in late January.

Major Wes's briefing would continue later. But first, I headed over to lunch at the Camp Doha mess hall—a vast warehouse, with enough tables and seats for over a thousand personnel—and then returned to the SOF area for a tour of the facilities.

Compared with the folks back at Camp Kalid in Bahrain, these soldiers had a comfortable life. Team members were billeted in air-conditioned, two-man rooms with common lavatory/shower facilities, and recreational areas. All had television sets (most were tuned to CNN or the BBC during the day). In the evenings, movies and popcorn were standard.

After the tour, I returned to the SOCCE-K/Iris Gold command center for the conclusion of Major Wes's briefing:

Operating in Kuwait necessarily placed limitations on U.S. personnel, he began. Though the Emirate is not as strict as Saudi Arabia and some of the other Persian Gulf States, it is still a Muslim country. Which means *no* consumption of alcohol by U.S. military personnel, *no* direct interaction with Kuwaiti women outside the Camp Doha compound, and a two-man rule on their rare visits to Kuwait City. These restrictions don't encourage tourism, and indeed, most U.S. personnel tend to stay inside the U.S. compound, except when they are out on exercise in the desert.

Next came my itinerary during the coming days: I was to visit a number of sites around the Emirate, starting tomorrow with visits to 5th SFG ODAs doing independent JCET training deployments.

He concluded by handing me a thick manila envelope, containing a folded map made of Tyvec paper (a synthetic paper that is waterproof and almost indestructible) and printed in camouflaged shades. This was an escape map used by aircrews and other at-risk personnel who work in this part of the Persian Gulf, and it showed details of Kuwait, southern Iraq, and northern Saudi Arabia that don't appear in tourist guides or local maps.

As he passed it over, Wes said, "So you'll know where you are . . . just in case." He did not need to say more. Iraq was less than an hour's drive away.

On that daunting note, Major Neil, Chief Wade, and I returned to the Suburban for the half-hour drive back to the Sheraton.

Sunday, November 22nd—Interior Ministry Training Range, Kuwait

Over breakfast, Neil gave me the latest on the local situation. Though the threat from the terrorist groups that had worried Neil and his bosses seemed to be declining, our vehicle would be out in the open without escort, and so two additional security personnel from the embassy would be joining us on our travels.

The more the merrier.

I grabbed my daypack and we all loaded up into the big Chevy. It was a beautifully haze- and dust-free day. It was going to be hot, but the absence of humidity made life bearable.

Heading north on a six-lane highway, we drove about 18 miles/30 km. until the

Special Forces soldiers from ODA 571 give soldiers of the Kuwaiti Interior Ministry a safety briefing prior to a live-fire training exercise north of Kuwait City. 5th Special Forces Group keeps a full company of soldiers in Kuwait at any given time.

JOHN D. GRESHAM

flat desert terrain began to rise. In more peaceful times this road had connected Kuwait City with Al Basrah in Iraq, and though it showed no signs of damage today, it had seen much fighting during the war. Soon we turned east onto a side road and went a few miles/kilometers until a series of walled compounds appeared on our left. These were the small-arms training ranges for the Kuwaiti Ministry of the Interior Police Force troops.

Here we would watch a team from the 3/5th SFG, ODA 571, train Interior Ministry troops in the use of M16 combat rifles, which have slowly been coming into service in Kuwait. Today they would be working on middle-distance shooting from various positions.

These particular trainees, I learned later, were essentially military police with training in special weapons and tactics (SWAT) procedures, and were learning the finer points of crowd and riot control. The ODA 571 guys considered them to be fairly well motivated, though hardly the crack soldiers you might find back home at Fort Campbell.

As we approached the range, several soldiers were attaching paper targets to wooden posts with staple guns, then pacing off various range marks. Others were breaking open cases of 5.56mm ball ammunition.

About this time a convoy of trucks arrived, carrying a platoon-sized detachment of Interior Ministry soldiers. As the men got out of the trucks, the ODA 571 team leader chatted with his Kuwaiti counterpart about how things should go this morning. This seemingly minor detail is actually important, for the Americans must not be seen as commanding the Arab soldiers. One of the first rules SF soldiers on JCET missions learn is to work *through* their host nation counterparts, not around or over them. By

5th Special Forces Group soldiers supervise marksmanship training with troops of the Kuwaiti Interior Ministry. These troops rarely receive such fine training, making it a treasured experience for the young Kuwaiti soldiers.

JOHN D. GRESHAM

doing this they avoid falling into the "ugly American" syndrome. (By *advising* the officer rather than telling him what to do, the status of the officer is enhanced in his own eyes and in the eyes of the young soldiers. Despite the temptation that "I can do it better myself," SF soldiers must be mentors, not masters.)

Some moments later, with the ODA 571 soldiers observing, the Kuwait officers led their soldiers a dozen at a time to the firing line, while the rest, for safety, were kept to the rear on a walled berm. After a short safety talk in Arabic, the soldiers on the line were shown firing positions and stances. If one developed a problem, an SF soldier of similar rank would work with him until he had the position down. When they all had their positions and stances down successfully, the Kuwaitis were taken through a series of dry-fire drills before live ammunition was distributed. Then ODA 571 personnel issued one full thirty-round magazine to each man and the firing began.

Each man was allowed to fully exercise his weapon from every position and a variety of ranges, while SF soldiers moved up and down the line to help those Kuwaitis who needed it. Clearly the young Arabs were enjoying the training. Most soldiers in this part of the world are lucky to get to a firing range more than two or three times a year. These lads were blowing off a year's worth of ammunition in a single morning, and they'd be doing it again later in the training.

When the first group had finished, the second group made ready, while the weapons were safed, ammunition was downloaded, and the targets were replaced. This took less than ten minutes, and soon another batch of troops were taking their turns on the firing line. These soon made room for the third and last group.

As they changed places, I glanced over at the ridge to our north. Though only 300 ft./100 m. tall, it stood out like a mountain over the flat local desert. A moment later it hit me that I was looking at something important, and I took out my escape map and GPS receiver to make sure. I was right. I was looking at Al-Mutlah Ridge and what had once been called the "Highway of Death."

An ODA 571 soldier counsels a trooper from the Kuwaiti Interior Ministry. Special Forces soldiers are careful to never "talk down" to foreign troops, and always respect local laws and customs.

JOHN D. GRESHAM

In 1991, coalition air forces had caught thousands of Iraqis there retreating from Kuwait City. Using the pass over the ridge as a choke point, the allied aircraft had bombed the first and last vehicles in the line, trapping the rest, which were then bombed at leisure. The images of the "Highway of Death," broadcast on TV and printed in papers, contributed to the early ending of the Gulf War. . . . In fact, most of the vehicles destroyed were not Iraqi military vehicles but stolen cars and trucks, carrying whatever loot from Kuwait City the retreating Iraqis could get away with. And when the bombing started, most of the Iraqis had sense enough to run off in the desert; very few actually lost their lives. It wasn't so much a "Highway of Death" as a "Highway of Abandoned Loot." Still, the burned out hulks of their vehicles had impressed Western civilians and Western leaders, and the war was ended.

Though today the highway is like any other freeway, it was for me a bizarre and compelling sight. A small but significant piece of history had happened here.

As I turned my attention back to matters at hand, ODA 571 was calling a halt to the morning's drills. There would be others following the noon meal. But I would miss them, as it was time to move along to my next event back toward Kuwait City.

Sunday, November 22nd—Emiri Guard Brigade Compound, Kuwait

It took forty-five minutes to drive to ODA 594 at the barracks compound of the Kuwaiti Emiri Guards, with Kuwaiti drivers zooming by in huge Chevrolet Impalas (according to Chief Wade, the most popular automobiles in the Middle East).

The Emiri Guards are just what they sound like: the personal security force for the Al-Sabah family, and they take their job seriously. During the Iraqi invasion in

Special Forces soldiers from ODA 594 teach pistol skills to troops of the Kuwaiti Emiri Guard. Assigned to defend the Kuwaiti Royal Family, these are elite troops with excellent equipment and skills.

JOHN D. GRESHAM

1990, many Kuwaiti military units just dropped their weapons and ran south. Only the desperate sacrifice of the Emiri Guards bought time for the Emir and the rest of the royal family to escape to Saudi Arabia. Casualties were heavy, and only recently have the ranks of the guards been fully filled.

The Emiri Guard barracks is a huge complex, perhaps five miles square, and protected by an impressive security fence and a full battery of Kuwaiti Patriot surface-to-air missiles (this says a *lot* about the importance of this brigade-sized security unit).

Because Arab armies have all been built after the British colonial period on a tradition of fully automatic personal weapons like the AK-47 and the M-16, they have no real tradition of precision marksmanship. This lack of capability is now turning into a serious problem in a part of the world where hostage rescue and antiterrorist situations can occur at any time. The Kuwaitis aim to remedy this by training Emiri Guards in precision marksmanship skills; and it was the job of ODA 594 to establish a certified sniper program.

After clearing the security checkpoints, we drove to the rifle ranges on the north side of the base. As we approached, we could hear the throaty sounds of heavy rifles and pistols being fired. We parked, grabbed packs and water, and walked to a covered range where a small flock of Emiri Guards were working with a half-dozen 5th SFG soldiers.

While the shooters set up the weapons for the next round of firing, an SF warrant officer named Sam filled in some background. Normally, he explained, the Emiri Guards are armed with the M16 combat rifle and the SIG 220-series 9mm pistol, hardly suitable for precision marksmanship. Meanwhile, even an elite unit in wealthy

Soldiers of the Kuwaiti Emiri Guards practicing with a Russian-made SVD sniper rifle. ODA 594 Special Forces soldiers were helping them develop a sniper capability for the Kuwaiti Army.

JOHN D. GRESHAM

Kuwait has limited funds for new weapons; they could not at the moment afford a first-class sniper system such as the American M24 or one of the Barrett-series rifles. Fortunately, there had been a few benefits (*not many*) resulting from their recent war with their unfriendly neighbor to the north. When the Iraqi forces abandoned Kuwait in 1991, they left behind a large stock of Soviet-made SVD Dragonov 7.62mm sniper rifles. Though not exactly state-of-the-art, the Kuwaiti soldiers had reconditioned the Soviet arms and were using them to train their first teams of combat snipers.[103]

Now the soldiers of ODA 594 were teaching the basics of zeroing and sighting to the young Kuwaiti gunners. Each of the six firing positions had two of the Emiri Guards assigned to it, with a single SF soldier coaching them along.

The Dragonov has an evil crack, and you could see puffs of dust kicked up from the big 7.62mm rounds hitting the berms and backstops downrange.

After a time, I could see that some of the Kuwaiti soldiers were showing a real aptitude for the sniper trade. An observation Chief Sam confirmed. A few were so good, he explained, that the SF guys were going to teach spotting to their most talented students, and perhaps bring out their U.S.-made M24 rifles to give them a taste of what might be in their future.

As I watched, a very talented young Kuwaiti marksman and an American began a friendly competition shoot at the targets downrange . . . which, in a way, is the whole point of the JCET program.

At this point, the chief offered me the chance to shoot a Dragonov for myself. I didn't have to be asked twice!

Soon I was prone on the warm concrete in the shooting position, steadying the

---

103 At one time, especially during World War II, sniping was a Russian specialty. In later years, the Dragonov SVD was among the finest sniper rifles in the world, and was especially feared in Vietnam, where its accuracy and hitting power in the jungle was impressive. Now, with its wooden stock and bed (as opposed to the fiberglass and composite units common in western designs) and poorly made sights and triggers, the SVD is somewhat dated. With the SVD, hitting targets at long ranges (greater than 547 yds/500 m) is almost impossible. Inside of 438 yds/400 m, however, it is still a useful and deadly weapon.

ODA 594 troopers counsel their Kuwaiti counterparts during sniper training at the Emiri Guards compound west of Kuwait City. The Kuwaiti soldiers learned quickly, and were quite competent in the use of the Russia-made SVD sniper rifle.

JOHN D. GRESHAM

SVD on a sandbag, and following the chief's suggestion to suck the stock hard into my shoulder. With my eye at a safe standoff from the sight, I pulled the trigger slowly until it broke. There was an ugly crack, and the stock punched hard against my shoulder. Downrange, there was a puff of dust behind the target. A moment later, Chief Sam on the spotter's scope scored me.

"Up at two o'clock" was his assessment.

I could just make out the hole in the paper target downrange through the sight, and adjusted my next round appropriately. The next few rounds were solidly in the center of the target. "Not bad!" I congratulated myself.

Recalling Fort Polk, I was reminded of the worth of good spotters. Now I was seeing that for myself.

(Back at the hotel, the shoulder bruise from the mule-kick of the Dragonov came on in all its livid glory. I was sore for days.)

It was time for the midday meal. The ODA 594 team gathered up their weapons and gear, and piled into a pair of rented Range Rovers for the ride back to their team house—a pleasant officers' barracks inside the Emiri Guards compound, with air-conditioners fighting hard against the midday heat.

After lunch with the SF soldiers, we headed back to Kuwait City . . . and into a haze that left a bite in our throats. "Kuwait cough," Chief Wade explained. "It's a combination of fine desert dust and the sulfur from oil production. Drinking water helps."

He was right; it did. But I was glad for the relatively cleaner air of the hotel, and a chance to rest and pack for home.

The remains of Iraqi armored vehicles along the Iraq/Kuwait border. Hundreds of such wrecks litter the desert, moot testimony to the fighting that took place here in 1991.

JOHN D. GRESHAM

Tomorrow would be my last day in the Persian Gulf. But before I left, there was a final major event scheduled.

Monday, November 23rd—Udari Bombing Range, Kuwait

After breakfast and checkout from the hotel, Major Neil and I met Chief Wade and the two security men from the embassy and headed west toward the Iraqi border. Our objective was the Udari bombing range, just under 6 miles/10 km. from Iraq (and about 60 miles/100 km from Kuwait City). Here the Iris Gold CSTs practiced their CAS skills. We were going to watch them work with Kuwaiti Air Force (KAF) F/A-18Cs.

On the way, we passed the huge Ali Al Salem airbase, home to many of the Kuwaiti, American, and British air units enforcing Operation Southern Watch, the "no-fly" operation that patrols southern Iraq. Four Tornado fighters were rising into the morning sky as we drove by.

On the edge of the base, you could see with field glasses what appeared to be a row of broken mounds. These were hardened aircraft shelters that had been destroyed by BLU-109-armed 2,000-lb. laser-guided bombs during Desert Storm—a still impressive statement about the power of U.S. weapons.

Also grimly intriguing were occasional stretches of road asphalt hit by cluster munitions during the war. They had left hundreds of large potholes, now patched. What they had done to living flesh could only be imagined.

After another half-hour we reached the turnoff for the Udari range. This brought us onto a rutted dirt road heading northwest. Putting the Suburban into four-wheel-drive, Chief Wade then kept the wheels carefully in the ruts. In a few minutes, we saw why. All around us were abandoned Iraqi fortifications and bunkers, built in 1990 and 1991; and scattered across the desert was an incredible array of weaponry—land mines, unexploded cluster munitions, antitank and surface-to-air missiles, and stacks of artillery shells—a devil's den of unexploded ordnance.

Though the oil fields and populated areas of Kuwait had been made relatively safe after the war, to walk in this area would be sure death.

"If we break down," Chief Wade warned (though no warning was necessary), "stay in the vehicle and wait for rescue. Don't walk *anywhere* without a guide."

Special Forces soldiers of ODA 595 controlling close air support aircraft at the Udari Range near the Iraq/Kuwait border. These troops operate in support of Operation Iris Gold, a joint U.S./Kuwait exchange program.
JOHN D. GRESHAM

By 1000 hours, we had arrived at the Udari Range, where we met a pair of CST teams from ODA 595, out to call in the bombing runs from GMVs (whose array of radio, navigation, and spotting gear allows them to call in almost any kind of ordnance from iron bombs to LGBs).

Over the next hour, flights of Kuwaiti F/A-18Cs called in and requested bombing coordinates. Once these were given by the CST teams, the aircraft made runs over the target arrays—a line of derelict Iraqi tanks several miles/kilometers away. The Kuwaitis were using the little BDU-33 7-lb. practice bombs, and they did a good job of placing their weapons (which the F/A-18 makes almost automatic).

After about an hour, the F/A-18s were headed back to Ali Al Salem, and I had a chance for a serious talk with the CST team.

It was short and to the point: If there were another Iraqi invasion, as long as the Kuwaiti brigades made any kind of stand, they would be able to call in enough firepower from above to keep the Emirate safe. These were confident young men, but they had no illusions about what would happen if the Kuwaiti forces did not make a stand.

After a careful walk back to the Suburban, we climbed aboard for the ride back to Camp Doha, where Neil and I would wait until our flight later that evening.

As Chief Wade threaded the vehicle along the rutted path to the highway, I could not help but wonder about the waste of war. "How long before this land is safe for humans again?" I asked myself. A Desert Storm officer I know once told me that archaeologists a thousand years from now will have a thrilling time digging up the ruins of the 1991 Kuwaiti battlefields with all that unexploded ordnance around.

In Kuwait City, at Major Neil's insistence, we made one last stop. In the southern

A pair of Kuwaiti Air Force F/A-18 Hornet fighter-bombers scream low past the Udari Bombing Range. These aircraft would be guided to their targets in wartime by U.S. Special Forces soldiers in Ground Mobility Vehicles.

JOHN D. GRESHAM

part of town is a two-story house that had been a safe house for Kuwaiti resistance fighters during the Iraqi occupation. Just prior to their retreat, the Iraqi secret police rounded up young men to use as hostages after the war (many of these are still held in Iraq—if they are alive at all). But when they pulled up to this house, the Iraqis ran into more than they counted on. More than a dozen heavily armed resistance fighters were waiting there to fight back. The Kuwaitis were so vicious the Iraqis had to call in a T-55 tank and armored personnel carriers to suppress them. Though most of the Kuwaiti fighters died in the carnage that followed, a few slipped away to tell the tale.

Today the building stands as the Resistance Martyr's Museum, and it is open to visitors.

When I entered, I found it exactly as it had been on that violent day in 1991. None of the bullet or shell holes had been repaired, and dried blood remained on the walls and floors—a stunning reminder that on this spot brave men had fought and died to oppose tyranny.

Monday, November 23rd—Camp Doha, Kuwait

After dinner at Camp Doha that evening, I was escorted over to the morale and welfare center, which was known to the troops as "Uncle Frosty's"—a large warehouse converted to look like a Stateside roadhouse. Here the troops can get free burgers, fries, hot dogs, and drinks, and listen to music or watch TV and movies on a large-screen projector. Tonight was "slasher" night: a trio of Jamie Lee Curtis horror flicks was playing. All around the troops were sucking down sodas and nonalcoholic beer, and blowing off steam.

All too soon, it was time to leave the howling crowd, and take one last ride in Chief Wade's Suburban—the first leg of the day-long journey home.

Thanks, Neil. It was a terrific experience.

The Kuwaiti Martyr's Museum in Kuwait City. Here over a dozen Kuwaiti resistance fighters made a last stand against Iraqi forces just prior to the liberation of Kuwait by allied forces.

JOHN D. GRESHAM

South of the Border: Venezuela

My journey to the Persian Gulf had given me a taste of the SF world downrange, but my appetite was hardly satisfied. I wanted to experience other kinds of SF missions in a greater variety of settings. Several opportunities presented themselves—among these, visits to the 7th SFG in Bolivia or the 1st SFGs UXO school in Cambodia—but I couldn't fit these into my schedule (and I've got to confess that traveling halfway around the world to watch people disarm ancient munitions did not strike me as fun).

Early in 1999, however, the right downrange opportunity fell in my lap: Venezuela. Strategically placed, mineral-rich, and one of America's strongest allies in Latin America now going through massive changes, here I'd see a side of SF downrange missions I hadn't yet experienced—focusing less on "here and now" contingencies and more on the building up of a nation's forces and capabilities. This was too good to miss, so I had my friend Major McCollum set a trip up for February 1999.

February 8th dawned cold and snowy around Washington, D.C., a misery compounded for travelers by the American Airlines pilots' union, who had initiated a nasty work stoppage . . . targeted, as luck would have it, against the routes handling traffic to Latin America and the southeast. The entire eastern half of the country was in a flying gridlock.

Despite the chaos, some talented reservations personnel managed to get me to the Miami International Airport, where I met Tom McCollum in a sea of disgruntled travelers.

Six hours and a switch of airlines later, I managed to shoehorn myself onto a flight to Venezuela, but had to leave luckless Tom McCollum in the mess at Miami (he caught up later in Venezuela); sometime past midnight local time, the aircraft settled down to Caracas International Airport, where I was met by a fine young 7th SFG sergeant named Carlos, who took me under his wing until the major could catch up.

The Caracas Airport is on the coast, some miles north of the city, and it took some time to get to our hotel. During the drive, Carlos filled me in on the local situation:

The week before, amid much pomp and controversy, a new president was in-augurated, Hugo Chavez. A onetime army officer—a paratrooper, in fact—Chavez led a failed military coup in 1992, and was jailed for two years. He now presents himself as a radical populist with big ideas about political reform. Essentially, his policy has been to toss the bastards out—the corrupt and self-serving political elite who have long run the country (as I write he is trying to restructure the courts and the National Assembly).

So far, the Venezuelan people seem to like him (he currently has a 70% approval rating).

All well and good.

However, Chavez has a strong authoritarian streak. There is little evidence that he listens to or fosters independent democratic voices, or has a serious plan for dealing with Venezuela's economic problems (even though oil prices have recently doubled, business mistrust of Chavez may lead to a 6% economic contraction this year); and in fact there's a better than even risk that he'll make things worse rather than better. A dictatorship under Chavez is not out of the question (though dictatorships are out of fashion in Latin America). On the other hand, the Venezuelan people treasure their democracy and their constitution. They're not likely to give these up easily.

The next couple of years in Venezuela are going to be *very* interesting (perhaps as in the Chinese curse about living in interesting times).

Of course, Venezuela's neighbor Colombia has been fated to suffer the effects of the Chinese curse. And worse, the drug-based insurgency there is threatening to throw the entire region into a major war. At the moment, the country is a nest of snakes. And even identifying the major power players is next to impossible. It's hardly as simple as left versus right, of poor against wealthy, or this faction against that faction; but many against many. It is possible, however, to identify the chief evil, and that's drugs and drug money. So the largest rebel group (they control an area roughly the size of Switzerland), the Revolutionary Armed Forces of Colombia (FARC), is nominally a force of the left, but, in fact, is not so much political as the paid army of the drug cartels. (They also get monetary support that comes from ransom payments derived from kidnapping wealthy or otherwise important persons.) Yet FARC is far from the only dark force in Colombia. And it's not the only gang to resort to kid-napping and other criminal tactics . . . the right-wing National Liberation Army is one example. And powerful ultra-right elements in the military cause plenty of trouble as well.

Few future scenarios for Colombia look happy. As in: a FARC overthrow of the elected government of President Andres Pastrana (far from unlikely) would make them the first narco-government. But a rightist takeover would hardly be an improvement.

In the event of a FARC takeover, Colombia's neighbors, including Venezuela, would likely go to war to change that. (There have already been cross-border clashes, and Venezuela has been slowly but deliberately expanding its army and national police forces.) Interesting times.

Meanwhile, U.S. policy in the region is in a bind: On the one hand, the current Clinton Administration wants to support the democratically elected regimes and to keep the lid as much as possible on the Colombian pressure cooker (good luck!). On the other hand, the Latin Americans are proud and independent people, and they are reluctant to accept full *Yanqui* partnership in their national security affairs. (They have not forgotten U.S. imperialism, even though that was decades in the past.) For both of these reasons, current American policy in this part of Latin America is based on improving the security forces of host nations, but not on putting U.S. forces on the ground. This support takes the specific form of Special Forces teams conducting JCET-type FID missions.

When I arrived in Venezuela, 7th SFG had four missions on the ground in Venezuela, involving four active teams (three ODAs and an ODB). My objective was to observe each of these teams in action.

We pulled into my hotel sometime after midnight, local time. A meeting was scheduled at the American embassy for early in the morning. Venezuela's a terrific place for a vacation, but that was not to be my fate.

Tuesday, February 9th—U.S. Embassy, Caracas, Venezuela

Caracas is a lovely city, set in a valley and surrounding hills. The American embassy is located on one of the tallest hills, and is more strongly fortified than a medieval castle.

Once Carlos and I had cleared security, we headed upstairs into the vaulted security area where the various military, intelligence, and legal missions are based.[104] Here officials from the military and Coast Guard, as well as the C.I.A., F.B.I., D.E.A., and other law enforcement and intelligence agencies operate under heavy security . . . and a cloak of discretion. While it is no secret that they are here (or in other countries), they keep a low profile.

When I arrived, I was met by a handsome and soft-spoken SF chief warrant officer (we'll call him Milwaukee), who was coordinating the four teams with the embassy. Chief Milwaukee ran me through the schedule for my travels throughout Venezuela.

---

104 All the law enforcement, intelligence, and military functions are conducted inside rooms that are essentially metal vaults. These can be locked and secured in the event of an attack or seizure, and are the last shelter in such an event.

Today's visit would be to a Guardia Nacional base east of Caracas. (The National Guard is the National Police and Security service.) I would then fly to the south and west of the country to see the other three SF teams and their missions. I was also told that Major McCollum would probably arrive sometime later that evening, assuming that the airline strike was no worse. With a wry smile at Tom's plight, I followed Sergeant Carlos back to his car for the ride out to Macarao, east of Caracas.

Tuesday, February 9th—Headquarters, Grupo de Acciones Comandos de la Guardia Nacional de Venezuela

As we drove east into the mountains and the El Ávila National Park (Venezuela is one of the first Latin American mainland countries with a serious environmental movement, and the government is backing it), Sergeant Carlos described the unit I would be visiting today. The Grupo de Acciones Comandos de la Guardia Nacional de Venezuela (known as GAC FAC for short) is roughly equivalent to our specialized antiterrorist units (such as the F.B.I.'s Hostage Rescue Team or the Army's Delta Force) in its mission, and is one of the most talented military units in South America— the elite of the elites (what U.S. planners call a "Tier 1" unit). Though technically flagged as a battalion, GAC FAC is actually sized more like an oversized U.S. company, with about 120 members, and is organized into three forty-man companies (each with two platoons). GAC FAC is a powerful little unit with all kinds of skills (it is far from limited to an antiterror role). Unlike other so-called Latin American elite military units that are there merely for show (they look grand and march straight, but could not lead a charge to the bathroom), GAC FAC is trained hard in skills ranging from riverine and underwater warfare, to hostage rescue, sniping, and demolitions; and the entire unit is jump and airmobile qualified, which means they can be inserted almost anywhere by any means imaginable. (Our own SOF commanders consider them to be easily the most capable Special Operations unit in the region.)

GAC FAC is part of the much larger Guardia Nacional, which is responsible for the nation's internal security (the Army, Navy, and Air Force have responsibility for external threats). In other words, the Guardia Nacional does all the jobs we would normally associate with our own Justice Department, Treasury Department, State Police, and some missions of the Army National Guard. And they have done a fine job in these powerful roles, with the result that they are quite popular with the local population. In fact, the Guardia Nacional is broadly perceived as the de facto protector of the nation's democracy and constitution. (It seems that in the crunch, they have always come down on the side of the democratically elected government. This consistency seems to have set the belief in the minds of the people that they can be trusted to do it again if necessary.) It was GAC FAC that put down the final stages of the 1992 coup led by Hugo Chavez. (Though the Guardia Nacional was keeping a wary eye on the new president, the past tension between Chavez and his security forces probably won't create present difficulties for either.)

All of this does not come cheap. GAC FAC is twice as expensive to maintain as a normal Guardia National battalion like the 69th I visited later. But its proven record of operations in the field against terrorists and drug smugglers is worth the

The entrance to the GAC FAC compound east of Caracas, Venezuela. GAC FAC is the finest antiterrorist unit in Latin America, roughly equivalent to the U.S. Delta Force.

JOHN D. GRESHAM

expense. In fact, because GAC FAC is a real asset in maintaining the stability of the whole region, it is in the best interests of the U.S. to support GAC FAC's high standards of training, and to provide them with new capabilities.

After an hour's drive though a beautiful mountain valley, we arrived at about 11:00 A.M. at the GAC FAC barracks. This compound is not large and flashy, with guards in dress uniforms. Rather, it reminded me of a boys' camp back home. But this was hardly a summer camp; it was a facility every bit as functional as the Delta Force compound back at Fort Bragg.

On the GAC FAC reservation, which spreads over several miles of the valley, the unit maintains firing and demolitions training ranges, obstacle courses, a small survival school, a shooting house for practicing breaching and assaults, and lakes for practicing rubber boat skills.

Though these facilities lack the technological sophistication of similar facilities back home, high technology is not the only way to train men for the commando trade. The observations of experienced NCOs can more than make up for an absence of closed circuit televisions and video recorders. . . . There is an old saying: "If it costs a dollar to train someone to 90% perfection, it costs ten dollars to reach 99%, and a hundred to reach 99.9%." GAC FAC was in the 99% range.

Once we had parked the car, Carlos escorted me to a small, rustic-looking barracks beside the road. This was the team house for ODA 763, a team from "E" Company, 2nd/7th SFG (and one of the teams that work for Lieutenant Colonel Joe Smith, who I met during JRTC 99-1). ODA 763 carried a complement of nine men, and was commanded by a captain named Marshall. During the coming weeks they

7th Special Forces Group soldiers of ODA 763 supervise members of GAC FAC in a sophisticated shoothouse exercise. Assigned to the Guardia Nacional, GAC FAC is an impresesive antiterrorist unit.

JOHN D. GRESHAM

would deliver a variety of training, advisory, and support services to GAC FAC. These would include the following:

- **Sniper Training**—ODA 763 would establish and supervise a program of refresher training for GAC FAC's sniper teams. This would include gunsmithing to improve system accuracy, training of spotters, and requalification of the entire GAC FAC sniper pool.

- **Mobile Interdiction**—To improve GAC FAC's counterdrug capabilities, ODA 763 would teach skills for interdicting the narcotics traffic routes into and through Venezuela. These skills included intelligence gathering, analysis and assessment, mission planning, and roadblock/search techniques.

- **Shoothouse Refurbishment/Training**—A shoothouse is a training facility that simulates a real building. Troops in training attack it with real ammunition. Though it was a well-designed facility the GAC FAC shoothouse, after years of use, had almost been shot to pieces. ODA 763 would initiate a program whereby the Guardia Nacional troops would refurbish the facility, and improve and expand its capabilities.

- **Survival Training**—ODA 763 would establish for GAC FAC a miniature version of the Survival, Evasion, Rescue, and Escape (SERE) school.

- **Tactical/Field Training**—ODA 763 would engage GAC FAC in a general course of field and tactical training maneuvers. These would include training in raids, ambushes, reconnaissance, land navigation, and other SOF-related skills.

Colonel Marcos Rojas, the commander of GAC FAC.

- **Delivery of Materials**—In support of all the other training objectives, ODA 763 would deliver to GAC FAC a large number of training manuals, maps, and other materials (translated into Spanish) prepared to support their expected threats, missions, and goals.

This was a lot to do in just eight weeks (the team had arrived in mid-January).

The team house was a large structure, with plenty of room for bunks and storage for weapons and gear. In one corner was the communications sergeant, with his array of satellite, HF, and other radios. He smiled as we walked by and gave us a "thumb's-up."

After a quick look-around, it was time to make a call on the commander of GAC FAC.

The headquarters building was a short walk up a hill. Once there, I was shown a chair on a small patio, and provided with a cold drink. After a few minutes I was introduced to the man many consider the finest officer in the Guardia Nacional: Colonel Marcos Rojas. As soon as I met him, I knew why. This was one super-high-caliber military professional. (I've been told he will shortly be made a general.) Powerfully built, with bright eyes and a serious look, even with his broken English, you could tell immediately how proud he was of his unit, and grateful to the U.S. for sending ODA 763 to make it better. With Captain Marshall as a translator, we talked about the roles and missions of the Guardia Nacional and GAC FAC and how they fit into the Venezuela of Hugo Chavez. He made it clear that they were as prepared to put down coups as they had been in the past.

Promptly at noon, he stood up and gestured for us to follow him down the hill

A GAC FAC soldier being given Survival, Evasion, Rescue, and Escape training.

JOHN D. GRESHAM

toward the road. What came then was a tour of the barracks facilities. These were predictably clean and orderly, and all the young men I saw around and about were lean and hard, bright and handsome lads.

Every man was a volunteer, the colonel explained, and he took it as a matter of personal pride that everyone had a good place to live, proper equipment and training, and the security to know that the Venezuelan people were behind them. As we passed, he addressed each soldier by name, and it was clear his men were glad to see him. You could feel their pride in knowing that he was *theirs*. This man was no old-fashioned Latin *"Jefe"* (chief, strongman), but the best kind of modern military leader.

A few minutes later, he led us into a dining area for the troops, directed us to the front table, and then took a seat himself. "This is the *only* mess hall in camp," Captain Marshall explained. "There are no separate facilities for officers and enlisted personnel. Everyone eats the same food together." Only the barracks were segregated by rank, and frankly I liked the enlisted quarters better than those of the junior officers.

This man shared *everything* with his men. Even in the U.S. military, vast cultural walls exist between officers and enlisted personnel (you see very little of that in the Special Forces, however). I was impressed!

That afternoon the ODA split in two. The two gunners and an assistant took a truck up to a new earthen dam down in the valley where they set up at a presurveyed sniper range, and continued the sniper course they had started the previous week. Four other team members took another company down the road to teach the basics of roadblocks and vehicle searches.

ODA 763 soldiers conducting sniper training with their GAC FAC counterparts. GAC FAC has a well-developed sniper capability, in support of their antiterrorist mission.

JOHN D. GRESHAM

I hopped in Colonel Rojas's truck and we drove up to the dam. Four Venezuelan snipers were practicing with full Gilly Suits on, the better to know the distractions and problems that can go into a "one shot, one kill" fire mission. As I watched, the two SF gunners went from man to man, checking sights, adjusting grips, and coaching the small details that make good snipers. Standing just behind the Americans, Colonel Rojas watched every move.

After a time, he lay down at one of the sniper stations, and proceeded to fire off ten rounds. The targets were at about 500 yards, medium range by current sniping standards, and he started scoring direct hits on his third shot, with no coaching from the spotters.

Then it was back to the truck for a drive to the roadblock and vehicle search training.

The GAC FAC company had marched down from the barracks area accompanied by a camp dog, a little one-eyed mutt who also joins the troops when they make parachute jumps and helicopter assaults. Even the GAC FAC dogs are jump qualified.

Once the company had arrived, the four SF soldiers sat them down under a tree, and laid out the procedures for setting up and running a roadblock, and for properly searching a vehicle—including basic rules about human rights of the suspects, a serious issue for SF troops on JCETs. After the "dirty" history of Latin American military forces toward civilians, such training is included wherever it will fit during a JCET mission.

Twenty minutes later, it was time to set up a roadblock. Soldiers from another GAC FAC company had volunteered to serve as the OpFor for this exercise; they would drive the truck that would be stopped and searched.

The GAC FAC leader set up some of his men (wearing body armor) on the road as control personnel. The rest were out of sight among the trees beside the road.

The roadblock itself was road cones and tire obstacle strips (metal plates with spikes). Vehicle traffic was stopped and checked. The passenger and engine compartments were inspected, the frame checked with a mirror and flashlight rig on a handle, and credentials examined. If the team leader or one of his men suspected that a further search was required, then the driver and occupants were moved into the trees, where they were searched and questioned by the security group posted there. More invasive searches were then conducted on the vehicle, until several packages of suspected (and simulated) drug contraband were located.

At this point, the exercise was stopped and critiqued by the SF soldiers. Then the GAC FAC personnel switched around, so everyone would get a turn on the road team.

The evolution was repeated half a dozen times. By the time it was over, the GAC FAC troops not only had the procedure down cold, but were coming up with improvements based on their own real-world experiences.

Colonel Rojas was understandably pleased.

Back in Caracas, Sergeant Carlos and I talked over plans and objectives for the rest of the trip. Tomorrow we would be headed south, to the town of San Fernando de Apure, where we would meet up with two more 2/7th SFG teams. Since Major McCollum was scheduled to arrive—finally—on the midnight plane, Sergeant Carlos would be able to return to his duties at the embassy.

Wednesday, February 10th—Guardia Nacional Barracks, San Fernando de Apure

An early wake-up call confirmed that Major Tom McCollum had indeed managed to get into Venezuela early that morning. I met him for coffee a little later, and then Carlos drove us to the airport.

Our destination, San Fernando de Apure (meaning the town of Saint Ferdinand on the Apure River), is the largest city (with a population of about 90,000) in the *Los Llanos* (the plains) region of Venezuela several hundred miles south of Caracas. *Los Llanos* is a mostly level plateau, with huge tracts of land dedicated to ranching and farming, and San Fernando de Apure, on the south bank of the river, is the hub of commercial activity in that part of the world. It is also a major headquarters for the Guardia Nacional.

That doesn't mean the place is easy to get to. You can either drive there or fly down on what we would call a commuter airline up here. We flew . . . in what must have been a fifty-year-old, twenty-seat Twin Beech (a twin-engine Beechcraft with two vertical stabilizers like B-25s, and in spectacular shape, with not an oil or bug spot on it). It had probably once been a VIP transport for the Venezuelan Air Force, and had then been sold to the airline after decades of loving care. I was amazed at how quickly the old beauty leapt off the runway, and climbed out, heading south on the minute flight to San Fernando de Apure.

The airfield at San Fernando de Apure was a single-runway affair, big enough

GAC FAC soldiers being trained in roadblock techniques by members of ODA 763. This training was designed to support counterdrug smuggling operations.

JOHN D. GRESHAM

for medium transports like C-130s, but not much else. In the small terminal building, we were met by Major Mark, the tall, sunny commander of ODB 740, which made him commander of Company Alpha, 2/7th SFG.

As commander of Company Alpha, he was charged not only with running his own headquarters team, but also with commanding the three ODAs scattered around Venezuela running their own missions—ODA 763 up with GAC FAC in Macarao, ODA 743 here in San Fernando de Apure, and ODA 746 in El Guayabo in the western part of the country. His ODB also provided communications and control support for 2/7th SFG missions in Guatemala, Ecuador, and Costa Rica. While not in actual command of these missions, he was responsible for ensuring that their regular reports got back to Fort Bragg and their support needs were met. (One ODB controlling between two and six ODAs operating around a particular AOR is a fairly standard deployment scheme.)

Our first stop was the ODB 740 team house, which was on the second floor of a walled barracks building assigned to the 69th Commando Rurales (Rural Commando Battalion). The 69th is a recently formed "regular" Guardia Nacional unit, part of the larger 6th Regional Command (a four-battalion brigade) assigned to the 1st Operation Theater (in southern Venezuela). Its mission, like the other "regular" units, was to defend against rebellions, provide law enforcement, and back up the Army as a reserve. Right now the troops of the 69th were living in an old prison, which had been abandoned by the Ministry of Justice.

This was hardly an elite unit like GAC FAC, and it showed.

The job of ODB 740 and ODA 743 was to teach basic tactical, fieldcraft, and firearms skills to the new recruits.

The team house for ODB 740 during their Venezuelan rotation in early 1999. These comfortable quarters were located in a vacant Guardia Nacional barracks in San Fernando de Apure.

JOHN D. GRESHAM

The ODB 740 team house was in an air-conditioned barracks. This was useful, since the climate in the *Los Llanos* region is hot and humid during our winter. At one end was a compact command center, with the communications gear being run by a senior communications sergeant (18E).

Each man had his own bunk and locker, and there were the usual team house amenities—a television with VCR, tables with laptop computers, a boom box or two, and lots of CDs and movies. Among the videotapes was the ubiquitous (among SF teams) copy of John Wayne's *The Green Berets* (whenever their host nation counterparts visit, the locals all want to see it). There was also a hotplate for making coffee and light cooking (the team normally ate with the 69th officers or in town at a local restaurant).

After a quick look around, Major Mark ran Tom McCollum and me into town for a late breakfast. Over eggs and ham links, we talked over our plans for the next couple of days. We then checked into what passed locally for a hotel (it had air-conditioning and running water), and drove back out to the team house for a briefing on his mission orders and objectives.

His entire operation, I was interested to learn, was funded out of the JCS operating budget, and a counternarcotics (CN) line number was used to designate each mission. The chart below lays each out:

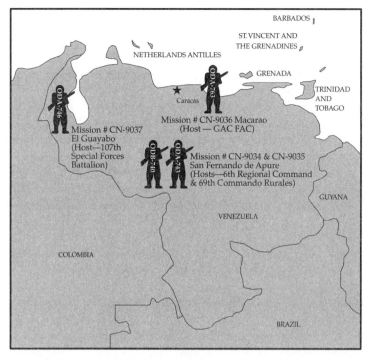

A map showing the disposition of the 7th Special Forces Group (Airborne) teams in early 1999 during their missions in Venezuela.

JCS Mission Number	Unit	Host Unit	Location	Mission
CN-9034	ODB 740	6th Regional Command (Brigade HQ)	San Fernando de Apure	Battle Staff Course Instruction
CN-9035	ODA 743	69th Commando Rurales	San Fernando de Apure	Light Infantry Training
CN-9036	ODA 763	GAC FAC	Macarao	Light Infantry/ Antiterrorist Training
CN-9037	ODA 746	107th Special Forces Battalion	El Guayabo	Light Infantry Training

Each SF mission was targeted at a particular Venezuelan unit, with specific plans tailored for each. This was important, since each Venezuelan unit had a different readiness status and mission within the country's national security structure. For example, GAC FAC was at the top of the Guardia Nacional food chain; it was their best unit and reported directly to the force's top leadership. Therefore, CN-9036 could carry out very advanced and difficult training with them. The 69th Commando Rurales was at the other end of the spectrum—brand-new and not yet terribly important.

Therefore, CN-9035 would deliver the most basic kinds of instruction . . . virtually "baby steps" for the new guardsmen.

Each mission called for its own training plan, and required separate measures for evaluating success or failure in its execution.

On top of all this, there are also numerous rules and regulations, such as human rights and, of course, financial guidelines.

Because of the Venezuelan units' limited budgets, most consumables (MREs, ammunition, targets, building supplies, etc.) had to be shipped in from the U.S. This meant that a lot of U.S. money had to be spent getting things down to Venezuela and distributed to the far-flung training sites. Because these U.S.-bought supplies were procured with JCS funds (controlled by Title 10 of the Federal Code), anything not actually consumed during the missions had to be returned Stateside for a full accounting. In the minds of Army auditors back home, this means not only bringing back unused ammunition, but every scrap of unused brass, and even the wooden packing dunnage!

This produces a catch-22: The value of materials returned to the U.S. does not match the cost of shipping it home. In order to eliminate any chance of waste and fraud, they make more waste. Go figure.

On the other hand, does all this activity cost U.S. taxpayers a lot? In fact, no. It actually costs very little:

Consider first of all that the SF soldiers, their weapons, food, and other basic operating necessities have to be paid for anyway, out of the normal Army operations and maintenance budget. Add to this ammunition, building supplies, food, and other expendables, and the costs for two months of cellular phones and rental vehicles. Also included must be the cost of shipping to Venezuela and back.

Put all this together, and you're hit with an amazingly low cost of $250,000 for all four missions (actually a little less). It would be hard to run a single aircraft carrier for an *hour* on that amount.

After Major Mark's briefing, we moved over to the small communications center at one end of the team room. Because seven missions were routing their communications through this small portal, the Sergeant (Drew) was a very busy man. His setup was a classic SF mix of ruggedized Army-issue gear (PRC-5/TRQ-43 radios, KY-99A/KL-43 encryption systems, and MST-20/BDC-400 modems), and civilian commercial systems (laptops running Windows 98, HP-97 palmtop computers, etc.). I also recognized one of the new PRC-137 combined radio/crypto units, that could plug directly into almost any kind of communications device, from a laptop computer to a Morse key.

Many people have an interest in overseas operations such as those in Venezuela. That meant a lot of demands were put on the communications setup. So for example, Special Forces Command, 7th SFG, SOCOM, and SOCSOUTH (Brigadier General James W. Parker) all had obvious operational concerns. But so also did various members of the diplomatic community: the U.S. Ambassador in Caracas, the Undersecretary of State for Latin American Affairs, and the Secretary of State all wanted updates as well. (Madeleine Albright gets a weekly briefing on the status of every

The communications sergeant (18E) of ODB 740 runs the team's communications center. From this tiny cubbyhole, ODB 740 ran three other teams around Venezuela, along with others in Latin America.

JOHN D. GRESHAM

JCET mission actually in the field. These missions are important at a *very* high level of government.)

There was also a regular flow of "housekeeping traffic" (personnel and supply reports, schedule changes, etc.) and personal e-mail.

As the hub for all this, Sergeant Drew was working an average of twelve to sixteen hours a day. Along the way he was also designing new interface cables, maintaining other teams' broken radio gear and computers, and trying to get in a few hours of sleep. And I've got to say he loved every minute of it. Whether it was conducting his twice weekly HF radio test "shots" up to the Chicken Road communications center at Fort Bragg, or finding a new way to connect old gear together to save the Army some money, this was a happy SF soldier.

Later that afternoon, Major Mark took me across the avenue from the barracks complex to a large, flat, and somewhat overgrown field, where a half-dozen SF troops from ODA 743 were engaged in training a company of Guardia Nacional soldiers.

Major Mark introduced us to the members of ODA 743. The team leader, a captain named Tom, took me aside to explain what they were up to. "We're teaching rudimentary ground tactics," he told me. "The groups are broken into ten-man fire teams, and then given walk-through instructions on formations, search procedures, and movement across terrain. Within a month, they'll be doing a live-fire assault onto an objective, complete with assault breaching demolitions." Such lessons are the basic building blocks of infantry training, and few armies do it better than ours. So the young guardsmen listened closely, and tried their best to emulate their *Yanqui* instructors.

Troopers of the Venezuelan Guardia Nacional 69th Battalion conducting field maneuvers near San Fernando de Apure.

Tom then left me to move from fire team to fire team, occasionally stopping to show guardsmen how to position themselves in ways that would allow them to both cover each other and maintain surveillance on their surroundings. This went on until he was satisfied; it took several hours.

Afterward, I rode with him in his rental SUV back to the ODA 743 team house on the other side of town.

This was located in a housing complex reserved for Guardia Nacional officers assigned to the 6th Brigade and reminded me of Army base housing on Stateside posts, and was quite pleasant. Cots had been set up in the bedrooms, gear stowed in the dining and kitchen areas, and a communications center (a half-sized version of Sergeant Drew's facilities) in the recroom.

In addition to the standard TV and VCR, ODA 743 had brought along an 18" DSS satellite dish, and had a college basketball game going.

"This is the best team house I've set up," Captain Tom told me. "It's comfortable . . . and it's separated from ODB 740." That is, he liked living away from the shadow of his company commander, and had the freedom to do things his way. SF soldiers like their independence.

After a diversion to an animal sanctuary across the Apure River to view some of the largest crocodiles and anacondas in the world (I saw there a crocodile more than twelve ft./four m. long, and was told a wild crocodile, estimated at sixteen ft./ five m., lived in the river nearby), we moved on to a nearby restaurant and dinner with Major Mark.

Guardia Nacional officer candidates conduct land navigation training under the supervision of Special Forces soldiers from ODB 740.

John D. Gresham

Wednesday, February 11th—Guardia Nacional Barracks, San Fernando de Apure

Early that morning, I was once again at the ODB 740 team house for a quick trip to one last training event.

The 6th Regional Command maintains at San Fernando de Apure a training academy for newly minted Guardia Nacional officers who will be assigned within the region's various units. At this academy, which is housed at the Guardia Nacional aviation complex at the local airport, young men learn the trade of soldiering and leadership from members of ODB 740. ODB 740 had set up there a small training cell where the students would get a U.S.-style dose of operational art.

When I arrived, the class of around a dozen in a small, well-appointed classroom was being taken through a land navigation and map reading course. Each student had been given a U.S.-supplied map of the area, a map protractor, and a series of UTM coordinates for specific locations. They were then split into two- and three-man teams, whose job was to plot out routes and timing for a hypothetical squad to march from one place to another.

The morning's lecture had covered march rates over various types of terrain; then the officer candidates broke up to work the problem out.

About twenty minutes later, the SF instructors asked them to show their solutions.

Roughly a third of the group had succeeded in plotting the course and developing the timeline. The rest took more attention.

After the class, a few of the young officers stayed on to work further with the SF instructors . . . igniting a nice smile from Major Mark. "These are the kinds of officers I look for overseas," he told me. "I take their names and keep track of them."

By midmorning, I was heading out to the airport.

Because the Beechcraft had suffered a generator failure on the ground in Caracas, it was three hours before a replacement aircraft, a classic DC-3, arrived to take us back to Caracas.

Colonel Jose Grant, commander of the
107th Special Forces Battalion, with a Special Forces soldier from ODA 746.

JOHN D. GRESHAM

From there, Major McCollum and I caught a quick flight over to Maracabo in the western part of the country. Though we had planned to continue on to El Guayabo, the earlier delay had nixed that, so we spent the night in a local hotel. Tomorrow, we would do a lot of traveling.

Thursday, February 12th—69th Parachute Battalion Barracks, El Guayabo

Starting early that morning, Tom McCollum and I caught a commuter flight (this time aboard a modern turboprop ATR-72) to the tiny airport at Santa Barbara, where we were met by a pair of SF soldiers from ODA 746 (which was assigned to work with the Army troops of the Venezuelan 107th Special Forces Battalion). After loading into their rented SUV, we headed southwest to the town of El Guayabo (which is only a handful of miles from the Colombia border). The country was pretty, with rolling hills and an abundance of lakes and rivers. In the distance you could see the Andes.

Here is located a barracks for the Venezuelan 107th SF Battalion, one of their finest units. The 107th is charged with securing the region against drug traffickers and raids by Colombia FARC rebels. Anywhere else, similar duties would probably be handled by police-type units, but here the scale is larger: It's a simmering low-level war. Recently FARC has been kidnapping for ransom wealthy Venezuelan ranchers. Since these thugs use every available means of travel—air, roads, and rivers—to conduct their operations, ODA 746 had been sent down to El Guayabo to provide the Venezuelans with new tools to fight back.

Unlike the somewhat makeshift Guardia Nacional barracks back in San Fernando de Apure, this was a true military barracks, with neatly trimmed grass and shrubbery, solid buildings, and lots of lean, healthy Venezuelan SF soldiers. As I looked around I couldn't help but feel that here the "first team" was running things, and that a good man had to be in charge.

Venezuelan soldiers of the 107th Special Forces Battalion learn trauma treatment skills from ODA 746 troopers.

JOHN D. GRESHAM

A good man *was* in charge, an officer in the style of the GAC FAC commander; his name was Colonel Jose Grant.

In the comfortable SF team room, I was introduced to Captain Jeff, the ODA 746 commander, who filled me in on what the team was up to.

Colonel Grant's soldiers, he explained, ran three- to five-day patrols along the border region—some on foot, some in helicopters, and some in trucks or 4WD vehicles. The one capability that they lacked was the ability to patrol and interdict traffic along the many rivers that crisscross the border region. To overcome this shortcoming, the Venezuelan Army had ordered for the 107th large inflatable rubber boats with powerful outboard motors (which would be arriving during the coming summer). To prepare them for this—as well as to improve their overall readiness—the U.S. had sent ODA 746. In addition to general light infantry refresher training, they were also training the Venezuelans to handle 12 ft./4 m. versions of the Zodiac-style units that would soon arrive.

Soon after that, I joined Colonel Grant and his men for lunch (like GAC FAC, the 107th has a single mess area for all personnel), after which I went off to a nearby ranch to observe a rubber boat class.

Ninety minutes later, I was clambering through a swampy meadow toward a large freshwater pond, where ODA 746 (under the supervision of Colonel Grant and Captain Jeff) would be exercising a company of Venezuelan SF soldiers.

The objective was to teach them how to rapidly assemble boats, get them into the water, and to safely handle them. Later would come other water exercises, including handling the boats under river conditions.

Since the men had already had some run through back at the barracks, they were

Soldiers of the 107th Special Forces Battalion conduct training in rubber boats. Their counterdrug mission includes riverine operations.

ready to go when they arrived. There were only a couple of safety matters to be dealt with, and then the exercise could start. Each man was issued a life preserver, and a sentry was set up with a loaded M4 carbine at the ready . . . not to ward off a FARC attack, but to scare off the 6 ft./2 m. long anaconda that lived in the pond. (It only made a single appearance that afternoon.) With safety issues under control, the fun began.

The 107th troops were broken into twelve-man teams, which then competed with one another through each phase in the training. Races were held for assembly and inflation of the boats, for moving them to the pond and getting them afloat, and for handling them in the water. This last involved rowing the boats out to the middle of the pond, overturning, righting, and reentering them, and then dashing back to shore. The competition was spirited, with a cliffhanger tie for first at the finish.

And that was it.

With the end of the boat races, my visit to ODA 746 came to a close. Now there was only the long flight home.

It had been a good, productive trip. And I'm grateful to my SF friends for the opportunity to share their labors. It's hard to imagine better ambassadors for our nation's deepest, strongest values.

Into the Twenty-first Century

It's always the guys that fight who count the most. Not technology. Not the hardware that emerges from technology. This is true of all branches of military service—and even of space warriors. But it is *most* true of Special Forces. The *people* in that community define the community, not the hardware they carry . . . or that carries them.

Sure, SF soldiers can't help but look lustfully at the "gee-whiz" technology their Army brothers and sisters will receive over the next decade. It's just that very little of the new gear will be of any value to the majority of SF missions: Over 90 percent of these will continue to be small training and assistance missions to developing countries, usually involving no more than a few A detachments, supported by a B detachment for command, control, and logistics assistance.

Still, new technologies—and high-tech gear—will play a role in SF missions, but it will play it primarily in the "big" ones. That is, in those large-scale operations where Special Forces are one constituent among many, such as, in the 1990s, the operations in the Persian Gulf, the Balkans, and Haiti.

Some of this gear will find its way into every SF rucksack.

Inevitably, there will be other changes—in planning, in communications, in systems. There must be. Let's look forward into the SF world of the twenty-first century and explore some of the likely ones.

The Twenty-first Century Special Forces

So, just what will SF soldiers look like in the years to come?

Just like they do today, I hope and pray. Right now, the mix of education, training, mental and emotional skills, and esprit approaches an optimum balance. Though there can always be improvements and increased efficiencies, it is likely that the standards and skills emphasized in the early phases of the SF Qualification Course at the JFK school can be retained in their current format for a long time to come.

The news is far from all good, however.

While the "Q" Course produces extraordinary men, and will continue to do so, the military force those men serve is in trouble. Like the rest of the U.S. military, Special Forces are having a tough time recruiting and retaining the personnel they need to carry out their assigned roles and missions. Worse, the demands on the SF community continue to grow, especially in areas like Foreign Internal Defense (FID) and Humanitarian Assistance (HA).

In some ways, the high qualities and standards of the SF community have created more problems for that community than any enemy efforts. Today the average SF ODA contains nothing like its official allotment of twelve soldiers. An ODA is considered lucky if it has a complement of just eight or nine. That means, simply, that there aren't enough people to do the work, and the average SF soldier assigned to a team spends over six months a year "downrange." The result is a plague of burnouts. Too many SF soldiers are resigning.

Clearly, if the qualities and capabilities the community requires are to be retained, the Special Forces Command leadership needs to take serious action. And that is happening. While the details of the leadership's thinking are highly classified, some outlines have filtered out:

The first twenty-first century SF challenge is recruiting the raw material of the teams—extraordinary men.

Over the last decade, the size of the U.S. Army has been reduced by about a third. Additionally, many of the billets previously held by active-duty personnel are now filled by reserve and National Guard troops. This translates into a huge recruiting problem for Special Forces Command.

Not only are too many SF soldiers leaving, the pool of possible replacements is shrinking.

The movement of a soldier through the traditional career path leading to an SF team is something like passage through a series of progressively finer filters. At each career stage—Airborne School, Ranger Training, etc.—fewer and fewer personnel are qualified or desire to move to the next step. At the same time, because the Army as a whole is smaller, only about two-thirds of the candidates that were available to the SF just ten years ago are available today.

An old engineering adage goes something like this: "You can have good; you can have fast; you can have cheap. Pick any two." Today, SF leaders are facing similar options . . . in their terms: quality, quantity, and operations tempo. "Quality" speaks to the overall attributes of the candidates admitted to the SF "Q" Course, the standards and toughness of that training, and the resulting SF soldiers that graduate. "Quantity" speaks to the number of billets needed to fill out the various SF units. "Operations Tempo" (OpTempo) is a measure of how much each SF soldier and unit can do, and the number of missions each unit can accomplish in a given period. OpTempo has a direct effect on the Army's ability to retain SF soldiers, and thus on the number of new men required to replace them.

Quality, quantity, and OpTempo are linked. A change in one affects the other two. Run OpTempos too high, and more SF soldiers will leave, requiring training of new personnel to replace them. But then if word gets back to recruits that veterans are resigning because of high OpTempos, fewer will take the "Q" Course, causing a further shortfall of numbers, which means that those left on the teams are run even harder. This negative feedback loop lies at the heart of the dilemma faced by Special Forces today.

What can be done to redress the shortfalls in recruiting, training, and retention?

One option, of course, is to reduce the standards for entry into the "Q" Course and for graduation into an SF team. As you might imagine, this is about as popular among SF types as an oil spill at a Greenpeace beach party. More than a few old SF soldiers still remember Vietnam, where the expansion meant that almost anyone could get into SF. Dilution of standards resulted in disaster. There's no reason to expect better results in the future. In other words, quality of personnel and training must remain a line etched in steel. It cannot be compromised.

The choice then is to adjust numbers and OpTempos. And Special Forces Command has been considering changes in both areas.

If the ODAs are to be brought back to their prescribed allotment of twelve men per team, the number of teams overall must be cut by roughly one third. Furthermore, the number of downrange missions must be cut by the same percentage, if the personal and professional needs of the SF personnel are to be met.

Such a move will of course inconvenience the customer base of the Special Forces—including foreign governments, regional CINCs, the Secretary of State, and sometimes the president—not normally a group that gleefully suffers inconveniences. In fact, if a message like this: "Sorry, we have to cancel the mission you've just assigned us; not enough bodies," were dropped on the State Department some Monday morning, you can expect the Secretary of the Army to be reading a blistering memo by early afternoon.

Inconvenience or not, only God can make something out of nothing, and it may well be time for the leaders of the "Green Machine" to inform their civilian masters that American military power has practical limits. Clearly, those limits have not only been reached but exceeded, and it is time for responsible military leaders to pull back and regroup. Quality has a price. The State Department, regional CINCs, and foreign governments will just have to accept the limited size of the active-duty Special Forces community. Simply, there will not be enough SF soldiers and teams to do everything they might desire.

In practical terms, the SF regrouping will probably result in a reduction of the number of ODAs in each SF company from six to four. This will allow the personnel thus freed to fill out the teams and bring them up to full strength. In addition, the company headquarters or Operational Detachment Bravo (ODB) will be reinforced, which will allow it to be split in two if needed, and thus to provide two support teams for downrange operations. The actual effects are shown in the table below:

	Present	Projected
ODAs per Special Forces Group	54	36
ODAs per Special Forces Battalion	18	12
ODAs per Special Forces Company	6	4

Regrouping is not the only means to make up the personnel shortfall. Another possibility is to expand the pool of "Q" Course candidates. But here also there are limits. Half the population, for starters, as long as Title 10 of the United States Code continues to exclude females in line combat units (and SF units belong in that classification).

Another source of candidates might be recruits from the other services. Not only are interservice transfers perfectly legal and proper, but there's no inherent reason why a few sailors, marines, or airmen wouldn't find life in the Special Forces an attractive alternative to their present assignments. Practically, however, recruiting from other services would almost surely raise up more problems than it solved. The other services have their own recruiting and retention problems; they wouldn't look kindly at poaching anyway, and the likely political firestorm would be both bloody and harmful.

A better idea might be to establish new National Guard SF Groups (in addition to the existing 19th and 20th SFGs, which have given outstanding contributions to supporting SF operations worldwide). These could be tasked to take over missions to some of the more "permissive" environments around the world. However, there are not enough candidates for National Guard SF soldier billets. This means that the Army is having problems filling even desirable National Guard slots. There are no easy answers to the question of finding more SF soldiers.

Twenty-first Century Tools of the Trade

After decades of living at the "rump" end of the military supply system, the Special Forces are finally getting control of their procurement system, and the new SFC G7 shop is starting to deliver the tools and supplies needed by their customer base.

Does that mean the SF soldier of the twenty-first century will be the computer-packing, phaser-shooting terror some Army lab engineers see in their PowerPoint briefing charts? Hardly.

The Special Forces have always been about people, and not the stuff they carry and use. Besides, as we've already seen, toting classy, new high-tech "gizmos" into a Third World country may not be the image our guys want to present to local troops, some just weeks out of backwater villages. If you have to train a native soldier whose kit consists of an antique AK-47, dusty rucksack, and worn-out sneakers, showing off a new twenty-first century infantry weapons system is at best patronizing, at worst insulting . . . not a clever way to build rapport and show sensitivity to their culture and situation.

So we'll see SF soldiers equipped with high-end, high-tech gear, but in a much more limited way than other Army soldiers, and most often when SF units are involved in major, joint operations.

So with these assumptions in place, what are the new technologies and equipment SF soldiers will likely pack when they head overseas to a major conflict? The following are good candidates:

• **Satellite Communications**—The revolution in wireless communications has taken another giant step with the recent launch of hybrid satellite/cellular phone systems.

Despite the likely failure of Iridium (a phone-satellite system that has not proved popular enough to make a profit), Orbital Science's competing Globalstar phone system should go online within months. Globalstar has potential for supporting SF operations, particularly in low-threat, permissive operations and environments. The actual hardware soldiers would carry is not significantly larger than cellular phones of a few years ago (batteries take up most of the weight and space); the baseline units have both voice and data transfer capabilities; and with prices under a thousand dollars and dropping, they could be issued to individual soldiers. Though they are currently limited to baud rates of less than 9,600, that speed is adequate for most present SF applications, and system improvements will probably increase throughput by several hundred percent within a few years. As a bonus, both systems are fully digital, meaning real-time encryption chips can easily be added to the sets. This could make such units credible backups in the event of a primary military SATCOM system failure. Already, the Department of Defense is looking closely at these and other commercial space services, which might in time include capabilities like one-meter resolution photographic imagery and direct broadcast teleconferencing.

- **Navigation**—No new technology has affected warfare more in the last decade than the NAVISTAR Global Positioning System (GPS). In less than that time, millions of military and commercial GPS receivers have been built, creating a new kind of service utility: positioning and timing. In the recent campaign against Yugoslavia, for instance, GPS-guided air-to-ground missiles and bombs carried much of the load.

Today, the drive in GPS technology is toward improving overall system accuracy, and imbedding receivers into an ever greater number of systems, so they can be used in an ever greater number of missions.

Greater accuracy will arrive with the launch and deployment of the new Block IIR-series satellites. Designed to replace earlier models of GPS satellites, the Block IIRs will be equipped with improved atomic clocks and more powerful computers. This means a roughly fifty-percent improvement in system accuracy, without any significant modifications to either receiver hardware or software. For military GPS users, system accuracy will improve to less than 23 ft./7 m. of ground truth. For GPS-guided munitions, the Block IIR upgrade means an accuracy approaching the current gold standard, laser-guided bombs. These improvements will also affect SF soldiers. Examples that come to mind include laying out humanitarian relief camps and planning ambush sites. Plan on seeing the Block IIR satellite system completed within a few years, with a follow-on GPS satellite vehicle (Block IIF) coming online not too long after that.

Meanwhile, on the ground, you can expect to see equipment and clothing imbedded with GPS receivers.

One simple and obvious example would be a multifunction wrist device, combining a digital wristwatch (such as the high-end Casio models favored by SF soldiers) with a miniature GPS receiver. If every SF soldier had such a device, hardly any of them would ever again "get lost," and the timing and coordination of small unit operations would greatly improve. GPS receivers with moving map databases could also be imbedded in other day-to-day devices, such as the Ground Mobility Vehicle, laptop/palmtop computers, or handheld radios. With civilian GPS receivers now selling for under $100, the cost of these advances is almost insignificant. But the benefits can only be imagined.

- **Ruggedized Palmtop Computers**—No SF deployment goes downrange without an array of laptop and palmtop computers, and there's no denying their enormous utility. The problem: The wear and tear is heavy. Right now, most off-the-shelf commercial computing products work in a fairly limited range of environments—temperature, humidity, dust, moisture, etc. And most break if dropped hard. While a forward headquarters or team house can usually handle—or work around—these limitations, equipment that fragile is hardly suitable for field operations. What clearly is needed is a ruggedized family of laptop/palmtop computers, capable of a variety of military and general tasks. These would include e-mail (with the ability to attach digital photos and other files), a small spreadsheet and database, drawing pad, and perhaps even an imbedded GPS receiver. This unit could then be plugged into a satellite phone to send and receive data.

- **Handheld Sensors**—One big victory in the fight against size and weight has been in the design of handheld sensors. In just a decade thermal imaging scanners (also known as Forward Looking Infrared—FLIR) have shrunk from small beer keg to soft-drink-can size. Similar improvements have been made in the quality and cost of other systems, including low-light scopes, laser designators, digital cameras, and GPS receivers. The next major advance will likely come in the form of a single unit combining many of the above systems—perhaps a large pair of binoculars that might also communicate through the satellite phone unit. Using such a system, a *single* SF soldier, acting as a sensor post, could transmit pictures and targeting coordinates back to higher headquarters in all weather and lighting conditions, and then call in precision firepower on a variety of targets—capabilities up to now unavailable to entire units.

- **Climate Adaptive Field Clothing/Gear**—The average SF soldier has a closetful of Battle Dress Uniforms (BDUs), each suited to a specific climate and terrain that might be encountered on deployment. Since the climates and terrains an SF soldier might encounter vary enormously—even during a single deployment—his rucksack can get terribly crowded with BDUs, socks, and jackets. It may well be, however, that rucksacks stuffed with clothing may soon be history. Clothing that adapts to local environmental conditions is now within reach. In the near future, conductive microfibers might be woven into a computer-controlled garment. This garment might possess a number of intriguing characteristics. It could have, for instance, a "chameleon" outer shell, which could change color and pattern to exactly match the surrounding terrain and conditions. It could have a bullet-resistant Kevlar interior layer, which could protect against fire from 5.56mm, 7.62mm, and 9mm projectiles at close range. The microfibers might expand under an electrical charge, increasing the garment's insulating properties. Electricity might be produced by a series of small generators in the joints. In other words, the wearer would make his own power. Such an overgarment might operate anywhere—in deserts, forests, mountains, and cities.

All of these projections, while bordering now on the fanciful, have a solid basis in existing technologies. Within a few years (and with the generous help of taxpayer dollars), SF soldiers will go into battle with a number of significant combat edges they do not now possess. Though the new gear will continue to offer only limited utility for low-end missions such as FID and HA, for high-intensity conflicts, such as regional wars and covert raids, it might prove decisive.

In fact, these higher end missions (and the equipment they require) are the subject of most of SOCOM's planning scrutiny these days, and for the same reasons that SF scenarios at JRTC and NTC are focused on operations in "big" conflicts. This is so not because the other SF missions are less important, but because the high-end missions are the most difficult in their mission spectrum, and thus require the greatest investment. In the "big" conflicts, the largest numbers of SF units and missions are run, the SF units themselves are large (often battalion-sized), and the risks and difficulties are the greatest.

How the new technology might apply to those missions is the subject of a series of ongoing field and laboratory experiments, examples of which will shortly follow.

Twenty-first Century Special Forces CONOPS

Combat is never more than one false step from screaming, raging, howling chaos. Thus the absolute necessity for what our military calls "command and control." Ideally, command and control involves easy communication up and down the lines of command. Never has this ideal been achieved. Never has there been sufficient bandwidth. (Smoke signals, flags, trumpets, telegraph, and even radio are *very* imperfect media.) And rarely, during critical moments, will warriors be able to divide their attentions enough to fight *and* talk.

Still, reducing chaos is always a goal.

The new computer and communications technologies offer a significant leap in the right direction.

How might these technologies help battalion- or group-sized SF units better accomplish their wartime missions? Perhaps even more important, how can the SF group/command organization and concept of operations (CONOPS) be changed so that smaller, better-equipped ODAs can more successfully accomplish all the various missions that will be handed to them?

For years, senior SF leaders have worked at creating a more efficient planning and tasking process, one that focuses better on the needs of ODA personnel, and allows input and contributions from a wider variety of personnel and organizations. This effort has included a top-to-bottom review of the entire mission planning and execution process. In particular, SF leadership has been looking for ways to use new technologies or systems to open up the planning process further, to improve team performance in the field, and especially to reduce the time required to plan missions and the size of the workload at every level of the mission planning and execution process.

Here are some of their early goals:

- **"Stovepipe" Elimination**—"Stovepiping" is a term that has become fashionable among both military and business types. It is a process with a fixed chain of tasks that *must* be followed in order for the goal of the process to be accomplished. To put this another way, if the goal is to be reached, the process can neither be accessed from outside the stovepipe, nor disrupted by anything, either in or out of the stovepipe.

  Good day-to-day examples of stovepiping are your local public utilities. If you want electrical power, telephone service, or cable TV, your only recourse (with *very* few exceptions) is to turn to large and fixed power, telephone, or cable companies. You get what they want you to have. That is, you have virtually no say in how you receive their services, and you pay the prices they want you to pay.

  It will come as no surprise that virtually the entire federal government is a hive of stovepipes, jealously guarded by bureaucrats whose professional lives center on the defense of "their" stovepipe. And you can take as a further axiom that in the government the higher the security "protecting" an organization or program, the more likely that organization or program is a stovepipe.

  Conversely, it will also come as no surprise that those who would make "revolutions" in military and business affairs have been working to destroy stovepipes—or at least to break into them—and allow new people and ideas to bring new life to previously closed communities, processes, and programs.

  Today, the process of tasking an SF ODA with a mission is a top-to-bottom stovepipe. The team has surprisingly little to say about that process. They are not expected to add much in the way of basic input or to suggest options for practically executing the overall mission.

  Of course, the teams make many specific choices about how they will carry out their assigned mission. No SF mission is executed without a tremendous amount of detail planning at the team level. However, the team rarely controls the broad strokes of these operations, as these are usually set at the top levels of the JTF or regional headquarters. In other words, the team's options lie at the bottom of the tasking chain—at the bottom of the stovepipe. This means their choices are severely limited . . . as is their participation in overall planning.

  So, for example, mission-critical issues, such as transportation to and from the target areas, rules of engagement, and radio net choices, are often simply handed to them; asking for other options is not open to them.

  If other options were open to them, then a team might request an infiltration by sea or submarine, instead of by air, in order to reduce the chances of enemy detection. Or, in order to reduce their risks, a team might like to change their tasking from direct action against a target (a self-contained raid) to special reconnaissance (observing), and then Terminal Guidance (designating the target) for weapons from an outside fire source (aircraft, artillery, or missiles).

Clearly, commanders will always have to have the final say, yet giving teams more input into high-level planning for their own missions would be a good thing, and Special Forces Command is looking very hard at ways to make that happen.

- **Reduction of Intercommunity Friction**—Every SF mission requires the cooperation and support of a number of government and military agencies. The transport aircraft and helicopters that carry the teams, the maps that show them the way, the clothing they wear, all come from everywhere *except* the Special Forces Command.

   One naturally expects cooperation and teamwork . . . and even better, *friendly* cooperation and *friendly* teamwork—especially during risky and dangerous operations where lives hang in the balance.

   That doesn't always happen. Too often, there's friction, competition, and rivalry—a situation often made worse by the sometimes heavy-handed ways of the SOF community. There are times when other services and organizations go out of their way to *avoid* providing what the Special Forces need to properly execute a mission.

   Such rivalry will never be entirely eliminated. However, the many different resources and services necessary for an SF operation require at least the reduction to comfortable levels of the impediments rivalries create.

   This is another example of what Clausewitz called "friction." Special Forces (like every other military organization) have no dispensation from friction. If they are going to make their missions work, they have to overcome the friction their community generates.

   One of the most powerful sources of friction is the system for delivery of intelligence from the intelligence agencies to its military customers. Special Forces (like every other military organization) vitally require accurate and up-to-the-minute intelligence data.

   Meanwhile, the various American intelligence agencies may well be the most stovepipe-ridden community in the history of humankind. This makes the process of tasking them to collect and then deliver accurate and timely intelligence information difficult—unless you happen to be the president, his immediate staff, or some few other high-level civilian government types. It's so much more gratifying to the ego to deliver your goods to customers who live at those heights rather than the guys slogging through the mud getting shot at. The security bottlenecks are so tight, it's hard for SF planners to know what they don't know, or *if* information is available *somewhere* that might help in the execution of the mission—or save lives.

   One way to get around these limitations is to set up tasking and distribution of the various intelligence collection systems at a central SF center. In this way, the teams can make their requests up the chain of command, which has the necessary clout and clearances to task agencies like NRO and NSA. Such a center might also provide other, similar services for the teams—like procuring special clothing, equipment, or food, or arranging special satellite paging and phone services.

- **Improved Connectivity**—Computers, data networks, and high-speed telecommunications have revolutionized just about everything you can think of . . . *except* SF mission planning. SF mission planners, with their deep tradition of "stubby pencil" planning in the field, have resisted these advances—often for solid, conservative reasons. Stubby pencils are *really* rugged.

On the other hand, not a long space separates solid and conservative from petrified and dogmatic. "This is the way we've always done it. It works. It doesn't break. I'll be damned if I do it different."

Where's the truth? For that, we have to answer a simple question. Can advanced sensor, computer, and communications technology give SF personnel (at all levels) a better situational awareness of their operating areas and missions? Will this technology allow SF soldiers to better accomplish their missions, or will it be a "gee-whiz" impediment to their core goals and objectives?

Many in the Special Forces community have already answered that question, by voting with their pocketbooks and yearly budget allocations. Already, laptop and palmtop computers, digital cameras, and other "gadgets" have begun to change the face of SF operations. At every briefing in an SF operations center, the presentation is delivered by means of a large-screen projector, fed by a computer running recent-generation presentation software imbedded with digital photos and video clips. Computerized mission-planning tools and high-speed digital communications are now also allowing team planners to get involved earlier in the tasking process. Historically, the earlier the participants are involved in planning a mission, the greater the chances it will be successful.

Meanwhile, in order to get an idea about performance of new technologies and systems outside of command centers, the SF community has hosted a series of laboratory experiments and field exercises. These have evaluated a wide variety of equipment and concepts, which could form the core of SF CONOPS and doctrine well into the next century.

We'll look more closely at all this, but before we do, a few words about the testing process itself.

People learn far more from their failures than from what works the first time. This truth lies at the core of the military developmental process.

The kinds of field exercises we tend to be familiar with are traditional force-on-force exercises, like those at JRTC and NTC. Experimental exercises (of the kind we're about to see) are a very different creature. Force-on-force exercises test training, preparation, and equipment under conditions of stress, surprise, mischance, and chaos that mimic as closely as possible the actual conditions of battle. Experimental field exercises are the military equivalent of scientific lab experiments. They don't test training (though they can have that effect); they test ideas, systems, technologies, and the like under controlled parameters. And they tend to be loaded down with a number of what people in the test and evaluation community call "artificialities"—unreal situations. Screwups happen in all field exercises—and they should—but they are more likely to occur in experimental exercises than in force-on-force exercises. The idea in experimental exercises is to validate particular concepts and procedures, not necessarily to "win" engagements or achieve objectives in the typical military sense.

Colonel Ed Phillips, USA, with his trademark basketball. Colonel Phillips was the commander of the 7th Special Forces Group during the high-tech R3 demonstration exercise.

Relampago Rojo: Rock Soup and a Vision

Because the 7th SFG has been at the forefront of new technology implementation within the SF community, and because Colonel Ed Phillips, their commander (he has since moved on), was a leader in the drive to prepare Special Forces for the new century, it will be no surprise that 7th SFG has been the testbed unit for new technologies and CONOPS concepts.

I first learned of Phillips's passion for new technology during a meeting in late 1998, when he outlined his vision for future SF CONOPS. It's a wide and "big" vision of future SF operations, in which SF no longer plays a subordinate role to conventional forces, but works as equals—or even takes the lead when that would be best. Here—in rough form, and a little cleaned up, for security reasons—is the vision he and a handful of others came up with:

Where Special Forces are concerned, the men on the teams have seen it all. SF soldiers live for downrange missions, where the only link home is a single high-frequency radio channel with a Morse key. All have also planned their share of exercises on a grimy sheet of paper with a broken pencil stub. They also know the value of the new technologies—computers, software, and networking. Still, the old methods have their place. Indeed, they are sometimes indispensable. But when you have complex operations and missions, you're better off using the new technologies. The missions will be more clearly presented to the participants, and the operations will be better coordinated.

The new vision, in other words, is surprisingly simple. Where a genius like Da Vinci might need only pencil and paper to sketch a masterpiece, it's better to give average artists a full pallet of brushes, tools, and pigments. That way, you probably won't get a great picture, but you'll get *more* picture. Technology can be a liberating force for the creative energies of Special Forces soldiers and Special Forces commanders. Technology allows the genius of each soldier to be more fully seen by a wider audience over a greater distance. And it allows commanders more choices (always a good thing: Every commander wants his enemy to run out of options before he does).

So, for example, the new technologies might allow the primary control center for large and widespread SF operations to be in a different time zone from the conflict. It might even be a permanent room at a group headquarters here in the U.S., which might permanently monitor and control a variety of missions through phone and satellite links to forward operations bases in the field.

Visionaries have a hard time in military organizations. It's not so much that military types are hostile to new ideas. They like new ideas, but only within the currently fashionable frame of reference (the stovepipe). What set the recent efforts of Ed Phillips apart from others was the ability to make the visions into a physical reality. In short, he "made rock soup," as George Patton used to call it.

During World War II, General Patton liked to attack faster and more aggressively than his superiors thought best. When his bosses tried to stop him, Patton "made rock soup": A hobo wants to make a pot of soup, but he has nothing to make it with, not even a pot. So he picks up a couple of stones and then borrows a pot of cold water, for "rock soup." Once he has the pot and water, he borrows a little of this and a little of that, gradually picking up meat, vegetables, and firewood—everything he needs to make "real" soup. Like the hobo, Patton would push a little here and a little there, and get into a small fight somewhere else. And before his superiors knew what was happening, he'd have a full-scale offensive going when he was supposed to be stopped dead.

In the same way, Phillips and his 7th SFG personnel built up a base of people, equipment, and opportunities to test their new ideas. Over several years, 7th SFG acquired computers, software, networking equipment, and other bits and pieces, and built the kind of command-and-control facilities SFC sees itself running in the future.

A key goal was to equip a testbed group-level headquarters with a maximum load of computers, communications, and networking equipment, and turn it loose in an actual field exercise. This test headquarters would control several widely separated SF battalions during the exercise (which itself would be imbedded in a larger theater-level training event), and would make maximum use of satellite communications links and a network of linked computers in a "mission control" configuration. In this way, the workload of a large, theater-level SF operation could be simulated, and the new planning and operational concepts and equipment evaluated.

The first test exercises were called *Relampago Rojo*-1 and -2 (R1 and R2 for short)[105] and they were run in 1997. These exercises had built up a base of experience for the coming larger event, which would be known as R3. R3 would take place in late February and early March of 1999 in the southeastern United States; it would try to fully implement the three major concepts described earlier: eliminating stovepipes, reducing friction, and improving connectivity; and it would include several extremely

---

105 *Relampago Rojo* is Spanish for "red lightning," a reference to the 7th SFG's Latin American mission, and their unit colors, which are primarily red.

intense SF operations, both multinational and joint. Active-duty, reserve, and National Guard units would be involved, as well as components from every part of SOCOM. And all of these would be formed into the SOF component of a larger Joint Task Force (JTF) . . . though with an unusual and innovative twist. While the larger conventional units of the JTF (carrier battle groups, amphibious units, etc.) would be operating elsewhere, the testbed SOF component headquarters would itself act as a mini-JTF.

After SOF units—acting as the lead elements—entered a hypothetical crisis area, the conventional units would arrive and take their orders from the SOF component commander (a reversal in policy from the usual U.S. joint operations doctrine, in which the SOF component is subordinate to the JTF commander). In fact, since the SOF commander probably has SF ODAs or other units on the ground already in the area, he is probably better qualified than the JTF commander to control the early days (at least) of a crisis. With his eyes and ears already in place, the SOF commander would relay close to real-time data back to higher headquarters, allowing for a smoother flow of conventional units into the theater, prior to handoff of the JTF command responsibilities to a normal headquarters structure.

At the close of our initial meeting, Colonel Phillips invited me to join him during the R3 exercise, to observe for myself (I'd act as an honorary Observer/Controller). I quickly accepted.

R3 turned out to be one of the most complex and difficult exercises I've experienced.

Relampago Rojo-3: A Unit/Task Breakdown

Though R3 was conceived to be primarily an experimental exercise, the concept was to be implemented within the context of a large, conventional force-on-force Joint Task Force Exercise (JTFEX) being run by USACOM.[106] This larger event (known as JTFEX 99-1) was being run to certify the USS *Theodore Roosevelt* (CVN-71) carrier battle group (CVBG), USS *Kersarge* (LHD-3) Amphibious Ready Group (ARG), and 26th Marine Expeditionary Unit—Special Operations Capable (MEU [SOC]) ready for their upcoming Mediterranean cruise.[107] This operation was being conducted off Puerto Rico and the Atlantic coast, and had already been running for several weeks. At the same time, a number of fleet units from NATO, as well as U.S. Army and Air Force units, were taking advantage of the huge training opportunity represented by JTFEX 99-1. R3 would derive its scenario from the larger exercise, and would operate as a component of the overall JTFEX plan. The basic breakdown of forces for JTFEX 99-1 is shown in the table below.

---

106 For more on JTFEX operations, see *Marine* (1996), *Airborne* (1997), and *Carrier* (1999).

107 These units would find themselves embroiled in Operation Allied Force against Yugoslavia within weeks of JTFEX 99-1. Later, the 26th MEU (SOC) would become the lead peacekeeping element of Operation Joint Guardian in Kosovo.

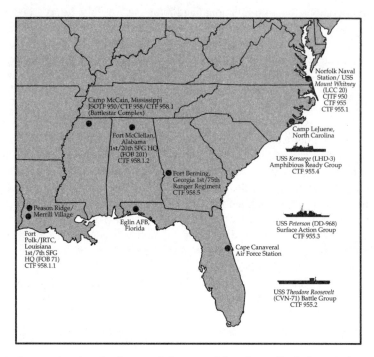

A map showing the layout of forces and locations of missions during *Relampago Rojo-3* in 1999.

Joint Task Force Exercise 99-1 Unit Organization

Component Designation	Acronym	Core Unit & Location/Base/Ship
Commander, Joint Task Force 950	CJTF 950	U.S. Atlantic Command/USS *Mount Whitney* (LCC-20)
JTFEX 99-1 Naval Component	CTF 955	U.S. 2nd Fleet/USS *Mount Whitney* (LCC-20)
Flagship, CJTF-955	CTF 955.1	U.S. 2nd Fleet/USS *Mount Whitney* (LCC-20)
***Theodore Roosevelt* Battle Group**	CTF 955.2	USS *Theodore Roosevelt* (CVN-71)
Surface Action Group (SAG)	CTF 955.3	USS *Peterson* (DD-968)
***Kersarge* Amphibious Ready Group/26th MEU (SOC)**	CTF 955.4	USS *Kersarge* (LHD-3)
Joint Special Operations Task Force 958	CTF 958	USSOCCOM/Camp McCain, MS

As you can see, the SOF component is contained in Combined Task Force (CTF) 958. This is the force that would make up the bulk of the units involved in R3.

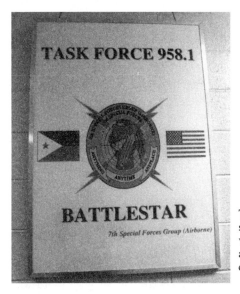

BATTLESTAR
7th Special Forces Group (Airborne)

The R3 emblem at the entrance to the Battlestar control center. R3 was designed to provide planning data on how to apply computer and network technology to twenty-first-century Special Operations.

JOHN D. GRESHAM

R3 would incorporate many of the features of NTC and JRTC rotations, including standard scenario terms and assumptions: The operating area included the "fictional" island of Cortina, and Koronans were the "bad" guys. (There were other "fictional" additions and complications, which I am ignoring to avoid confusion.)

For R3, the JSOTF would have to deal with two major near-simultaneous crisis situations. The first involved weapons of mass destruction in northwest Florida, near Eglin AFB. Here SCUD-type missiles with WMD (chemical) warheads were being prepared. An extensive SOF effort would be required to destroy the threat. Guidance from the JTFEX 99-1 CINC was to prosecute this effort aggressively, to prevent any enemy use of WMDs on allied forces planning to operate along the eastern seaboard.

The second situation was a growing insurgent effort by Koronan forces on the island of Cortina (in reality Louisiana, Mississippi, and Arkansas, with most of the activity at Fort Polk, Louisiana), highlighted by the ethnic cleansing of some villages and an emerging chemical weapons threat. This mission would require the prosecution and destruction of the insurgents and their WMD stockpiles, as well as the repatriation of the local residents into their homes and villages. This meant that a full-spectrum SOF effort would be required from all the participants, including Special Reconnaissance (SR), Direct Action (DA), Civil Affairs (CA), and Humanitarian Relief (HR) missions.[108]

To accommodate these various jobs, SOCOM had provided the R3 leadership with a variety of SOF units and personnel.[109] These included:

- **Commander, Task Force (CTF) 958**—Normally, a Joint Special Operations Task Force (JSOTF) headquarters would be a theater-level headquarters operation; it

---

108 In December, I decided that the 1/7 SFG's operations at Fort Polk would be a better event for me to observe than the 20th Group's SCUD hunt at Eglin AFB, which would have been more difficult to cover and included classified elements that would have been denied to me.

109 The nomenclature "Commander, Task Force" (thus: CTF) is standard. I have no idea why it is used.

would be commanded by an O-7 (Army or Air Force brigadier general or rear admiral); and would be assigned minimally a full SFG and other SOF units (helicopters, transport aircraft, Rangers, SEALs, etc.). For R3 (because it was an experiment), the 7th SFG headquarters functioned as the JSOTF, and Colonel Ed Phillips as the JSOTF commander. CTF 958 was based at Camp McCain, Mississippi.

- **Commander, Task Force (CTF) 958.1**—The Army SOF forces operated under an organization known as CTF 958.1. Technically called the Army Special Operations Task Force (ASOFTF), CTF 958.1 was also played by Colonel Phillips and the 7th SFG headquarters staff, based at Camp McCain.

- **Commander, Task Force (CTF) 958.1.1**—The first of the two SF units assigned to the R3 exercise was the 1st Battalion of the 7th Special Forces Group (1st/7th SFG). Commanded by Lieutenant Colonel Mike Adams, 1st/7th SFG would operate out of Forward Operating Base (FOB) 71 at Fort Polk. For R3, the SF soldiers from 1st/7th SFG were to be reinforced with a company of infantry from the Bolivian Army.

- **Commander, Task Force (CTF) 958.1.2**—The other SF unit assigned to R3 was 1st Battalion of the 20th SFG (1st/20th SFG) from the National Guard. They would work from FOB 201 at Fort McClellan, Alabama, which was near home for many of the guardsmen of the 20th. Lieutenant Colonel Paul Roberts commanded CTF 958.1.2 during R3.

- **Commander, Task Force (CTF) 958.2**—Along with Army SOF personnel, other services contributed to R3. One of these was the Navy Special Warfare Command, which controls SEAL teams and their Special Boat Squadrons (SBSs). Operating as CTF 958.2, the Navy Special Warfare Task Group was composed of units from Navy Special Warfare Group Two (NSWG-2) and SBS-2 out of Little Creek, Virginia. They supplied SEALs and boats to support littoral SOF operations during R3. (Colonel Phillips did not, in fact, command these forces, but their comms were linked through the JSOTF center to the JTFEX command, thus putting more stress on the system—desirable as part of the experiment.)

- **Commander, Task Force (CTF) 958.3**—Along with naval and ground SOF units, R3 also required aviation muscle to accomplish its goals. Because this might involve flying units from Army, Navy, and Air Force commands, a Joint Forces Air Component Commander (JFACC) headquarters was established as CTF 958.3. Known as the Joint Special Operations Aviation Command (JSOAC), CTF 958.3 was based at Camp McCain with the JSOTF center.

- **Commander, Task Force (CTF) 958.4**—In addition to U.S. units, R3 also involved SOF personnel from Great Britain. While I was asked not to take too great an interest in their participation, the United Kingdom Special Forces Task Group (UKSFTG, operating as CTF 958.4) contributed personnel and equipment from the Special Air Service (SAS).

- **Commander, Task Force (CTF) 958.5**—To provide JSOTF with some serious striking power, SOCOM provided the services of A Company from the 1st Battalion of the 75th (1st/75th) Ranger Regiment. These would come from Hunter Army Airfield, Georgia, and would be flagged as CTF 958.5.

When all of the pieces were laid out, they looked like this:

R3 Special Operations Unit Organization

Component Designation	Acronym	Core Unit & Location/Base/Ship
Commander, Joint Task Force 950	CJTF 950	U.S. Atlantic Command/USS *Mount Whitney* (LCC-20)
Joint Special Operations Task Force 950	CTF 958	USSOCCOM/Camp McCain, MS
Army Special Operations Task Force	CTF 958.1	USASOC/Camp McCain, MS
Forward Operating Base (FOB) 71	CTF 958.1.1	1st Battalion/7th Special Forces Group (1st/7th SFG)/Fort Polk, LA
Forward Operating Base (FOB) 201	CTF 958.1.2	1st Battalion/20th SFG (1st/20th SFG—National Guard)/Fort McClellan, AL
Navy Special Warfare Task Group	CTF 958.2	NSWG-2 and SBS-2/Various locations
Joint Special Operations Aviation Command	CTF 958.3	U.S. Air Force Special Operations Command/Camp McCain, FL
United Kingdom Special Forces Task Group	CTF 958.4	22nd Regiment, Special Air Service/Various locations
1st Battalion/75th Ranger Regiment	CTF 958.5	1st/75th Ranger Regiment/Fort Hunter Army Airfield, GA

The concepts being tested in R3 would be proved or disproved at the SCUD hunt at Eglin AFB, Florida, and at the counterinsurgency/humanitarian effort at Fort Polk. And each of these was designed to simulate the information workload for an entire Special Forces Group (a point to keep very firmly in mind).

From the time the exercise would begin Phillips and his JSOTF staff would have less than two weeks to plan out these two major operations and to get the forces to their operating areas. At the start of the exercise, most of the R3 SOF units were still at their home bases, awaiting the tasking that would come out of the R3 control center that was even then still being built. While the units and their commanders had a general idea of what would be happening, the details of the operations were kept from them. This was designed to simulate the real-world uncertainties that go with any military operation, and would keep people on their toes throughout R3. It would be an ambitious set of tasks.

In terms of actual tasking, the JSOTF team had two basic missions to perform. The first would be to conduct the search and destruction of enemy SCUD missiles and their launchers at Eglin AFB with the 1st Battalion of the 20th (1st/20th) SFG. 1st/20th would establish a FOB 201 at Fort McClellan, which would act as their home base, and would be supported by a variety of joint SOF aviation and ground units. The plan was for 1st/20th to insert a number of SR teams into the area of Eglin AFB, which would locate a number of simulated SCUD transporter erector launchers (TELs). Once the TELs had been targeted, the SR teams would provide Terminal Guidance with laser designators onto the targets, which would then destroy the launchers with fire from U.S. Air Force (USAF) AC-130 Spectre gunships.

The second mission, which would be run nearly simultaneously, would be more complex. At Fort Polk, the 1st Battalion of the 7th (1st/7th) SFG would be tasked to establish FOB 71. Their mission was to liberate a village north of the main post at the JRTC live-fire range at Peason Ridge. There, insurgent troops had driven out the local villagers ("ethnic cleansing" on a small scale) in order to utilize the town as an assembly area for chemical land mines and other WMDs. The plan was for 1st/7th to insert SR teams into the Peason Ridge area, and then to reconnoiter the town (known as Merrill Village) and surrounding areas. Once the area was under surveillance, A Company of the 1st Battalion of the 75th (A/1st/75th) Ranger Regiment would be parachuted into the area by USAF Special Operations MC-130 transports supported by AC-130 gunships. When safely on the ground, the Rangers would assault the village, with a primary mission of killing or capturing all the insurgent troops. Once Merrill Village was secured, the Rangers would hand off control to a multinational ground task force of 1st/7th Special Forces soldiers and troops from Bolivia. This force would then set up a secure perimeter around the town, clear any antipersonnel hazards (mines, booby traps, etc.), and make it ready for the return of the displaced villagers (being played by JRTC roleplayer personnel). The mission would then continue for several more days, allowing the SF/Bolivian task force to practice their humanitarian relief and civil affairs skills.

Both missions were much like "normal" SOF missions that might be run anywhere in the world. The difference was this: In R3 both missions would occur at the same time and be run out of a single JSOTF command center at Camp McCain (roughly two hundred miles from each event). SFC was looking to learn whether the new command-and-control system could actually handle the tremendous quantity of information flowing through it, and whether the greater connectivity created by improved communications systems would not only increase the flow of info, but create a greatly improved situational awareness both for the command center and for the guys in the field. The command center would act as a clearinghouse for planning, support, and intelligence, and would push necessary information and services down to the teams planning their missions. And it was hoped that much of the "stovepiping" that slows down SF operations could be eliminated, making the entire mission planning and execution more efficient and less time consuming.

While there would be many "artificialities," R3 would provide enough information to let Special Forces Command know if what was being tested had merit in the real world.

Camp McCain, Mississippi, February 21st

My journey to R3 started with a road trip into the heart of old Dixie. Driving toward Camp McCain, the site of the testbed headquarters, I passed through towns and villages with haunting names—Selma, Meridian, and Granada (where I stayed)—all mileposts on the great civil rights marches of the 1960s. Camp McCain is an Army National Guard base in northern Mississippi, and normally home to a battalion of tanks and other armored fighting vehicles, along with a company of the 20th SFG. But for the next few weeks, it would host the leadership of the 7th SFG and other units of Special Forces Command. Here would be situated what Colonel Phillips dubbed the "Battlestar," the concrete realization of the vision for the R3 SF mission control center.

The headquarters was set up near the National Guard billeting area (where the headquarters staff would be housed), in what normally is the base mess and recreational complex. Here 7th SFG troops had built up a Joint Special Operations Task Force headquarters, including a simulated force protection perimeter, though there would be no OpFor units to attack them here (those limited resources would be reserved for the actual field operations). Senior officers take such matters quite seriously these days, even if the threat is only "imagined." Many senior SOF and SF generals would be passing this way in the weeks ahead, and anything less than a full-blown force protection scheme would not do.

After receiving a security badge, I was led into the compound. Since I would spend the exercise flagged as a JRTC O/C, I'd have a "God's-eye view" of the entire exercise. This placed on me certain responsibilities. For instance, I had to be careful in conversations with all personnel that were "in play." Loose lips might give one side or another an unrealistic advantage and skew the results of the exercise. Fully appreciating my enhanced status as an observer, I went into the center.

The weather was raw and cold (it would snow before the day was out). Inside the security tent, my old friend Major Tom McCollum, the USASOC public affairs officer greeted me and led me inside the perimeter. For this exercise, Tom was acting out the role as the R3 JSOTF PAO, and would take part as a roleplayer in a number of the coming actions.

We went first to the headquarters support center, where day-to-day paperwork and other administrative tasks were handled. There I was given a cup of coffee, and then got a quick update from Tom as I waited for Colonel Phillips, who was to show me around. The 7th SFG personnel had arrived several days earlier, and had constructed this center in just two days. In addition to the Battlestar itself, smaller "feeder" centers had also been set up in other rooms to support intelligence, planning, communications, and other functions within the headquarters.

After a few minutes, Colonel Phillips came in and began his tour.

As we moved through the centers for communications, planning, and other functions, it became clear that Special Forces Command had committed a significant percentage of their deployable communications, computer, and networking resources to R3. Outside were enough satellite communications vans and antennas to support a conventional Army division or corps headquarters. Almost as impressive was the networking gear for these communications channels, all being routed into a custom-built local area network (LAN). Every important headquarters function, from e-mail to reconnaissance satellite tasking, would flow through this LAN, making it key to the success or failure of the R3 exercise.

The Battlestar operations center during R3. Much like a space mission control center, the Battlestar is designed to provide Special Operations leaders with a clearer picture of downrange operations.

JOHN D. GRESHAM

The JSOTF headquarters also sported some unusual additions—a space filled with stacks of Styrofoam sheeting and plywood, for instance. This material would become terrain models to support planning and briefings for the major R3 missions . . . and an important component of yet another experiment. The hope was to run some of the various R3 operations without the traditional full dress rehearsals that SOF units prefer. Phillips and his men planned to run a few of these missions after only "virtual" rehearsals, extensively using video teleconferencing and limited face-to-face meetings between unit commanders. Called Operation Rock Drill, these "virtual" conferences would simulate the pulling together of widely separated SOF units from around the world, throwing them into a fast-breaking crisis.

Next we proceeded down a hallway into what had been a gymnasium, but was now the Battlestar control center, the heart of the upcoming R3 operation. What was once the basketball court was now partitioned with plywood walls, all covered with maps, photographs, charts, and a variety of graphics useful to the personnel who would spend the next three weeks in this cyber-rustic workspace.

Stepped back a short way from the front of the large area that was the actual Battlestar control center were three semicircular rows of folding tables, now covered with computers, printers, networking equipment, and a variety of other high-tech paraphernalia. And in front of all that were four large-screen television projectors, which could be programmed to show a variety of programming and materials. While we were visiting, the screens were programmed with:

- A continuous loop of satellite cloud activity over the eastern U.S, downlinked from a National Oceanic Administration (NOA) GOES-series weather satellite. This provided everyone there with an up-to-date pictorial depiction of the weather situation.

- A computer-generated display of the eastern United States and adjacent waters, showing the location of ships and aircraft involved in the coming exercise. This display was being fed from a joint system, which displayed the information in real-time, making it a useful tool for keeping track of the overall strategic situation in the JTFEX 99-1 exercise, as well as units assigned to R3.

- A high-resolution ground map of the southeastern U.S., covering the area of operations for the SOF units involved in R3. Overlaid onto this were ground and air unit symbols, which could be moved and controlled from a small computer in the Battlestar center.

- *CNN Headline News*, a source of continuous study for everyone in the room. With the 1999 NCAA basketball playoffs only days away, every sports junkie there was keeping one eye on game highlights.

A number of other programs and displays could also be shown, including classified feeds from intelligence agencies, and several hundred channels of commercial programming from a DSS satellite dish in back of the center.

Tying everything in the building together was a state-of-the-art Intranet system, with feed-out to various classified networks, and even the commercial Internet. All of the data sources were fed through a commercial Cisco Systems network router, so that to the operators in the Battlestar and other parts of the building, everything they saw on their computer screens looked like conventional World Wide Web sites or pages.

After my Battlestar tour, I returned to my hotel rooms to prepare for the following day's briefings . . . and to enjoy some local barbecue.

Camp McCain, Mississippi, February 22nd

This Monday morning began early, so I could attend the morning shift change briefing at 0700, which would bring me up to speed on the R3 scenario, and the units involved. After I gathered up my badge at the security checkpoint and grabbed a cup of coffee, I was escorted into the Battlestar center where I was given a seat in the front row between Colonel Phillips and his command sergeant major.

Promptly at 0700, everyone came to attention, and the briefing commenced. One at a time, the various staff section heads went to a podium and presented a slideshow about their area of concern on one of the large screens. Like most present-day electronic briefings, each presentation was mastered in Microsoft PowerPoint.[110] Computers have so deeply imbedded themselves in our military that major planning can't get off the dime until the PowerPoint slides are done; and the most powerful and valuable person on a headquarters staff is often an officer called the "PowerPoint Ranger" (the "producer-director" of briefings, who integrates text, graphics, photos).

---

[110] PowerPoint is a computer-based program for mastering and presenting briefing slides. Easy to use and quite powerful, PowerPoint has become a staple for American business and military personnel trying to get their message across. More recently, all NATO briefings during Operation Allied Force were presented in PowerPoint, including video clips and photographs.

Colonel Phillips had his own PowerPoint Ranger (a very bright and skilled young SF captain on the 7th SFG staff) who produced his briefings.

This day's briefings covered a wide range of topics, most of which centered on the R3 scenario. While technically R3 was already underway, the most intensive parts were still almost two weeks in the future.

Meanwhile, the larger exercise it was part of, JTFEX 99-1, was in many respects a restaging of the various JTFEXs I had observed over the past four-plus years. Since this one was taking place in wintertime, the deep-water segments (designed to test and certify the Navy and Marine components) were taking place in the warm waters near Puerto Rico, while the main thrust of the exercise was an Iraqi-style invasion of a hypothetical country in the "Gulf of Sabini" (the coastal waters of the Carolinas). Marines from the 26th MEU (SOC) were rushing up from Puerto Rico to evacuate civilians from the danger zone, and the *Theodore Roosevelt* CVBG was moving into the area to support the operation. Simulated enemy SCUD missiles were raining down on Philadelphia, and more were being prepared in denied territory in Florida. Navy and British SAS SOF units were scouting the area around Cape Canaveral, where the missiles were being assembled (the enemy inventory of SCUDs was assessed at over a hundred). At the same time, a U.S. Navy Aegis cruiser, the USS *Vicksburg* (CG-69) steamed into the Gulf of Mexico to provide ballistic missile defense for the island of Cortina, if the enemy fired any that way.

Right now, the R3 units were only playing on the periphery of the action, but that would change in a few days. So for the time being, the pace of operations in the Battlestar remained brisk but calm.

Once the briefing was done, I headed over to an excellent breakfast cooked by the 7th SFG sergeants. Since the regular cooks and support troops work long hours putting meals on the table, the group NCOs take over the job one day out of seven. The rib-sticking, Southern-style meal they laid out was a wonderful way to combat the unusually cold weather.[111]

After breakfast, I spent the rest of the day poking into the other centers of activity within the JSOTF headquarters.

Later, as the sun was sinking into the west and I was about to head back to Granada and my hotel, I got a surprising invitation from Colonel Phillips. "Why don't you join us for the COA briefing tomorrow?" he asked.

"Sure, I'd love to," I answered in a shot.

The Course of Action (COA) briefing would decide the operation plans for the CTF 958.1.1 at Fort Polk. Such briefings, even during exercises, are usually highly classified. It was a great honor.

I had a lot to look forward to the next day.

---

111 Because R3 went 'round the clock, breakfast was the only meal that overlapped a shift change for the Battlestar personnel. Colonel Phillips therefore designated this as the main meal of the day, and his food preparation personnel did their best to make it special. Most days, they had eggs to order or pancakes, as well as biscuits and gravy, breakfast meats, fruit, and excellent coffee. This also was the time when Battlestar personnel could pick up their midday meal, an MRE.

Camp McCain, Mississippi, February 23rd

Next morning I again attended the shift change briefing at 0700. Taking my place at the front table near Colonel Phillips, I sipped coffee and took in overnight developments during JTFEX 99-1, where most of the activity still centered on the carrier and amphibious groups, which were beginning to enter the Gulf of Sabini.

The R3's part of the briefing was more interesting.

Colonel Phillips ran these sessions with a pleasantly relaxed, yet forceful style. He'd enter a room with a basketball under his arm and set it down on the table next to him. Whenever anyone screwed up his briefing—by being muddy or by missing a vital point—Phillips called out, "You've got the ball!" and heaved the ball at the briefer. Penance for screwing up was to carry the ball until the next briefing, and—more important—to make good on the shortcomings and be ready to brief the material again if asked.

Such antics offered more than just comic relief and a goofy way to handle mistakes. They were a significant element in Phillips's command style. His easygoing, nonthreatening, yet tough, technique helped him build deep-seated loyalty among his SF soldiers. Nobody wanted to "get the ball," yet getting it hurt a lot less than other ways of pointing out screwups. And it was not a bad way to motivate others to give their best effort, either.

As for the R3 itself: The units assigned to JSOTF were beginning to move to their assigned exercise locations. A C-17A Globemaster III transport aircraft from the 437th Airlift Wing at Charleston AFB, South Carolina, had picked up eighty Bolivian soldiers, and was moving them to Fort Polk via Roosevelt Roads in Puerto Rico. The lead elements of 1st/7th SFG had arrived in Louisiana the day before with seventy-two SF soldiers, and had begun to build FOB 71 in the same complex where JRTC 99-1 was played a few months earlier. The 1st/20th SFG also began to move, and would establish FOB 201 at Fort McClellan a few days later. R3 was beginning to move, and you could feel the energy building inside the Battlestar.

A few hours later, I was escorted into a small room for the COA briefing for what was now being called Operation Marauder (the overall name of the operations to be conducted at Fort Polk). I was about to get a look at something rarely seen—the process of deciding just how a military operation would be run in the field.

This particular COA would be unusual for a number of reasons. For starters, to test Battlestar's power and comm capability, only Colonel Phillips and his immediate 7th SFG staff from the Battlestar would be physically present. Unlike normal briefings of this type, the various unit commanders who would actually carry out Marauder were all miles away. Having already made their inputs via the satellite uplinks to the Battlestar Intranet, they would be informed of the JSOTF's intentions via e-mail and video teleconference.

Now a quick overview of what Marauder would involve:

The basic scenario centered on a small-town complex in the Peason Ridge area on the Fort Polk live-fire range. Known as Merrill Village, the complex has a dozen or so small buildings, where Military Operations in Urban Terrain (MOUT) training is normally conducted. For the purpose of R3, Merrill Village represented a sort of rural county seat, with several dozen inhabitants. As the R3 scenario opened, these civilian personnel had already been driven from their homes by Koronan insurgents, who wanted to use the village as a base to fill chemical munitions with mustard gas. The goal of Operation Marauder was to reverse this situation. Five phases were planned:

- **Phase I**—SF ODAs and other reconnaissance assets put the village complex (called Objective Frank) under surveillance, and maintain the effort until an assault force can be inserted.

- **Phase II**—Air Force Special Operations AC-130 Spectre gunships and three MC-130 Hercules transport aircraft deliver A Company of the 1st/75th Rangers by night parachute drop near the village. The Rangers will then assault Objective Frank, killing or capturing as many of the Koronan insurgents as possible.

- **Phase III**—Once Objective Frank is secured, a ground task force of SF soldiers from the 1st/7th SFG and the Bolivians (operating as a multinational coalition force) relieves the Ranger company and takes over control of the village. This will be followed by the repatriation of the villagers from a displaced persons' camp elsewhere on Fort Polk.

- **Phase IV**—To help bring life in the village back to normal, a civil affairs team will be assigned to provide relief, and a rebuilding effort will be initiated. At the same time, the combined SF/Bolivian task force will establish a security perimeter to protect the complex for the duration of hostilities.

- **Phase V**—When hostilities cease, the security/civil affairs teams will be withdrawn, and hopefully normal life in the village will resume.

If all its elements worked, Marauder would generate important results for the JTFEX 99-1 commander off of the Carolina coast. It would eliminate a major WMD problem for the 26th MEU (SOC), which would soon invade in the Gulf of Sabini; and it would provide a significant political advantage in the overall scenario, which translated into more time for the Navy and Marines to act in the primary action along the Atlantic coast.

While the basic plan seemed fairly straightforward, there were some important decisions to be made. Key among these was the guidance that would be given to combat units assigned to accomplish Phase II, arguably the most difficult part of the operation, as much for the many interlocking parts that had to be synchronized as for the potential combat power of the insurgents at the objective.

The overriding question: How will the units approach and assault the village, with a minimum of friendly casualties and collateral damage?

The briefing, which was run by the 7th Group Operations Officer (S-3), began with a short talk about the area where Marauder would take place.

Peason Ridge is mostly rolling, wooded terrain, but with a number of open, grassy meadows. Though rising fairly high out of the swamplands of the Louisiana low country, much of the area is still soggy. Merrill Village is located on the edge of a wooded ridge, running northwest to southeast. The area around it is lightly wooded, dropping down to an open meadow to the north. Numerous hard-packed dirt roads run throughout the area, and there is lots of ground cover.

The key issue discussed at the briefing was this: Should the Ranger company handle *both* the assault and their flank/drop zone (DZ) security, or should one or more of the other ground elements join them in the assault and relieve them of some of these problems?

Before the briefing, various courses of action had been proposed for the recapture of Merrill Village. These had been distilled into four assault plans by the S-3 (operations) Battlestar staff. And then the S-3 shop had laid out for each assault option a set of Mission Essential Tasks Lists (METLs) and scored each according to standard Army success/risk criteria. These options were then presented to Colonel Phillips and his staff, who discussed them seminar-style. Presenting all the materials and analyzing the options took several hours.

In the end, a consensus was reached that matched up with Colonel Phillips's command judgment, and the option was chosen that placed the bulk of the security and assault responsibilities upon the Rangers.

There were several reasons for this decision: First, it seemed to offer the best chance to fully utilize the Rangers' well-known ferocity and combat power. (Rangers are not subtle; they light their cigars with blowtorches.) Second, it offered a good likelihood that blue-on-blue casualties might be avoided in the confusion and darkness of the assault. Third, it offered the greatest chance of catching the insurgents by surprise, which was vital to the successful taking of the village.

The plan had weaknesses: The assault plan called for them to maneuver from their DZ north of the village around to the west and then an attack from the south. In that way surprise should be maintained and the most likely enemy escape route would be cut off (if they tried to move north, they'd have to cross meadows exposed to the Air Force Spectre gunship). Therefore, failing to follow the plan risked losing surprise . . . *and* losing the insurgents.

Given the limited forces available, Colonel Phillips felt that the plan's strengths outweighed its weaknesses, and he ordered his staff to send the battle plan out over the network to the various R3 CTF commanders. At his insistence, it was going to be an intentionally tough exercise, fraught with risks and some chances for foul-ups. Though some of the leaders and planners were worried that the absence of a full-scale dress rehearsal by all the units together might cause serious problems, it was hoped that the teleconferencing, networking, and other capabilities being tried in R3 would make up for that. In Phillips's view, making the scenario easy, and going less than all the way with the experiment, would corrupt the testing process. You have to admire his intellectual honesty.

Time would tell if he was right.

After the meeting, I was escorted into the room where the Rock Drill terrain model was being built. Already the contours of the Peason Ridge area were taking shape. Scattered around the worktables were the many small replicas of the Merrill Village buildings, as well as trees and other terrain features. Clearly, the model would be an excellent briefing tool for the planners and leaders when they gathered for their conference the following weekend.

My own plan was to leave the exercise for a few days and return when the action got hot. I wanted to be there for the Ranger assault on Objective Frank.

When I returned, I was informed, Lieutenant Colonel Mike Adams 1st/7th and Mike Rozsypal's JRTC Special Operations Training Detachment (SOTD) Observer/Controller personnel would be ready for me.

Main Post, Fort Polk, Louisiana, Friday, March 5th

After my many visits over the past four years, Fort Polk was starting to feel very familiar. In the morning, I drove to the post public affair office to meet my old friend Paula Schlag (the Fort Polk/JRTC PAO) for instructions, maps, and briefing materials.

It was a clear and beautiful late winter day, with only a touch of breeze in the cool air. All around, you could see and hear the hum of activity. Coincidentally with R3, a brigade of the 101st Airborne Division (Air Assault) was coming in for their annual rotation. The exercise they were to take part in, JRTC 99-3, would overlap the JTFEX 99-1/R3, making this one of the busiest times in the history of the center.

As she passed over the instruction packet, Paula asked me to report to the Special Operations Training Detachment (SOTD—the SOF O/C organization) headquarters, just across the street from where the 1st/7th SFG had FOB 71. I then drove the few miles over to SOTD, where I met up with old friends from JRTC 99-1, Lieutenant Colonel Rozsypal and Major Bill Shaw. Rozsypal's big news was his promotion to full colonel; he would soon be turning over command of SOTD to Lieutenant Colonel Joe Smith (who'd been commander of 2nd/7th SFG during JRTC 99-1).

It was a good and cheerful moment, but inevitably attentions turned to the coming operations.

The day-to-day R3 roleplaying had not, in fact, generated many changes. Already three SR teams from 1st/7th SFG were watching the area around Peason Ridge, passing along their observations to FOB 71 and the JSOTF. Two of these were assigned to watch Objective Frank (Merrill Village), while the other was to provide surveillance of the Ranger DZ, known as Burma.

Plans had the Rangers dropping onto DZ Burma at 2100 the next evening (Saturday, March 6th), with the assault on the objective an hour after that. Assuming that all went well, the link-up with the ground relief force, known as Task Force Sparrow (after Major Bernie Sparrow, the commander of the SF company that made up part of the force), would take place the following morning around 0900. This would be followed by a hand-off from the Rangers to Task Force Sparrow, who would then take over control of the village. The Rangers would then maneuver back to an exfiltration site to the north, where the MC-130s would land and pick them up for the flight home.

Meanwhile, back at Merrill Village the SF soldiers and Bolivian infantry would be policing the area for mines, booby traps, and other unexploded ordnance, so that the villagers could return ASAP. That event was scheduled to take place on Monday the 8th, with rebuilding and CA actions following that.

Once these goals had been accomplished, Operation Marauder would be over by the end of the week. All in all, a well planned and tidy schedule.

Now if events proved to be equally tidy . . .

I laid out my maps and SOTD-supplied briefing books, and quickly worked out the places I'd visit and my observation points.

My first trip took me to the camp where Internally Displaced Persons (IDPs—the current State Department babble for "refugees") from Merrill Village were located.[112] The IDP compound, about a mile from the SOTD headquarters in a pleasant little forest clearing, was completely surrounded by antipersonnel obstacles and wire, and contained a small tent village, complete with mess hall, showers, and recreational facilities. Inside were around two dozen IDP roleplayers (TRW contractor personnel), as well as a number of other "players," including representatives of the local constable's office and representatives of the Cortinian government who actually ran the IDP camp. Protecting the IDP facility were the Bolivian infantry that had flown in some days earlier via C-17. The Bolivians were being supervised by a 1st/7th SFG ODA team, who provided translation services as well as logistical support.

Though initially everything seemed quiet and pleasant, that wasn't exactly the case. Because of the simultaneous running of JRTC 99-3 for the 101st Airborne, Opposing Force (OpFor) assets were thin for R3. Nevertheless, there had already been several sightings of insurgent scouts around the IDP camp, as well as a sniper attack on the compound. Though nobody had been hit, the IDP roleplayers were getting edgy. And as I passed inside the wire, they were beginning to show unruly signs, and there were shouts: "When are we going home? When will the Americans win it back? When will our own government take charge again?"

Because of obvious Operational Security (OPSEC) considerations, the IDPs would not be told the details of Operation Marauder until after it was completed. Therefore, they would just have to sit tight until Merrill Village was liberated.

After I left the IDP compound, I headed back to my billeting area. Since I was scheduled to spend the entire night of the assault in the field, I'd need some "down" time for rest and preparations. It was good that I had that.

Fort Polk Live-Fire Range, Louisiana, March 6th, 1999

I slept late on Saturday . . . intentionally: I knew I'd get very little rest the coming evening. I gathered my gear, dressed in military Battle Dress Uniforms (BDUs), and headed out into a beautiful day that looked to warm up to the mid-80° F/30° C range.

By midafternoon, I had connected with Lieutenant Colonel Rozsypal at the Fort Polk live-fire range control complex. Located some miles north of the main post, this was the entrance to the Peason Ridge area. We parked our vehicles, climbed into an O/C HMMWV with our gear, and headed north toward Merrill Village. A half-hour later, we arrived at the settlement and parked a few hundred meters away. Walking in from the east, we identified ourselves as O/Cs and began to look around.

Just under two dozen OpFor personnel occupied the village (they'd been borrowed

---

112 If you think this sounds like recent headlines, you are right. Operation Marauder came very close to running exactly like a real-world ethnic cleansing/repatriation event in, say, Rwanda or Kosovo. Plan on seeing a lot more of these in the years ahead.

from the 101st for a few days). As the young captain (O-3) commanding the "insurgents" showed us around, it quickly became obvious that the Marauder plan was already beginning to leak a little.

One of the three SR teams on Peason Ridge had accidentally been discovered by the OpFor. About half had been "killed," while the four remaining had been taken prisoner. Meanwhile, a half-dozen Merrill villagers had been taken hostage by the insurgent soldiers, and were being held in one of the main buildings.

Clearly, the captain commanding the Rangers was going to have his hands full. One of his only sources of intelligence about the village was now out of action; and he was in total ignorance of both the SF POWs and the hostages. If any of these wound up "killed" as a result of "friendly fire" during the assault, that could later be judged as a "mission failure."

But the war gods tend to hand out bad luck evenly; and so, as it happened, the "rebel" intelligence proved to be just as bad. Interrogation of the captured SR team members had resulted in no information about the coming assault. In fact, they thought the main attack would come from SF soldiers on their western flank (not a bad guess—the woods in that direction offered plenty of cover, and the hill sloped down into the village).

Meanwhile, the OpFor was planning to face a force with superior numbers and firepower. To protect their position, they had spread over two dozen simulated land mines, fortified several of the village buildings, and scouted several escape and evasion (E&E) routes, including one that allowed them rapid evacuation with a commandeered truck.

Not surprisingly, in view of the lay of the land, their E&E routes all went south—right into the lanes planned for the coming Ranger assault. If the Ranger assault plan went forward as ordered, the insurgents would be retreating right into the attacking Rangers.

As the sun dipped behind the trees to the west, it was looking like the Rangers were going to have a very easy time when they made the assault scheduled some four hours hence.

But then, just as we were about to hand victory to the Rangers, Mother Nature came along and reminded us of who is the *real* boss. A fast-moving storm front was pushing in from the northwest, and the warm winter day, which had made our afternoon tour of Peason Ridge such a joy, began to rapidly change. Soon, the temperature plunged (by morning, it would drop to around 27° F/-3° C, bringing misery to everyone on Peason Ridge), and a fierce, gusting wind blew in from the northeast. For the attacking Rangers, this was potentially a worse problem, since the wind was blowing exactly 90° off-axis from DZ Burma and running at over 20 knots, with gusts over 25 knots. The strong off-axis winds meant that chances for the Rangers to successfully parachute into DZ Burma were rapidly heading into the toilet. (JRTC range safety rules dictate that drops with crosswinds over 12 to 15 knots should be waved off depending upon the gusts.)

If the wind kept up, the aircraft would circle for as long as possible, trying to slip in a drop between gusts. If the drop proved impossible, then the MC-130 transport aircraft would divert to the Army airfield at Fort Polk, and the Rangers would be bussed into DZ Burma. This would mean a delay of several hours, and might even cancel the night's operation entirely.

It was dark as I drove with Colonel Rozsypal in the HMMWV to the southern end of DZ Burma, and things were not looking good. We took shelter in the HMMWV, and grabbed a short dinner break (the colonel's driver had brought along a case of MREs and a thermos of hot coffee). After we finished, we camouflaged our faces with black and green paste (a JRTC O/C rule), and did what we could to stay warm.

Around 2000 hours, the O/C radio net came alive with the reports of observers reaching their posts and checking in. Overhead, we could hear an Air Force Special Operations AC-130 Spectre gunship moving into orbit (it would provide observation and fire support for the drop). Though the winds had faded a bit, they were still strong enough to make the drop problematic, and still cold enough to make life miserable.

We uncased our PVS-7B night vision goggles (NVGs) to look around the ridge for signs that the night's action had started.

A short time later, the AC-130 began to fire its "simulated" 105mm howitzer at nearby targets. All around us, JRTC contractor personnel were throwing fire markers that went off with bright flashes and loud bangs. At the same time, the rebels launched simulated man-portable surface-to-air missiles (called MANPADS for Man-Portable Air Defense Systems), which filled the night sky with rockets. It was an impressive fireworks display.

Meanwhile, the O/C drop zone team monitoring the situation at DZ Burma reported that wind conditions were marginal. If the crosswinds grew no worse, then the drop just might take place, albeit with a high degree of scatter. There also was concern that the wind might blow the Rangers into the tree line along the southwestern edge of the DZ.

A few minutes before 2100 hours, we heard turboprop engines to the northwest. Squinting through the NVGs, we could just make out the subdued running lights of the three MC-130s, flying in line-astern formation with about a mile separating them. Over the radio circuit, the O/C on the lead MC-130 was talking to the DZ team, trying to determine if a drop was still possible. The jumpmasters waved off the first two passes, but on the third pass they finally okayed a live jump. This window only opened briefly. For only a handful had exited the aircraft before the wind again gusted over 25 knots, and the drop was scratched by the jumpmasters on the lead MC-130. (In a real war, the jump would have gone off anyway.)

Meanwhile the half-dozen parachuting Rangers were drifting rapidly toward the tree line, and were quickly lost to our view. The MC-130s made one more pass, but the winds rose even stronger, and that was it.

The DZ O/Cs called the cancellation over the radio net, and the transports were ordered to head for Fort Polk. After a delay of several hours, the Rangers would be bussed back to DZ Burma, where they would be turned loose for their movement to Objective Frank. With the night's planned execution schedule in ruins, there was nothing for the O/C teams to do but round up the handful of Rangers who had been blown into the tree line, and try to stay warm. (The Rangers would be allowed to rejoin their companions when they arrived at the DZ, and would continue in play.)

We headed back to Merrill Village, pulled on our coats, and walked toward a campfire in the middle of the settlement. There we joined a dozen or so other O/Cs, and an impromptu planning meeting broke out around the warm blaze. Meanwhile, the OpFor, the "hostages," and the "POWs" snuggled down in sleeping bags and waited. Overhead in the circling AC-130, the O/C radioed down that he could see us on his thermal imaging system—one bright blob with a circle of smaller blobs around it.

It took almost five hours for the buses to get the Rangers to their line of departure at DZ Burma, and even longer for them to maneuver the several kilometers through the trees to Objective Frank.

It was coming up on 0300 hours Sunday morning when the OpFor troops were rousted out of their bivy (bivouac) sacks. Two minutes later, all the OpFor defensive positions were manned, and silence returned to the clearing.

The O/Cs doused their fire, and began to move to their observation positions. I quietly headed with Colonel Rozsypal over to a position at the base of a simulated water tower on the eastern side of the village where we would watch the attack. Standing at the base of the tower, we made sure we were visually marked as O/Cs (soft camouflage caps, etc.), trying to make sense out of the conflicting reports coming in over the O/C net on the colonel's radio. Clearly something was going awry with the Rangers' movement from the DZ.

Bear in mind that the original Marauder assault plan had the assault coming in from the south, following a march along the western edge of the village. Thus, in theory, we should have been seeing Rangers charging in from our left and moving uphill to our right. Now we were getting reports of the Rangers deploying to the north of the village, and the OpFor clearly was shifting their attention to that axis.

Suddenly, the predawn darkness was split by the blast of an air horn, the OpFor signal that attack was now imminent. Down to our right, we could see movement through our NVGs a few hundred meters away. The Rangers were moving up to the obstacles and wire barriers along the north side of Merrill Village, getting ready to make a direct assault on the main buildings in the complex. At least a full platoon was already directly in front of the large chateau in the center of the village, and another was flanking to the west.

Though it seemed like an eternity, no more than twenty seconds after the air horn blast several parachute flares fired from Ranger M203s flew into the sky and lit the scene with a golden glow. This was followed immediately by the chatter of Ranger-manned M249 SAW light machine guns laying down suppressive fire.[113] The fire was quickly returned by six OpFor insurgents in the main village chateau, and in moments the firefight was general.

Farther to our right, a Ranger M240G machine gun also began to pump fire into the chateau, while engineers began to move forward to blow breaches in the wire and obstacles. For several minutes, the fire between the insurgents and Rangers went on

---

113 Though R3 was held on the JRTC live-fire range, all engagements were conducted by personnel wearing MILES gear and firing blanks. The only live ordnance used were illumination rounds and some demolitions for clearing obstacles.

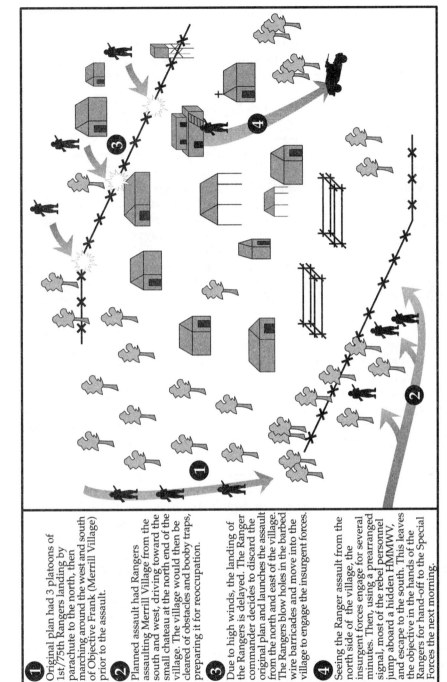

1 Original plan had 3 platoons of 1st/775th Rangers landing by parachute to the north, then marching around the west and south of Objective Frank (Merrill Village) prior to the assault.

2 Planned assault had Rangers assaulting Merrill Village from the south and west, driving toward the small chateau at the north end of the village. The village would then be cleared of obstacles and booby traps, preparing it for reoccupation.

3 Due to high winds, the landing of the Rangers is delayed. The Ranger commander decides to discard the original plan and launches the assault from the north and east of the village. The Rangers blow holes in the barbed wire barricades and move into the village to engage the insurgent forces.

4 Seeing the Ranger assault from the north side of the village, the insurgent forces engage for several minutes. Then, using a prearranged signal, most of the rebel personnel jump aboard a hidden HMMWV, and escape to the south. This leaves the objective in the hands of the Rangers for hand-off to the Special Forces the next morning.

A diagram of the attack upon Objective Frank during Operation Marauder.

RUBICON, INC. BY LAURA DeNNNO

unabated, until a loud explosion signaled the detonation of the first breaching charge. Seconds later, another charge was fired farther down the barriers, and Rangers began to flow into the open ground north of the chateau.

As soon as the Rangers began to pass through the obstacles, the captain commanding the insurgents again blew his air horn, signaling the rest of his command to begin their E&E to the south. Seconds afterward, almost a dozen insurgent soldiers were running like mad out the back of the chateau to the truck next to the church. Despite the intense cold, the engine started on the first try, and the rebels sped away in a spray of sand and gravel.

Though a number of insurgents had been "killed or wounded," eleven had escaped with their weapons. These included a mortar with twenty rounds and a MAN-PAD SAM launcher. Had this been a normal JRTC rotation, that force could have made a nightmare of planned operations over coming days. But because the R3 was an experimental scenario, the 1st/7th SFG would pay very little for the Rangers' mistakes. The lack of a dedicated OpFor (the R3 insurgents were borrowed from the 101st Airborne) meant that friendly actions the next few days would go unopposed.

Even so, we had just witnessed a major fiasco.

The O/Cs at the base of the water tower stared in wonder as the rebels escaped without so much as a notice from the Rangers, who continued to pour fire into the buildings of the village. (The Rangers were living up to their blowtorch reputation, firing at everything that moved.) Only a couple of the OpFor soldiers, probably cut off from the rest of their band, continued to return fire, as they tried to find a way out of the firefight.

Though firing would go on for a few more minutes, the battle was already over. By 0330 hours, the firing had stopped.

The Rangers had taken the objective, and as luck would have it, the hostages and POWs had survived the thousands of "rounds" poured into the building where they had been held. That was good news. Even so, the Rangers' problems would continue: The stiff wind had blown several Ranger illumination rounds into the ground cover to the west, and a number of small brushfires had started just outside the village. (It had burned several acres before the range service personnel got it under control; and it burned itself out.)

Meanwhile, there were OpFor minefields to deal with. Though the Rangers had entered the village through an unexpected—and therefore unmined—line of advance, it seems they got cocky, or reckless, or were pursuing the rebels, or were simply cold and exhausted (it's hard to say why), and a half-dozen Rangers stepped on simulated land mines in rebel-laid fields on the other side of the village, doubling the number of casualties taken during the assault.

Despite the Ranger-caused fiascoes, the good guys had won, Merrill Village was in the hands of the U.S. Army, and R3 could now move to Phase III.

As for me, it was time to retreat to the warmth of the HMMWV with Colonel Rozsypal for another cup of coffee and some rest. We stayed there until Task Force Sparrow arrived around 1000 hours Sunday morning.

It's time for serious questions: Isn't the point of the exercise to show how a more sophisticated command system, with better comms all around, can be made to

JRTC observer/controllers (including Lieutenant Colonel Mike Rozsypal, far left) look over Merrill Village the morning after the Ranger assault.

JOHN D. GRESHAM

work? What good did the increased info flow back and forth to Battlestar do? If Colonel Phillips had close to real-time info about Ranger actions, why didn't he just step in and order them to do what he'd wanted them to do in the first place?

The answers to these questions are complex: I said before that it's hard to fight and talk at the same time. Good commanders know that. Good commanders don't micromanage. They trust their subordinates to take the best actions under the circumstances they face. (A system that does not allow mistakes will never allow creativity; it will never grow.) So as soon as the Rangers left the DZ, they were for all intents and purposes offline, and this was part of the operational plan. The Ranger captain may well have seen risks on the ground that the plan did not foresee. So he may well have felt that the best option was a frontal assault on the village from the north. More likely, he screwed up. However, the Battlestar staff was unable to do anything to change the situation.

Fort Polk Live-Fire Range, Louisiana, March 7th

Dawn broke cold and overcast. The bad weather was expected to continue.

As we waited for Task Force Sparrow, we ate a breakfast of MREs and drank the last of Colonel Rozsypal's hot coffee. As we sat there trying to keep warm, questions filled the HMMWV: Why did the Ranger commander scrap the original flanking maneuver to the south and opt for a direct assault on the north side of the village? And why did he take himself and his men out of the Marauder plan, thus creating a command-and-control screwup?

No one had an answer, but we could make a likely guess: Hours late, exhausted, probably hassled by his own battalion commander (who was present and probably wondering why he was being bothered with this exercise in the first place), he simply decided to blow off the plan and take the objective in the most direct and quick way possible. It seems that intercommunity friction between the Rangers and Special Forces had again flared up, and the Ranger commander had been more interested in getting the assault over with than following orders from an SF commander.

And now Task Force Sparrow was an hour late, as a result of a navigation error by a lead vehicle in one of the convoys. Another lesson learned: Even satellite-based GPS receivers and perfect maps cannot overcome the mistakes of tired men with too much to do.

Because they were late, when Sparrow arrived their handoff with the Rangers was rushed, and went off poorly. Not only were the MC-130s due very soon on the dirt exfiltration field north of DZ Burma, but the Ranger company commander would rather leave than stay and explain how things had gone to Lieutenant Colonel Adams and Major Sparrow.

I can only imagine how frustrating these situations must have been for Colonel Phillips and the JSOTF staff back in the Battlestar center, who had followed the entire evolution of the exercise via the satellite communications links. They must have felt like the war gods had abandoned them.

Still, R3 had a long way to go. There would be almost another week of sustainment operations in Merrill Village, more than enough time to find out whether Battlestar could control two widely separated SOF missions at the same time.

But now it was time for me to call it a day. I had been up for almost twenty-four hours and needed rest.

Fort Polk Live-Fire Range, Louisiana, March 8th

By Monday morning the storm had moved off, and the day was clear and pleasant, a perfect day to head back up to Peason Ridge to watch the Merrill Village IDPs return home. Today I would ride up with Major "Fitz" Fitzgerald, another of the SOTD O/Cs I'd worked with in JRTC 99-1.

We drove up to a small clearing south of the village, where the rest of the O/Cs had parked their vehicles, and then walked past the checkpoint erected the previous day and into the village.

Overnight, the 1st/7th SFG and the Bolivian infantry had set up a tent camp just south of the village. They had closed up the obstacles and wire left behind by the OpFor, and now the whole village could be patrolled and secured. Major Sparrow had MP patrols (supported by UH-60 Blackhawk helicopters from the Kentucky National Guard) hunting for the escaped OpFor unit. (The Blackhawks had been provided to 1st/7th SFG after the 160th SOAR proved unable to support both the Eglin and Fort Polk R3 operations.) Clearly, the major was trying hard to make good the shortcomings of the previous day. He had a tight compound, a "big dog" presence outside the wire, and was ready for the next part of the operation: the repatriation of the Merrill Village IDPs.

The IDP convoy—four trucks to haul the villagers and their belongings—was surrounded by a phalanx of armed HMMWVs and had an overwatch escort of two Kentucky National Guard UH-60s. Along with the escort came a civil affairs detachment, which would run the repatriation effort in Merrill Village.

The convoy of internally displaced personnel (refugees) return to their simulated home at Merrill Village during R3. R3 not only simulated combat operations, but also peacekeeping and counterproliferation missions.

JOHN D. GRESHAM

With the help of the Battlestar center, Lieutenant Colonel Adams had carefully coordinated the movement of the convoy from the north side of Fort Polk to Peason Ridge with all the other elements involved. The convoy was kept in constant contact with the FOB at Fort Polk and Task Force Sparrow at Merrill Village. Today everything ran perfectly, and the IDPs arrived promptly at 1000 hours.

As the convoy passed through the checkpoint, I was joined by Major Tom McCollum who was now playing the part of the 1st/7th PAO. Along with the CA mission, USASOC was trying out a number of new ideas and technologies for their "Media on the Battlefield" program, and Tom was here to apply them.

When the convoy pulled up to a stop in the village square, soldiers from the security force helped some two dozen IDPs down and escorted them over to the gazebo at the center of the square, where they all sat to listen to the head of the civil affairs detachment (a female captain in the Army reserve) welcome them back to their homes. "Things are still a little rough," she told them, "and some of your homes have not yet been cleared of booby traps or mines that may have been left behind. So please be patient.

"I also hope," she went on, "that you'll understand the soldiers protecting the village might not always understand you or appreciate your customs. But please be aware that they'll do their best. And also be aware that Americans 'died' to free your village from the 'insurgents.' "

Her words didn't go over all that well with the IDP roleplayers. Already they were growing restless (they were a fractious lot): Some were unhappy that their homes were not yet cleared for moving in. Others were unhappy that Bolivian soldiers of the security force had dug a machine gun position in the middle of their livestock corral. And the next day, Major Fitzgerald explained, there would be a preplanned (but unknown to the SF players) civil disobedience incident.

I had no doubt that Major Sparrow's troops had their work cut out for them.

Fort Polk Live-Fire Range, Louisiana, March 9th

Once again, I rode up to Peason Ridge with Major Fitzgerald. It was another fine winter day.

A simulated riot breaks out in Merrill Village between contractor roleplayers. Such events provided R3 leaders a chance to deal with fast-breaking situations to test their new command-and-control systems. *JOHN D. GRESHAM*

Our plan was to discreetly enter the village, and be there when the preplanned "incident" took place (around noon). The idea was to stress the security and civil affairs teams, and see how they reacted to a fast-breaking crisis. While all the TRW contractor roleplayers and O/Cs were aware it was coming, the American and Bolivian soldiers had no clue.

When we arrived, the Americans and Bolivians were constructing a new clinic between the chateau and the church, and were focused on their work. We chose to wait out the situation on the second floor terrace of the chateau. Meanwhile, Tom McCollum, who'd sensed that something was up, had joined us with a loaded camera. Tom's an old SF team leader, and has a nose for such things; he was ready when trouble broke out.

Around noon, several trucks and vans full of people unexpectedly arrived at the compound security gate—"civilians" from another town seeking refuge from the insurgents until U.S. and Cortinian forces could resecure their town. They were admitted and directed into the village square.

Here things got messy. The Merrill villagers did not at all like sharing their village and its limited resources with the new IDPs (the two villages were rivals), and a small riot broke out.

After a time, local constables and the SF security detachment separated the two groups and called in the civil affairs team to sort things out. The Merrill villagers were moved to the gazebo, while the new IDPs were sent to an open area near the church, where a large tent was erected to provide shelter, and MREs and water were sent over.

Several hours of back and forth negotiations followed.

In a remarkably short time, thanks to the well-organized communications links, a Cortinian government official arrived and settled things down. Schedules were worked out for sharing facilities like cooking, bathing, and the church (for worship services). And because of the robust computer network linkages (in this case via satellite communications link), extra supplies, tents, and other necessary items were delivered via truck and helicopter in just a matter of hours.

In other words, properly employed, Colonel Phillips's Battlestar computers and communications links had made a difference in a fast-breaking situation in the field.

Other potentially messy situations over the next days were handled with similar dispatch.

Meanwhile, over at Eglin AFB things had also gone well (and bear in mind, this very complex operation was run in parallel with the Fort Polk mission): After a SCUD hunt of several days, the combat portion of the mission had climaxed with a nighttime raid on a missile depot. Aided by Terminal Guidance by 20th SFG teams on the ground, Air Force AC-130s had destroyed the missiles in their storage areas.

I went home convinced. In spite of the Ranger fiasco, and some ordinary mistakes (shit happens), the Battlestar concept of controlling SOF operations has demonstrated its ability to handle wartime data/communications loads . . . and to do that from the get-go: The effect of the better comms and computer power started at the COA briefing. They gave Phillips and his commanders more and better options, and went a long way toward eliminating stovepiping. During the exercise, they handled a pace and flow of data that no normal SF command center could have handled. Changes were accommodated and problems were resolved faster than ever before.

Battlestar works . . . to the degree that information can influence events. Even so, broader questions arise: More than a few SF soldiers, while impressed with the SF Battlestar concept, are concerned about misuse of the technology. They've seen too many commanders who are tempted to overcontrol. Micromanaging comes easy. I'll repeat: Good commanders trust their subordinates (and help them learn from their mistakes). Bad commanders micromanage. A few older hands remember when SF commanders used to ride around in helicopters and call down instructions to troops on the ground below. A *very* bad idea.

Today, with UAVs, satellites, and other imaging platforms, the potential for micromanaging exists on an even larger scale. A group commander or general at Fort Bragg could give orders in real time to SF soldiers on the other side of the world. Commanders will have to fight hard the temptations that capability offers.

Another question is more subtle: A command center that's thousands of miles from the action is thousands of miles from the risks and the dangers the guys in action are facing. Situational awareness and improved comms and improved flow are all good. But there's also a counterargument: The absence of stress and intensity and the "feel" for the action that comes from being near the battle might well hurt the performance of commanders. Which setup will work better? The answer remains very much open.

On a more positive note, the prototype Battlestar equipment exists today, ready to be deployed, if needed, in support of an overseas contingency. Given the current pace of SF operations, I would be surprised if that did not happen very soon.

Meanwhile . . .

- In Thailand and Laos, 1st SFG continues to remove mines, and in the Philippines to run force-on-force training exercises.
- 3rd SFG continues to train African troops as part of the ACRI program.
- 5th SFG continues its liaison operations with the Kuwaiti military.
- 7th SFG continues its counternarcotics and counterterrorist efforts in Colombia.
- 10th SFG continues its ongoing peacekeeping efforts in Bosnia and Kosovo.
- 19th SFG continues its efforts in South Korea and Southeast Asia.
- 20th SFG continues its work in Central America.

These are only fractions of the whole. The work goes on and on . . .

Operation Merdeka

"*Merdeka*" is Indonesian for "freedom." For Indonesians, as with all people, freedom is more than a value in itself, it also implies truth, justice, dignity, the absence of oppression, and a good life for oneself and one's family. For many people, Indonesians among them, these values understandably carry a sacred force. And this was especially the case in Indonesia during the heady years following the expulsion of their Dutch colonial masters, the years of the Sukarno presidency—years of grandiose, highly visible, and expensive "projects" and little economic or political progress. The word *merdeka* was a mantra with Sukarno. The national holiday, their Fourth of July, is called Merdeka Day. And Sukarno named his most grandiose projects and monuments "Merdeka This" or "Merdeka That." Thus, in Jakarta there is a Merdeka Square (on one side is the U.S. Embassy; on the other, the Presidential Palace) and a Merdeka Stadium. All over Indonesia, there are Merdeka parks and Merdeka bus terminals. For a time *merdeka* was a greeting, like "salaam," or "shalom."

Over the years, tens of thousands of Indonesians have died fighting for *merdeka*. And tens of thousands more have been murdered or massacred because they were thought to threaten it—Chinese, who had lived in the country for generations, because it was believed they had undeservedly taken wealth from the native born; Christians because they were not Muslims; Muslims because they were not Christians.

What did these losses gain? Not a lot over the years. Though there have been the trappings of democracy—president, cabinet ministers, and parliament, the Army has by and large run the country from behind the scenes. Instead of a government of, by, and for the people, it has been largely a government of, by, and for the Army. Outlying provinces have been operated as private fiefs by Army generals, for their own benefit. Many officers and soldiers hold murder and looting to be their legal right. The more thuggish and murderous of local militias (gangs used to put down opposition to the government, i.e., to the Army) have been supported and supplied by the Army. And in places like East Timor, the Army has been a force of anarchy and destruction rather than order and justice.

The Army has in fact a legal "justification" for its power position in the state. It was specifically charged by the Indonesian constitution to protect, guard, and nurture the nation. Army generals took that to mean they were licensed to run things the way they wanted. Some folks get more *merdeka* than others (as George Orwell observed in another context).

In the mid '60s, the corrupt but charismatic Sukarno was replaced by the corrupt but uncharismatic Suharto (an army major general before assuming the presidency) and a clique of equally corrupt cronies. Suharto brought greater order, and a measure of economic progress, but this was more than offset by his and his cronies' looting. They stole more wealth than they created—billions of dollars. Then they parked it offshore, where it would do the nation no good.

Indonesians are a volatile people, for whom rioting is an art form. In 1998, Suharto was driven out of office after weeks of increasingly violent riots. He was replaced by a friend and crony, Dr. B. J. Habibie, a technocrat of the most shallow kind, and a lover of extravagant and grandiose high-tech projects. Habibie was a joke, but his presidency was blessedly short-lived. He was replaced—democratically—by President Abdurrahman Wahid, a Muslim cleric, and by all accounts a man of integrity. His mandate was to reform the government (read for that defang the Army). As of this writing (early in 2000), he has made a brave start toward that goal . . . but it is a difficult and perilous journey, and Wahid's fragile health may not stand up to the hard job ahead.

What does all this say about *merdeka*?

It has yet to be realized for the two hundred million citizens of what *could be* the world's third largest democracy. Yet there is hope . . . and reason to fear.

2005

During his years in office, President Wahid had some modest successes, yet he failed to make Indonesia work. His body was simply not up to the strain . . . though it is arguable that *no* body could handle that much strain. He faced—and failed to solve—two intractable problems:

First, the Balkanization of the military.

It actually makes sense that a nation of thousands of islands provide itself with an effective navy and air force to provide protection against Indonesia's few external enemies (smuggling and piracy are greater threats than invasions). Conversely, a large army is not required (though a small, highly trained, and quick-moving strike force could come in handy).

Wahid managed to diminish the power of the army by getting rid of some of the more flagrant Neanderthals, thieves, and murderers within the officer corps, by starving it of money, and by playing factions against one another. At the same time, he funneled greater funds into the Navy and Air Force, and gave plum jobs to the relatively more honest and trustworthy, and better educated, Navy and Air Force officers. All of this did not, of course, sit well with the old-line Army officers who survived Wahid's assaults. They missed the constitutional perks that made them the guardians and "nurturers" of the nation, and they missed even more their easy access to the nation's money teats.

Second, the Balkanization of the country.

By 2004, Aceh (on the northwest corner of Sumatra) and Irian Jaya (western new Guinea) had become virtually independent, while sectarian fighting in the Moluccas (once the Spice Islands, now called Maluku by the Indonesians) had seen the killing of thousands and the destruction of much of the islands' infrastructure. By 2001, destruction by rampaging militias (Christian and Muslim) had devastated the provincial capital of Kota Ambon (Ambon City) on Palau Ambon (Ambon Island). There was scarcely a building untouched by gunshot or crude, homemade bombs. Tens of thousands of people tried to find shelter in the burned out, roofless buildings that had once been their homes. The militias destroyed water, power, transport, communications, hospitals, and schools. In 2002 the Army, abdicating responsibility (while continuing to support the more violent Muslim militias), abandoned the province to the mobs.

The Moluccas are not a chain. They are simply those islands in the Indonesian archipelago that lie scattered between the larger islands, Sulawesi and New Guinea, on a roughly north-south line. Because they were once the jewels of the Dutch empire and the prime source of Holland's spice wealth (in 1492, Columbus was headed in their direction), Dutch influence is heavy, and the islands had at one time a Christian majority (they were probably the most Christian area of Indonesia). But by the turn of the millennium, an ever growing influx of Muslims had made Christians a minority (though a large and powerful one).

For a time friction between Christians and Muslims was minimal. In fact, during the Suharto years (think of him as an Indonesian Tito), the two sides could actually be called friendly. Muslims would help Christians build churches, and Christians would help Muslims build mosques.

But with him gone, chaos . . . much of it inspired by Army agitators. Backward-looking officers seemed to think a grateful nation would welcome them as saviors: "You have to love us for snatching you out of the fire that we lit!"

Wahid died in 2002. After his death, the new administration had a weak president, Gajah Mada, and a popular vice-president, an Air Force general named Ratu Adil. Adil was popular with the nonarmy military and with a substantial portion of the ordinary people.

By 2004, the American-educated Adil (a B.S. from UCLA, and graduate work at the National Defense University in Washington) had managed to bypass his mostly ineffective presidential superior, and set in motion a small (but carefully thought out) number of positive initiatives. Among these was the JISF, a "Joint (i.e., multiservice) Indonesian Special Forces" group. This small, but highly trained (by U.S. Special Forces) organization was immediately put to good use in the Moluccas, where a JISF team, aided by U.S. Special Forces, succeeded in separating the warring factions, enforcing an uneasy peace, and making a strong start at rebuilding the islands' devastated infrastructure.

December 2005

This tenuously emerging peace in the Moluccas did not please everyone, and it especially displeased the Sons of the Jihad (the SJs), a violently fanatical Muslim sect based in Java, Indonesia's most populous island, and its economic and agricultural center. In retaliation for what they saw as a betrayal of their coreligionists in the Moluccas (and secretly urged on by the Army), thousands of SJs embarked on a holy jihad by boat flotilla to set things right. On 10 December, ten thousand Muslims sailed toward Ambon.

They could not be allowed to land there.

They were intercepted by the Indonesian Navy and diverted to an anchorage near Suli, a town on the east side of Baguala Bay, and about ten kilometers east of Kota Ambon.

Though they were prevented by Navy and JISF units from completing their "crusade," the situation was tense.

ODA 142 Team House
Pattimura Airport
Ambon, Indonesia
0526 25 December 2005

"Shit!" said Captain Carlos Valdez, Commander ODA 142, as the intense early dawn flash yanked him awake. The glare came from the direction of the rising sun, but it was incredibly brighter. Valdez, almost without thinking, rolled out of bed and put the cot—admittedly not much protection—over him. He had a pretty good idea what caused the flash. And it was just about the *last* thing he imagined he'd run into in Ambon. He covered his head with his arms and counted seconds. "One thousand one, one thousand two, one thousand three, one thousand four . . ."

The sound of the blast came. Noisy, but he'd been in thunderstorms as bad. Seconds later, the wind whipped through, fierce to be sure; yet again, not as bad as it could have been. Bad would have been 200 meters from ground zero (because you are instantly dead). Worse would have been three kilometers from ground zero (because you might live for a little while). If his rough and ready second counting was anything close to accurate, he estimated the nuke had been set off something like 20–30 kilometers away . . . 15–20 miles. "Good, the farther the better."

Valdez stood up, went over to his window, and threw open the shutters. Several kilometers away to the east, dark against the gray dawnlight, a lightning-splashed mushroom cloud was roiling up.

"Jesus!" he shouted at the top of his voice, without realizing it.

He had not yet begun to form serious questions. But on the outer edges of his consciousness a few were starting to take shape: The nuke hadn't hit the city, which was ten kilometers across Ambon Bay. It was to the east of that. *Where? Somewhere near Baguala Bay, probably.* But mostly, *Why?*

"Jesus!"

He thought of Karen and the boys. *Was this a worldwide thing?* he wondered. *The Big Madness? Or just a local insanity?* Something in him told him they were okay . . . that he was in the middle of some local insanity. *But I got problems!*

Another thought hit him: *Shit, Merry Christmas!*

Somebody was standing in his doorway (there was no door). "Sir, you okay?"

It was Valdez's warrant, Max Buser (called Bruiser by his friends), looking just about as dazed as Valdez felt. Like Valdez, he was wearing boxer shorts and a T-shirt.

"Yeah," Valdez answered. "You, Bruiser?"

"Ticking."

"Okay. Then let's get moving," Valdez said, realizing that they had a lot to do. Somebody had set off a nuke. And he knew he and the rest of his ODA had been instantly elected to do what they could to help survivors and start the cleanup.

Luckily, his guys were not alone. They would be aided by a few good friends.

The team was not actually located on the airport proper, but a stone's throw away in the village of Laha, on Ambon Bay. They had boats there, which gave them an edge in mobility. The ODB commanding them (ODB 140) was located at the airport itself, housed in a loaned Indonesian Air Force facility. Another ODA (146) was in Kota Ambon, and a third (144) at Passo, a town on the narrow isthmus that separated the two peninsulas that made up Palau Ambon.

It hit Valdez just then that Passo, which was east of the capital, would have been awfully damned close to ground zero. "Shit," he muttered to himself, "we're going to have to get help to them, and pretty damned fast."

He turned his mind again to available forces:

They would have Indonesian help. Especially useful would be Lieutenant Colonel Kumar's two companies of JISF guys. The JISF had replaced the army in the peace-keeping role in the Moluccas, which was the prime reason the islands had achieved something like peace and stability. Kumar was a good guy; he and Valdez had grown close over the months they'd been working together. (He remembered just then that JISF units were at Siri, on Baguala Bay, forming a firewall against the madmen of the Sons of the Jihad. *Shit*, he thought. *That can't have been far from ground zero.*)

There was also the local police—newly created and far less effective and reliable than the JISF, but sure to do more good than harm.

Valdez and Bruiser were by then at the team's comms center, a few doors down from Valdez's room. And moments after that they learned that their comms were actually (as designed) hardened against EMP (Electro-Magnetic Pulse) effects from nuclear weapons. That meant the SF guys could communicate with each other, and with their 1st SFG superiors in Okinawa and the U.S. It also meant that they were probably the only people on the island who could communicate with anybody (with the possible exception of the JISF, but there was no word from Kumar yet). The EMP had surely fried transistors in phones, cell phones, radio, TV, and computers . . . and probably all the navigation and safety systems at the airport.

Meanwhile, ODA 142 got its marching orders from Major Ron Carver, the ODB commander. The team was to be split. Valdez would take half over to the Kota Ambon side of the island and get himself up to the top of Gunung Sirimau, the 950-meter high hill that would provide the best visibility of Baguala Bay. It was Carver's estimate (like Valdez's) that the nuke had probably been set off somewhere on or near the bay. Carver also had a pretty good idea what the nuke had been set off to destroy—the Sons of the Jihad flotilla anchored off of Siri. Though who had done it, and why, remained a very open question.

Valdez's job was to gather information about damage, and get some idea about survivors.

The other half of the team would race over to Passo (there was a decent road along the coast), and do what they could for the team there. The ODA in Kota Ambon would link up with Kumar's people. Carver estimated it might be two days before serious relief help arrived. Until then, it was going to be largely up to them and the JISF to organize the medical and relief efforts.

The White House
Washington, D.C.
1713 24 December 2005

"So what gives?" the president asked, visibly out of joint, as he entered the Situation Room. The furthest thing from his mind was a call from Admiral Len Croce, the Chairman of the Joint Chiefs of Staff, urgent enough to pull him out of the Christmas Eve party his wife had set up for the rest of their very large and usually very spread-out-across-the-country family—sons, daughters, and their husbands, wives, and children. He enjoyed his family; he did not like to be dragged away from them on the most joyous holiday of the year.

The president, a tall, lanky, loose-limbed man, was wearing a pastel-colored cardigan, and he was accompanied by a Corgi dog. He had the almost too-relaxed manner of a Mister Rogers, and this had charmed the electorate into believing he would be another presidential grandfather like Eisenhower or Reagan. The manner was deceiving; he was not as easygoing as he looked (any more than Eisenhower and Reagan had been). He had served with distinction in the Gulf War, successfully run for Congress, and then was elected governor of a populous western state (which he had governed well). He was tough, decisive, and short-tempered.

And the dog was obedient. The president murmured a command and it lay down quietly next to the chair the president usually occupied. Then the president looked around, expecting to see more than the two top advisors now present . . . until it hit him that it was Christmas Eve. They were accompanied by a pair of high level gofers whose names escaped the president.

The expression on Croce's face was grim. Next to him stood Richard Callenbach, the president's National Security Advisor, also grim.

"Mr. President," Croce announced, "word came to NMCC from Colorado Springs a few minutes ago that our DSP Pacific bird has picked up a double-flash in Indonesia." He paused for a second to let that sink in; and in case it didn't, he added, "Somebody has set off a nuke."

The National Military Command Center at the Pentagon is the clearinghouse for military significant events. Defense Support Program satellites, in geosyncronous orbits, sense bursts of high-intensity thermal and other radiation. They see, in other words, events like rocket launches and nuclear detonations. The double-flash the DSP satellite observed in Indonesia was a sure signature of a nuclear explosion. The DSP bird then relayed the news to the 11th Space Warning Squadron at Shriever AFB near Colorado Springs, who fed the data to the NORAD warning center at Cheyenne Moun-

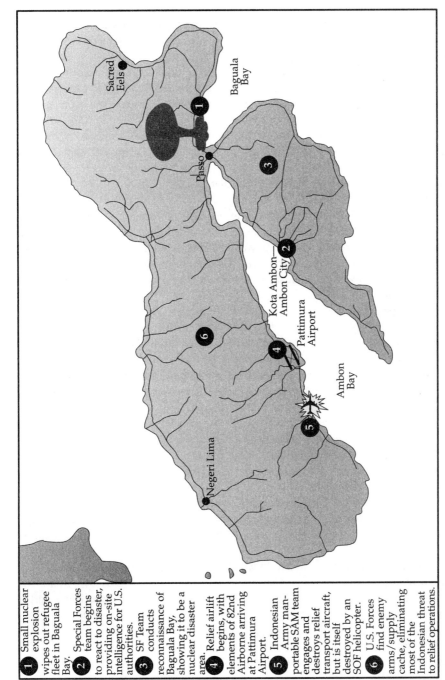

1. Small nuclear explosion wipes out refugee fleet in Baguala Bay.

2. Special Forces team begins to react to disaster, providing on-site intelligence for U.S. authorities.

3. SF Team conducts reconnaissance of Baguala Bay, showing it to be a nuclear disaster area.

4. Relief airlift begins, with elements of 82nd Airborne arriving at Pattimura Airport.

5. Indonesian Army man-portable SAM team engages and destroys relief transport aircraft, but is itself destroyed by an SOF helicopter.

6. U.S. Forces find enemy arms/supply cache, eliminating most of the Indonesian threat to relief operations.

Sacred Eels

Baguala Bay

Passo

Kota Ambon—Ambon City

Pattimura Airport

Ambon Bay

Negeri Lima

RUBICON, INC, BY LAURA DeNINNO

tain, who then relayed it to the NMCC and the president. If a clear and present danger to the nation had been perceived along that path (such as missile launches whose warhead trajectories ended in the United States or near U.S. facilities overseas), the president would have been informed in a few score seconds. In the current situation, where the risk to the U.S. was seen as more remote, it took half an hour. During that time the CJCS and other high-level national security types availed themselves of that interval to inform themselves of current American military and relief capabilities in and around Southeast Asia. They wanted to be able to give the president some options.

"Where exactly?" the president asked.

"Early estimates put it in the Moluccas, on the Island of Ambon," Croce answered. He had come prepared with an open map, marked with the spot. Then he added, with a puzzled look, "There is nothing militarily significant there, or strategically or economically significant either, for that matter."

"You're saying it's an accident?"

"No . . . though it could be. I'm saying we have no idea why—barring an accident—anyone would want to set off one of those things there. Indonesia has no real enemies. None of the nearby nuclear powers—China, India, Pakistan—has any reason to be angry. The Indonesians themselves have never lusted after nuclear weapons. They don't even have any nuclear power plants. Local oil covers all their energy needs."

"So it could have been an accident," the president mused. "Or they could have done it to themselves . . . assuming they got nukes. Which we know nothing about." This last was a subtle rebuke. U.S. Intelligence *should* know who has nuclear weapons.

"It's possible," Admiral Croce allowed.

"What I'm thinking is that there's been a lot of shit hitting the fan in that part of the world. Muslims fighting Christians and vice versa and crap like that. Not a lot of folks wear haloes."

"Possible," Croce repeated.

"But why would anybody nuke themselves," the president continued to muse. "I heard of shooting yourself in the foot . . . done it myself more than once." He smiled at his own wit. "But this goes a little far." He glanced over at his National Security Advisor. "So what do you think, Dick?"

"What you say, Mr. President, makes sense." He shrugged. "But Indonesia is an Asian country—a muddle wrapped in a mystery, wrapped in misdirection—and I wouldn't venture to try to explain events there until I had a lot more facts than we do."

"So let's get some facts. What do we have over there? Anything? Anybody? . . . And where are the carriers?" he added.

"There we may be in luck, sir," Croce responded. "We've got the better part of a Special Forces company actually on Ambon, working with an Indonesian special forces unit and the local police, doing peacekeeping, communications and police training, and civil affairs infrastructure things. I've got people trying to get in touch with them as we speak. You have to understand, sir, that communications will be initially dicey. The EMP."

"I understand."

"I also talked to CINCPAC on my way over here. He'll be giving me a list of units he can swing into Indonesia fast . . . And we may be in luck here, as well. There's a CVGB on a port visit in Perth, Australia, along with its Marine MEU (SOC) and ARG. We should be able to get them up near Ambon four days after you give the word."

"Tell CINCPAC to start them moving. If we have to stop them later, we can do that."

"They probably have already received the warning order. I'll flash the go-ahead to CINCPAC." He gave a nod to his aide, who moved to the side of the room and picked up a phone.

"And what else?"

"I have anticipated that we'll need to go to DEFCON 4. And I recommend DEFCON 3 for those units in the region, or bordering it."

"Go ahead, do that," the president ordered.

DEFCON numbers represent states of military alertness. There are five of them. Peace is DEFCON 5 (peace in the sense that we have nothing serious to worry about right now). At DEFCON 4, command authorities are beginning to get a little nervous. At DEFCON 3, forces go on increased alert. At DEFCON 2, the threat looks imminent. DEFCON 1 is war. At DEFCON 1, pray for the survival of the human species.

"And tell me what you hear from those Special Forces guys. I want to know what's going on out there. And I want to know now."

"Yes, Mr. President," the CJCS and the National Security Advisor said as one.

"Meanwhile," the president said, finishing up, "we are going to very soon get inundated with questions and alarms from the media. I don't want to deal with them until we have some kind of handle on this thing. But have a statement for them from me drafted by morning. And have my speechwriters rewrite my Christmas address."

"It will be done."

"Oh yeah, unless there's an overriding need, I don't think you'll need to call in other advisors tonight. You two will be enough . . . and it is Christmas Eve."

The White House
Washington, D.C.
0245 25 December 2005

"Captain Valdez, how are you?" The president spoke into the phone receiver. The line had been patched through to Valdez via SATCOM to Pattimura Airport, from where there was a good line of sight to the top of Gunung Sirimau, where Valdez and his team had set up for observation. "Can you hear me okay?"

"Just fine, sir," Valdez answered.

"So tell me what you see."

"Yes, sir," Valdez answered. "We're situated at the top of a small mountain, sir, about three thousand feet high. It gives us a good view of Baguala Bay. Ground zero was maybe five kilometers—three miles—from our position.

"There was a flotilla of small boats across the bay anchored next to Siri, a little town there, sir. They called themselves the Sons of the Jihad."

"I know about that," the president interrupted.

"Okay, sir," Valdez said. "It looks to us like the bomb was set off in the water, close to shore, or maybe on shore a little ways. Whoever did it didn't like the Jihad. The flotilla's vaporized, sir. And so is the town.

"We've also got heavy blast damage all around the bay. And it raised up a pretty big wave. There were six or seven towns around the bay. Not much of them is left . . . wiped clean, sir. We had an ODA—an A-Team, sir—at one of them, Passo. I don't think they made it." The president could hear the other man choking up on that.

"I'm sorry," the president said, knowing how lame that must sound. "They will be in our prayers."

"Thank you, sir." Then he continued, not wishing to linger on the loss of friends. "The JISF—Indonesian Special Forces we've been working with, sir—also lost some guys over at Siri. They have already sent some other guys in along the bay on Land Rovers. I don't know yet if they have found survivors.

"The mountain we're on, sir," Valdez continued, "has given the city, Ambon, good protection. Shadow effect. I doubt if there is much damage there . . . maybe a few broken windows. And the airport is on the other side of another bay—Ambon Bay—from the city. The airport's okay, too. That means the airport can handle relief aircraft . . . and Ambon Bay can handle ships."

"Good. So the damage was pretty much limited to the other bay area?"

"It appears so, sir. It could have been a lot worse."

"Do you have any idea, Captain, who did this thing? Or why?"

"Not really, sir. Somebody didn't like the Jihad."

"So it appears. Somebody with a bomb."

"Yes, sir." Valdez anticipated the next question. "But we have no information, sir, about nuclear weapons in this part of the world. They shouldn't be here."

"They shouldn't be anywhere," the president murmured, almost inaudibly.

"So what about fallout?" the president asked, moving on (he had a list). "Can you give us some clues about where that might go?"

"It was a dirty weapon, sir, a ground burst. It had to have picked up lots of water and lots of dirt and other stuff. That's the bad news. The good news is the prevailing winds tend south this time of year . . . the good news for us," he amended. "It doesn't look like we'll get any rain today. I'd worry if we were. But south of here they could have problems. Timor's maybe just over 300 miles downwind, to the southwest. And Darwin in Australia is less than a thousand. They could get some bad shit, if you pardon me, sir."

"I've heard worse. And it describes the situation only too well. I don't think our Australian friends will be very happy."

The president moved the phone receiver away from his face. "I want to talk to the prime minister when I finish with the captain," he said to his National Security Advisor.

"We have U-2s up from Kadena AFB, Mr. President, in Okinawa," Admiral Croce broke in. "They'll be monitoring the fallout situation and taking samples. Analysis of these should tell us within seventy-two hours exactly where the weapons were made. And what kind of fallout situation we can expect. We will also send a DOE

NEST team"—Nuclear Emergency Search Team—"from Las Vegas to monitor the situation on the ground."

"Good. That will be something. Meanwhile, our Aussie friends are going to be mega-pissed." And then a spark lit his eyes. "Which is not necessarily a bad thing. They're going to want to take some action. They could be a big help."

"They will be, Mr. President," Croce said. "I already have people talking to people in Canberra."

"Fine, fine," the president said, "we have to move fast." He then resumed his conversation with Valdez. "Anything else you can tell me, Captain?"

"No, sir. Not now, sir."

"Thank you, Captain."

"Yes, sir. Thank you, Mr. President."

It was now three A.M. in Washington.

Richard Callenbach's female aide approached the president. "Mr. President," she announced softly, "I think you need to look at a report we've just taken off the BBC World Service." She pointed a remote at a TV screen, and a nice-looking blonde Brit female news reader appeared:

"Minutes ago," she announced, "Indonesian Major General Nusaution appeared on all the Indonesian national networks to make a startling announcement with reference to the even more startling nuclear explosion in the Moluccas early this morning." The face of the general appeared onscreen. "According to General Nusaution," she went on, "the Indonesian Armed Forces have been in possession of nuclear weapons for the better part of a year. These weapons, and I quote, 'were obtained for purely defensive purposes, and were placed under the very highest security. Even so,' the general continued, 'through treachery at the highest and most trusted level, one of these weapons was stolen, and passed into the hands of Moluccan Christian radical separatist fanatics. They detonated that weapon in order to destroy the Sons of the Jihad . . . and to permanently end the possibility of Muslim–Christian coexistence in Indonesia. We will provide conclusive evidence of this Christian conspiracy shortly.

" 'These fanatics pose imminent danger to the nation,' the general concluded. 'The Army will, as always, protect the nation from all enemies—internal or foreign.'

"General Nusaution has left more questions unanswered than he has answered," the BBC announcer concluded. "First, how did they come to acquire nuclear weapons, and from whom? Second, *why?* And third, how could one of these weapons be stolen from a presumably secure facility?

"So far, there are no good answers to these questions. We hope to have more answers soon. This is Linda Sillitoe reporting from Jakarta."

The aide clicked off the screen.

"Not a bad analysis," Richard Callenbach observed.

"It still leaves more questions than answers," Admiral Croce answered.

"It does confirm one thing," the president said. "You were right, Dick. The place is a muddle wrapped in a mystery wrapped in misdirection. Do you all realize that there may well be not a single truthful word in that general's statement?"

"How do you know that?" Richard Callenbach asked. He was the president's resident skeptic.

"My nose itched, Dick. My thumbs prickled. And ask yourself this: What Christian would set off a nuclear weapon on Christmas Day? Mark me on this: Some idiot who doesn't know the first thing about Christians has set the Christians up."

Callenbach raised a skeptical eyebrow. But Croce's gaze was more thoughtful. "If you're right about that, sir," he said, "then we may have much bigger problems in Indonesia than disaster relief in the Moluccas."

"You bet," the president said, pleased that the admiral had caught his train of thought. "There are two hundred million Indonesians. We could be seeing something starting to go down there worse than former Yugoslavia.

"Could the nuke have been the first shot in a civil war?

"Whatever's going down there, I don't want to be caught flat-footed. Let me know by morning what we can do . . . if we have to do something."

"We'll do that," Admiral Croce said.

"We'll need to put together a coalition," Callenbach added. "It can't be an American affair. And the existing Asian security collectives don't really cover the case . . . especially if it turns out there's a civil war."

"It's too bad this thing is not in the NATO sphere," the president added to that thought. "Yeah, this can't be an American affair: We need to bring in the Aussies and the Brits, of course, but also Thailand, the Philippines, Singapore, and Malaysia (they'll be initially reluctant, but they'll come aboard after the others do), and any other suspects. Get working on that now.

"And by the way, the Indonesian government—or *somebody* over there . . . somebody crazy enough to use it—has got their hands on at least one nuke. If there are others, find the bastards . . . *now*!

"Today's was the first nuke fired in anger since Nagasaki. I want to make sure those crazies don't fire off another one . . . in, say, Jakarta."

Kota Ambon, Moluccas
1750 25 December 2005

JISF headquarters was located in what had once been police headquarters in Kota Ambon, on the corner of Jalan[114–115] Raya Pattimura and Jalan Ahmad Yani. Carlos Valdez hoped to find Lieutenant Colonel Kumar there, and he was in luck, but only just barely. Kumar was on the way out.

"Hi, Kumar," Valdez greeted his friend. "What gives?"

"I'm on my way out to meeting Sam Fireside and I have set up with all the various local leaders." Captain Sam Fireside was Commander of ODA 146. "We've rounded up all of them: Christians, Muslims, militia commanders, the whole catastrophe. And then we are going to draw water from the moon."

114–115 Indonesian for *street*.

"Water from the moon?"

"An Indonesian saying: 'Do the impossible.' They *will* cooperate, with us and with each other. If they don't, they'll get no transportation, no communications, no support, and no medical aid."

"That should encourage them to listen to sweet reason."

Kumar made a sad, lopsided grin. "You're welcome to join us."

"I'd like to. Sparks will fly . . . before sweetness prevails. But I can't. I'm on my way back to Pattimura to brief Major Carver; I decided to stop here on the way for a heads-up."

Kumar was short, slender, and very trim. His English was fluent (though Valdez was comfortable speaking Indonesian); he had been educated in the States, at Texas A&M.

"Here, take a look." He handed Valdez a piece of paper, printed on both sides in Indonesian. "We used our printing press you gave us to turn out thousands of these. Your Chinooks have been dropping them over the eastern parts of the island all afternoon." (The Chinooks had come with CH-47D [4] of the California Army National Guard, on scene to provide the Special Forces with air support and transportation.)

The leaflet told Valdez what he expected to find: "There has been a nuclear explosion." (*In case you don't already know.*) "Below are directions to move to safety. If you or someone close to you have the following symptoms—nausea, vomiting, diarrhea, fatigue, headache, shortness of breath, rapid heartbeat—you need immediate medical care.

"Medical care can be found at aid stations located in the following towns: Rutung, Lateri, Hunut, and Tulahu." (These were the closest relatively undamaged towns to ground zero.) "Everyone must obtain and take potassium iodide pills to ward off radiation sickness. These would be available soon at the following locations." (A list followed. The pills were being flown in from Australia, and Valdez was eager to start taking some himself. They helped sweep the zapping nasties from your body.) "Seriously injured would be transported to a hospital in Kota Ambon. If you know of anyone unable to help themselves, please inform officials at the above locations or any JISF soldier or officer you encounter." There were maps and other graphics.

Leaflets were a longtime Special Forces specialty. It was the world's oldest technology for getting word out to large numbers of people, but still effective—especially in situations, as here, where the more technologically advanced media were inoperative. Valdez was pleased that Kumar and his JISF guys had learned the lesson so well.

"Looks pretty good," he said to Kumar. And then, "How are things going out there?"

"We have people in boats and SUVs combing through what's left of the towns around Baguala Bay. There aren't many survivors there."

"Your guys at Siri?"

Kumar's shrug showed more than resignation. There was anger, too. "There's nothing left there. Wiped clean. But they've been able to pull a few people out alive a few kilometers away . . . and across the bay."

Another disturbing thought occurred to Valdez, "There's no protective gear here. Your people on the bay will be taking more rads than they should."

"We'll lose a few of them," Kumar snapped bitterly. "Americans aren't the only heroes."

Valdez gave his friend a sharp but pained look. "I'm sorry."

"*I'm* sorry," Kumar replied quickly, immediately repentant for his outburst (which to an American was hardly an outburst; to an Indonesian it was a serious breech). "I shouldn't have said that."

Valdez could only guess at the pain and stress his friend was feeling. These were his people out there suffering.

"Your people are mostly backing us up with communications and C and C," Kumar went on, "but your medics have joined ours out in the four frontline towns."

"And how is it out there?"

"Ugly. Very ugly. We're getting initially walk-in survivors, of course—blast and thermal damage, flying debris. Not much radiation yet—and what we do find are certain to die; it was a dirty bomb—but there'll be more, surely."

He gave Valdez a suddenly impatient look. "I have to go."

"We'll get through this," Valdez said, by way of farewell.

"*We* will," Kumar answered bitterly.

The Ministry of Defense Command Center
Merdeka Square, Jakarta
1930 25 December 2005

The Indonesian Military Command Center was a large, high-ceilinged room furnished with ranks of long tables and computer terminals. On the front wall were three large screens, on which could be projected maps, slides, or video.

The Indonesian vice-president, Radu Adil, sat at the front table, taking in the current situation. Currently dreadful. Nusaution's announcement, and its follow-up "proofs," had had the expected effects: The nuclear weapon exploded inside their country had sent students and other customary rioters berserk. Sectarian rioting had broken out in Jakarta and all over the country, especially in Java. Though the riots were "reportedly disorganized," the initial signs were bad. Christians and Chinese (always the scapegoats in Indonesia) were being hunted down and murdered. It could get worse.

"*Reportedly disorganized.*" That was, of course, official bullshit, and Adil knew it. The riots were the work of Army instigators. They were foreplay leading up to some kind of orgasm that would spark an Army takeover attempt. The big question now for Adil: How and when would it come?

He and his friends and allies were prepared for it. Had they prepared enough? Another big question.

Next to Adil sat the Minister of Defense, Untung Sutopo—like Adil, an Air Force general—and the commanders of the Army, Navy, and Air Force: General Yani, Admiral Suwandi, and General Omar Dhani. All of them allies of the president, Gajah

Mada. (Adil himself had come from a group technically opposed to Gajah Mada. He was made vice-president as a consensus-building measure.) The president himself was in his office in the Presidential Palace, but there was a link-up, and he occasionally made remarks through the public address system (usually inane, in Adil's view).

All eyes, except Adil's, were riveted on one of the large screens on the front wall, where General Nusaution (the official Army spokesman) was making another announcement over state TV. Adil had directed his face dutifully toward the screen, but only half his attention was there. Nusaution's words, delivered in an "authoritative" and patronizing tone, were predictable—diatribe and invective and unfounded charges aimed at Christian fanatics and Moluccan "splittists" (a Chinese coined term he had picked up to denote separatists and secessionists). They had brought the day's tragedy on themselves, he intoned in a voice dripping sanctimony. Yet it should also come as a warning to other "splittists" and Balkanizers. Disorder and anarchy will not be tolerated. Martial law has been declared, and the Army, under the direction of a group calling itself "The Committee for the Restoration of the Republic" is restoring order. Keep calm. Stay home. Don't resist.

"So they're moving now," Adil said to himself, not exactly surprised.

At that moment he lifted a phone receiver and punched in a number. After fourteen rings someone came on at the other end.

"Merdeka," the voice said.

"Activate Delphi," Adil said, then called the president on his private number. There was no answer. Unsurprised, he replaced the receiver in its cradle and waited.

He did not have long to wait. Seconds after Nusaution had finished his speech, army troops in combat gear were standing in all the exits. They were led by a colonel Adil knew vaguely. His name was Cancio.

Very quickly and smoothly Cancio moved in, and was soon standing in the space in front of the screens.

"Be calm," he announced politely, though with none of the deference you'd expect he would offer military superiors. "This is a precaution to restore order. Please do not resist."

He then approached Adil and leaned down close to his ear.

"The president is dead," he whispered. "You can cooperate or not. Your choice. Your family are," he paused significantly, "in our care. Your cooperation will make you useful to my superiors. I suggest that you comply. You will be taken by helicopter to a safe place."

Adil gave a brief nod that might be taken as assent. He knew he had no choice.

Cancio pointed in the direction of a major. "He'll be responsible for you. You'll be safe with him."

Cancio then slipped his pistol out of its holster, and, with four quick, accurate shots, put bullets into the heads of the Minister of Defense, General Yani, Admiral Suwandi, and General Dhani. They slumped across the table.

"Traitors," he said calmly, then led the major and Adil to a helicopter waiting on the rooftop pad.

Jakarta
2330 25 December 2000

Jakarta was a madhouse. The news of the Army intervention did not calm the rioters, it only inflamed them more. Buildings and cars were torched, shops were looted. There were dozens of deaths and hundreds of injuries. Though considerably reinforced Army troops had tried to restore order, they were clumsy and ill-trained for the job; as the night progressed, the mayhem in the streets had actually increased . . . and it had been terrible during the afternoon. (The coup leaders had predicted an easy transition to their rule; this was not their only, or their worst, miscalculation.)

Paradiso 2001 was a small Chinese vegetarian restaurant down an alley off of Jalan Sabang, and a ten-minute walk from the American Embassy. Two men, an Indonesian and an American, met there very late and took a quiet booth, with the expectation that chances were slim that either would be recognized. Both were in civilian clothes. The Indonesian was wearing tan slacks, batik shirt, and a *pitji* cap, the Indonesian national headgear. The American was dressed like a tourist, in shorts, flowered shirt, and baseball cap (New York Mets). The American was not a tourist; he was the American Air Attaché, Air Force Colonel Anthony Meyer (who had been in-country long enough to know that Indonesians frown on shorts). The Indonesian was Radu Adil's top aide, Widodo Suratman.

The meeting was Delphi.

Suratman, who had not eaten since morning, ordered braised Chinese broccoli, fried rice, and tea. Meyer sipped on a Tsingtao beer while Suratman waited for his meal.

"I have been authorized by Vice-President Adil," Suratman said, after a decent diplomatic interval, "to pass over to you certain sensitive information. He will also make, through me, requests of the United States, which he hopes your country will honor.

"But," he added, with pleading eyes, "in whatever way you use this information, and whether or not you honor the vice-president's requests—you must understand that this meeting never happened."

"Agreed," Meyer said.

"You must also understand that the president has been executed. Yani, Suwandi, Dhani, and Sutopo were all murdered at the Ministry of Defense Command Center. The vice-president was observed to leave the ministry in a helicopter with an Army colonel named Cancio and an unidentified major. He can be presumed to be alive— they could have killed him with the others, but did not."

"Did he leave voluntarily?"

"If you mean by that, 'Is he one of the conspirators?' Hardly. They evidently feel they can use him. He is respected in and out of the military. He would make a useful figurehead."

"Is he weak enough to stand for that?"

"I think he would choose to stay alive until the alternatives look worse."

Suratman moved on: "The coup now underway may well fail. I'd put the odds in its favor as no better than even. The conspirators have miscalculated their support among the people . . . and among the military. The Navy and the Air Force will not back them. Nor will all the Army outside Java. But they are very strong in Java.

"The conspirators call themselves the Committee for the Restoration of the Republic—the CRR," he explained. Meyer nodded; he had heard the name earlier. "Their leader is General Tono Bungei, the Army commander of Java."

"Not Nusaution?"

"He is a spokesman only, though the others have led him to believe he is more than that . . . that he is, in fact, number two; but the real leaders use him only as a . . . how do you say? A stalking horse?"

"Close enough."

"We have prepared a list of the top people in the CRR, and other relevant information—military units likely to back them, units likely to oppose them, and units likely to stay neutral." He passed over a Zip disc. The American slipped it in a shirt pocket.

"The one monkey in the works . . ."

"Monkey wrench," Meyer corrected, with a friendly smile. "My Brit friends call them spanners."

"Monkey wrench then," Suratman corrected himself. ". . . is the nuclear weapons."

Meyer looked at the other closely, his eyes steely.

"I must speak very plainly," he said. "It has never been the intention of my government to acquire nuclear weapons. *Never*. The weapon that exploded this morning was *never* in the possession of my government. It was one of five acquired by Tono Bungei and his Army rogues, for their own use."

Meyer took that in for a time, then asked, "Who'd they get them from?"

"We don't know, but my guess would be Pakistan. The generals there, like ours, are Muslim; to them there is a mystique about a Muslim bomb . . . It is only right to share this gift of Allah with Muslim friends . . . And besides, the Pakistanis need money. They grow more impoverished by the second."

"And why did you wait to tell us this?"

"It is still our country. We have our pride.

"I want you to know also," he continued, "that the story the rogues have given out about this morning's tragedy is a lie. The rogues themselves are completely— *totally*—responsible.

"They thought to kill four birds with one stone. First, to *really* hurt the Christians by putting the blame on them. Second, to set off chaos elsewhere, especially in Java. (In that they have succeeded.) Third, to encourage the others. As in: 'Don't forget, people of Indonesia, that we have nuclear weapons, and we will use them if we must.' And fourth, to give the conspirators justification for a government takeover (to restore order and stability—the usual disguise for a power grab)."

"It's not a bad plan . . . if you have the morals of Hitler. Who would use WMDs on their own people? . . . Who outside of Saddam Hussein?"

"Exactly. It is a plan from Seten"—from Satan.

"Vice-President Adil would like these instruments of Seten to be removed from our country."

"And he'd like us to do it?"

The other did not answer him.

"The rogues are keeping the nuclear weapons at an army facility near Bandung . . . adjacent to Bandung's Husein Sastranegara Airport." This was once a multimillion-dollar showpiece aircraft plant, Merdeka Aircraft (promoted by Habibie when he was Suharto's Minister of Research and Development; it was one of Habibie's dream children). After its inevitable failure, it was transformed into a clandestine Army facility.

"We have obtained schematics and blueprints of this facility, as well as maps, photos, and other relevant data. You'll find them on the disc I gave you."

Meyer looked at the other with greatly increased respect.

"It is likely, I will add, that they have taken Vice-President Adil there. I hope you will use this information carefully and wisely. All of this is a momentary irritation for a great power such as the United States. It is a historical turning point for my country."

"Count on it."

The White House
Washington, D.C.
1525 27 December 2005

The Chairman of the Joint Chiefs of Staff greeted the president as he entered the Oval Office. In his hand was a folder containing what he thought of as very exciting show-and-tell. He was about to brief his boss on the Indonesia situation.

Len Croce himself showed signs of wear and tear. He hadn't gotten a great deal of sleep over the past forty-eight hours. The president, by contrast, was well rested. He had returned only minutes before from a Christmas swing through his home state. Adoring crowds energized him. The president was wearing a bright red cardigan, partly in honor of the season and partly in honor of his mood, which was the emotional equivalent of Manifest Destiny.

"So, Len, where do we stand?" the president asked the chairman brightly. He expected good news.

"We've made real progress, Mr. President," Croce answered. He passed the folder to the president, who dropped it on his desk, unopened. "Briefing material, charts, and such like," he added, by way of explanation. "You'll find it helpful."

"I'll look it over," the president answered distractedly. He was famously uninterested in military briefing materials.

"The first thing we have," Croce began, "is an early analysis of the atmospheric particles the U-2 picked up." The president gave him a go-ahead nod. "It was a Pakistani-made weapon, based on a Chinese design, probably built about four years ago (it was an early Paki model), and it had a yield of between 50 and 60 kilotons. A nasty piece of work, but not big—as weapons go; a nuke, not a thermonuke."

"I'll have State get on that," the president mused. "We can turn some pretty big screws on the Pakis and the Chinese. They both could use knocking down a peg or two," he added with less than perfectly battened-down delight. Sticking it to the Chinese always played politically. "This will give us nice leverage."

"Yes, sir," Admiral Croce agreed, and quickly moved on. "As for post-detonation effects . . ."

"Fallout?"

"Right. The weapon was not a clean design to begin with, and the blast—a ground burst—lifted up a lot of local materials. Timor, which is south of Ambon, got a heavy dose yesterday. There'll be casualties."

"Deaths?"

"Very likely."

"What will it take to get help to them?"

"There is still a UN presence in East Timor, and it is very heavily Australian. The Aussies have agreed to augment that with medical personnel. West Timor—the Indonesian side—will also accept Australian help."

"Then it is not our problem?"

"Not all problems are ours."

"Yeah!" the president agreed with some force.

"The Aussies, of course, are having problems of their own with the fallout. It's beginning to register in Darwin."

"Bad?"

"Not so far . . . and we don't expect it to be nearly as serious as Timor. The bad stuff has had several more hundred miles to dissipate.

"Of course," he added, "there could be local hot spots. These things never take their course with a nice, predictable smoothness."

"And the Aussies . . . ?"

". . . Are pissed," Croce finished. "As we knew they would be. The diplomatic traffic between Canberra and Jakarta has been even more blistering than the PM's public statements—and they have been very tough."

"Good," the president said, unsurprised. This confirmed his own estimates of the Australian reaction.

"Needless to say, the Aussies have taken a strong position in the Southeast Asia Coalition." The hastily formed coalition to deal with the problem had quickly come to be called SEAC. "They're totally onboard—both in the relief end and the military end. They would have gone with us anyway, but when they started getting a dose of rads . . . and then heard what Adil had to tell us . . ." He let that thought go uncompleted.

"Terrific," the president said, very pleased indeed. "And how about the rest of SEAC?"

"We're not telling all of them everything. But State has been feeling them out about military actions. We think they'll all approve in the end. Nobody wants to see nukes going off, especially in their own neighborhood. And everybody would like to see Indonesia stable and peaceful. But they're nervous about us intervening. The idea is to frame it all carefully, so everything we need to do appears absolutely unavoidable and necessary. State is working on that."

"That's fine."

"And I'd like to go on to relief efforts, Mr. President."

"Go ahead."

"They've started to reach the site," Croce said. "But it will take another couple of days for the whole thing to get there. Essentially, we'll have the 82nd Airborne in there for blast site relief, and the 82nd Airborne commander will also double as JTF commander. We'll have the CVBG from Perth in the area within another couple of days. And we'll be beefing up the Special Forces units already on scene (who have carried the whole weight of this thing so far—they and their Indonesian counterparts; they are doing an *outstanding* job). There'll also be air and logistical support.

"The Time and Phase Deployment Schedule that's in the folder will give you some idea of the way that will work."

The president opened the folder and gave those pages a glance. "Right," he said.

Unit	Start Location	Transport Mode	Transport Time	Delivery Location
Units On-Site in AOR				
ODB 140 (Balance Petrol)	On-Mission, Indonesia	N/A	N/A	N/A
ODA 142 (Balance Petrol)	On-Mission, Indonesia	N/A	N/A	N/A
ODA 144 (Balance Petrol)	On-Mission, Indonesia	N/A	N/A	N/A
ODA 146 (Balance Petrol)	On-Mission, Indonesia	N/A	N/A	N/A
CH 47D (4) California Army National Guard (ANG)	On-Mission with ODB 140, Indonesia	N/A	N/A	N/A
13th MEU (SOC) and USS *Bataan* (LHD-6) ARG	Port Visit, Perth, Australia	Self-Steaming	A+4 Days	As Required
USS *Abraham Lincoln* (CVN-76) CVBG with CVW-11	Port Visit, Perth, Australia	Self-Steaming	A+4 Days	As Required
Regional Units				
Company B, 1/1st SFG	Okinawa	4—C-130 (374th AW/ Yokota AFB)	A+2 Days	As Required
Company F, 2/1st SFG	Okinawa	4—C-130 (374th AW/ Yokota AFB)	A+3 Days	As Required
HQ (FOB 11) 1/ 1st SFG	Okinawa	4—C-130 (374th AW/ Yokota AFB)	A+2 Days	As Required

Unit	Start Location	Transport Mode	Transport Time	Delivery Location
Regional Units				
AC-130U Spectre Gunships (4)	Hurlburt Field	Self-Deploy	A+4	As Required
MC-130H/P (4)	Kadena AFB	Self-Deploy	A+2 Days	As Required
MH-53J Pave Low Helicopters (4)	Kadena AFB	4—C-17A (62nd AW/ Fairchild AFB)	A+3 Days	As Required
SOCPAC HQ	PACOM HQ, Pearl Harbor	2—C-17A (62nd AW/ Fairchild AFB)	A+2 Days	As Required
Army MPS Squadron	Agana Harbor, Guam	Self-Steaming	A+6 Days	Blast Site for Disaster Relief/ Peacekeeping
MPS Squadron-2	Diego Garcia	Self-Steaming	A+4 Days	Blast Site for Disaster Relief/ Peacekeeping
III MEF	Okinawa	Assorted Airlift	A+6 Days	Blast Site for Disaster Relief/ Peacekeeping
CONUS Units Deploying to AOR				
1/505th PIR	Fort Bragg/ Pope AFB	6—C-17A (437th AW/ Charleston AFB)	A+36 Hours	Blast Site for Disaster Relief/ Peacekeeping
2/505th PIR	Fort Bragg/ Pope AFB	6—C-17A (437th AW/ Charleston AFB)	A+48 Hours	Blast Site for Disaster Relief/ Peacekeeping
3/505th PIR	Fort Bragg/ Pope AFB	6—C-17A (437th AW/ Charleston AFB)	A+56 Hours	Blast Site for Disaster Relief/ Peacekeeping
505th PIR HQ and Attached Units	Fort Bragg/ Pope AFB	12—C-17A (437th AW/ Charleston AFB)	A+56 Hours	Blast Site for Disaster Relief/ Peacekeeping
1/75th Ranger Regiment	Fort Benning	6—C-141B (SOF) (305th AW/McGuire AFB)	A+36 Hours	Nuclear Storage Depot
NEST Team	McCarren International Airport, Las Vegas	1—C-130 (Department of Energy)	A+24 Hours	As Required
JTF Headquarters (82nd Airborne Division HQ)	Fort Bragg/ Pope AFB	6—C-17A (437th AW/ Charleston AFB)	A+36 Hours	Blast Site for Disaster Relief/ Peacekeeping

Unit	Start Location	Transport Mode	Transport Time	Delivery Location
CONUS Units Deploying to AOR				
1/XVIII Aviation Brigade (OH-58D, CH-60, CH-47E)	Fort Bragg/ Pope AFB	24—C-17A (437th AW/ Charleston AFB)	A+5 Days (Gradual Buildup)	Blast Site for Disaster Relief/ Peacekeeping
Company C, 1/1st SFG	Fort Lewis	4—C-17A (62nd AW/ Fairchild AFB)	A+3 Days	As Required
Company A, 1/ 19th SFG (ANG)	Buckley, WA	4—C-17A (62nd AW/ Fairchild AFB)	A+5 Days	Blast Site for Disaster Relief/ Peacekeeping
Company C, 1/ 19th SFG (ANG)	Murray, Utah	4—C-17A (62nd AW/ Fairchild AFB)	A+6 Days	Blast Site for Disaster Relief/ Peacekeeping
III MEF	Okinawa	Various Airlift	A+6 Days	As Required
7th PSYOP Group	San Francisco, CA	3 C-5B 60th AW/Travis AFB	A+2 Days	Blast Site for Disaster Relief/ Peacekeeping
2/358th Civil Affairs Brigade (USAR)	Norristown, PA	5 C-5B 60th 436AW/ Dover AFB	A+3 Days	Blast Site for Disaster Relief/ Peacekeeping
Allied Units				
Tactical Assault Group (TAG), Australian SAS Regiment	Perth, Australia	Embarked with 13th MEU (SOC)	A+4 Days	As Required

The president closed the folder, then asked, "And the Indonesian authorities?"

"Too busy with their own problems to do more than make gloomy noises. There have been statements attributed to Adil, who is the nominal head of state, condemning SEAC on general principles. But they can hardly complain very much about our relief efforts. What are *they* doing to help, after all?

"More to the point. The new government has not been able to take control of Java, much less the rest of the archipelago. In other words, they don't carry any real weight. They don't like us moving into their country, but all their complaints are just pissing in the wind."

"Can they win?"

"Will their takeover succeed, you mean? It's very doubtful, Mr. President. But the longer they hold the reins—even if it's a phantom horse—the more trouble they can cause. Civil war is a real possibility. That would be a terrible catastrophe, with decades of very bad long-term consequences."

"We have to prevent that," the president said, and then added, "and they have nukes."

"They have nukes. And they have demonstrated no qualms about using them against their own people. These are very bad guys, Mr. President."

"So then . . . ?" the president asked, with a *come on* gesture.

"The materials from Adil are priceless, Mr. President."

"And it's certain that the bad guys are using him . . . that he hasn't gone over to them."

"As certain as we can be. They want a respectable figurehead. He fits the profile."

"He's a great patriot," the president said. "And far more courageous than I am. I hope he survives. I'd like to meet him."

"With those materials, sir, we have a damned good shot at getting those nukes. And we'll do our best to make sure he survives.

"The operation itself is relatively simple," he continued, "not unlike some things we did in Panama a few years ago. We have a Ranger regiment now transiting to Darwin. They're the class act when it comes to taking airports. They can secure just about any airport in the world in twenty minutes. They'll take the airport at Bandung. And the Aussies' SAS has a Tactical Assault Group who are ideal for taking the nuclear storage depot."

"Good idea, using the Aussies."

"Yeah, and they're totally right for the job."

"We will also probably want to use a pair of B-2s to soften up opposition," the admiral added.

"When will this all go down?"

"The night of the 31st."

"Thanks, Len. And by the way, get some sleep."

"I'll try, Mr. President."

Jakarta, Java
0430 28 December 2005

Two large, long-range CH-53E Super Stallion helicopters, from USS *Bataan*, set down in Merdeka Square near the U.S. Embassy, after a lengthy flight (assisted by inflight refueling) from the ARG/CVBG steaming north from Perth.

The previous day, the embassy had informed the Indonesian Foreign Office that a detachment of Marines from 13th MEU (SOC) would arrive by helicopter to beef up embassy security. The Foreign Office saw this as a reasonable request (most embassies in Jakarta, including America's, were by then being emptied of all except essential personnel), and it was duly acknowledged and approved. A no-brainer: The rioting had continued to grow in intensity, and ever increasing Army counterviolence had done little to calm the anarchy in the streets.

The Marines would arrive on detached diplomatic duty, and they would, of course, have diplomatic immunity.

As it happened, the U.S. Embassy had suffered very little at the hands of the mobs—a few tossed stones and eggs. With the expectation that this low-threat situation would continue, the Marines had come primarily armed with nonlethal weapons. But to be on the safe side, they also had a variety of lethal antipersonnel weapons.

The Marines, as it also happened, were not all Marines. Joining them on one of the CH-53Es were a pair of ODAs (163 and 168) and a six man ODB (161) from Company F, 2nd/1st SFG, based on Okinawa (all of them in Marine drag). The ODB set up in the embassy, while their comms went on the roof, among the embassy antenna arrays. All electromagnetic emissions became one to those who might have liked to listen in.

Meanwhile, the ODAs turned in for a good day's sleep. They would need it. Starting that evening they would be very busy boys indeed.

Pattimura Airport
Palau Ambon
28 December 2005

Three days after the nuclear explosion, Pattimura had taken on the look of Tempelhof in the days of the Berlin Airlift. New and (as it happened) much improved air traffic control equipment, flown in by the earliest flights from Kadena Air Force Base on Okinawa, had replaced the EMP-fried Indonesian electronics. Streams of aircraft—an air bridge—were now taking off and landing. Containers and shipping pallets had been piled in every available open space. To carry off all that stuff to where it was needed, local transport had been taken over by JISF. At any given moment, most of this could be found either at Pattimura or moving to or from it, while commandeered buses connected the refugee camps with the capital, and doubled as ambulances.

Field hospitals had been set up in the camps, with triage stations closer to the blast site; specialized units to deal with severe thermal or radiation burns and other serious traumas had been set up in Kota Ambon.

By this time, the most immediately pressing actions had been accomplished: Survivors had been coaxed, carried, or driven out of the danger zone near the blast and herded into camps; most of those who required medical attention had received some kind of care; and everyone on the island with any sense was taking potassium iodide tablets.

The refugee camps were crowded, and shelter was scarce and far from comfortable, but overall conditions were far from appalling . . . and they were improving daily.

Meanwhile, the major portion of the 82nd Airborne had arrived and set up adjacent to the airport, along with various headquarters facilities: the 505th PIR HQ (under a brigadier general); the JTF HQ (under a major general, the 82nd Airborne commander); and an enlarged Special Forces HQ (FOB 11, 1st/1st SFG, under a lieutenant colonel) to supplement ODB 140.

Airport security was tight. There was *much* to protect—arriving American servicemen and servicewomen (thousands of them), medical and technical people and equipment (including teams from NGOs like Doctors Without Borders), and billions of dollars worth of hardware. A single C-17A transport, for example, weighed in at around $220,000,000. That's a lot of school lunches.

Happily, Ambon Island was far from being "denied" territory. The JISF troops were friendly, cooperative, and effective; the majority of the Ambonese people had also proved to be friendly and grateful (the better than yearlong U.S. Special Forces presence had ensured that); and even previously warring religious factions were keeping the peace. And yet, unhappily, there was no scarcity of unfriendlies in Indonesia.

Some of these made their presence felt on 28 December.

The MH-53J Pave Low helicopter is big, fast, and a kludge—not so much purposefully designed for Air Force Special Forces operations[116] as cobbled together out of available systems (inside it looks like Dr. Frankenstein's laboratory in one of its comic manifestations). It is built around a basic CH-53D Sea Stallion air frame, it is heavily armed, heavily protected, heavily equipped with electronic equipment (FLIR, terrain-following radar, the works), it carries a five-man crew, and it leaks fluids[117] like rain. But kludge or no, don't mess with one. It does the job.

Air Force Major Al Tatum commanded the Pave Low detachment flown in from Kadena. As soon as his four birds were checked out as flyable, he asked ODA 142 commander Carlos Valdez to accompany him on an orientation flight. He wanted to get a good look at the island, the blast site, the camps, and anything else he needed to be aware of—or that might pose a potential threat. They took off on that flight at 0830 on the morning of the 28th.

At 1020, they were hanging around over the Bay of Ambon, waiting for clearance to land at Pattimura. Tatum was then in the right-hand commander's seat, chatting with Valdez, who was in a jump seat behind him. The copilot, Bob Thornton, was at the controls.

The flight path for fixed wing aircraft put the normal final approach over the villages of Hattu and Leke, west of the airport. Their Pave Low was south of that.

As they waited, a C-130 was passing over Hattu (it was carrying medical supplies, they learned later), when Thornton cried out, shocked, "SAM!" and pointed to a pair of corkscrewing trails of smoke beyond and below the big plane.

Valdez watched, fascinated, not sure what he was seeing . . . But also wondering with a chill down his back if the missiles had been shot at them.

"Christ!" Tatum groaned, turning away from Valdez to look. "Goddamn!" And then, "I've got it." He took the controls, his hand on the throttle, shoving it forward.

Meanwhile, in answer to Valdez's fears, the corkscrews ended near the port engines of the C-130, instantaneously followed by twin flashes as their warheads blew. The starboard wing lifted, and then the aircraft twisted and tumbled out of the sky. As Valdez watched, transfixed, it plunged into the forest just off the coast road, two thirds of the way between Hattu and Leke.

The Pave Low by now was traveling at high speed, 160 knots, heading for the spot where the twin corkscrews had emerged from the forest. Valdez saw an opening there, probably a yam patch some farmer had hacked out of the jungle.

In addition to the pilot and copilot, Pave Lows are manned by two gunners, who operate a pair of 7.62 mm Gatling guns. A third Gatling, aft, is manned by the crew chief. These don't give you heavy-duty firepower, but they make up for that (in most cases where you need them) by laying down a *fast* stream of lead. Gunners fire them the way firemen use a fire hose. One sweep will cut a man in two.

As they hurtled toward the coast, Tatum called out instructions to his gunners,

---

116 The Air Force is not famous for paying a lot of parental attention to its Special Forces component.
117 The joke goes: "If it don't leak, it ain't a Sikorski . . . or else you're out of hydraulic fluids."

his voice clear, calm, precise, yet tense with rage: "Gentlemen, we're gonna get the bastards that took out our C-130. Check out your guns, please, gentlemen."

This order was quickly followed by a series of clicks and snaps, as the gunners prepped their guns.

By this time, Valdez was himself caught up in the rage he could feel swelling through the aircraft.

Transport aircraft are vulnerable, and essential, in an operation like the one then underway. Without the air bridge, the relief effort would starve. Whoever had shot down the C-130 had wanted to threaten that. *Why?*

At the same time, the United States Air Force takes threats to any of their aircraft *very* seriously. And even transports come equipped with protective measures—chaff, flares, and other tricks of the trade. In fact, the larger aircraft can move with surprising agility if they have to. Even they can dodge missiles (man-portable SAMs have short legs—their maximum range is about five km., but their optimal range is only one or two km.). Tragically, no one had expected such an attack. This was a bad guess. *On the other hand*, Valdez was thinking, *if you shoot down a U.S. Air Force aircraft don't expect the other cheek to get turned.*

A rack contained four M-4 carbines. He worked his way out of his jump seat and grabbed one, checking it over quickly to make sure it was ready to fire. It was. He placed himself to one side of one of the now open doors.

By then they had crossed the coastline and were descending; Tatum was throttling down, starting a tight circle that had the little field as its center. It had taken the big chopper less than two minutes to cover the distance from the bay to the SAM site.

The standard procedure for SAM shooters involves a quick in and out—shoot and scoot. And that was what the bad guys were doing. There were four of them, two shooters and two spotters, and they were hustling toward the jungle, maybe fifteen meters from its hope of safety (a triple-canopy forest wilderness covered the interior of the northern peninsula; only the coast was inhabited), when the Pave Low arced behind them. None of the four expected the cavalry to gallop over the hill that fast; and they all panicked. Three of them tried to put on a burst of speed; the fourth dove for the ground. It turned out that he made the best move. The Gatlings make a noise that has been described as the fart of the gods. Valdez listened, fascinated, to the gods farting, as he watched a laserlike stream of 7.62 mm projectiles cut through the three runners. The gunner then sent the briefest of bursts in the direction of the man on the ground, to encourage docility.

The Pave Low made a couple of fast circuits around the field to make sure there were no other bad guys . . . and that the three that were down were truly down. Then it settled to the ground, not gently; the two gunners and the crew chief, armed with M-4s and sidearms, leapt out, with Valdez following.

Valdez headed for the fourth man; the others for the three nearer the forest.

His had been hit . . . not directly, it appeared, but by ricochets. He was still alive, and he was wearing the uniform of an Indonesian Army officer (a captain, Valdez recognized); an AK-47 lay where he had dropped it, not far from one of his hands, and a holstered pistol was at his side. He had been hit in the thigh and shoulder, and was in a great deal of pain, though the wounds weren't life threatening.

Valdez was a little surprised to find the man in uniform . . . because of this very eventuality. Why would the Indonesian military want to proclaim responsibility for shooting down a U.S. aircraft? Did they have Saddam's crazy chutzpah?

"*Bangsat!*"[118] Valdez called out to the other man in Indonesian as he approached, his carbine leveled. "Can you hear me?" he continued in Indonesian.

"Yes," the captain murmured.

"Get rid of your pistol. And then give the Kalashnikov a good toss."

The Indonesian officer gave him a pained look, indicating his wounds.

"I don't give a ratfuck how much you hurt, motherfucker! Get rid of your weapons!" Valdez screamed out in English. Even so, the other man got the idea, and very delicately removed his pistol from its holster and flipped it away into the yam patch. He then crawled to the AK-47, struggled with it for a second, but managed to give it a heave.

"Okay," Valdez said, satisfied. He moved closer. "Now let's see about patching you up."

As he said that, one of the gunners showed up to announce that the other three were truly and finally out of the picture forever. Then he went off into the yam patch, to find the discarded launch tubes. A few minutes later, he reappeared. "They were Russian SA-16s," he told Valdez, then went over to give the same message to Major Tatum, who by this time was out of the Pave Low and checking out what had been wrought.

Valdez, meanwhile, was thinking: *Unless these bastards are acting on their own—not very likely—they have a cache somewhere in the jungle. If we find where that is, no more SAMs . . . probably.*

Later, after they had clambered back into the helicopter, and the Indonesian had been safely stowed with his wounds patched up enough to allow him to be moved, Valdez took Al Tatum aside and cocked his head in the direction of the wounded man. "This guy needs to have a date with a friend of mine, Kumar, the JISF commander over here," he said. "Do you think you can run me and the Indonesian back to Kota Ambon? I kind of think Kumar will take him into a room and shut the door while I go out and have a beer. When I come back, I'm pretty damned sure Kumar will be able to tell me where they have cached their other SA-16s."

Tatum gave him a tight, pleased smile. "Fine by me," he said. "Can I join you . . . for that beer? I hear they make a pretty good brew in Ambon."

"Sure thing."

———————

By the time the Pave Low was lifting off from the yam field, Air Force traffic controllers back in Pattimura had already placed local airspace in high-security mode. A pair of OH-58D helicopters (all that were available at that point) were put on watch along the approaches to the airport. The OH-58Ds are FLIR-equipped, and armed with a variety of antipersonnel weapons (rocket pods and 50-caliber machine guns). They could reply to other SAM launches swiftly and decisively.

---

118 The rough Indonesian for "bastard" or "asshole."

In order to warn aircraft of actual launches, teams of ground spotters were sent out along the airport approaches.

And finally, air traffic had to be slowed down, and everything coming in that was not essential (or low on fuel) had to be put off until after nightfall. That meant a slowdown on the air bridge, but that couldn't be helped.

Man-portable SAMs are simple beasts that do not work well at night. They are visually aimed and visually tracked. Darkness makes that difficult (darkness or bad weather cut vulnerability to such missiles by 80–85%). On top of that, the missile's ability to home in on heat sources comes in the form of a simple sensor on the missile itself. There is no thermal-imaging capability in the aiming and ground guidance system, nor any kind of sophisticated radar guidance. All of these nice things come in packages that are too heavy for people on foot to handle. In other words, man-portable SAMs are nothing but simple bazooka-type systems with a heat-seeking nose. Even at that, they weigh in the neighborhood of fifteen kilos. That's a big load if you're walking.

All this also requires some kind of central storage location.

And that was a big reason why Carlos Valdez wanted to find where that was hidden.

He was not wrong in thinking he would not have long to wait.

RAAF Base Darwin
Darwin, Australia
28 December 2005

Flying very long distances is hard work. You lose lots of water. You lose lots of electrolytes. You lose lots of time zones. You come out of the silver tube a dehydrated zombie, your body clueless about what the hell time it is.

You need downtime—rest, rehydration.

Rangers are mean, and they are *tough*. One big reason why they are trained to be in top physical condition is to give them the ability to get on an aircraft in battle gear and then get off it eighteen hours later and swarm out fighting. (These aircraft, it should be noted, do not come equipped with cute stewardesses, in-flight movies, or seats you'd want to sit in for more than about ten minutes.)

That they can do that is a good thing. But they are also human. They'd rather not. And if they can, they'll take a day or two off after a world-spanning flight to get their bodies back in synch. That's what they did when they arrived at RAAF Darwin on 27 December.

Meanwhile, their soon-to-be partners, the Tactical Assault Group of the Australian SAS, who had arrived at RAAF Darwin on the 26th, were busy building what looked like very crude stage sets—two-by-fours, butcher paper, canvas cloth. Special Operations in many ways parallel theatrical performances—performances with very high stakes. Carpentry, lighting, and stagecraft skills come in handy. Rehearsals are crucial. And if you are a special operator, the more time you have for rehearsals, the happier you are. (The bad guys at Entebbe gave the Israeli Special Ops guys three days to prepare. That rehearsal time sealed the bad guys' fate.) What you want to have is mock-ups of your target (they don't have to be elegant) that will allow you to experience and internalize spatial relations at your target, proportions, layout, exits, sight lines, lines of fire, routes and timing and locations of obstacles and hostiles. You want to also synchronize all the pieces of your own actions.

So, while the 1st/75th Ranger Regiment rested, the Aussies built a stage set, representing the one-time Merdeka Aircraft Plant that was now the nuclear weapons storage site.

On the 29th, the SAS TAG and the Rangers would start rehearsing together, with buildings on the base (like the control tower, for instance) doubling as likenesses of buildings at Bandung's Husein Sastranegara Airport.

The Rangers can take 99% of the airports in the world in twenty minutes. The SAS TAG expected to have the nuclear weapons and the Indonesian vice-president (assuming he was being held at the storage site) within a similar time frame.

It would not be pretty. But it would be fast.

Husein Sastranegara Airport
Bandung, Indonesia
1625 28 December 2005

Radu Adil was confined in a small but comfortable room, which he correctly took to be underground. It was in fact about 100 meters from the hastily constructed storage vault for the nuclear weapons, and a few doors down a hall from a much larger room that served as a comms and C-and-C center. General Nusaution had been left in Jakarta to continue to act as spokesman, while the rest of the conspirators had retired to the greater safety of their facility at Bandung.

At this moment he was being graced by the presence of the conspiracy leader, General Bungei, and Colonel Cancio. Bungei was in his fifties, portly and prosperous looking. Cancio was ten years younger and a good hand taller; and unlike his boss, he was fit and hard. Under other circumstances, Adil might have liked the man, and he might have been proud to have Cancio serve under him. It was difficult to understand why such a man had thrown in his lot with these thugs. Both men were dressed in BDUs. Cancio carried a leather folio case.

Adil watched them both closely, searching for signs that might tell him something about what was going on outside his four walls and tiny bathroom.

Meanwhile, his jailers had so far maintained the "official" fiction that he was their guest; and he had so far maintained an "official" blind eye to that. He had tried to preserve an "official" neutrality. He knew orders had been going out in his name (as interim president). There was no way he could stop them. He had even allowed himself to be photographed with Bungei. This was a calculated compromise. He hoped it would gain himself and his family time.

On the other hand, there were circumstances that might compel him to sacrifice himself and his family. He was under no illusions. He expected to face one of those circumstances soon.

Now what do they want? He wondered, as General Bungei settled into one of the two easy chairs that had come with the room. Adil took the other. Cancio remained standing.

Like most Asians, Indonesians do not come quickly to the point. During his time in America, Adil had grafted onto his personality a measure of American impatience. His fears for his family magnified that. As Bungei went through his obligatory circling around and around, Adil churned. Though he endured the general's courtesies with polite, yet stony-faced replies, he almost screamed inside: "Get on with it!"

Cancio, a man of few words, looked on impassively.

"I have a request to ask of you, Radu," Bungei said, at last coming to the point of the visit, his face a mask of friendliness.

"Yes?" Adil replied carefully.

"We're at a point in our restoration where the people of our country need a word of encouragement from a respected figure . . ."

". . . Such as the interim president."

"Exactly. We would like you to address the nation. We would like you to reassure the people." He brought his finger and thumb to a near touch. "We are on the very edge of success, my friend; we are that close." He gave his hand a little flutter. "But we need someone . . . of your high stature . . . to bring our nation over that edge. A man of the hour is required. You can be that man."

Adil stared at the other man, his mind churning. "I'm not sure what you mean," he said.

"You will have the support of the CRR to assume the presidency. But we will, of course, require gestures of support on your part. The relationship could be mutually beneficial."

"And if I find that I can't help you?" Adil asked, using all his strength of will to keep his voice casual and uncolored by the turmoil he felt. It was clear to him that the coup was not going well. If it had been, they would not have needed him for this.

It was probably for such an eventuality that they had kept him alive.

How can I use that? he asked himself. *How can I turn this to my advantage? . . . Shall I agree to go along with them, and then say what I must say when I'm in front of the cameras? . . . Of course not. They will tape the speech. If I try that, I'll be dead in seconds. . . . No, not before they show me my wife and daughters as they rape and torture them to death.*

"I can't imagine how you could refuse your nation in its time of trial," Bungei said smoothly. "Yet the examples of Sutopo, Yani, Suwandi, and Dhani point toward the consequences of a negative choice. And there are other consequences." He glanced at Colonel Cancio, who produced from his folio case a seven-by-nine photograph and passed it over to Adil.

The photo showed his nineteen-year-old daughter, Reni, under fierce, glaring lights, standing naked and terrified against a featureless cinderblock wall, her hands behind her back, certainly bound. Adil had not seen his daughter unclothed since she was a child.

The sight of her that way now seared his soul . . . enraged him.

There were no marks on her . . . as yet. Their continued absence was clearly a condition of his future cooperation.

Adil stifled the impulse to lash out. It would do no good (his eye had already caught Cancio's hand resting casually yet alert on the gun holstered by his side). He also stifled the equally useless verbal abuse he wanted to scream out.

He made his decision.

The bastards had made another mistake. They had tried to push him to submit. Instead, they had pushed him toward resistance. Adil had seen through their pressure (which wasn't hard to do) . . . leaving Adil with a granite certainty: Reni and Suya and Nuri were dead. And so was he. In hours. Or days. Soon. They would not be allowed to live. Cooperation would only delay that.

With that the case, honor won.

"No," he said quietly, his voice a near whisper. "I can't join you."

"Do you want to elaborate on that?" Bungei asked, visibly surprised. Cancio, on the other hand, was staring at Adil with something like respect.

"No," Adil said. "I don't think I have anything to add to that."

"Your choice will have consequences," Bungei said, the surprise now melting into disappointment; beneath which was anxiety, and swiftly emerging from that was rage. He had been counting on Adil's weakness. With Adil on their side, the CRR could win without having to rattle their nuclear sabers. Without him, they would have no other choice but to do that. And there was no telling what would come then.

He decided to delay. It was a weakness, he knew—and so did Adil—but there was no helping it. He *must have* Adil, for the moment at least, on his side.

"You should think for a time," he said, cursing the man, and hating it that he needed him. "Think about your daughter. A pretty thing. Look at her." He gestured at the photograph as he rose from his chair. "We'll return later."

Adil picked up the photograph and tore it slowly into small pieces. The pieces fluttered to the floor like moths.

Bungei and Cancio were out of the door before he had finished destroying it. The general's face was rigid with fury.

The United States Embassy
Merdeka Square
Jakarta, Indonesia
2247 28 December 2005

The Marine guards at the embassy were not happy. Earlier that evening, Indonesian Army troops had fired at rioters. Some of the shots had "strayed" and hit a corporal and a private. Both had been wearing flak vests, which worked out well for the corporal, but the private's right wrist was shattered. The Marines had been ordered not to shoot back unless directly threatened, and this incident was officially an "accident" (though they suspected, rightly, that it was intentional), but that didn't prevent the Marines from being pissed. They were not in a friendly mood toward Indonesians.

When the Indonesian approached the Marine first lieutenant (his name was Kelleher), Lieutenant Kelleher tried to shoo him away. He did this automatically, and he wasn't particularly gracious about it. At least not after two "You'll have to come back tomorrow when the embassy is open" tries had failed to send the man away. He was just an ordinary-looking Indonesian, batik shirt, *pitji* cap, polite, patient.

"Back off, motherfucker," Kelleher commanded, making a "get lost" gesture with the butt of his M16.

"My name is Widodo Suratman," the man persisted. "May I ask you again to tell Colonel Anthony Meyer that I'd like to see him? Please tell him it is urgent."

Yeah, Kelleher was thinking, *like you want visas for your family.*

On the other hand, a contrary thought was beginning to intrude into his thinking: He began to see that this man was intelligent, and he had an air of authority. *And if he really did have reason to see Colonel Meyer, then my ass is grass if I don't tell the colonel about him.*

A few minutes later Suratman and Colonel Meyer were seated in the colonel's office.

"So what gives, Widodo?" he asked, glad to see the man . . . glad to see that he was alive. He hadn't put his chances as very high the last time they parted.

"I must tell you this . . . officially: The shootdown of your C-130 earlier today was the responsibility of the outlaws who call themselves the CRR. It was an Army operation. They inserted a SAM team to embarrass you. I hope they did not succeed."

"We had already figured that out," Meyer answered. "But thanks for your concern. It will be noted.

"We had a Pave Low," he explained further, "on scene when they shot down the C-130. It took out three of them and managed to capture a fourth. He talked. What he said connected the attack with the CRR. It gives us justification to reply with force."

"Which you don't need," Suratman said softly.

"No, not really, but it will firm up the nervous Nellies among the coalition partners."

Suratman nodded understanding, and then continued. "Now for the real purpose of my visit," he said. "I told you before that the Air Force and the Navy would not back the CRR. That is true. I can also tell you that there will be no Air Force or Navy hindrance to SEAC movements. Or to military actions . . . say, in the Bandung area, if that is contemplated." He stared at the other with masterful impassivity.

"Meanwhile, the CRR remain technically in control of the capital, but, in fact, the city is currently hardly a degree or two away from anarchy, and no one believes they can hold it. Bands of young people have been killing soldiers in less than platoon strength. And the Air Force has been interdicting Army reinforcements trying to move into Jakarta. The Army is increasingly isolated. The only strong backing they have is certain Army units . . . but that will melt away in time.

"They've made terrible miscalculations," he added. "And they have misread the people of this country. After the initial shock, few believed their lies. No one who took the time to think about it believed their claim that the Christians stole the bomb. It was one big lie too many. No one believed in their legitimacy. The CRR is another big lie.

"We will die unless we have the democracy, the freedom, the *merdeka* that is our right. Anything less is not a start-up."

"You mean a nonstarter?" Meyer corrected, with a smile.

"A nonstarter? All right."

"So how desperate are they?" Meyer asked, his tone suddenly sharp.

"You mean, I take it, 'Are they desperate enough to use their nuclear weapons?' The answer: 'I don't know.' One can hope they will see reason. But with them reason has been in short supply." He caught Meyer's eye. "I hope *immediate* action will be taken by someone to neutralize those weapons."

Meyer did not reply to this.

"One final word," Suratman added. "I have received definite confirmation that Radu Adil is being held at the former aircraft factory near the airport at Bandung."

"I'm glad that he is alive."

"I must leave," Suratman said.

"Will you be safe? If you'd like, I'll find a place for you here . . . and your family," he added, "if necessary."

"Thank you. No. I'll be okay. And my family are safe now on Bali. I can be more useful outside."

"Well, then, good luck, Suratman. *Selamat jalan.*"

"*Selamat tinggal,*[119] my friend."

During the time Widodo Suratman and Anthony Meyer were having their conversation, four vehicles left the embassy's underground garage, at intervals of between five and fifteen minutes. The first was a Range Rover. The second was a sixteen seat minibus (a sign on its side read COUNTRY WALKERS in Indonesian and English). The third was an identical minibus. And the fourth was an old Mitsubishi Montero SUV.

Half an hour later, the Range Rover was on the toll road to Bandung, a distance of about 120 kilometers.

Bandung, Indonesia
0530 29 December 2005

The city of Bandung is set in a large valley surrounded by 2000+-meter-high mountains. The airport is on the northwest side of the city, just off the toll road to Jakarta. The lower slopes of the volcano Tangkuban Prahu rise a couple of kilometers north of the airport. Its summit is thirty kilometers north of the city. (It has not erupted seriously since 1969, but it fumes and rumbles.)

If, like the two ODAs now enroute to Bandung, one wanted to view the airport unobserved, one could do worse than find a relatively inaccessible spot on the volcano's lower slopes. There were disadvantages, of course (you were hoping for easy?). For example, the distances were on the long side: You might find yourself with a five kilometer sightline. On the other hand, five-kilometers is no more of a problem than five hundred meters for modern optics and thermal-imaging equipment. Consideration

---

119 "Goodbye." In Indonesia, the person staying says. *"Selamat jalan;"* the person leaving, *"Selamat tinggal."*

had been given to placing a series of TV minicams near the one-time aircraft plant (it was on the north side of the field), but that idea was rejected. The risk of their discovery, though small, was too great. No one in the plant must suspect that they would soon be the target for a number of nasty surprises.

———

The SUVs and minibuses, driven conservatively, had started arriving in the Bandung area by 0130. An hour and a half later, they had deposited their passengers and equipment by the side of one of the roads up the mountain. An hour after that, the two ODAs (each of them a couple of men understrength, as it happened) had split into two teams of five men each and set about digging hide sites. They placed these at the corners of a rough-sided box, about 200 meters on a side.

The idea was to get a clear and exhaustive two-day view of the workings of the airport and the bomb storage depot. One team would keep track of air traffic. A second would watch ground traffic at the terminal and its facilities. A third would watch the goings and comings at the former aircraft factory—entrances, exits, loading docks, security arrangements around the building and on the roof, and the like. And the fourth would put together a "thermal map" of the facility. Human beings, for instance, shine brightly in infrared, even at a distance of five kilometers. Getting a thermal picture of the inside of the plant was more problematic. Still, sleeping spaces, dining areas, work areas, command-and-control and communications areas—one could make a pretty fair guess about the locations of such places by examining closely the thermal signatures coming out of the building.

But far more important: Nuclear weapons need to be kept cool. Heat is a normal byproduct of highly radioactive materials. A five-pound lump of plutonium is warm to the touch.

A number of critical parts within a nuclear device must be able to move in very precise ways if the device is going to work as designed. If you heat up these parts too much, they expand and don't move the way they should. Ergo, you want to keep the bomb chilled.

Keeping bombs chilled is not hard to do. Refrigeration technology has been around a long time. It works by heat exchange. That is, cool air comes out of one end of, say, an air-conditioner, and warm air comes out of the other.

But, of course, a good thermal imager can tell you a lot about what is going on in such a system. Even better, in an emerging Third World country, where you don't always have absolute confidence in the power grid, you will probably want to set up a separate generating system to power the refrigeration system that keeps your nuclear weapons cool. And for solid practical reasons, you'll probably place this generator not far from the vault where you are keeping your weapons. Generators generate a lot of heat. That means—all other things being equal—if you can find the generators, you're pretty damned close to the bombs.

Palau Ambon
2200 29 December 2005

It had not taken the Indonesian captain long to reveal the location of the SAM cache. He was not eager to suffer for the Committee for the Restoration of the Republic.

Earlier that day (during the morning of the 29th), another four-man SA-16 team had tried to take out a Chinook carrying a NEST team to the blast site. The Chinook drivers (unlike the C-130 pilots the day before) proved to be ready for the twin corkscrews of smoke that headed their way, launched from about three kilometers to their port rear. Flares were dropped and the Chinook took violent evasive action. The NEST people got shook up (one dislocated a shoulder), but the missiles missed.

Unfortunately, this time there were no MH-53Js or OH-58Ds around to follow up, and the bad guys successfully slipped away into the rain forest.

Later, a Pave Low, operating at 2,000 meters, made a pass near the spot the Indonesian captain had identified as the SAM cache location. The Pave Low's FLIRs indicated that he had been telling the truth.

At 2200, a Chinook carrying ODA 142 was hovering behind a hill near the cache site. They were accompanied by an OH-58D and a Pave Low. Meanwhile, an AC-130U Spectre was at 2,500 meters, circling the cache site, setting up to fire its 105mm short-barreled howitzer. This is, quite simply, one hell of a weapon to fire from an airplane. It's like placing a howitzer on the best possible high ground . . . high ground you can move where you need it most.

At 2202, the Spectre started firing its 105mm. It stopped firing at 2208 to allow the smaller birds to go in for a closer look. There wasn't much to see except flames and smoke, punctuated by the occasional fiery burst of a cooking SA-16 warhead. But just to be on the safe side—and because they also wanted to get in a few licks of their own—the guys in the OH-58D launched a series of rockets from their pod at the peripheries of the jungle camp, while the Pave Low hosed it down with their Gatlings.

At 2210, having located a decently clear landing spot half a kilometer from the cache, the Chinook set down so ODA 142 could clean up what was left.

They found nothing undamaged, and no one alive. There were fifteen shredded corpses and thousands of shards of weapons and gear. Body parts were everywhere. It was as though somebody had put everything in the camp through a big snow blower (with a missing blade).

It was, of course, possible that one or two of them had managed to escape into the jungle when the pounding from the Spectre started, but they were toothless and clawless. They wouldn't cause any more harm.

Meanwhile, there was intelligence to be gathered, and Valdez and his ODA did that for the rest of the night. Much as he and his guys hated what these people had done to Americans, and were prepared to continue doing, it was still a ghastly duty that the ODA would have preferred not to do.

Just after dawn, they trudged back to the Chinook carrying bags of "evidence" that the analysts would do their thing with.

In the Chinook, Valdez was sick at heart. He was also a realist and a warrior, who understood the consequences of war. Those guys had been enemies. They deserved to be treated with extreme violence.

Yet the killing and the destruction of war never failed to yank hard at his insides. Those guys had wives, girlfriends, children. Somebody would be weeping for them the way Karen might be weeping for him if the situation was reversed. It was insane, but that was the way it was.

And besides—these moments aside—he loved the job.

Husein Sastranegara Airport
Bandung, Indonesia
0100 31 December 2005

Nuclear weapons do funny things to people. Or at least that was the message Captain Chuck Verbalis, the ODA 163 commander, had gotten during a briefing at the U.S. Embassy in Jakarta by Dr. Ben Sobel, one of the NEST team from Nevada. (There would be a NEST component during the final grab of the weapons.) "When people have nukes as close neighbors, they go nuts" was the way Sobel had put it. "That's going to be particularly the case when people come into possession of nukes who aren't used to the damned things . . . not that anyone will ever get used to them.

"What you can expect to see is some really strange things. The villains are going to get overprotective. They're going to look real paranoid. It's like the ring in Tolkein's books. The longer you have it, the more power it has over you. If they could wear the fuckers around their necks, they would.

"You'd think having nukes would make you feel mega-macho," he went on. "It doesn't work that way. You look for enemies everywhere. It's like showing a million-dollar diamond necklace on the New York subway. You don't know who is going to snatch first." From his accent, it was clear Dr. Ben Sobel had done a lot of time on New York City subways. "So the nuke guys will go for overkill where protection is concerned."

After two days at airport, Verbalis had concluded that Sobel had been right. He and the others on the teams surveilling the airport had expected the CRR generals to present a low profile . . . They'd expected them to let the civil airport run normally, and to keep their security measures more or less invisible. "Why call undue attention to yourself?"

But things didn't work out that way. As Sobel had predicted, the generals got increasingly paranoid (Verbalis called that the "Sobel Factor"). They closed down the airport to civilian traffic and brought in a battalion from Kostrad, Indonesia's 15,000 man, well-trained and well-equipped strategic reserve. The Kostrad battalion secured the perimeters of the airport, set up AAA and SAM batteries, and fortified the former aircraft plant.

Two days of observations had yielded the following information, which had been relayed by SATCOM to the mission controllers at the FOB in Darwin (the mission itself was now called Operation Merdeka):

Guarding the airport against air attack, there were:

- Five batteries of Swedish-made Bofors 40mm/L70 pompoms, with four guns per battery. (These were a direct descendant of and very similar to the Bofors-made pompoms everyone has seen firing from ships in World War II movies. They are still very much in use all over the world . . . because they still do the job very well.) The Bofors fire time, impact, and proximity fused ammunition, and are useful against both air and ground targets. Two batteries were placed near each end of the main runway, and the fifth was placed closer to the Merdeka factory.
- At each end of the main runway was also placed a British-made Rapier SAM battery. Rapiers are purpose-designed for airport defense. They're day and night capable, all-weather, and effective against aircraft flying at low to medium altitudes. Each battery has three or four launcher units, with each launcher holding four ready missiles (which are eight feet long). These require a direct hit to kill a target (there is no proximity fuse), but they are very accurate.

On the ground:

- One battalion (three companies plus a headquarters—approximately 600 men) from the elite Kostrad division. Two of these companies, on twelve-hour shifts, guarded the plant perimeter in platoon-sized units (a platoon was on the roof) from fortified (usually sandbagged) positions. The Kostrad troops were billeted in a tent camp set up about two hundred meters north of the former Merdeka factory.
- At strategic and fortified positions around the airfield had been placed .50-caliber machine gun positions, as well as lighter machine guns. It was clear to the ODAs that these light machine guns could fire at aircraft as well as ground targets.
- The Kostrad garrison was also augmented with six French-built AMX-13 light tanks (armed with a 105mm cannon and light machine guns), positioned just outside the plant perimeters.
- A number of quickly improvised obstacles had been placed within the perimeter fences of the plant—primarily twelve medium (5-ton) trucks loaded with concrete blocks and scrap iron to limit access to the loading docks and main plant entrances.
- There were sniper positions on the terminal buildings and control tower across the runway, and on hangars and other buildings on the plant (north) side of the field.
- Along the main runway was a string of six medium trucks, also loaded with concrete blocks. If needed, they could be driven onto the runways to act as obstacles to landing aircraft, and quickly disabled . . . The Indonesians actually used a belt-and-suspenders approach: They could remove the ignition rotors (easily reinstalled if the trucks had to be moved again). But if more permanent obstacles had to be created, they had attached 20-kilogram demolition charges (TNT with a burning—not electrical—fuse) to the truck beds beneath the concrete and scrap.

Inside the plant:

- Thermal-imaging systems are not X-ray vision, yet they provide an approximation of that. That is to say, the ODAs' thermal imagers could not provide "guaranteed" exact locations for the nuclear weapons storage vault or for Vice-President Adil, but analysts armed with the ODA-provided thermal imaging information and the building plans provided by Widodo Suratman could make reasonably accurate estimates, based on generator and air-conditioning signatures and other heat concentrations. These estimates were downlinked to the Australian SAS TAG.

Meanwhile, a pair of B-2s had taken off from CONUS, armed with JSOWs (AGM-154 Joint Standoff Weapons—1000-pound glide bombs with INS/GPS guidance) and JDAMs (Joint Direct Attack Munitions—2000-pound GPS-guided high-explosive bombs). The JSOWs—standoff munitions—can be released from a safe distance, glide over their target, and spew out cluster munitions—a mix of explosives, incendiaries, and shrapnel. JSOWs are very useful against antiaircraft positions and other more or less soft sites. JDAMs, on the other hand, can be used against more hardened targets, bridges, and buildings. Both are carried on a rotary launcher within the B-2's bomb bay.

During the previous two days, ODAs 163 and 168 had carefully mapped antiaircraft positions at the airfield with PAQ-10 Ground Laser Target Designators, which had been linked to the GPS system. These coordinates had been uplinked to FOB Darwin, and eventually downlinked to the B-2s. The bombs on the B-2s were then programmed with this information. It made them accurate within three or four meters.

The coordinates of several other strategic positions on the airfield were also noted and uplinked.

The "grab and snatch" that was the essence of Operation Merdeka presupposed an essential sequence of actions (which were downlinked back to ODAs 163 and 168):

- The antiaircraft positions at Husein Sastranegara had to be neutralized.
- The runways had to be cleared.
- Defensive ground positions had to neutralized and obstacles cleared.
- And, in general, the defenders had to be placed in a condition of confusion, havoc, and panic. The closer to total paralysis the better. Thus, an early goal was to create shock and mayhem . . . That was about to happen.

During the attack, the ODAs would provide fire control and instant BDA (Bomb Damage Assessment).

By 0100 on the 31st, the two ODAs had packed their nonessential gear and cleaned up their positions (you'd have to look hard after they left to tell that they had been there). The vehicles that had driven them up from Jakarta two days earlier were now waiting for them a short distance away on one of the mountain roads.

They could not leave yet, though. They had loose ends to tie.

Just after 0100, Chuck Verbalis and his companions went silent, listening intently. Seconds later, they heard what they were listening for—the faint but distinctive whooshing sound of JSOWs, almost instantly followed by the bright flashes of cluster

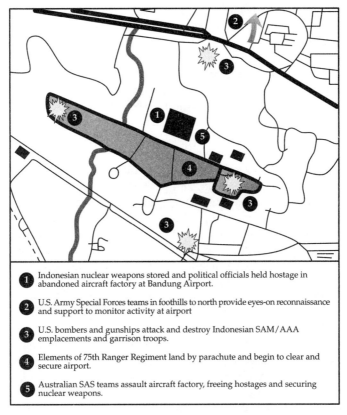

1. Indonesian nuclear weapons stored and political officials held hostage in abandoned aircraft factory at Bandung Airport.

2. U.S. Army Special Forces teams in foothills to north provide eyes-on reconnaissance and support to monitor activity at airport

3. U.S. bombers and gunships attack and destroy Indonesian SAM/AAA emplacements and garrison troops.

4. Elements of 75th Ranger Regiment land by parachute and begin to clear and secure airport.

5. Australian SAS teams assault aircraft factory, freeing hostages and securing nuclear weapons.

RUBICON, INC., BY LAURA DeNINNO

munitions at the ends of the Husein Sastranegara runway. (Firecracker pops, traveling at the speed of sound, arrived later.)

"Scratch two Rapier sites," Verbalis said to himself. Moments later, the Bofors gun sites met the same fate. And moments after that, he observed more flashes over the Kostrad camp to the north of the Merdeka plant. Verbalis counted on perhaps two to three hundred troops to be sleeping there. They would sleep a *very* long time. (Later 266 Kostrad dead were counted.) When the firecracker pops ceased, discreetly murmured cheers came from the guys in the ODAs.

As all this was happening, Verbalis's comms sergeant was passing a running report to the B-2s, to the second wave of Spectre gunships and Pave Lows waiting nearby, and back to FOB Darwin by SATCOM.

After the JSOWs came the JDAMs. It was not a long wait. There were flashes, followed seconds later by low crackling rumbles, and the airport control tower was a pile of shards and rubble, the terminal building was a smoking ruin, and hangar and administrative buildings on both sides of the field were "no longer functional." That meant that most Kostrad sniper positions were likewise "no longer functional."

That success was communicated to the various players and controllers.

With their primary job done, the B-2s were released from their primary role. They would now destroy local communications facilities and approaches to the airport—by taking out a selection of bridges and overpasses (this would hinder potential reinforcements).

Once the B-2s had moved out, a pair of AC-130U Spectre Gunships (at 3000 meters) and three MH-53J Pave Low helicopters (closer to the ground) began taking out targets selected by the two ODAs with their PAQ-10 GLTDs.

Verbalis watched as the Spectres' 105mm howitzers and 20mm Gatlings demolished machine gun positions and AMX-13 tanks. Soon the tanks were immobilized and burning, while machine gun positions ceased to be operational. Once these were neutralized, the Spectre howitzers focused on the trucks poised to obstruct the runway. Meanwhile, the Pave Lows hosed the roof of the former aircraft plant, its perimeter defenses, and anything else that caught their gunners' interest.

At 0110, the Spectres and the Pave Lows checked fire, and the Pave Lows pulled back to the airfield perimeters. This was in order to deconflict the airfield airspace. It was also the ODAs' signal to go passive. From that moment on, they no longer had an active fire control function, though they would continue to report BDAs.

At 0114, Verbalis turned his attention to the former Merdeka Plant. Over it hovered three Pave Lows, from which the Aussie SAS TAG (a 36-man company split into three 12-man teams) were fast roping down to the factory roof, each of them carrying a noise- and flash-suppressed H&K 9mm submachine gun.

Though Pave Low Gatlings had earlier eliminated rooftop security, a handful of Kostrad troops had rushed up to the roof after the initial ruckus ended and were getting off shots at descending SAS troops (hitting one man, Verbalis learned later). But this proved to be only a brief inconvenience for the SAS guys. TAG H&Ks quickly cut the bad guys down. (The SAS man's wound was not life threatening, but it proved to be serious enough to take him out of action. He was helicoptered back to the CVBG, which was now in position south of Java.)

Once they were on the roof, the TAGs split up. One team remained on the roof, for security and to give the Ranger company fire support; the other two raced down an airshaft stairs for the cellar.

From then on, Chuck Verbalis had to wait. He consoled himself with the thought that if they made a major slip up, his end would probably come instantly and painlessly.

The wait was by no means without incident: Even as the TAGs were roping down from their Pave Lows, three companies of Rangers, augmented by armored HMMWVs equipped with .50-caliber machine guns, 40mm machine guns, and TOW missiles, were parachuting onto the airfield. Two of the companies, and all of the HMMWVs, fanned out to establish security and prepare the runway to receive air traffic (their biggest problem was clearing used parachutes—these could create a *big* problem for C-130 props). The third Ranger company launched an assault on what was left of the opposition around the Merdeka plant. The side of the plant closest to the airport's main runway consisted of a huge, high-ceilinged hangar-type shed, where finished aircraft had once been assembled. The Rangers attacked toward the shed's big sliding doors.

Verbalis watched a brief skirmish with the remnants of the Kostrad resistance. Then charges were placed on sliding doors. There was a flash, followed a few moments later by a dull *whump*. And the Rangers were inside.

By 0135, it was essentially over. One or two bull-headed snipers remained to be suppressed, but aside from these, the Kostrad forces had either surrendered or were dead.

At 0145, a NEST C-130 arrived, and the NEST team, accompanied by a Technical Escort Unit (TEU) from the Defense Non-Proliferation Agency at Fort Belvoir, Maryland, who handled security, were escorted into the plant by Rangers. Half an hour later, a HMMVW emerged through the shed doors and drove out to the NEST C-130. Verbalis examined it closely. There was a pallet on its truck bed. The pallet contained a gray, lethal-looking lozenge, about a meter in length.

Verbalis was a Catholic who did not pray often. He prayed then.

After three other warheads were safely transported onto the C-130, Verbalis gave the order for his guys to move out. A half hour later, ODAs 163 and 168 were headed north toward the coast, and then west on the coast highway to Jakarta. Ever the "quiet professionals," they had slipped in and out of their hide sites as stealthily as B-2s.

Later, Verbalis learned that the TAG had found Radu Adil in a cell (converted from an office) not far from the large room used by the CRR leaders as a temporary command and control center. This was an "action central" that was both close to the nuclear weapons (another example of the "Sobel Factor") and safely out of the chaos that Jakarta had become.

Though the guards posted outside Adil's cell had been prepared to kill him—and had expected to do that—the execution order never came. The TAG put 9mm shots into them before they even realized that the men in black who suddenly appeared in the corridor were not friends.

Adil himself was visibly uninjured, but spiritually much shaken. His wife and daughters had each been shot in his presence the day before the American and Australian assault (their unmarked graves were discovered by Rangers later that morning).

The choice he had made had been the right one, but its consequence had been the murder of his family. The pain of that would remain with him for the rest of his life.

In due course, Generals Bungei, Nusaution, and the other conspirators were rounded up. Within weeks, all of the conspirators had been tried and executed.

Colonel Cancio (whose job it had been to order Adil's execution . . . Adil never learned whether this lapse was deliberate) was never found.

Adil privately believed that he had survived.

At 0230, the NEST C-130, containing the nuclear weapons, lifted off for Darwin.

The next day the weapons were placed in a C-17 bound for the USA ... and an inspection by expert scientists.

Kota Ambon
1100 25 December 2006

Carlos Valdez was a man of strong emotions, usually held under professional control. But it was hard for him to do that this Christmas morning. He and several hundred others—the President of the United States, President Adil of Indonesia, the commanding general of SOCOM, the commander of Special Forces Command, various other participants, American, Australian, and Indonesian (including his friend, now Brigadier General Kumar), and (far from insignificantly) Karen and his two boys—were waiting in Taman Victoria, a park in downtown Victoria, for the ceremony to begin.

The big shots, including Kumar, were on a platform beside a draped statue. Speeches were made, which Valdez ignored. The two presidents then together undraped the statue: It was bronze and showed several figures—suffering Indonesian children and an Indonesian mother being helped by an American Special Forces and an Indonesian JISF soldier. Valdez had seen the statue, of course, before the dedication (he had come to Ambon three days before—three days of partying with Indonesian friends), but it never failed to move him. And he was choked up now.

He was even more choked up when the President of the United States called him up to the platform. The Indonesians evidently wanted to give him some kind of decoration. Karen gave his hand a squeeze as he set off through the very unwelcome applause.

Shit! he thought. *Why the hell do they want to do that?*

Glossary

AAR After Action Review—group assessment and evaluation of a just-completed mission. Ideally an occasion for honest criticism and self-criticism, without regard to ego-tripping, pulling rank, or careerism.

AC-130 Nicknamed "Spectre," Lockheed C-130 4-engine "gunship" equipped with night targeting sensors and a mix of heavy weapons, typically including a short 105mm howitzer, 40 mm Bofors automatic cannon, and 20 mm 6-barrel "Gatling" machine gun. Flown by Air Force Special Operations Squadrons. Devastating against ground targets.

ACRI African Crisis Response Initiative—U.S. diplomatic attempt to promote development of a trained and effective multinational African peacekeeping force. Initial participants in 1996 included Ghana, Malawi, Mali, Senegal, Uganda, and Benin.

AFSOC Air Force Special Operations Command—based at Eglin Air Force Base, Florida. Consists mainly of specialized helicopter and transport aircraft units and supporting personnel.

ALICE All-purpose Lightweight Individual Carrying Equipment—obsolescent U.S. Army pack and frame system.

ANG U.S. Army National Guard.

AOR Area of Responsibility—Geographic region that a Unified CINC or other senior commander is responsible for.

ATV All-Terrain Vehicle—one-man 4×4 off-road vehicle based on commercial motorcycle technology.

BDU Battle Dress Uniform—standard U.S. military field uniform, made of cotton or cotton-polyester blend. Produced in several different camouflage patterns. Very comfortable and practical, but often criticized for baggy appearance.

Blue Light Code name for a small Army counterterrorist unit formed in Europe in the 1970s.

C4 Military plastic explosive used for sabotage or demolition of obstacles.

CA Civil Affairs—SOF missions designed to promote cooperation (or minimize interference) by local populations with friendly military operations.

CBT Combating Terrorism—SOF mission aimed at preventing or neutralizing the actions of hostile terrorist groups, often in close cooperation with law enforcement and diplomatic agencies. (Also abbreviated CT.)

CD Counter-Drug Operations—SOF missions designed to assist host nation in preventing the production, processing or distribution of illegal narcotics.

CENTCOM U.S. Central Command—unified command responsible for the Middle East. CENTCOM exercised combatant command over the forces that fought the 1991 Gulf War. Its area of responsibility was extended to Central Asia in 1999.

CINCSOC Commander-in-Chief, U.S. Special Operations Command—usually an Army general with extensive combat experience in Airborne, Ranger, and Special Forces units.

COA Course of Action—a briefing or paper that systematically and logically presents the alternatives that a commander can follow to achieve a mission objective. One of the key things a good staff officer does for a commander is to simplify decision making with clear COAs—ideally not more than three choices at one time.

Combat Talon   Lockheed MC-130 transport aircraft equipped for special operations transport missions. Operated by Air Force Special Operations Command.

CONOPS   Concept of Operations—a brief statement describing how a mission is to be accomplished. Reflects a military commander's plans, intentions, and understanding of how a particular operation will unfold.

CONUS   "Continental United States"—military jargon for the forty-eight contiguous states. The opposite of overseas, or "downrange."

CP   Counter-Proliferation—a critical SOF mission, aimed at preventing the acquisition or development of weapons of mass destruction (nuclear, chemical, biological, or radiological) by potential adversaries.

CRD   Chemical Reconnaissance Detachments—small Army teams with protective equipment and detectors trained to rapidly assess possible areas of toxic contamination. A national asset, subordinate to Special Forces Command.

CS   Coalition Support—SOF missions that assist friendly states typically by combined training, exercises, or "military diplomacy."

CSAR   Combat Search and Rescue—SOF mission to locate and retrieve military personnel or downed aircrew behind enemy lines.

CSEL   PRQ-7 Combat Survivor Evader Locator—miniaturized encoded radio "beacon" carried by aircrew, allowing search-and-rescue teams with a special receiver to safely locate and confirm identity of lost or downed personnel. Finally scheduled to enter service around 2001 after a shamefully long development delay.

CST   Close Support Team—Special Forces team equipped and trained as ground observers to locate targets and direct strike aircraft.

CTF   Commander, Task Force (sometimes slurred into "Commander's Task Force")—a component of a Joint Task Force, under a designated commander. CTFs are usually temporary, can be of any size, are tailored for a specific mission, and are numbered with decimals according to Navy convention, such as CTF 958.1.2.

DA   Direct Action—SOF mission involving short, intense raid to seize, capture, recover, or destroy specific hostile personnel, equipment, or facilities.

Delta Force   Secretive U.S. Army counterterrorist unit based on the training and tactics of the U.K. Special Air Service. Delta participated in the abortive 1980 Iran hostage rescue mission.

Downrange   Army slang for "overseas on hazardous field mission"—originally applied to live ammunition firing ranges; adopted by explosive ordnance disposal teams and other specialists in dangerous activity.

DZ   Drop Zone—a clear terrain area where parachute troops or supplies can be delivered safely (hopefully). Should be as close as possible to the objective.

E&E   Escape and Evasion—tactics, techniques and procedures (some very simple, some highly classified) for avoiding capture behind enemy lines and returning safely.

ECWCS   Extended Cold Weather Clothing System—worn over BDU in severe winter or arctic climates. Produced in two weights, both using Gore-Tex (a breathable, synthetic waterproof insulation material).

EUCOM   U.S. European Command—unified Command responsible for combatant command of forces in Europe and Africa. Headquarters in Stuttgart-Vaihingen, Germany. CINC EUCOM is also NATO Supreme Allied Commander, Europe (SACEUR).

FARC   Revolutionary Armed Forces of Colombia—originally a leftist guerrilla group, rapidly evolving into a multinational narco-terrorist enterprise.

FID   Foreign Internal Defense—SOF mission aimed at strengthening security forces of friendly host nations. Usually requires great cultural sensitivity and may involve ethical risk of complicity in human rights abuses.

FLIR   Forward-Looking Infrared—An electro-optical sensor that provides a visual display based on detecting small differences in temperature rather than emitted or reflected light. Allows precise navigation and targeting at night or in adverse weather.

FOB   Forward Operating Base.

Force Protection   Catchall term for measures to prevent terrorist attack on U.S. forces and facilities, including access control barriers, restrictions on off-base activities, perimeter surveillance, and physical hardening of facilities against blast and fragmentation (e.g. no exterior windows on new construction).

G Bands   Special Forces jargon for guerrilla groups.

G7   Military staff designation for an equipment development and procurement office or "shop."

GAC FAC   Grupo de Acciones Comandos de la Guardia Nacional de Venezuela—elite counterterrorist unit of the Venezuelan armed forces. Rated as a battalion, but about the size of a U.S. reinforced company.

Gilly Suit   Loose, shaggy overgarment worn by snipers and designed to blend with ground vegetation. Extremely effective camouflage. Name derives from *"ghillie,"* a Scottish term for game wardens, who have worn similar outfits for centuries.

GLTD   PAQ-10 Ground Laser Target Designator—portable (5.5 kg) device used to mark targets for air-launched precision-guided weapons. Range up to 10 km.

GMV   Ground Mobility Vehicle—standard Army HMMWV modified for Special Operations.

Goldwater-Nichols   Legislative Act passed in 1986; reorganized combatant command of U.S. military forces under regional or functional joint "Unified Commands," such as PACOM (Pacific Command), EUCOM (European Command), and STRATCOM (Strategic Command).

GPS   Global Positioning System—A constellation of orbiting satellites that broadcast extremely precise navigational signals to compact, low-cost receivers. Includes a wide range of military (encrypted) and civil applications.

HA   Humanitarian Assistance—SOF missions designed to support relief operations during natural disasters, refugee crises, or other complex mass emergencies.

HAHO   High Altitude, High Opening—Specialized jump technique using steerable parachute release above 9000 meters. Allows gliding range up to 50 km. from drop point.

HALO   High Altitude, Low Opening—A difficult parachute technique involving extended free fall with oxygen breathing apparatus. Can be used to insert Special Forces teams into denied territory.

HD   Humanitarian Demining—SOF mission to assist host nation in safely locating and neutralizing land mines and hazardous unexploded munitions; typically relying on simple training and manual methods rather than high-technology equipment.

HMMWV   High Mobility Multipurpose Wheeled Vehicle—nicknamed "Hummer." Rugged 4×4 light truck, replacing the famous jeep. Produced in many variants (ambulance, command vehicle, weapons carrier) and widely used by all U.S. military services.

IDP   Internally Displaced Persons—jargon for "refugees."

IO   Information Operations—All actions (by SOF and other forces) designed to disrupt enemy information systems, computers, and control networks, by introducing disruptive software, inserting deceptive information, physical destruction, or other means.

ISOFAC   Isolation Facility—barracks or campsite where troops are isolated before a Special Forces mission, both to prepare mentally and to preserve operational security.

JCET   Joint Cooperative Engagement Training—an exercise (usually planned at the CINC level, but carried out by small units) designed to share expertise and build good working relationships with selected forces of a host nation.

JCS   Joint Chiefs of Staff—advises the national command authorities on military matters. Includes a Chairman and Vice Chairman who may be appointed from any service, the Army and Air Force Chiefs of Staff, the Chief of Naval Operations, and the Commandant of the Marine Corps. Controls a substantial budget and supporting personnel (The Joint Staff) headquartered at the Pentagon.

JRTC   Joint Readiness Training Center, Fort Polk, Louisiana—intensively used military training area in the remote wilderness of northern Louisiana. One of the few extensive nondesert ranges still available in the U.S.

JSOC   Joint Special Operations Command—Secretive brigade-sized joint military unit combining ground and aviation combat elements. Responsible for sensitive counterterrorist missions. Based at Fort Bragg, North Carolina.

JTFEX   Joint Task Force Exercise—an extremely large exercise, usually involving forces from every military service, run six times each year by U.S. Joint Forces Command (formerly U.S. Atlantic Command). Serves as a "final exam" for Navy carrier battle groups and Marine Expeditionary Units.

LCE   Liaison Coordination Element—a small Special Forces Detachment, strong in language and signal communications skills, assigned to coordinate allied operations with a foreign military unit.

LRP Ration   Long-Range Patrol Ration—freeze-dried vacuum-packed food lighter and more concentrated than MRE. Originally called MCW (Meal, Cold Weather) and designed for mountain troops.

LVRS   Lightweight Video Reconnaissance System—compact, rugged still-frame videocamera that connects to a variety of data links or recording devices.

LZ   Landing Zone—a relatively unobstructed area where helicopters can unload, usually hovering just off the ground for the shortest possible time. A "hot LZ" is one under enemy fire.

M4 Carbine Lightweight, short-barreled modification of the standard M16 automatic rifle.

MBITR Multiband Intra-Team Radio—new communication system able to provide secure VHF and UHF voice and data transmission in AM or FM modes.

MERC Mobility Enhancing Ration Components—new family of compact, long shelf-life rations resembling "pocket pastries" designed for quick eating and high troop acceptance.

METL Mission Essential Task List—a very structured "to do" list for a military operation. Includes success criteria and risk assessments. Used mainly for training exercises.

MEU (SOC) Marine Expeditionary Unit (Special Operations Capable)—U.S. Marine battalion-sized force integrating ground and air combat elements. Normally deployed with a three-ship U.S. Navy Amphibious Ready Group (ARG).

MILES Multiple Integrated Laser Exercise System—training simulator based on eye-safe coded laser transmitters mounted on weapons and laser detectors worn by individual soldiers or mounted on target vehicles. Similar to commercial "laser tag" games, but more serious and capable, especially if you become a "casualty."

MIPM MultiPurpose Infantry Munition—one-shot shoulder-fired rocket launcher designed to give infantry some capability against tanks and bunkers out to a range of 500 meters. Scheduled to enter service around 2002.

MOLLE Modular Lightweight Load-carrying Equipment, Individual—soldier's pack system adopted by U.S. Marines to replace ALICE gear. To be adapted for Army Special Forces.

MOS Military Occupational Specialty—an alphanumeric code (two or three digits and one letter) that specifies general categories of Army skills. Special Forces MOSs make up the 18-series.

MOUT Military Operations in Urban Terrain (jargon for "street fighting")—one of the most difficult tactical challenges, especially for a force that wants to avoid casualties and the destruction of the urban infrastructure.

MRC Major Regional Contingency—military jargon for a war against a regional power like Iraq or North Korea.

MRE Meals Ready to Eat—Standard U.S. military field ration package. They come in about a dozen different menus, can be stored for long periods and eaten without cooking, and provide plenty of calories and nutrients, but also a lot of inedible waste plastic and cardboard.

MSS Mission Support Site—a secure hide site for a Special Forces detachment during a mission. Should be well concealed but located near a source of potable water.

NAVSPECWARCOM U.S. Navy Special Warfare Command—based at Coronado, California, and responsible for training, equipment, and doctrine for U.S. Navy SEAL teams and supporting special boat squadrons, and other units.

NCO Non-Commissioned Officer—the "glue" that holds any military organization together. Technically, a soldier, sailor, airman, or Marine in any pay grade between E-3 and E-9.

NRO National Reconnaissance Office—secretive, lavishly funded agency, headquartered in Chantilly, Virginia, that procures and operates U.S. military reconnaissance satellites.

NSA National Security Agency—secretive, lavishly funded U.S. agency responsible for encrypted communications, code-breaking, and global electronic surveillance, headquartered at Fort Meade, Maryland. Nicknames include Puzzle Palace and No Such Agency.

NTC National Training Center, Fort Irwin, California—located in rugged desert terrain, this high-tech training facility gets much of the credit for the U.S. Army's amazing performance in Operation Desert Storm (1991).

Nunn-Cohen Legislative Act passed in 1987 that created U.S. Special Operations Command (SOCOM), and provided it with its own independent funding sources. Excluded U.S. Marine forces from subordination to SOCOM.

NVG Night Vision Goggles—based on 3rd-generation optical image intensifier technology. Battery powered, worn strapped to the head. Standard Army ground model is currently the PVS-7D.

O/C Observer/Controller—senior personnel assigned to supervise, record, and evaluate a training exercise. May also be responsible for range safety.

ODA Operational Detachment Alpha (previously called A-Team)—a twelve-man Army Special Forces team, combining combat, language, engineering, medical, and communications skills. Roughly equivalent to a platoon, and normally led by a captain (O-3).

ODB Operational Detachment Bravo—Special Forces Company Headquarters unit, capable of controlling multiple ODAs in the field.

OPFOR Opposing Force—units assigned to represent the enemy in a training exercise or wargame. May be trained in enemy doctrine and tactics; equipped with real or simulated foreign equipment, and fictional insignia, to avoid offending any specific real country.

OPSEC Operational Security—All measures taken to prevent disclosure of operations, plans, or capabilities to hostile forces. Can be as simple as "No comment," or as complex as an elaborate deception plan.

OpTempo Operational Tempo—A measure of the total demands placed on a military unit, typically the number of days per year the unit is deployed away from its home base or station.

OSS Office of Strategic Services—"cover" name for Joint U.S. War Department headquarters formed in 1941 to coordinate special operations behind enemy lines. OSS veterans played key roles in the postwar intelligence community.

PACOM U.S. Pacific Command—unified command responsible for forces in the Pacific, Far East, and Southeast Asia. Typically commanded by a Navy admiral, and based in Hawaii.

PAO Public Affairs Officer, or Public Affairs Office—individual or organization in a military unit responsible for media relations. Often a reservist, trained as a journalist.

PASGT Personal Armor System, Ground Troops—Lightweight helmet and vest (flak jacket) based on Kevlar synthetic fiber.

Pave Hawk Sikorsky MH-60K/L helicopter, specially modified for Special Operations (including in-flight refueling, night, adverse weather, and low-level terrain following flight).

PAVE LOW Sikorsky MH-53J helicopter—a large, long-range aircraft specially configured for low-level night flight over hostile terrain in support of Special Operations.

Peace Operations SOF missions that may include monitoring of peacekeeping operations or support to peace enforcement.

PERC Performance Enhancing Ration Components—High-nutrition drink mix and food bars developed for Special Forces. Reflect latest research on physiology and sports medicine.

PLGR AN/PSN-11Portable Lightweight GPS Receiver—hand-held, battery-operated device weighing less than 1.5 kg., providing extremely accurate 3-dimensional position, time, and velocity measurements based on GPS satellite transmissions.

PSYOP Psychological Operations (replaces outdated term "psychological warfare")—SOF missions designed to influence attitudes and behavior of enemy forces, noncombatants, or others.

"Q" Course Special Forces Qualification Course—three-phase training course for Army personnel who pass the SFAS course. At the end of the "Q" Course, soldiers receive the Green Beret and become members of the 1st Special Forces Regiment.

Ranger (1) U.S. Army 75th Ranger Regiment—elite unit of two airborne battalions, trained for unusually hazardous or difficult missions. (2) A qualification awarded to all U.S. Army soldiers who have completed the demanding Ranger training course. (The "Ranger" tab is worn above the unit insignia on the right sleeve.)

Robin Sage Demanding field exercise that comprises the "final exam" portion of the Special Forces "Q" Course.

ROE Rules of Engagement—detailed military orders that specify exactly how, when, where, and by whom deadly force may be used against hostile forces. The right of self-defense is never denied, but everything else is subject to unit, CINC, and national guidance.

S-3 "Operations Officer" or "OpsO"—staff officer responsible for implementing a commander's intentions by drafting orders, managing headquarters resources, coordinating movement in time and space, and generally making the commander's life easier by anticipating his or her needs.

SA Security Assistance—congressionally mandated programs to provide training and assistance to host nations receiving U.S. military equipment.

SA/MTT Security Assistance/Mobile Training Team—Detachment formed to train host nation security forces in particular skills, or to provide local security for a VIP.

Saber Radio Motorola PRC-126—portable radio; sometimes called a "brick" radio, from its shape. Popular with military and police forces worldwide. Range up to 10 km.

SAW Squad Automatic Weapon—M249 light machine gun based on a Belgian design firing the same 5.56mm ammunition as the M4 carbine and M16 rifle.

SCUBA Self-Contained Underwater Breathing Apparatus. Consists of tanks, valves, regulator, and mouthpiece. Invented in the early 1940s by French Navy Captain Jacques-Yves Cousteau.

SCUD NATO reporting name for widely exported Russian-designed short-range mobile ballistic missile, originally introduced in 1965. Obsolete and inaccurate, but copies and variants are still produced by China, Iran, North Korea, and other states.

SERE   Survival, Evasion, Resistance, and Escape—an extremely tough course designed to prepare personnel at risk of becoming prisoners of war. Reportedly, one of the few training programs in the U.S. military where troops are systematically subjected to real physical and mental abuse.

SFAS   Special Forces Assessment and Selection—physically and mentally demanding entry-level course used to select personnel suitable for further Special Forces training.

SFG   Special Forces Group—roughly equivalent to a regiment, a unit of three small battalions plus support elements. In early 2000 there were five active and two Army National Guard SFGs, each with a designated geographical focus.

SMRS   PRC-137F Special Mission Radio System—portable satellite communications terminal with built-in encryption for voice and data transmission.

SOCCE   Special Operations Command and Control Element—a "cell" of a few officers and enlisted technical specialists established at a Joint Task Force headquarters to coordinate special operations with the CINC's overall battle plan.

SOCCENT   Special Operations Component of U.S. Central—Command. Headquarters, commanded by a brigadier general (though a colonel in Desert Shield/Storm) responsible for U.S. Special Operations in the Middle East and Central Asia. Major assets include Army 5th SFG.

SOCEUR   Special Operations component of U.S. European Command. Includes 10th SFG. Focused on Balkans and Eastern Europe.

SOCKOR   Special Operations Command, U.S. Forces Korea. Commanded by a brigadier general. No major units in country, but can rapidly be reinforced from Okinawa and other locations.

SOCOM   U.S. Special Operations Command—a unified command, headquartered at MacDill Air Force Base, Tampa, Florida. Responsible for training, equipment, and doctrine of Special Operations Forces (SOF).

SOCPAC   Special Operations component of U.S. Pacific Command. Headquartered in Hawaii, focused on East and Southeast Asia. Includes 1st and 19th SFGs.

SOCSOUTH   Special Operations component of U.S. Southern Command. Includes 7th SFG. Focused on counternarcotics missions, tropical jungle expertise, and Latin American cultures.

SOF   Special Operations Forces—collective term for Army, Navy, Air Force, and Joint military forces assigned to U.S. Special Operations Command.

SOPMOD   Special Operations Modification—a series of upgrades and attachments to the standard M4 carbine.

SOUTHCOM   U.S. Southern Command—unified command responsible for forces in Latin America and the Caribbean. Exercised combatant command of U.S. forces that participated in 1981 invasion of Panama. Headquarters relocated from Panama to Miami, Florida in 1998.

SR   Special Reconnaissance—a traditional SOF mission requiring covert (clandestine, and usually deniable) reconnaissance and surveillance in "denied territory" (behind enemy lines).

Stosstruppen   German for "shock troops"—special units formed in 1917, based on the ideas of a relatively junior officer named Hutier. Trained to infiltrate enemy positions by bypassing strongpoints. Equipped with a high proportion of light automatic weapons.

SUV   Sport Utility Vehicle—a popular type of light truck favored as a rental vehicle by Special Forces troops overseas.

SVD   Russian Dragonov sniper rifle—a famous WWII weapon firing a powerful 7.62 mm cartridge. Kicks like a mule. Manufactured in huge numbers, lacks the precision and range of modern sniper rifles.

T-Rations   Precooked meals packaged in large aluminum trays, designed for garrison situations where troops can be fed in groups.

TEL   Transporter Erector Launcher—a big truck, often with off-road capability, equipped with nearly everything needed to transport, prepare, aim, and fire a missile, usually a short-range ballistic missile such as the Russian SCUD. (U.S. military forces are obsessed with SCUD-hunting, which we did rather ineffectively in the Gulf War.)

TFR   Terrain-Following Radar—a specialized sensor, usually linked to automated flight controls, allowing an aircraft to fly with relative safety at night and/or in bad weather at extremely low altitude, with low risk of detection.

Title 10   Section of the U.S. Code dealing with the national defense establishment. Defines the legal and financial authority for U.S. military operations. Prohibits assignment of females to "combat" jobs.

TRANSCOM U.S. Transportation Command—A unified command including Air Mobility Command, the Navy's Military Sea Transportation Service, and the Army's Military Traffic Management Command (rail and truck).

UAV Unmanned Aerial Vehicle—a remote-controlled drone aircraft, typically used for reconnaissance and surveillance. Aviators are understandably very resistant to the idea of autonomous "killer" UAVs.

USASOC U.S. Army Special Operations Command—includes Special Forces (Green Berets), Ranger Regiment, Special Operations Aviation, JFK Special Warfare Center and School, and other units. Based at Fort Bragg, North Carolina.

UXO Unexploded Ordnance—jargon for "dud" bombs that are waiting to blow up when disturbed or carelessly handled.

WMD Weapons of Mass Destruction—jargon for nuclear, chemical, biological, and radiological weapons. CounterWMD missions include counterproliferation and consequence management.

Bibliography

Books:

Bosnia: Country Handbook, US Department of Defense, 1995
Combined Operations: The Official Story of the Commandos, Macmillan, 1943
Conduct of the Persian Gulf War, US Government Printing Office, 1992
GPS—A Guide to the Next Utility, Trimble Navigation, 1989
"Guardia Nacional de Venezula" The National Guard of Venezuela, Venezuelan National Guard, 1998
Jane's Balkan Handbook, Jane's Information Group, 1999
Sky Soldiers, Time Life Books, 1991
Special Forces and Missions, Time Life Books, 1990
The World's Missile Systems, General Dynamics, 1988
TRW Space Data, 4th Edition, TRW, 1992
Adams, James, *Secret Armies: Inside the American, Soviet and European Special Forces*, Atlantic Monthly Press, 1987
Adan, Avraham (Bren), *On the Banks of the Suez*, Presidio Press, 1980
Adkin, Mark, *Urgent Fury: The Battle for Grenada*, Lexington Books, 1989
Admiral U.S.G. Sharp, *Strategy for Defeat*, Presidio Press, 1978
Albrecht, Gerhard (Ed.), *Weyers Flotten Taschenbuch 1992/93 (Warships of the World)*, Bernard & Graefe verlag, Bonn, Germany, 1992
Alexander, Joseph H. and Bartlett, Merrill I., *Sea Soldiers in the Cold War*, Naval Institute Press, 1995
Ambrose, Stephen E.
——*D-Day, June 6, 1944: The Climactic Battle of World War II*, Simon & Schuster, 1994
——*Pegasus Bridge: June 6, 1944*, Simon & Schuster, 1985
Asprey, Robert B., *War in the Shadows: The Guerrilla in History*, Morrow, 1994
Atkinson, Rick, *Crusade: The Untold Story of the Persian Gulf War*, Houghton Mifflin, 1993
Axelrod, Alan, *The War Between the Spies: A History of Espionage During the American Civil War*, Atlantic Monthly Press, 1992
Bank, Col Aaron, USA (Ret.), *From OSS to Green Berets*, Pocket Books, 1986
Barnett, Jeffery, R., *Future War: An Assessment of Aerospace Campaigns in 2010*, Air University Press, 1996
Baxter, William P., *Soviet Air Land-Battle Tactics*, Presidio Press, 1986
Beaumont, Roger A., *Joint Military Operations: A Short History*, Greenwood, 1993
bin Sultan, Khaled, *Desert Warrior: A Personal View of the Gulf War by the Joint Forces Commander*, Harper Collins, 1995
Bishop, Chris and David Donald, *The Encyclopedia of World Military Power*, The Military Press, 1986
Blackwell, James, *Thunder in the Desert: The Strategy and Tactics of the Persian Gulf War*, Bantam Books, 1991
Blair, Arthur H., Colonel U.S. Army (Ret.), *At War in the Gulf*, A&M University Press, 1992
Blair, Clay, *The Forgotten War: American in Korea, 1950–1953*, Times Books, 1987
Bolger, Daniel P., *The Battle for Hunger Hill*, Presidio, 1997
Bowden, Mark, *Black Hawk Down: A Story of Modern War*, Atlantic Monthly Press, 1999

Bradin, James W., *From Hot Air to Hellfire—The History of Army Attack Aviation*, Presidio Press, 1994

Briggs, Clarence E. III, (1Lt, USA), *Operation Just Cause: Panama, December 1989*, Stackpole, 1990

Burrows, William E. and Robert Windham, *Critical Mass*, Simon & Schuster, 1989

Cardwell, Thomas A. III (Col. USAF), *Airland Combat*, Air University Press, US Air Force, 1992

Chant, Christopher, *Encyclopedia of Modern Aircraft Armament*, IMP Publishing Services Ltd., 1988

Chetty, P. R. K., *Satellite Technology and Its Applications, 2nd Ed.*, McGraw Hill, 1991

Clancy, Tom

————*Carrier: A Guided Tour of an Aircraft Carrier*, Berkley Books, 1999

————*Rainbow Six*, G. P. Putnam & Sons, 1998

————*Executive Orders*, G. P. Putnam & Sons, 1997

————*Airborne: A Guided Tour of an Airborne Task Force*, Berkley Books, 1997

————*Marine: A Guided Tour of a Marine Expeditionary Unit*, Berkley, 1996

————*Fighter Wing: A Guided Tour of an Air Force Combat Wing*, Berkley, 1995

————*Armored Cav: A Guided Tour of an Armored Cavalry Regiment*, Berkley Books, 1994

————*Debt of Honor*, G. P. Putnam & Sons, 1994

————*Submarine: A Guided Tour Inside a Nuclear Warship*, Berkley Books, 1993

————*The Sum of All Fears*, G. P. Putnam & Sons, 1991

————*Clear and Present Danger*, G. P. Putnam & Sons, 1989

————*The Cardinal of the Kremlin*, G. P. Putnam & Sons, 1988

————*Patriot Games*, G. P. Putnam & Sons, 1987

————*Red Storm Rising*, G. P. Putnam & Sons, 1986

————*The Hunt for Red October*, Berkley Publishers, 1985

Clancy, Tom with Horner, Chuck (Gen., USAF, Ret.), *Every Man a Tiger*, Putnam, 1999

Clancy, Tom with Fred Franks, Jr. (Gen, USA, Ret), *Into the Storm: A Study in Command*, Putnam, 1997

Clark, Robert M., *Intelligence Analysis: Estimation and Prediction*, American Literary Press, 1996

Cohen, Dr. Eliot A. and Gooch, John, *Military Misfortunes—The Anatomy of Failure in War*, Free Press, 1990

Cohen, Dr. Elliot A.

————*Gulf War Air Power Survey Summary Report*, U.S. Government Printing Office, 1993

————*Gulf War Air Power Survey Volume I*, U.S. Government Printing Office, 1993

————*Gulf War Air Power Survey Volume II*, U.S. Government Printing Office, 1993

————*Gulf War Air Power Survey Volume III*, U.S. Government Printing Office, 1993

————*Gulf War Air Power Survey Volume IV*, U.S. Government Printing Office, 1993

————*Gulf War Air Power Survey Volume V*, U.S. Government Printing Office, 1993

Cooling, Benjamin F. (Ed.), *Case Studies in the Development of Close Air Support*, Office of Air Force History, 1990

Coyne, James P., *Airpower in the Gulf*, Air Force Association, 1992

Crampton, William, *The World's Flags*, Mallard Press, 1990

Crowe, Admiral William J., Jr., *The Line of Fire—From Washington to the Gulf, the Politics and Battles of the New Military*, Simon & Schuster, 1993

Darwish, Adel and Alexander, Gregory, *Unholy Babylon—The Secret History of Saddam's War*, St. Martin's Press, 1991

David, Peter, *Triumph in the Desert*, Random House, 1991

Dawood, N. J. (Ed.), *The Koran*, Penguin Books, 1956

De Jomini, Baron Antoine Henri, *The Art of War*, Green Hill Books, 1992

Dean, David J., *The Air Force Role in Low Intensity Conflict*, Air University Press, 1986

Dempster, Chris and Dave Tomkins, *Firepower*, St. Martin's Press, 1980

Devereaux, Tony, *Messenger Gods of Battle*, Brassey's, 1991

Doleman, Edgar C., Jr., *The Vietnam Experience—Tools of War*, Boston Publishing Company, 1985

Donnelly, Ralph W., *The Confederate States Marine Corps: The Rebel Leathernecks*, White Mane, Shippensburg, Pennsylvania, 1989

Dorr, Robert F.

————*Desert Shield—The Buildup: The Complete Story*, Motorbooks, 1991

————*Desert Storm—Air War*; Motorbooks; 1991

Doubler, Michael D. *Closing with the Enemy: How GI's Fought the War in Europe, 1944–1945*, University Press of Kansas, 1994

Dunnigan, James F., *Digital Soldiers: The Evolution of High-tech Weaponry and Tomorrow's Brave New Battlefield*; St. Martin's Press, 1996

Dunnigan, James F. and Albert Nofi, *Victory and Deceit: Dirty Tricks at War*, Quill, 1995

Dunnigan, James F. and Austin Bay

———*A Quick and Dirty Guide to War, 3rd ed.*, Morrow, 1996

———*From Shield to Storm*, Morrow Books, 1992

Dunnigan, James F. and Raymond M. Macedonia, *Getting It Right: American Military Reforms After Vietnam to the Gulf War and Beyond*, Morrow, 1993

Dupuy, Col. T.N. USA Army (Ret.)

———*Future Wars—the World's Most Dangerous Flashpoints*, Warner Books, 1993

———*Saddam Hussein—Scenarios and Strategies for the Gulf War*, Warner Books, 1991

———*Future Wars; The World's Most Dangerous Flashpoints*, Warner Books, 1993

———*Understanding Defeat—How to Recover from Loss in Battle to Gain Victory in War*, Paragon House, 1990

———*Attrition: Forecasting Battle Casualties and Equipment Losses in Modern War*, Hero Books, 1990

———*Understanding War—History and Theory of Combat*, Paragon House, 1987

———*Numbers, Predictions & War—The Use of History to Evaluate and Predict the Outcome of Armed Conflict*, Hero Books, 1985

———*Options of Command*, Hippocrene Books, Inc., 1984

———*The Evolution of Weapons and Warfare*, Bobbs-Merrill, 1980

Dydynski, Krzysztof, *Venezuela*, Lonely Planet, 1998

Edwards, Maj. John E., USA (Ret.), *Combat Service Support Guide—2nd Edition*, Stackpole Books, 1993

Eshel, David, *The U.S. Rapid Deployment Forces*, Arco Publishing, Inc., 1985

Ethell, Jeffrey and Alfred Price, *Air War South Atlantic*, Macmillan, 1983

Evans, Thomas J. and James M. Moyer, *Mosby's Confederacy*, White Mane Publishing Co., 1991

Fall, Bernard B., *Street Without Joy*, Schocken, 1972

Felix, Christopher, *A Short Course in the Secret War*, Madison Books, 1992

Follett, Ken, *On Wings of Eagles*, Morrow, 1983

Francillon, Rene J., *World Military Aviation*, 1995, Naval Institute Press, 1995

Frank Chadwick, *Gulf War Fact Book*, Game Designers Workshop, 1992

Friedman, Norman, *Desert Victory: The War For Kuwait*, U.S. Naval Institute Press, 1991

Gallagher, James J. CSM (USA, Ret.)

———*Combat Leaders Field Guide, 11th Ed.* Stackpole, 1994

———*Low-Intensity Conflict*, Stackpole, 1992

Gibson, James William, *The Perfect War—Technowar in Vietnam*, Atlantic Monthly Press, 1986

Goldstein, Donald L. et. al., *D-Day, Normandy: The Story and the Photographs*, Brassey's, 1994

Goldstein, Frank L. (Col. USAF), *Psychological Operations: Principles and Case Studies*, Air University Press, 1996

Gordon, Michael R. and Trainor, Bernard E., *The General's War: The Inside Story of the Conflict in the Gulf*, Little Brown, 1995

Gray, Colin S., *The Leverage of Sea Power*, Free Press, 1992

Griswold, Terry and D. M. Giangreco, *Delta: America's Elite Counterterrorist Force*, Motorbooks, 1992

Grove, Eric, *Battle for the Fiords: NATO's Forward MARITIME STRATEGY IN ACTION*, Naval Institute Press, 1991

Haas, Michael E. (Col, USAF, Ret), *Apollo's Warriors: United States Air Force Special Operations during the Cold War*, Air University Press, 1997

Halberstadt, Hans

———*Desert Storm—Ground War*, Motorbooks International, 1991

———*Army Aviation*, Presidio Press, 1990

———*NTC: A Primer of Modern Land Combat*, Presidio Press, 1989

Hallion, Dr. Richard P.

———*Storm over Iraq—Air Power and the Gulf War*, Smithsonian Books, 1992

———*Strike from the Sky—The History of Battlefield Air Attack 1911–1945*, Smithsonian, 1989

Hansen, Chuck, *US Nuclear Weapons: The Secret History*, Orion Books, 1988

Hansen, Victor Davis, *The Western Way of War—Infantry Battle in Classical Greece*, Alfred Knopf Publishers, 1989

Hart, B. H. Liddell, *Strategy*, Frederick A. Praeger, Inc., Publishers, 1967

Hartcup, Guy, *The Silent Revolution: Development of Conventional Weapons 1945–85*, Brassey's, 1993

Hastings, Max, *Overlord*, Simon & Schuster, 1984

Heinlein, Robert A., *Starship Troopers*, Ace Books, 1959

Hersh, Seymour M., *The Samson Option*, Random House Publishers, 1991

Hogg, Ian, *Jane's Guns Recognition Guide*, Jane's Information Group, 1996

Hudson, Heather E., *Communication Satellites—Their Development and Impact*, Free Press, 1990

Hughes, David R., *The M16 Rifle and Its Cartridge*, Armory Publications, Oceanside, California, 1990

Isby, David, *Weapons and Tactics of the Soviet Army*, Janes, 1981

Jessup, John E., Jr., and Coakley, Robert W., *A Guide to the Study and Use of Military History*, US Government Printing Office, 1991

Jones, Virgil Carrington, *Gray Ghosts and Rebel Raiders: The Daring Exploits of the Confederate Raiders*, Promontory Press, 1956

Kaplan, Robert D., *Balkan Ghosts: A Journey Through History*, Vintage, 1994

Keany, Thomas A. and Cohen, Eliot A., *Revolution in Warfare? Air Power in the Persian Gulf*, Naval Institute Press, 1995

Keegan, John

———*A History of Warfare*, Alfred A. Knopf, 1993

———*The Second World War*, Viking, 1989

———*The Illustrated Face of Battle*, Viking, 1988

Kelly, Mary Pat, *"Good to Go" The Rescue of Scott O'Grady from Bosnia*, Naval Institute Press, 1996

Kershaw, Robert J. *D-Day: Piercing the Atlantic Wall*, Naval Institute Press, 1994

Kinzey, Bert, *US Aircraft & Armament of Operation Desert Storm*, Kalmbach Books, 1993

Kohn, George C., *Dictionary of Wars (Revised Edition)*, Facts on File, 1999

Kyle, James H. (col, USAF, Ret), *The Guts to Try: The Untold Story of The Iran Hostage Rescue Mission by the On-scene Desert Commander*, Orion Books, 1990

Lake, Donald, David and Jon (Eds.), *US Navy and Marine Corps Air Power Directory*, Aerospace Publishing, Ltd., 1992

Lambert, Mark, (Ed.), *Jane's All the World's Aircraft, 1992–93*, Jane's Information Group, 1992

Langguth, A. J., *Patriots: The Men Who Started the American Revolution*, Simon & Schuster, 1988

Luttwak, Edward and Koehl, Stuart L., *The Dictionary of Modern War—A Guide to the Ideas, Institutions and Weapons of Modern Military Power*, Harper Collins, 1991

Marquis, Susan L., *Unconventional Warfare: Rebuilding U.S. Special Operations Forces*, Brookings, 1997

McConnell, Malcolm, *Just Cause: The Real Story of America's High-Tech Invasion of Panama*, St. Martin's Press, 1991

McNab, Andy

———*Immediate Action*, Dell, 1995

———*Bravo Two Zero*, Dell, 1993

McRaven, William H., *Spec Ops: Case Studies in Special Operations Warfare*, Presidio, 1995

Meigs, Montgomery C., *Slide Rules and Submarines*, NDU Press, 1990

Meisner, Arnold, *Desert Storm—Sea War*, Motorbooks International, 1991

Mets, David R., *Land-based Air Power in Third World Crises*, Air University Press, 1986

Michell, Simon, ed., *Jane's Aircraft Upgrades, 5th ed. 1997–98*, Jane's Information Group, 1997

Middlebrook, Martin, *Task Force—The Falklands War, 1982*, Penguin Books, 1987

Miller, Charles E. (Lt Col, USAF), *Airlift Doctrine*, Air University Press, 1988

Morgan, Tom, ed., *Jane's Space Directory, 14th ed. 1998–99*, Jane's Information Group, 1998

Morse, Stan, *Gulf Air War Debrief*, Aerospace Publishing Limited, 1991

Newhouse, John, *War and Peace in the Nuclear Age*, Alfred Knopf Publications, 1989

Norton, Oliver W., *The Attack and Defense of Little Round Top (reprint of 1913 edition)*, Morningside Bookshop, Dayton, Ohio, 1983

O'Ballance, Edgar, *No Victor, No Vanquished*, Presidio Press, 1978

O'Grady, Scott (Capt., USAF), *Return with Honor*, Doubleday, 1995

Pagonis, Lt. General William G. with Cruikshank, Jeffrey L., *Moving Mountains—Lessons in Leadership and Logistics from the Gulf War*, Harvard Business School Press, 1992

Peebles, Curtis, *Guardians-Strategic Reconnaissance Satellites*, Presidio Press, 1987

Pelton, Robert, *The World's Most Dangerous Places, 3rd edition*, Fielding, 1998

Polmar, Norman and Floyd D. Kennedy, *Military Helicopters of the World*, Naval Institute Press, 1981

Prados, John, *Presidents' Secret Wars: CIA and Pentagon Covert Operations from World War II through the Persian Gulf*, Ivan R. Dee, Publisher, Chicago, 1996

Rapoport, Anatol (Ed.), *Carl Von Clausewitz on War*, Penguin Books, 1968

Rhodes, Richard, *The Making of the Atomic Bomb*, Simon & Schuster, 1986

Richelson, Jeffrey

————*America's Secret Eyes In Space*, Harper & Row Publishers, 1990

————*American Espionage and the Soviet Target*, William Morrow and Company, 1987

————*Sword and Shield—Soviet Intelligence and Security Apparatus*, Ballinger Publishing Company, 1986

————*The US Intelligence Community*, Ballinger Publishing Company, 1985

Ricks, Thomas E., *Making the Corps*, Scribner, 1997

Robison, Gordon, *Arab Gulf States*, Lonely Planet, 1996

Rommel, Erwin, *Infantry Attacks*, Presidio, 1990

Santoli, Al, *Leading the Way: How Vietnam Veterans Rebuilt the U.S. Military*, Ballantine Books, 1993

Scales, Brig. General Robert H., Jr. (USA), *Certain Victory: The US Army in the Gulf War*, Brassey's, 1994

Schmitt, Gary, *Silent Warfare—Understanding the World of Intelligence*, Brassey's (US), 1993

Schneider, Wolfgang (Ed.), *Taschenbuch der Panzer (Tanks of the World) 7th edition*, Bernard & Graefe Verlag, Bonn, Germany, 1990

Serber, Robert, *The Los Alamos Primer: The First Lectures on How to Build an Atomic Bomb*, University of California Press, 1992

Shaara, Michael, *The Killer Angels*, Ballantine, 1974

Sidell, Frederick, William C. Patrick III, Thomas R. Dashiell, *Jane's Chem-Bio Handbook*, Jane's Information Group, 1999

Silber, Laura and Alan Little, *Yugoslavia: Death of a Nation*, Penguin, 1997

Skorzeny, Otto, *Skorzeny's Secret Missions: War Memoirs of the Most Dangerous Man in Europe*, Dutton, 1950

Smith, Gordon, *Battles of the Falklands War*, Ian Allen, 1989

Smith, Peter C., *Close Air Support—An Illustrated History, 1914 to the Present*, Orion Books, 1990

Sokolski, Henry, *Fighting Proliferation: New Concerns for the Nineties*, Air University Press, 1996

Staff, US News and World Report, *Triumph Without Victory—The Unreported History of the Persian Gulf War*, Random House, 1992

Stevenson, William, *90 Minutes at Entebbe*, Bantam Books, 1976

Summers, Colonel Harry G. Jr. (Ret.)

————*A Critical Analysis of the Gulf War*, Dell Publishing, 1992

————*The New World Strategy*, Simon & Schuster, 1995

Sutherland, LTC Ian D. W., USA (Ret.), *Special Forces of the United States Army: 1952/1982*, R. James Bender Publishing, 1990

Suvorov, Viktor, *Spetznaz: The Inside Story of the Soviet Special Forces*, Norton, 1987

Swanborough, Gordon and Bowers, Peter

————*United States Military Aircraft since 1909*, Smithsonian, 1989

————*United States Navy Aircraft Since 1911*, Naval Institute Press, 1990

Thornborough, Anthony, *Sky Spies—The Decades of Airborne Reconnaissance*, Arms and Armour, 1993

Toffler, Alvin and Heidi, *War and Anti-War-Survival at the Dawn of the 21st Century*, Little Brown, 1993

Von Hassell, Agostino, *Strike Force: US Marine Special Operations*, Howell Press, Charlottesville, Virginia, 1991

Wagner, William

————*Fireflies and Other UAV's*, Midland Publishing Limited, 1992

————*Lightning Bugs and Other Reconnaissance Drones*, Aero Publishers, 1982

Waller, Douglas C., *The Commandos—The Inside Story of America's Secret Soldiers*, Simon & Schuster, 1994

Warden, Col. John A., III, USAF, *The Air Campaign—Planning for Combat*, Brassey's Punishing, 1989

Ware, Lewis B., *Low-Intensity Conflict in the Third World*, Air University Press, 1988

Watson, Bruce W., Bruce George, MP, Peter Tsouras and B. L. Cyr, *Military Lessons of the Gulf War*, Greenhill Books, 1991

Watson, Bruce W. and Peter Tsouras Editors, *Operation Just Cause*, Westview Press, 1991

Wedertz, Bill, *Dictionary of Naval Abbreviations*, Naval Institute Press, 1977

Weinberg, Gerhard, *A World At Arms: A Global History of World War II*, Cambridge, 1994

Weinberg, Caspar, *Fighting for Peace: Seven Critical Years in the Pentagon*, Warner Books, 1990

Weissman, Steve and Herbert Krosney, *The Islamic Bomb*, Times Books, 1981

Winnefeld, James A. and Johnson, Dana J., *Joint Air Operations: Pursuit of Unity in Command and Control 1942–1991*, Naval Institute Press, 1993

Woodward, Robert, *The Commanders*, Simon & Schuster, 1991

Woodward, Sandy (Admiral, RN), *One Hundred Days: The Memoirs of the Falklands Battle Group Commander*, Naval Institute Press, 1992

Zaloga, Steven J.
———*Inside the Blue Berets: A Combat History of Soviet & Russian Airborne Forces, 1930–1995*; Presidio Press; 1995
———*Red Trust—Attack on the Central Front, Soviet Tactics and Capabilities in the 1990's*, Presidio Press, 1989

Zurick, Tim (Cpt, USAR), *Army Dictionary and Desk Reference*, Stackpole, 1992

Pamphlets and Manuals:

A Short History of Support to Special Operations, U.S. Army Special Operations Command, 1995

Close Air Support and Close-in Fire Support, Headquarters, U.S. Marine Corps, 1992

FM 100–5, Operation, June 1993, US Army, 1993

FM 101–10-1/1 Staff Officers' Field Manual, Organizational, Technical and Logistical Data (Volume 1), Headquarters, U.S. Marine Corps, 1987

FMFM 0–9 Field Firing for the M16A2 Rifle, Headquarters, U.S. Marine Corps, 1995

FMFM 5–40, Offensive Air Support, Headquarters, U.S. Marine Corps, 1992

FMFM 5–42 Deep Air Support, Headquarters, U.S. Marine Corps, 1993

FMFM 5–60, Control of Aircraft and Missiles, Headquarters, U.S. Marine Corps, 1993

FMFM 6–18 Techniques and Procedures for Fire Support Coordination, Headquarters, U.S. Marine Corps, 1992

FMFM 6–8, Supporting Arms Observer, Spotter and Controller, Headquarters, U.S. Marine Corps, 1994

FMFM 6–9, Marine Artillery Support, Headquarters, U.S. Marine Corps, 1993

FMFM 7–32, Raid Operations, Headquarters, U.S. Marine Corps, 1993

FMFRP 0–55, Desert Water Supply, Headquarters, U.S. Marine Corps, 1990

FMFRP 0–59, The Environment and Its Effects on Materiel, Personnel and Operations with Special Emphasis on the Middle East, Headquarters, U.S. Marine Corps, 1990

FMFRP 12–18, Mao Tse-tung on Guerrilla Warfare (Reprint of 1961 Edition, Translated by Brig. General Samuel B. Griffith), Headquarters, U.S. Marine Corps, 1989

FMFRP 12–33, The Defense of Duffer's Drift, Headquarters, U.S. Marine Corps, 1991

FMFRP 12–46 Advanced Base Operations in Micronesia (Reprint of Unpublished 1921 Manuscript), Headquarters, U.S. Marine Corps, 1992

FMFRP 4–34 Battlefield Damage Assessment and Repair, Headquarters, U.S. Marine Corps, 1993

Former Yugoslavia Handbook, Department of Defense, 1993

General Design and Construction Criteria for Kuwait, Headquarters, U.S. Marine Corps, 1990

GPS: A Guide to the Next Utility, Trimble Navigation, 1989

Joint Pub 0–2, Unified Action Armed Forces, Joint Chiefs of Staff, 1995

Joint Pub 1–01.1, Compendium of Joint Publications, Joint Chiefs of Staff, 1995

Joint Pub 3–02.2, Joint Doctrine for Amphibious Embarkation, Joint Chiefs of Staff, 1993

Joint Pub 3–05.5, Joint Special Operations Targeting and Mission Planning Procedures, Joint Chiefs of Staff, 1993

Joint Pub 5–0, Doctrine for Planning Joint Operations, Joint Chiefs of Staff, 1995

Joint Pub 6–0, Doctrine for Command, Control, Communications and Computer (C4) Systems Supports to Joint Operations, Joint Chiefs of Staff, 1995

Ranger Handbook, Desert, Ranger Training Brigade, 1992

Remote Sensing Field Guide, Desert, Headquarters, U.S. Marine Corps, 1990

Sine Pari, U.S. Army Special Operations Command, 1995

Small Wars Manual (Reprint of 1940 Edition), Headquarters, U.S. Marine Corps, 1987

Space Log–1993, TRW, 1994

Standing Up the MACOM: The U.S. Army Special Operations Command 1987–92, U.S. Army Special
    Operations Command, 1995
To Free From Oppression, U.S. Army Special Operations Command, 1995
United State Special Operations Command History, U.S. Army Special Operations Command, 1998
Worldwide Geographic Location Codes, U.S. General Services Administration, 1987

Magazines:

Air and Space Smithsonian, Smithsonian Institute
Air Forces Monthly, Key Publishing, Ltd.
Air International, Expediters of the Printed Word, Ltd.
Airpower Journal, United States Air Force
Aviation Week and Space Technology, McGraw Hill Publications
Command: Military History, Strategy & Analysis, XTR Corporation
Joint Forces Quarterly, National Defense University
KORUS, IMC
Naval History, United States Naval Institute
Naval War College Review, U.S. Naval War College
Military Heritage, Sovereign Media
Military Review, U.S. Army
Proceedings, United States Naval Institute
Sine Pari, U.S. Special Operations Command
The Economist, The Economist
The Hook, The Tailhook Association
The Rucksack, U.S. Army Special Operations Command
U.S. News and World Report, U.S. News and World Report
World Airpower Journal, Aerospace Publishing Ltd., Airtime Publishing, Inc.

Videotapes:

America's Commandos, Hoagie Films
ArmyTACMS, Loral Vought Systems
C-17 the 2nd Year, McDonnell Douglas-Teleproductions
CIA—The Secret Files Parts 1–4, A&E Home Video, 1992
Fighting Men: The Green Berets, Sunwood Entertainment Company
Hercules and Beyond, Lockheed Aeronautical Systems Company
Hercules Multi-Mission Aircraft, Lockheed Aeronautical Systems Company
Heroes of the Storm, Media Center
It's About Performance, Sight & Sound Media
Joint Stars, Grumman
Joint Stars One System Multiple Missions, Grumman
Predator Presentation & 2 MPV Shots, Loral Aeronutronic
The Canadian Forces in the Persian Gulf, DGPA-Director General Public Affairs
War in the Gulf Video Series–1–4, Video Ordinance Ino., 1991
Wings over the Gulf–Volume 1, 2 and 3, Discovery Communications Inc., 1991

CD-ROMs:

Army Experiment Six: Training the Forces of Army XXI, US Army, TRADOC
DESERT STORM: The War in the Persian Gulf, Warner New Media, 1991
EADTB Demonstration Suite, Raytheon, 1999
Encarta 96 Encyclopedia, Microsoft, 1996
Infopedia, Future Vision Multimedia, 1995
Warplanes: Modern Fighting Aircraft, Maris, 1994
WINGS (4 CD set), Discovery Communications, 1995
World Factbook 1995 Edition, Wayzata, 1995